NEW
TRENDS IN
SOVIET
ECONOMICS

NEW
TRENDS IN
SOVIET
ECONOMICS

Edited by Martin Cave,
Alastair McAuley,
and Judith Thornton

M. E. Sharpe, Inc.
Armonk, New York
London

47

Translated by Martin Cave.

Published previously as vol. XVII, nos. 2, 3, and 4, and vol. XVIII, no. 1, Winter 1980-Fall 1981, of *Matekon*.

Library of Congress Cataloging in Publication Data

Main entry under title:
New trends in Soviet economics.

Translated from the Russian.
Selections from: Matekon.
Includes bibliographical references.
1. Economics, Mathematical—Soviet Union—Addresses, essays, lectures. I. Cave, Martin. II. McAuley, Alastair, 1938-   . III. Thornton, Judith. IV. Matekon.
HB135.N49   1982   330'.01'51   82-835
ISBN 0-87332-206-1   AACR2

Printed in the United States of America

Contents

Part 4

Natural Resources Economics

Foreword

Martin Cave, Alastair McAuley,
and Judith Thornton

Our aim in preparing this selection of recent Soviet economic
writing has been to give the Western reader a sample of some
of the major tendencies in Soviet economics. Much of the work
of major innovators in Soviet economics such as Kantorovich
and Novozhilov was carried out or first published in the 1960s
and is now fairly well known to Western readers. Less famil-
iar are the ways in which subsequent writers have developed
or extended these original ideas and applied the new techniques
to other areas of analysis. The present volume is intended to
fill this gap.

We have not attempted to give an exhaustive survey of contemporary Soviet economics. Our emphasis has been on mathematical contributions, not because this is the only field in
which important developments have been made but because it
is the area which has seen the most obvious advances. We have
also concentrated on a limited number of major topics. One of
them (Part 2 on planning models) is a traditional area of concern of Soviet economists. Other topics have come to the fore-
front more recently. The analysis of consumption behavior
(Part 3) now receives far more attention from economists and
policy-makers in the USSR than was the case ten or fifteen
years ago. Equally, natural resource economics (Part 4) has
come into much greater prominence now that the importance
of natural resource prices and pollution is more fully recognized. These three sections are preceded by a group of arti-

cles dealing with a number of fundamental issues in planning.

Many of the techniques used by Soviet economists are the same as those used by their Western colleagues, and are often borrowed from the latter. But the different institutional arrangements in the USSR naturally alter the thrust of Soviet economic research. Although the analysis is sometimes abstract, it usually has as its aim the production of a specific input into economic planning and management. This predominant interest in the numerical rather than the general pervades much Soviet economics. Any assessment of its quality and practical usefulness should take this special context into account.

The materials below first appeared in <u>Matekon,</u> a journal of translations from Soviet and East European mathematical economics. Each section is preceded by an introduction by one of the editors, which attempts to place the extracts in context and refers the reader to other Soviet writings available in English. The translations were prepared by the first-named editor with assistance from his colleagues; the only amendments made in the translations have been corrections of errors in mathematical notation.

Martin Cave,
Brunel University

Alastair McAuley,
University of Essex

Judith Thornton,
University of Washington

Part 1

Conceptions of the Planning Process

Introduction

Martin Cave

The following selection contains articles on the broad theme of how the economy and the planning process are conceived in contemporary Soviet economic literature. The earlier belief that the planning problem required merely that the Soviet government or Party identify the goals of economic development, compile a plan to achieve those goals, and implement it by administrative fiat has now given way to a recognition that none of these three stages is simple. This group of articles gives a sample of the various approaches taken toward different aspects of the planning problem in recent Soviet theoretical writing on the economy.

The first article, by E. Z. Maiminas, starts from the proposition that the economy is just one part of the socioeconomic system and that the goals of economic development and the system of economic management must be shaped with reference to the other components of that system. Maiminas is the author of an influential book on informational aspects of economic planning [1] that draws on cybernetic concepts popularized in the USSR in the late 1950s and 1960s. In the present article, he argues inter alia that the socioeconomic system contains three types of structure: a technological structure, a social structure, and an organizational structure. Very crudely, the social structure articulates values and interests which, insofar as they can be realized through material production (the technological struc-

3

ture), are implemented by means of a hierarchical organizational structure. The three structures, however, are also interdependent in complex ways.

The conclusions drawn from this analysis are neither straightforward nor directly helpful to planners. Maiminas gives priority to changes in technology as the motive force in the development of the socioeconomic system, but he accords a degree of autonomy to the other structures. In particular, at any moment alternative forms of control of the system are conceivable, though the author offers no guidance as to how the choice between them should be made. One major conclusion is that it is wrong to treat the objective function for the economy as something given from outside. Rather, it is a creation of the socioeconomic system as a whole.

This same theme is taken up in the second article included here, written by N. Ia. Petrakov, a deputy director of the Central Economic Mathematical Institute (TsEMI). He argues that planning is characterized by various types of uncertainty, affecting (among other things) the goals of the economy and the implementation of the plan. As far as the former is concerned, Petrakov restates the argument that the goal of a socialist economy is maximum satisfaction of the needs of its members, but he asserts that those needs depend upon the level of economic development, which itself is determined by the plan. The objective function thus shapes the plan, but the plan, when implemented, also affects the parameters of the objective function. Moreover, to add to the uncertainty thus created, there are other problems resulting from inaccuracies — deliberate or accidental — in communications between agents.

The second type of indeterminacy arises from the probabilistic nature of plan fulfillment. According to Petrakov, uncertainties arise here partly from failures of coordination between enterprises and their superiors and partly from planners' errors. But there is also an irreducible technological uncertainty which is aggravated (though not totally caused) by technological progress.

With a colleague, Petrakov has elsewhere analyzed the implications of this second aspect of uncertainty [2, 3]. He takes an input-output representation of the economy with the simplest form of objective function (maximizing a given structure of consumption). Uncertainty over the gestation period of investment projects makes capacity levels indeterminate; the planning problem thus becomes one of stabilizing economic growth. The conclusion is that uncertainty reduces the rate of economic growth to an extent which depends upon the number of sectors in the economy; it is noted that, since new industries are continually being created, the rate of growth will decline.

Both Petrakov and Maiminas are preoccupied with the problem of the objective function. A conference on this theme was held in Moscow in April 1979 and the published account shows the wide diversity of views [4]. Some speakers disputed the position advanced by Petrakov and Maiminas and argued that the objective function for the economy was given a priori. Others emphasized its socioeconomic nature, stressing that it depended on forms of social organization as well as on the outputs of the economic system. Standard forms of objective function were enumerated, but other speakers emphasized the links through duality theorems between cost minimization and welfare maximization criteria. Kantorovich in his contribution cast doubt on the possibility of or need for a single global and absolute criterion, arguing that the optimality criterion should incorporate qualitative elements in the plan as well as such attributes as stability and flexibility. This, too, implies a generalization of the objective function and is a possible response to uncertainty.

One way around the problem of specifying an optimality criterion involves the identification of so-called goal-related programs. It is suggested that the authorities be given a set of possible major programs to choose from, each program being designed to achieve a specified goal at a specified resource cost. The goals themselves may be derived either informally or, as in some planning schemes, by more elaborate methods [5, pp. 62-63, 74-78]. The general approach based on the identification and implementation of programs is highly favored in the USSR. The article by Danilov-Danil'ian included here considers some of the problems that arise when programs are incorporated into a system of optimal planning, as an addition to the standard sectoral and regional elements in the plan.

The author first identifies the circumstances in which programs can appropriately be devised. The goal must be operational; its attainment must be feasible in a resource sense; the objective must go beyond a mere combination of targets for lower-level bodies; and, finally, a program must involve activities that are not simply routine continuations of existing procedures.

Such programs clearly complicate the planning procedure. The choice of programs to be incorporated into the plan must be made at a stage preliminary to the compilation of sectoral and regional plans while leaving as much latitude as possible for the latter. The author proposes a two-stage approach. A provisional set of programs is identified, largely by informal methods; the details (including the resource cost) of implementing this set is then discovered using a network model. If this proves to be beyond the resources available to the economy, the set of programs is amended (see [6] for a full account).

The discussion leaves many questions unanswered; in particular, the serious organizational problems of monitoring and coordinating the implementation of the programs fall outside the scope of Danilov-Danil'ian's article. At the conceptual level, however, the program approach has the advantage of presenting strategic planning choices in a helpful way, and, in the absence of agreement about the status or form of the objective function, this is a clear benefit.

The fourth article in this selection examines a later stage in the planning process — the interaction between a superior and subordinate organizations, each of which is assumed to have its own objective function. Moiseev, joint author of the article with Vatel', is head of the Computer Center of the USSR Academy of Sciences. Their article surveys a body of work carried out by that center on problems of coordination. Their approach is characterized by a number of special features — in particular, emphasis on the strategic nature of the interaction, the problem of incentives, and the incorporation of uncertainty. These complications are analyzed within the framework of an extremely simple model, yet the authors demonstrate or describe some interesting results. For example, apparently complicated assumptions concerning the knowledge about each other held by superior and subordinate collapse to simpler cases; the model is shown to imply an unusual and discontinuous bonus function; and it can incorporate "learning behavior" by the center. The interest of the article, however, lies not merely in the results of the models but in the comparative sophistication of their formulation.

Some noteworthy discussions of other basic issues in planning have been omitted for lack of space. For example, procedures for plan implementation have been treated in a particularly interesting way by Makarov and Perminov, who devise rules of thumb for lower level plan executants hampered by "bounded rationality" [7]. In addition, interesting research has been done into the problem of choosing an optimal organizational structure for planning and management (for a survey, see [8]).

Both these contributions and the ones printed below show the diversity of problems tackled and the diversity of approaches adopted. As Fedorenko, the director of the Central Mathematical Economics Institute, has recently observed, "if the first theoretical models for optimizing the economy mainly described technical relationships (outputs and the material and labor inputs needed to produce them), today the interrelationships incorporate all the major components of planning and management of the economy, including the process of planning itself, operational control, and regulation of the activity of all the subsystems in the economy; this also includes improvements in the organizational structure, management techniques and economic instruments, as well as the development of the required basis in information technology" [9, pp. 1228-29]. This widening of the agenda raises all sorts of practical and methodological problems, as indicated in the articles that follow.

Martin Cave

REFERENCES

1. Maiminas, E. Z. Protsessy planirovaniia v ekonomike. Moscow: "Ekonomika" Publishers, 1971.
2. Petrakov, N. Ia., and Rotar', V. I. "On the Problem of a Mathematical
Economic Model Incorporating Uncertainty." Matekon, 1980, 15(3), 13-33.
3. Petrakov, N. Ia., and Rotar', V. I. "On One Approach to the Problem of
Stabilizing Economic Growth." Matekon, 1979-80, 16(2), 42-70.
4. Ekonomika i matematicheskie metody, 1979, 15(6), 1045-93.
5. Cave, M. Computers and Economic Planning: the Soviet Experience.
Cambridge: Cambridge University Press, 1980.
6. Danilov-Danil'ian, V. I., and Toroian, V. O. "Model' tselevoi programmy
v sisteme optimal'nogo perspektivnogo planirovanniia." Ekonomika i matematicheskie metody, 1978, 14(4), 654-68.
7. Makarov, V. L., and Perminov, S. B. "On Some Aspects of Modeling the
Process of Plan Fulfilment," Matekon, 1979, 16(1), 67-86.
8. Leibkind, A. R. et al. "Models for Forming Crganizational Structures
— a Survey," Matekon, 1981, 17(3), 102-35.
9. "O rabote TsEMI AN SSSR," Ekonomika i matematicheskie metody, 1979,
15(6), 1228-35.

THEORETICAL PROBLEMS OF MODELING
THE SOCIOECONOMIC SYSTEM

E. Z. Maiminas

The objective laws governing the development of our society at
the present time make it urgently necessary to study and model
the socioeconomic system in an integrated way. As was stated
at the Twenty-fourth and Twenty-fifth congresses of the CPSU,
they require that planning and management be oriented more
purposefully toward the goals of economic activity, thus ensuring the satisfaction of social needs and, above all, continuous
increases in the material and cultural standards of the population. Increasing the welfare of the working population becomes,
in turn, one of the major economic preconditions for a fast rate
of growth of output. The development, efficiency, and quality
of production depend, like many social processes, on the accel-
eration of scientific and technical progress and the correct
choice of direction in this regard. The relationships between
our economic development and highly complex problems of international politics and the extension of scientific and economic
cooperation are becoming continuously more diverse. There is
a qualitative change in the interrelation between the economy
and society as a whole on the one hand and the environment on

Russian text © 1979 by "Nauka" Publishers. "Teoreticheskie problemy modelirovaniia sotsial'no-ekonomicheskoi sistemy," Ekonomika i matematicheskie
metody, 1979, vol. 15, no. 4, pp. 653-67.

the other (Materials of the XXV Congress of the CPSU [Materialy XXV s''ezda KPSS] [Moscow: Politizdat, 1976]).

All these processes are linked closely to material production, with which they make up a single system. This system is controlled as a whole in accordance with the new constitution of the USSR on the basis of state plans for economic and social development. Methods of socioeconomic planning incorporate our overall experience in compiling and implementing a national economic plan. The latter determines such things as the social program and the development of the nonproductive sphere, science and technology, and external economic relationships, and these are linked with the structure and growth of material output. Using this foundation, we must now extend the content of the plan and develop its integrated character as a plan for economic and social development. The major issue is the fuller coverage and deeper internal coordination of socioeconomic processes together with a general extension of the planning horizon.

In economics, particularly in research on optimization of the economy, this set of problems has occupied a central place in recent years; this is the result both of the requirements of planning in practice and of the internal logic of the development of theoretical analysis. The major motive force behind this analysis is a generalization and deepening of optimization, from the planning of production to the operation of the socialist economy [1]. The next step leads naturally to the socioeconomic system, and this issue is becoming more and more prominent in a whole set of inquiries — in analyses of the structure, objectives, and mode of operation of the economy, in studies of socioeconomic interests or of the socioeconomic consequences of scientific and technical progress and the use of the environment, and in the composition of numerous sets of models, including simulation models, and so on (for more details, see, for example, [2-4]). This theoretical and applied research now enables us to formulate in a preliminary (and highly provisional) way some theoretical problems encountered in modeling the socioeconomic system.

The Basic Propositions

The concept of the socioeconomic system is not yet clearly defined — still less, uniquely defined. Often it is used as a synonym for the economy to underline its social aspects. Sometimes the socioeconomic system is identified with the social system as a whole or with a particular historical type of social formation. Most frequently (although not explicitly) some intermediate definition is adopted, because of the need to view the economy and other directly related social processes as a system.

It is questionable whether we can decide which processes should be assigned to the first layer surrounding the economic core of the socioeconomic system by measuring how closely those processes are related to material production, especially since we have no reliable way of determining this quantitatively. In methodological terms, we should find a qualitative criterion for what constitutes the system, and then search for some quantitative measure. "Society," as Marx wrote, "does not consist of individuals, but is the totality of the ties and relationships those individuals have with each other" (K. Marx and F. Engels, Works [Sochineniia], vol. 46, part 1, p. 214).

The economy is defined by social relationships between people in the process of production, exchange, and distribution of material goods. These relationships are also the basic ones in the socioeconomic system and in society as a whole. However, the daily life of individuals, of social groups, and of society as a whole is not maintained and reproduced by production of material goods alone. A broader spectrum of resources is needed to satisfy varied individual and collective needs and to support the operation of the social system. This includes psychic benefits, a pleasant environment, numerous and varied sources of information, and a developed social infrastructure. This of course embraces labor too — the quality of work and its psychological and social basis, including attitudes toward work, working habits and arrangements, and the moral atmosphere in production and daily life [4].[1]

Material production does not simply play the role of an external factor in ensuring that these resources come into being; structurally, it permeates every aspect of the process by which they are created, transformed, distributed, and used in society, and conditions their "social makeup." At the same time, material production increasingly betrays the pervasive influence of these processes — through new technology, through the productive and general educational culture of the work force, and the conditions of their daily lives and work, through natural forces, etc.

This interaction allows us in some sense to generalize the concept of "production" to any transformation of resources in society, while continuing to treat material production as its major and decisive element.[2] Viewed overall as a continuous process of renewal, this transformation ensures that the life of society is reproduced, and its full cycle involves all processes of consumption.

The transformation is regulated by highly complex information processes through which social values, interests, norms, and incentives are created, transformed, and come into effect; through which the goals of the respective agents and subsystems of society are determined; and through which resource requirements are specified, adjusted, and met. These processes involve informational feedbacks, in the form of observation, control, and analysis of results. This whole socioeconomic mechanism (which includes an economic mechanism) is a highly important informational resource for the socioeconomic system, and in many ways it predetermines how effectively the system operates. As in the economy, the central problems here are those of incentives and of finding a social evaluation of the benefits of the transformation to compare with its costs in terms of resources — an evaluation based on the concept of socially necessary labor (depending on the conditions under which output is both produced and consumed). It is no exaggeration to say that we can define as socioeconomic any process, relationship, or interaction for which such an evaluation has meaning, and where it exists or operates to control the transformation of resources.

This informational criterion does not allow us unambiguously to define the socioeconomic system as a structural subsystem or to distinguish socioeconomic processes from other social phenomena. The issue is that of distinguishing a functional subsystem of society. In a broad sense [6], social production combines operations by man on nature and by man on man (Marx and Engels, Works, vol. 3, p. 35). Man and his relations with others identify the whole set of these processes, starting with material production. Their socioeconomic aspect involves a transformation of resources and a social evaluation of this transformation; this allows us to distinguish the socioeconomic system as a functional subsystem supporting the existence of society. The socioeconomic relations between men not only include production relations as a major constituent but also the many relationships existing in the superstructure formed on the basis of production relations — juridical, political, and ideological. Socioeconomic aspects dominate in all these relationships, and it is from their interaction that a particular way of life emerges [8]. They are clearly reflected, for example, in processes such as urbanization, and they are observed in cultural affairs as well as in politics and ideology.

In our view, the plan for economic and social development must in the final analysis be a plan for the socioeconomic system and for the processes through which it functions and develops (although the latter are by no means all subject to direct influence by the plan, particularly in the short or medium term). This makes it particularly important to model and analyze the socioeconomic system.

Preconditions for Modeling the Socioeconomic System

As a unit to be modeled, the socioeconomic system is not simply "larger" or more complex than material production alone, or even the economy as a whole. It requires a qualitatively new approach to modeling; new principles are needed to devise models, and these cannot be reduced to the assumptions underlying optimal planning of production or even optimization

of the functioning of the economy. In the case of the socioeconomic system, the very notion of optimization takes on a meaning that is different in principle from the original and strictly
formal definition.

"Traditional" optimizing models in mathematical economics
are intended to choose the best way of using given (current or
future) resources with the aim of satisfying demands that are
in some way specified. What was earlier assumed to be given
from outside — both in the objective function and in the constraints — is now subject to "endogenous" modeling. In the case
of a socioeconomic system, it is meaningless to appeal to a
supersystem that determines resource availabilities and the
criteria by which society evaluates the returns to them. The
socioeconomic system is modeling itself [9].

The presuppositions for optimal planning have by now been
set out fairly strictly and formally and are embodied in detailed
models. But we cannot yet say the same about the presuppositions for modeling the socioeconomic system. It is still too
early for them to exhibit the normal requirements placed on
axiom systems: independence, avoidance of contradiction, and
completeness. To generalize the arguments of a series of
studies (in particular [1-4, 9-13]), we can only point to certain
propositions that must be taken into account in modeling the
socioeconomic system:

(1) The socioeconomic system is a complex (multistructured)
hierarchical dynamic system.

(2) As a unit to be modeled, the socioeconomic system is
unique (on the scale of human society as a whole); it is incom-
pletely observable, containing many important latent factors,
interrelationships, and processes. It exhibits a high degree of
indeterminacy both in its structure and in its development —
this requires stochastic approximation, at the least. Many of
the processes occurring in the socioeconomic system either
cannot be quantified directly, or cannot be quantified at all. It
is an important principle that the socioeconomic system embraces both the observers themselves and instruments of measurement; this affects the researchers' attitudes and the pro-

gram of observations, the quality of the human "observation equipment," and the content of the information coming from the units under observation.[3]

(3) The socioeconomic system is a combination of material and physical processes, and informational processes; it constitutes a self-regulating system[4] that includes the object of control and the system of regulation (or control); hence, it is necessary to construct and combine models of the units to be controlled and of the process by which they are regulated (or controlled).

(4) The resources for developing the socioeconomic system, the motivation for doing so, and the outcome of the process require a broad treatment at the level of society as a whole and must be evaluated in conjunction with the nature and development of social values, interests, goals, and norms.

(5) Such an evaluation of the functioning and development of the socioeconomic system can be realized only through a set of criteria reflecting the totality of the social and economic interests through which the economic relationships of the society are revealed; these criteria are not always formulated a priori, but are generated, amended, and interact[5] as the socioeconomic system develops.

(6) As a result, the most important qualitative properties in the growth of the socioeconomic system are the stability and adaptability with which it develops, combining both structural equilibrium and disequilibrium (this combination is sometimes called "dynamic equilibrium").

(7) The mechanism by which the socioeconomic system operates is formed at the level of metacontrol of the socioeconomic genotype,* which reflects the qualitative aspects of the system and ensures that the interests of its elements and subsystems are coordinated in a way that takes account of emergent results; at the same time, centralization of the higher functions and strategic decisions is combined with independence for local organizations to function "vegetatively" and to make tactical decisions.

---

*A genotype is a group sharing a specified genetic makeup — Editor.

(8) Regulation (or control) of the socioeconomic system cannot be completely incorporated into an algorithm, and its most important blocks must include heuristic procedures, particularly insofar as they concern social aspects of decisions.

(9) Hence, in the foreseeable future it is impossible completely to formalize the modeling of the socioeconomic system or to construct a single, integrated, formal model for this complex system; what is required is a combination of formalized models and informal approaches.

(10) For this reason, we must use political economy and sociology as a methodological basis for integrating the approaches and results of a number of other social and natural sciences.

Propositions (1)-(4) relate primarily to an analysis of the socioeconomic system; (5)-(7) concern its subsequent synthesis, while (8) and (9), and indeed (5), are warnings of the "impossibility theorem" type. All the theoretical propositions above are essentially the result of collective creative scholarship. They are related and form a fairly integrated starting point for modeling the socioeconomic system. In the exposition below, we seek to demonstrate this interrelationship, starting from a representation of the socioeconomic system as a complex system.

The Socioeconomic System as a Complex System

Like any complex system,[6] the socioeconomic system is characterized by diversity both in its states and in its structures. The operation and development of the system is conditioned primarily by the internal interaction of a number of structures that are combined in any element or link in the system. To each structure there corresponds a particular angle or aspect of research into the socioeconomic system, and these must be combined to model it as a system. At the same time, we have to consider all the structures and their interrelationships — in terms of their content and their spatial and temporal properties, and in terms of the relationship within them between material or physical and informational processes.

The chief issue is the qualitative nature of the structure; this

allows us to distinguish three major types of structures interacting within the socioeconomic system. These types (but certainly not all the detailed structures of each type!) are common
to the economy and to the socioeconomic system and, in a sense,
to the social system as a whole, since "the mode of production
in material life conditions social, political, and intellectual life
generally" (Marx and Engels, Works, vol. 13, p. 7). The difference lies in the impact, scale, and mode of operation of any type
of structure in each process under consideration. Obviously,
changes in the productive forces directly influence the organization of production and lead to changes in the relations of production; but it is only after a long time, and indirectly through
the economic structure, that they affect politics and social attitudes. Politics, law, and ideology in their turn, although generated by the economic base, have a certain autonomy and react
back in various ways onto that base (Marx and Engels, Works,
vol. 37, pp. 393-97, 414-22).

The figure illustrates in as simplified a form as possible the
three types of structures in the socioeconomic system and their
interrelationship. In this classification, we provisionally identify (by the small cube) the
core of the socioeconomic
system, the system of material production.

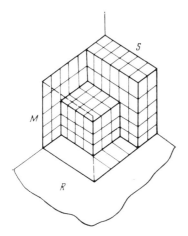

The first type consists of
resource-technology structures R. In this group, the
major structure is the technology of material production.
It conditions the range of material goods produced and the
"technology" of consumption
and of daily life; it influences
the technology of science and
education, the health service,
management, warfare, etc.
The major line of development

in this type of structure is the link between science and production. As Marx foretold, production in the present day has become a technological extension of science. The view of science as a direct productive force applies more and more strongly to every aspect of the transformation of resources in society. In the broad sense of production given above, all type R structures can correctly be regarded as technological structures based on the productive forces.

Technological structures in themselves are flat rather than hierarchical. In the generalized resource plane R in the socioeconomic system, they take the form of a more and more ramified, multiform network of detailed technological operations linked with one another by flows of resources — which may be material or informational depending on the stage of transformation [12]. This system of flows and stages, dispersed in time and space, is not only found in the technological interaction of the workers with one another and with the means of production; nor is it exhibited only in the supply of goods to consumers or interrelationships in the consumption process itself. The technological interactions of people through management, education, and other socioeconomic processes are created in the same way.

"Vertical" relationships between superior and subordinate, teacher and pupil, the informal leader of a group and its other members — even if they are technologically determined — belong by nature to other types of formal or informal structures — social and organizational. On the basis of shared technological inputs, processes, or outputs, or by virtue of the nature of their production processes or the uses to which their outputs are put, blocks in R can be gradually built up into enterprises, technological (or "pure") sectors, and multisector complexes. They can also, on the basis of their location, be aggregated into territorial complexes. These successive levels of aggregation are sometimes called the technological "hierarchy." In fact we are talking about successively more aggregated informational representations of technological blocks. Until a true control block within the organizational structure has been incorporated to direct them, any such representation is no more than an informational model, generated by the researcher.

The next type consists of purely social (society-based) structures S. They come into existence, develop, and change under the predominant influence of the development of the productive forces and of type R structures, although they have a feedback — in an encouraging or restraining way — into the latter. As noted above, what is basic for the socioeconomic system and for society as a whole is the structure of the relations of production — i.e., the relations between people as concerns the means of production; this determines their class position and the distribution of the output. It is in this structure that the technological relations between people take on a particular historical social form. It is under the impact of this structure (in S) that a social evaluation of the costs and benefits of production is made and that evaluation is registered in this structure. Under commodity-money relations the evaluation is realized, in particular, through resource flows in opposite directions using flows of money as carriers of valuations.

In the final analysis, the basic economic structure determines the way of life that is typical for a particular formation — through the combination of the labor and other activities undertaken by the members of society, their consumption, their leisure activities, and so on [8]. Ideological, political, and family relationships are created, together with their corresponding structures, on the basis of the economic structure. It determines the nature of society's socioeconomic genotype — its system of social values, socioeconomic interests, and objectives and norms of control [13].

Social structures "in the plane" appear as a diverse intersecting network of social relationships between individuals. But in fact many of these relationships, as distinct from technological structures, have a true hierarchical character. The existence of social groups and classes in society as well as relationships of dominance and subordination in antagonistic socioeconomic formations is an objective fact of life under certain production relations. Such an economic structure is also reflected in class consciousness through conscious regulation and control processes in the socioeconomic system.

When social and technological processes take on an organizational form, the third and last type of structure in the socioeconomic system comes into existence — organizational and formal institutional structures (M). In terms of content, these structures are obviously social. Informal institutions (such as the family, a school of thought in science, and so on) are woven directly into the fabric of social relations. There is no clear and watertight boundary between these and formal institutions.

The dependence of M on S takes its principal concrete form through the political structure of the society — that is, in the organizational relations between classes and other communities in terms of power and control [5]. Consequently, type M social structures (as distinct from other structures) are created consciously in the form of organizationally permanent social institutions with fully specified tasks, internal structures (usually hierarchical), and interrelationships. Examples are the system of management of the socialist economy, the state and legal structure of the USSR, or the structure of productive or social organizations. Normally, functions are allocated and rights and responsibilities clearly specified in the corresponding regulations laid down either by society as a whole or within the corresponding organization.

Obviously, the nature of all organizational structures changes over time, and some change more rapidly than others by virtue of being linked more closely with shifts in R. Organizational structures bear the imprint of the interaction between technological and social structures. This is shown most clearly in the organizational structure of the economy, in the construction of sectoral and regional units at different levels, and in the identification of functional organizations controlling production, supply, sales, finance, construction, etc. But even the organization of other subsystems in society — such as state control, the courts, the procurator's office, or defense — must, when broken down into units within a framework of vertical and horizontal links, necessarily take into account such "technological" aspects as the nature of the activity under control, the spatial characteristics of the units involved, etc.

Thus the socioeconomic system operates through the interaction of three types of structures, R, S, and M; in modeling the
system, each of them is one "coordinate." Man, being an active
element in this complex system, should also be included in the
system of coordinates. On the technological plane, man plays
the role of a labor resource and a consumption unit. Human
interrelationships take many complex forms in social structures
and in organizations. Only the interaction of these relationships
can explain the behavior of an individual, either overall or in
each isolated act, as producer or consumer, as a member of a
work collective or of a social organization, in a family or in a
group of philatelists.

Spatial and Temporal Aspects

The structural complexity of a socioeconomic system is
matched by the complexity of its spatial and temporal attributes.
Space is one aspect to be considered within each structure, but
it has to be treated differently in each case. In technological
structures, we are dealing with the space in which resources
(including labor resources) are located, relocated, and transformed. In social structures, it is the spatial element in the
life, development, and contacts of man and of the various social
organizations. In organizational structures, we are dealing
with fixed areas of operation of particular organizations or of
dominance of particular control units; certain resources are
subordinate to these in technological space, and they operate
in a particular social space.

A particular region is, as it were, a field of interaction in
this multidimensional space — a fact that is often neglected
when the location of the productive forces or migration is analyzed in isolation or when the responsibilities of regional administrative bodies are determined. In some cases, this is ap-
parent in a collision between departmental and local interests.

In a sense, the temporal properties of the processes occurring in the socioeconomic system (its diachronic structure [24])

are also complex. The key process of development of the productive forces, which causes changes in the relations of production, takes place unevenly in historical time and space, and its
impact on the development of other structures in the socioeconomic system is variable. All these processes differ in important ways in their time and duration, from the fast changes observed in technology, to long investment lags, to even longer
changes in goals or demographic and social trends, and finally
to very slow shifts in value orientations. Even the very concepts of "fast" and "slow" are formed in the ambiguous time
scale of human decisions, which varies in accordance with the
historical epoch, the culture or subculture, and the control
level. Marx and Lenin frequently noted that in periods of revolution historical time is, so to speak, "compressed," and the
rate of socioeconomic transformation speeds up: "revolutions
are the engines of history." An inhabitant of a large modern
city and an Australian aborigine conceive time quite differently, as do an austronaut and a gaucho.[7]

The problem of synchronizing the parameters and elements
in all these various temporal processes is one of the most difficult in the modeling of the socioeconomic system and in forecasting and planning its development. Here we have to take into
consideration the variety of parameters to be controlled and the
origins of indeterminacy at the various time horizons of a forecasting or a planning model.

In the short run, these parameters concern principally the
allocation of current material and financial resources which
(together with spare productive capacity) are used to overcome
technological imbalances and accidental departures from the
plan (random disasters, accidents of production or seasonal
disruptions, a sudden change in foreign trade conditions, etc.).

In the medium term, more importance attaches to activities
associated with investment and construction — the structure
and quality of fixed capital and the date of its installation. There
are also cumulative departures from plan for short-term reasons (affecting design work, shipments, construction work,
etc.). At the same time, particular social and organizational

factors, as well as technological factors, begin to play an increasing role. There are changes in the parameters of the economic mechanism (the system of planning and incentives,
prices, taxation, credit, wages, or management organization);
the structure or level of demand alters, and patterns of migration are affected.

The long term not only sharply increases freedom of maneu-
ver with all types of resources, but also changes the very concept of resource potential; here the most important elements
are those concerned with science and technology, investment,
education, natural resource potential, and the overall development of the infrastructure. The goals toward which development is oriented become particularly important, because of the
broad range of possibilities available; at the same time, we
have to take account of the probability of changes in particular
goals and their interrelationship, as well as shifts in value systems and in the qualitative structure of the socioeconomic
mechanism. On the other hand, short-term fluctuations disap-
pear over a long time horizon; it is more difficult, however, to
assess the impact of many medium-term changes, including
changes in the parameters of the economic mechanism or in the
organization of management.

Thus it is obvious that, just as the interdependence of the
time paths of structures R, S, and M becomes stronger as the
time horizon is extended, so its nature changes. We must start
from this proposition when we devise a continuous system of
short-term, medium-term, and long-term plans and when we
establish systems of plan indicators. Our armory of models
for carrying out the appropriate computations, however, is
presently oriented primarily toward plane R. This allows us,
by using expert estimates of particular parameters and design
data, to foresee changes in resources and technology over the
course of the life of a capital project (from its design to its
commissioning and the completion of its life cycle as a production system) on average for seven, ten, or even fifteen years.
Beyond these limits, an approach of this kind inevitably leads
to a view of the more distant future characterized by inertia.

It is quite natural that there should be widespread interest in the use of various simulation models, with experts participating actively in both their design and their operation. It is particularly important, however, to appreciate the subjective basis of these models: the quality of the results obtained depends entirely on the ability of the experts to devise a "creative reality" and to operate in that reality in the same way as in the real socioeconomic system.

The Controller and the Controlled in the Socioeconomic System

We can provisionally distinguish material and informational processes within the socioeconomic system in accordance with their underpinnings. In fact, they interact in each block of the system, and the issue is rather what kind of product is expected as the output. Thus technological and other types of control information are used in material production processes, yet we correctly classify these processes as material or physical. Conversely, all forms of mental output (science, culture, education) are informational in character, even though more and more powerful material inputs are being used to produce them, from proton synchrotons to computers.

Consequently, resource and technological structures combine both material or physical and informational processes. Purely social and organizational structures — the relationships between people in these structures and the processes that take place within them — are informational in character. Physical equipment for communication and control — from a communication system to armed forces — also belong to technological structures, for management, propaganda, defense, and so on.

Within the social and organizational structures of the socioeconomic system, information also fulfills the specific function of control of the system. Information for control is also generated in R — in the form of knowledge about the natural environment and society (as well as technical knowledge, of course) and in the form of feedback about the implementation of the

controls and their results. This information is transformed
into control information in structures S and M, in which new information is generated as well. The basic source of control information is the interaction of these structures, although it is
clearly realized primarily through M.

In fact an informational analysis of the socioeconomic system
allows us to distinguish controlling units from controlled units
in this self-regulating system,[8] since it is only the content of
the informational flows that determines the relationship between
them. Generally speaking, processes in the socioeconomic system (for example, creative processes in mental work) are regulated not by relationships formed in an organized way (and at
certain stages there is no institutionalized regulation system),
but directly by scientific or aesthetic attitudes or by social values
(although these regulations are themselves formed through the
joint operation of all the structures). Control presupposes the
existence of some organizational structure, through which control information passes and is acted upon. It does not consist
entirely of information flows in M, but, as a starting point, it
is most convenient to view control through the prism of organizational structures.

As noted already, these structures are themselves formed
through the interaction of resource and technological factors,
on the one hand, and of social factors, on the other. In the final
analysis, control in the socioeconomic system regulates the
processes by which resources are transformed and must conform with the principle of requisite variety. As the productive
forces develop, the informational variety of the processes increases. "Mastering" them requires a corresponding increase
in the variety of the system of regulation, which at certain historical stages leads to a qualitative change in the social form
of regulation of the socioeconomic system; a change occurs in
the social structures and, in particular, in the system of economic relations [20]. To give shape to the operation of these
factors within the framework of the socioeconomic formation,
organizational hierarchies appropriate to the mode of production come into existence, grow, and adapt. The initial com-

plexity of the socioeconomic system is broken down within these
hierarchies into informational blocks formed on the basis of
their interrelationships and control levels. At the same time,
each block processes only an insignificant part of the information circulating in the system; the capacity required is reduced
by many orders of magnitude (compared with total centralization of control in a single block). Informational constraints,
however, are only a general precondition for the formation of
hierarchical organizational structures. The true distinction
between control units and the units they control arises from the
complex interaction of technological and social factors, which
determines the area of dominance of any particular organization
in the structures.

On the resource and technology plane, certain transformers
of resources are subordinated to control blocks and are thus
controlled units in this respect. Special features of the technology play some role here, but the nature of production relations is decisive, particularly the form of ownership of the
means of production. These determine what kind of economic
units are distinguished, how large they are, and how they are
interrelated with and subordinated to each other.

In an organizational hierarchy, any given controlling unit has
subordinate units at a lower level under its direct control. Only
the lowest level controls technological operations directly, and
among workers and groups of workers — the elementary agents
of control at this level — socioeconomic interests arise that
reflect both production and other relationships in the socioeconomic system. These are further refracted at subsequent levels, forming a complex set of social, institutional, group, and
personal interests.

The socioeconomic system contains individuals, groups, and
organizations, and this ensures a dialectical relationship between controlling units and the units they control which is lacking in technical systems. Thus the collective in a socialist enterprise is both a unit to be controlled by the management and
superior organizations and, at the same time, a controlling
unit in relation to its own members and a link in the system of

management of society. Control information is formed through the interaction of instructions from the controlling bodies and the internal interests of their subordinates.

The actual activity of the latter is not regulated by a simple vertical hierarchy (in fact, we often find here dual subordination, by sector and by region). Even within organizational structures based on laws, a productive enterprise, for example, is for many of its functions under the control of a whole series of controlling units (the bank, national control bodies, health, fire, and other regulations, and so on). The operation of each link and cell in the socioeconomic system is influenced by material incentives and sanctions and is governed by legal standards; moreover, every member of society acts in accordance with certain moral standards and a certain world view and ideological attitude, and conforms with the behavior of his or her small group. In other words, in terms of the many social dimensions in S, a man is both a unit under control and a controlling unit outside the fixed organizational structures.

This whole, highly complex combination of regulators created by the socioeconomic system makes it difficult to identify controlling units, particularly for modeling purposes. In modeling the system, it is much easier to identify the informational inputs and outputs by treating each block as a unit. Moreover, we can follow the flow of the information in various directions and, by stopping at some stage, we can identify the group of organizations that transforms that information.

We are thus able to construct and compare two types of models: a model of the unit of management that describes the transformations taking place within that unit, and a model of the process of management that shows the movement and transformation of information associated with the regulation of that unit [20]. Generally speaking, each information transformer supplying our "unit" with information can be identified as a controller. We would be justified in classifying them in accordance with some threshold value of a measure of their impact on the behavior of the unit, if such a measure existed. Hitherto, as noted, we have been restricted to qualitative indices of the organizational hierarchy. But such an approach clearly does not give a sufficiently detailed map of control in a socioeconomic system.

When we model the socioeconomic system as a whole, it becomes difficult in principle to subdivide units and processes under control, and this applies even more to controlling units. In the first place, a high degree of aggregation is unavoidable, and standard aggregation principles must take account of the complexities of the structure of the units under study; otherwise, modeling will be confined to a single plane of the socioeconomic system.

The chief difficulty here lies in the choice of standpoint of the researcher himself. He must identify himself explicitly or implicitly with some constituent in the socioeconomic system as the starting point for his account, and this influences how the blocks are established, the extent and principle of aggregation, and the breakdown of major interests and objectives. Could a researcher building an integrated model of the socioeconomic system conceivably distance himself from the various standpoints? In fact, the builders of simulation models of socioeconomic systems try to do so when they appoint experts in decision-making units to "voice" the interests of the corresponding elements in the system. But the illusion disappears as soon as the question arises of interpreting and using the results.

Quality and Variability in the Operation and Development of the Socioeconomic System

Even if we assume that the problem of modeling socioeconomic systems is resolved, three major questions traditionally face the researcher: how to evaluate the operation and development of the system, how to choose the best alternative, and how to implement the alternative chosen. In any case, these are correct questions to ask regarding the design of technical systems or the selection or genetics of biological organisms, although here too they may have unforeseen or underestimated consequences. How to treat these questions and find answers to them remains a central issue in studies dealing with the optimal planning and functioning of the socialist economy. The closer the researchers are to a particular block in the resource-technology structure and the shorter the planning horizon they consider, the more reliable are their recommendations.

For the case of a socioeconomic system, as is clear from its definition and the assumptions on which it is modeled, we must first examine the very formulation of the questions. The formulation will differ in essential respects depending on whether we view it provisionally as operating in a stationary regime or whether we are studying its development, since our formulation will be quite different if we are operating within the confines of a particular socioeconomic formation from what it will be if we are considering the transition to later formations.

Each socioeconomic order works out and establishes within its genotype a system of criteria for evaluating the operation of a particular socioeconomic system appropriate to its qualitative properties. This can take the very direct form of management attitudes or "accepted" technical rules for running the economy.

In accordance with these rules, one first evaluates technological and organizational alternatives and makes a choice from among them, then does the same with alternative forms of control. In complex systems there is generally no clear and unique correspondence between structure and function. Within limits, the same structure can perform a whole series of functions, and conversely the same functions can be performed by a class of structures. But these limits are quite different for different types of structures of the socioeconomic system. Technological structures R are the most dynamic and variable; they can be evaluated and selected comparatively successfully using the operating criteria of the system. Organizational structures M are relatively more stable, but here too we may use the same criteria. Shifts in social structures S take much longer and — this is most important — it is these shifts that shape the very criteria by which the operation of the socioeconomic system is evaluated. Although in any historical epoch these criteria are formed in the past and extrapolated into the future, they remain the creation of that epoch, since the superstructure depends on the base of the corresponding socioeconomic formation.

Consequently, when we are speaking of a socioeconomic system that is developing and in transition from one historical type to another or discussing major qualitative changes in its mode of operation, it is unsuitable to have criteria for evaluating the operation of the system that are specific to each type. "Society," wrote Marx, "if it is following along the natural law of its development..., can neither jump over natural phases of its development nor sweep aside the latter by decree. But it can shorten or lengthen the birth pangs" (Marx and Engels, Works, vol. 23, p. 10). The key to a scientific evaluation of society lies in knowledge of the objective laws of the natural historical process of its development.

General laws for the development of the socioeconomic system are revealed in the specific forms and criteria of operation of an individual formation, since the operation and growth of a system form a single process. The linkage between the two aspects of the process is particularly important for an overall evaluation of how it changes. On the one hand, the development of the socioeconomic system is reflected in the continuous increase in the productivity of social labor. In the R plane this is shown by the development and transformation of resources for society and by the level of output and variety of the output structure. On the other hand, in S (and R) this increase leads to a change in the nature of work, in other kinds of activity, and in the whole way of life of the members of society; it also leads to the development of their capabilities.

In societies divided into antagonistic classes, this process takes place in the class form appropriate to each society. With the liquidation of antagonistic contradictions, social progress is ensured directly: "all the attributes of man as a social being are cultivated, and he is created a being with the richest possible capacities and relationships, and hence needs — man is the most valuable and universal product of society (since in order to use the materials available, man must be capable of using them, i.e., he must be a person with a high cultural level)" (Marx and Engels, Works, vol. 46, part 1, p. 386). Thus, the extent to which the human personality can develop freely and harmoniously, together with the extent and breadth of the incorporation of the human personality into society, is a criterion for the development of the socioeconomic system.

It is only possible to deal with the problem of evaluating the growth process of a socioeconomic system if we combine the general and the specific. And, as we switch from the economic base toward politics and ideology (particularly over comparatively short historical intervals), the more variable the development of any particular structure becomes, "the more it moves in a zigzag. If you trace the line along an axis, then you will find that, the longer the period and the wider the area under study, the closer that line approximates the axis of economic development, and the more closely parallel to it it becomes" (Marx and Engels, Works, vol. 39, p. 176). Within the historical limits set by the objective laws of development of the socioeconomic system, how far a particular variant can be deliberately implemented depends on how well these laws are understood, how well society is organized, how forcefully it can act on the basis of those laws, and the extent to which society's members share social or economic interests.

Thus sociology and political economy are of great value from a methodological point of view if we are to solve the theoretical problems of modeling the socioeconomic system. "At the present stage of the country's development the need for further creative theoretical work is not diminishing but, on the contrary, is becoming even stronger. New opportunities for creative research both of a general theoretical and fundamental nature and of an applied character are opening up at the interfaces of different sciences, particularly the natural and social sciences. These opportunities must be fully exploited (Materials of the XXIV Congress of the CPSU [Materialy XXIV s''ezda KPSS] [Moscow: Politizdat, 1976], p. 72). These remarks apply equally to integrated research into the socioeconomic system, for this will give us a scientific basis for improving our planning and control of that system.

NOTES

1. By a resource we mean any stock or flow of a material or intellectual input actually or potentially available for transformation (or use), situated at the entrance of any block in the social system and necessary for its operation.

2. One encounters more and more often in the literature the concepts of "mental, nonmaterial production" [5, 6] or "the production of knowledge or information" [7]. We do not classify as production the transformation of resources in nature itself, unless it is associated with human activity (the manufacture of peat, for example, or the natural reproduction of noncultivated flora or fauna); nor do we classify as production transformations of resources in society, unless they are linked with social needs (psychopathological activity, for example).

3. The material observed — people and groups with their own interests and wills — are not indifferent to the content of the scientific hypotheses adopted and the forecasts to be tested; the latter may in some cases be falsified for this reason.

4. It would be more accurate to describe the socioeconomic system as a self-improving system, capable of changing its program of regulation (i.e., self-teaching) and its structure (i.e., self-organizing) over a growing set of elements.

5. If criteria "interact," it means that the evaluations obtained on the basis of those criteria are not additive.

6. Research into complex systems of a general methodological nature can be found in [14-16]; for applications to society, see [8, 17, 18, etc.]; and to the economy, see [19-23, etc.].

7. It may turn out to be useful in this connection to have a generalized concept of space-time in the socioeconomic system. M. M. Bakhtin introduces this concept, applied to spiritual and aesthetic values, as "chronotopy." Many participants in the debate concerning "the Asiatic mode of production" have also adopted this view.

8. Control assumes the existence both of a regulator — which, in accordance with a given program, ensures that specified states or outputs are achieved by the unit regulated — and of a block — which specifies those properties and the program.

REFERENCES

1. Fedorenko, N. P. Optimizatsiia ekonomiki. Moscow: "Nauka" Publishers, 1977.

2. Maiminas, E. Z. "Razvitie sistemnogo podkhoda k narodnokhoziaistvennomu planirovaniiu." Ekonomika i matematicheskie metody, 1974, vol. 10, no. 5.

3. Baranov, E. F.; Danilov-Danil'ian, V. I.; and Zavelskii, M. G. "O sisteme optimal'nogo perspektivnogo planirovaniia." Ekonomika i matematicheskie metody, 1971, vol. 7, no. 3.

4. Danilov-Danil'ian, V. I., and Zavel'skii, M. G. Sistema optimal-nogo perspektivnogo planirovaniia narodnogo khoziaistva. Moscow: "Nauka" Publishers, 1975.

5. Perfil'ev, M. N. Obshchestvennye otnosheniia. Leningrad: "Nauka" Publishers, 1974.

6. "Aktual'nye aspekty materialisticheskogo ponimaniia istorii." Kommunist, 1978, no. 17.

7. Afanas'ev, V. G. Sotsial'naia informatsiia i upravlenie obshchetvom. Moscow: Politizdat, 1975.

8. Butenko, A. P. Sotsialisticheskii obraz zhizni: problemy i suzhdeniia. Moscow: "Nauka" Publishers, 1978.

9. Petrakov, N. Ia. Kiberneticheskie problemy upravleniia ekonomikoi. Moscow: "Nauka" Publishers, 1974.

10. Mikhalevskii, B. N. Sistema modelei srednesrochnogo narodnokhoziaistvennogo planirovaniia. Moscow: "Nauka" Publishers, 1972.

11. Kornai, J. Anti-equilibrium. Amsterdam: North-Holland, 1971.

12. Problemy optimal'nogo funktsionirovaniia sotsialisticheskoi ekonomiki. Moscow: "Nauka" Publishers, 1972.

13. Maiminas, E. Z. "Upravlenie khoziaistvennym mekhanizmom i ekonomicheskaia kibernetika." Ekonomika i matematicheskie metody, 1976, vol. 12, no. 4.

14. Problemy metodologii sistemnogo issledovaniia. Moscow: "Mysl'" Publishers, 1970.

15. Blauberg, I. V., and Iudin, E. G. Stanovlenie i sushchnost' sistemnogo podkhoda. Moscow: "Nauka" Publishers, 1973.

16. Sistemnye issledovaniia. Moscow: "Nauka" Publishers, annually, 1969-78.

17. Afanas'ev, V. G. Nauchnoe upravlenie obshchestvom. Moscow: Politizdat, 1973.

18. Sotsiologiia i problemy sotsial'nogo razvitiia. Moscow: "Nauka" Publishers, 1978.

19. Cherniak, Iu. I. Sistemnyi analiz i upravlenie ekonomikoi. Moscow: "Ekonomika" Publishers, 1975.

20. Maiminas, E. Z. Protsessy planirovaniia v ekonomike: informatsionnyi aspekt. Moscow: "Ekonomika" Publishers, 1971.

21. Saltykov, B. G., and Tambovtsev, V. L. "K probleme postroeniia dereva tselei sotsial'no-ekonomicheskoi sistemy." Ekonomika i matematicheskie metody, 1973, vol. 9, no. 6.

22. Gavrilets, Iu. N. Sotsial'no-ekonomicheskoe planirovanie: sistemy i modeli. Moscow: "Ekonomika" Publishers, 1974.

23. Fedorenko, N. P. "K voprosu o 'kletochke' sotsialisticheskogo proizvodstva." Voprosy filosofii, 1978, no. 4.

24. Serov, N. K. Protsessi i mera vremeni. Leningrad: "Nauka" Publishers, 1974.

THE OPERATING MECHANISM OF A SOCIALIST ECONOMY AND THE PROBLEM OF THE ECONOMY'S OPTIMALITY CRITERION

N. Ia. Petrakov

One of the major ways of improving the system of economic planning and management mentioned in the report of L. I. Brezhnev, general secretary of the Central Committee of the CPSU, to the Twenty-fifth Party Congress, was the problem of orienting the whole system of planning indicators to reflect the end results of economic activity. If this problem is to be solved, then research must be intensified in the area of devising criteria to evaluate the activity of every agency in the economic system.

The problem of the national optimality criterion is among the problems that are most generally and vigorously debated in the current economic literature. Interest in this problem is generated by the fact that the formulation of the criterion is one of the pivotal factors in the theory and practice of organizing economic management. This problem is clearly not an invention of mathematical economics (although discussion of it in recent years has been stimulated by the work of mathematical economists) but is linked organically with such fundamental categories of political economy as "socialist ownership," "the basic

Russian text © 1976 by "Nauka" Publishers. "Mekhanizm funktsionirovaniia sotsialisticheskoi ekonomiki i problema narodnokhoziaistvennogo kriteriia optimal'nosti," Ekonomika i matematicheskie metody, 1976, vol. 12, no. 5, pp. 941-53.

economic law of socialism," and "the nature of planning." For this reason the problems encountered in developing the political economy of socialism have ensured that the issues concerning the economy's optimality criterion have been the subject of study and debate.

In our view, there is need for a broader exchange of views on the problem of criteria. The urgency of such a debate stems not only from the importance of the problem from the standpoint of the theory of political economy and the further development of theoretical and methodological principles for the management of the socialist economy; it also follows from the fact that, when the debate first started, for various reasons certain issues disappeared from sight (or were overshadowed) which experience has shown to be of exceptional significance both in a theoretical and in a practical sense. An important role here belongs to the development of the category of social welfare from the standpoint of the basic economic law of socialism. In specifying in detail the requirements for this fundamental law of the socialist mode of production, we focus attention on the problem of weighting the social and economic interests of different groups of workers and using this as a basis for comparing the goods that can be used to benefit those interests.

As research intensifies on the goal stage of planning as part of the development of program-goal techniques of plan compilation, we encounter the serious methodological problem of linking these developments with our view of how the economy's optimality criterion is derived.

It is vitally important, of course, to regard the stage of identifying and formulating the economy's criterion not as a stage prior to the plan, but as an organic element in an entire operating mechanism that includes the stages of forecasting, plan compilation, implementation, control over fulfillment and, where necessary, correction. Closely related to this is a set of issues including the question of how the purposive control of the planned economy should be organized in circumstances where the interaction of all the elements in the economic system is not strictly determinate at all stages in its operation.

Since we cannot within the confines of a single article discuss all the issues listed, we restrict ourselves to the last of those mentioned, bearing in mind their relative novelty and, in our view, their undoubted importance.

On Some Trends in the Development of the Theory of Control over the Economy

The notion that deliberate and active control of the economy is a practical problem is a creation of the twentieth century. It has certain specific features. The fact that control of the economy is a practical possibility is only indirectly the result of developments in science and technology or in the productive forces. Solving the problem of the control of the economic system involves primarily the solution of social (rather than technical) problems, and this is a natural consequence of the nature of the entity to be controlled. Development of the productive forces only creates the necessary material conditions for fundamental changes in the social basis and helps to create conditions for the transformation of production relations or for their replacement through a revolutionary process. Mankind's conquests in the field of the management of economic processes have been directly conditioned by fundamental social changes such as have taken place over the past decades. These changes consist, first, in the transformation of a capitalism based on free competition into state monopoly capitalism and, then, in the emergence of a new economic system based on socialist ownership of the means of production.

It would of course be incorrect to assert that the issue of whether purposeful control of the economy is necessary has arisen solely in the twentieth century. The history of economic thought includes a number of organizational proposals for control of the economic system that are as brilliant as they are utopian. They all envisaged the elimination of the existing mode of operation of the economic system and the formation of economic relationships based on new principles. The theory of scientific communism, which set out the fundamental ideas for the control of the socialist economy, also — as is well known — presupposes the elimination of the capitalist system and the socialization of fixed capital as a necessary precondition for the switch to a consciously controlled economic system. "There is the same difference here as between the destructive power of electricity in lightning and the tamed electrical current in the telegraph system or the electric lamp; the same difference as that between a conflagration and a fire burning in the service of mankind" (K. Marx and F. Engels, Works [Sochineniia], vol. 20, p. 291).

As far as the apologists of bourgeois society are concerned, their position directly or indirectly comes down to asserting that, the less the economy is controlled, the greater the "social welfare." Only since the time of the "great depression" of the late 1920s and early 1930s has the need for active state regulation of the development of the economy been fully discussed in bourgeois economics, through the efforts of Keynes and his followers.[1] But this was a period when the social and economic structure of capitalist society was already seriously deformed as a result of the activities of the large monopolies and of finance capital.

The notion of conscious and purposeful control of the economy as a problem that not only requires a practical solution but also can be solved in practice within the framework of objective social conditions is a feature of the socialist economic system. There is not and cannot be a single system of management irrespective of the social nature of the unit, its scale, and the degree of complexity. The nature of the unit determines the nature of the control.

In order to identify the control techniques appropriate to the organization in question, obviously we must first identify its special features; i.e., we must correctly describe the unit to be controlled. Naturally, we attach a well-defined meaning to the notion of "a correct description." We mean that a model must be devised for the unit (whether a mathematical or heuristic model) that incorporates its major properties. Identifying these properties is a primary part of the analytical research

work and is an indication of how well the unit is understood.
This is particularly important since, for the overwhelming majority of more or less complex units, it is impossible in principle to construct a model that exhaustively describes the unit.
As Norbert Wiener perceptively observed, the ultimate model of a cat can be only another cat, irrespective of whether it was obtained by the normal method or in a laboratory.

Over the course of the development of economics, a great many types of models have been proposed to describe the economy, including models using mathematical techniques. These models can be classified in various ways. The most widespread subdivision is based on the distinction (and, in some degree, the contrast) between two major groups of models: balance models and extremal models. This classification is useful in many respects. First, it corresponds to the actual historical process by which the modeling of the economy developed from basically equilibrium or balance models to an account of the economy as a system developing toward some goal. Second, it underlines how mathematical tools are used in different ways to interpret economic processes (in one case, most use is made of systems of differential equations and linear algebra; in the other, of mathematical programming and game theory). Third, such a classification is useful to demonstrate the scientific methodology that lies at the basis of the various models for describing the economy: in one case, emphasis is placed on the view of the economy as a system developing mainly in a process characterized by inertia; in the other, priority is given to the active role of management bodies in redistributing economic resources in the decision-making process.

At the same time, this classification has certain limitations. First, extremal models are normally equilibrium models. In any case, it is quite obvious that the procedure for solving mathematical programming problems consists in finding a situation that is an equilibrium in a particular clearly specified sense. The difference between such models and balance models lies at another level. In extremal models, economic interrelations are not specified exogenously on the basis of external information, but are found through the decision process, on the basis of the properties of the objective function, the availability of resources and the degree of substitutability between them, and the technologies available for using those resources. The problem also involves finding a combination of characteristics that will ensure that the system emerges into an operating regime which is optimal from the standpoint of the chosen criterion. Thus extremal models embody in a clear form the concept of a system that is purposeful. If, by control, we mean that the elements of a system operate to change that system's parameters in order to move it from its original position to one that is superior (in the view of the controlling body), then it is not hard to conclude that an extremal model in which the criterion for the development (or state) of the system is clearly expressed would be very suitable for analyzing control problems. A criterion or objective function expresses and hence reflects our conception of the system's purposes. By formulating that criterion, we make the solution of the management problem substantially easier. It is for this reason that in recent years the methods and techniques of operations research have been quickly developed and given recognition. But we should bear in mind that the solution is made easier at the cost of simplifying the formulation of the control problem. Assuming that the objective function is given exogenously is in many cases (particularly for complex economic systems) too strong an assumption.

As far as purely balance models (of the input-output type) are concerned, these embody no clear formulation of the notion of a purposeful system and represent for the controlling body a part of its passive economic information about the state of the system. In such models the problem of the criterion remains "out of bounds." But it surfaces whenever it is suggested that a use be made for control purposes of the information contained in the balance models. For example, if the existing structure of the economy is held to be optimal, then this presupposes some optimality criterion. Assumptions about changes over time in the coefficients of the input-output model, changes in the structure of final demand, and so on are essentially exogenously specified hypotheses about possible changes in the state of the system, and if these changes are considered to be desirable or are rejected, then there is every basis for saying that some criterion for evaluating the state of the system exists, even if it is only formulated by the control body at an intuitive level.

When we consider control problems, it is important to establish the extent to which any models for describing the economy can be viewed as describing purposeful behavior. Insofar as a socialist economy is a controlled economy, this is important for the evaluation of the adequacy of any model of an actual system. Analysis shows that most mathematical models of the economy can be interpreted directly or indirectly in terms of a goal and of the means for achieving it. Thus purposefulness as a specific property of the system to be controlled has been fairly well reflected in the modeling of economic processes.

The situation is very much worse when we turn to the analysis and hence the modeling of the process of interaction between the controlling bodies and the controlled unit. Although outwardly simple, in our view the problem has one aspect of major significance that has not yet received the attention in the literature its importance warrants.

The nature of the controlling body's actions is determined by its notion of the unit it is controlling and of the global objective function. On the basis of its conceptions of these, it chooses control parameters and ways of intervening with the controlled unit, and it evaluates the responses to these interventions. In relation to economic systems, we may say that the control parameters themselves are fairly well known. The allocation of investment and of primary productive resources among the various spheres of economic activity is a powerful means of exercising a controlling influence over the nature and tempo of economic development. At the macro level production functions are used to express how changes in the outcome of the economic process (growth of national income, for example) depend on how intensively primary productive resources are used. At the sectoral level, in order to describe the relationship between inputs and outputs, use is made of the properties of technological relationships in production (input coefficients, indices of capital and labor input per unit of output, norms for the use of materials, including raw materials, etc.). Overall, we can say that highly significant achievements have been recorded in the area of modeling the inputs and outputs of economic processes, at various levels of aggregation of information.

Economists, however, have almost completely avoided the question of how determinate are the processes described by the models, and how accurate is the actual information exchanged between the controlled unit and the controller. At the same time, it is generally recognized that this issue is becoming more and more urgent as the system grows more and more complex. As information flows multiply and become more complex, we lose the simplicity in the response to control signals that we would like. Indeed, these signals do not always appear as strictly determinate instructions to the system and its separate elements. When we bring a control mechanism into operation in a complex system, we can expect only to achieve the desired outcome with a given probability. The indeterminacy of large systems (and these include economic systems) is so obvious that this statement cannot be contradicted either by economic theorists or by practitioners. Here, though, we must emphasize one terminological aspect of considerable importance for theoretical economists. Indeterminacy in a centrally controlled system is not identical in meaning to randomness in the development of economic processes. Randomness works against conscious control or planning. But conscious, purposeful action to control the economy does not mean that all the processes taking place within the system are strictly determinate.[2]

If we recognize the existence of indeterminacy in economic processes and in the behavior of the controlled unit,[3] it may seem that this aspect should be regarded as the major distin-

guishing characteristic of the control process. This feature of
the operation of economic systems, however, has in practice
been little studied. As far as the qualitative formulation of the
question is concerned, uncertainty (and here we must recognize
our debt to the cyberneticists) was already present in one form
or another in the first elaboration of the general theory of control of complex systems. The introduction of the concept of the
"black box" as a nondetermined element, the principle of external augmentation, and the enlistment of Beer's version [3] of
Godel's theorem concerning the incompleteness of language, are
all attempts to "legitimize" indeterminacy in describing processes of control of complex systems. In spite of a certain ar-
bitrariness in the treatment of some concepts, we must recognize that the founders of cybernetics have succeeded overall at
only a qualitative level. This applies in particular to description of the control of social systems. Wiener considered the
principle of indeterminacy so important a feature of social systems that, in his view, the mathematical apparatus developed
to describe physical or even biological processes was not generally suitable for socioeconomic systems. "The use of mathematical formulae," he noted, "had accompanied the development of the natural sciences and become the mode in the social
sciences. Just as primitive peoples adopt the Western modes
of denationalized clothing and of parliamentarianism out of a
vague feeling that these magic rites and vestments will at once
put them abreast of modern culture and technique, so the economists have developed the habit of dressing up their rather im-
precise ideas in the language of the infinitesimal calculus. . . .
An econometrician will develop an elaborate and ingenious theory of supply and demand, inventories and unemployment and
the like, with a relative or total indifference to the methods by
which these elusive quantities are observed or measured. To
assign what purports to be precise values to such essentially
vague quantities is neither useful nor honest, and any pretense
of applying precise formulae to these loosely defined quantities
is a sham and a waste of time" [4, pp. 98-99, 100] .

In our view, two factors explain why such a severe verdict is recorded against attempts to formalize economic processes. In the first place, an attempt is made to warn against mechanically transferring methods for describing in mathematical terms units at one level of complexity to units with a qualitatively different structure and mode of operation. And here we must pay particular attention to the views of the distinguished scholar. Second, we should not forget that Wiener had before his eyes the capitalist system with its random nature and with a number of highly important features that are in principle uncontrollable. As a result, we can say that his pessimism regarding the application of cybernetic ideas to the economic aspect of human activity is fully justified in the sense that such a possibility arises only in a centrally controlled socialist economy. At the same time, it would be wrong to view these obvious advantages of a socialist system as indicating that determinate models are more suitable to describe a planned economy and probabilistic models more suitable for a capitalist economy (while, in fact, bourgeois econometrics relies more heavily on determinate models in mathematical economics). The problem must evidently be posed more broadly: either indeterminacy in the behavior of the elements in the system is not a major property of a complex economic system, or models that do not take account of indeterminacy cannot pretend to give a correct description of an actual unit or to set down its basic properties adequately.

What, then, is the true state of affairs in the economy? What factors determine whether randomness or indeterminacy appear in the economic system?

The Principle of Indeterminacy and the Choice of an Optimality Criterion for the Economy

Among the factors causing indeterminacy in the socioeconomic system, we must include above all the formulation of the optimality criterion for the economy. So far, as we have seen, the optimality criterion in economic models at the national

level has been given exogenously. In fact, however, if we are
talking at the macro level of choosing a development strategy
for the socioeconomic system as a whole, then a distinctive
feedback loop operates. Since the criterion for the growth of a
socialist economy is maximum satisfaction of the needs of the
members of society, whatever form they take, the controlling
agency must necessarily refer to the controlled unit to get information concerning the level and structure of, and trends in,
individual and social needs. At the same time, account must be
taken of the fact that the control body is itself an element in the
same socioeconomic system for which it is formulating the optimality criterion.

Thus the very procedure for determining, say, the part of the
criterion that reflects the level and structure of demand for
personal consumption goods means that the parameters of the
criterion are only approximately determined and that the latter
must subsequently be coordinated and corrected in accordance
with feedbacks received from the controlled unit. It is still
more difficult to foretell how the weighting of the parameters of
the objective function will change over time. This depends on
an enormous number of social and production factors, which in
any case interact with one another. This special feature of the
economy as a unit to the controlled was noted in particular by
Wiener, who wrote that "the economic game is a game where
the rules are subject to important revisions, say every ten
years" [4, p. 100].

After analyzing the problem of finding an optimality criterion,
the present author was able, even in 1971 [5, p. 27], to draw
the conclusion that, when axiom systems are being determined
for optimal planning and management of the socialist economy,
the postulate that there is a criterion of optimality for the economy should be augmented by the following postulate: that this
criterion is in the final analysis indeterminate and that a mechanism for finding, revising, and correcting the criterion as the
system operates is needed. Introducing the principle that the
criterion is ultimately indeterminate into the axioms for optimal operation of the economy entitles us to view the system as

self-regulating and self-improving. In this approach, development involves not finding the shortest route to a clearly defined goal, but simultaneously searching for and correcting the development goals. This argument — for seeking the criteria as the system is changing and for developing a means of organizing the search — is a consideration that is qualitatively new in principle and distinguishes highly complex systems from the systems studied by specialists in operations research.

Thus a refusal to view the problem of the national criterion as a problem above and outside the socioeconomic system is sufficient grounds for establishing the principle that the ultimate indeterminacy of the criterion is one of the key aspects in the operation of the economy. Indeterminacy in the economic system, however, is also caused by a number of other factors — among them, the question of how accurate economic information is.

In social systems, there is the special problem of establishing social mechanisms for giving the unit to be controlled an incentive to transmit accurate information both to its superior and to units operating at the same level (from one enterprise to another, for example). The "concealment effect" is explained by conflicts of interest (or criteria) between different parts of the economic system. In a capitalist economy, such conflicts are objectively conditioned by the social orientation of the system as a whole. Illustrations of this are the protection of commercial secrecy, concealment of incomes to evade taxes, the policy of monopolies over patents, techniques for limiting the diffusion of technological inventions, and so on. In a socialist economy, the position is diametrically opposite. In our economy too, however, we encounter relative and nonantagonistic conflicts of interest between different parts of the economic system and the global objectives of the system. This is explained by two factors: first, by subjective and temporary deficiencies in organizing the system of planning and incentives; and, second, by the objective impossibility of complete and perfect coordination of all the interests of the separate blocks in the system at each moment of time.

As far as the first consideration is concerned, this factor is being eliminated as a result of the active policies adopted by the CPSU and the directive bodies of the Soviet state both to improve the system of prices, charges for the use of productive resources, and fines for pollution of the environment, and to develop the system of planning indicators for evaluating economic activity (local criteria) and the incentive system.

The second consideration is the result of special features in the interaction of the controlling body and the unit controlled, which are mentioned above. When the controlling body is establishing a model for the objective function, it must have constant recourse to the social system, which acts as a "higher court" both when the controlling body attempts to find such a model and when it chooses the form and frequency of its control signals. This makes it objectively impossible to achieve complete, determinate consistency in the chain from control signal to expected outcome. The economic system that is being controlled is in a constant state of flux. What was right yesterday may turn out to be wrong today. These changes in the responsiveness of the system to the control signals can be forecast only within a certain degree of accuracy.

The unit to be controlled, although a subsystem of the national economy, at the same time retains features of a self-teaching and self-improving system. The operation of the principle of indeterminacy is revealed here in the fact that the language of the local criterion in which the control signal "converses" with the unit to be controlled constantly becomes obsolete and requires correction. This process takes a varying amount of time. The lag creates conditions for a wedge to appear between the local and global criteria. We should add that the global criterion itself changes as the overall socioeconomic system changes. Moreover, the way in which it changes cannot be reduced to changes in its separate components.

The example which follows is a very simple illustration of the proposition formulated above. We know the role played by material incentives in increasing productivity and intensifying the use of labor. If, however, we try to specify how the increase in output depends on bonuses, it turns out that the effect of bonuses even in this respect depends at a minimum on the following factors: (1) the initial level of income; (2) the nature of the production process (flow-line production, the scale of output, the organizational structure); (3) the availability of benefits provided fully or partly through social consumption funds (the provision of kindergartens, nurseries, canteens and domestic services, medical facilities, etc.); (4) the availability of goods to satisfy the additional money incomes; (5) special regional and occupational features of the consumption structure; (6) the relationship between the system of material incentives and the system of moral incentives. All these factors are constantly changing and interacting with one another. It is practically impossible accurately to foretell their impact in each particular case. By adapting to an existing system that has operated for a greater or lesser period of time, an enterprise or association naturally seeks a compromise between that system and the constantly changing circumstances in which it uses its labor force. This search also creates a range of local interests in the unit under control, which will not necessarily correspond strictly to the social interest.

Questioning whether criteria at different levels are irreducible to one another is alien to the formulation of extremal control problems. This is quite understandable, since, if we take systems that are not developing qualitatively (so far we have understood by economic growth a purely quantitative increase in the scale of production and hence in the system as a whole), there is no need to take any account of "noise" or indeterminacy as a necessary property of such systems.

The Mechanism for Running the Economy and the Generation of New Information

In the terminology of the theory of control of complex systems, an operating mechanism first must minimize the social costs of seeking a criterion for the system's development (this is part of the system's self-organization process); second, it must ensure that the system moves at the optimal speed to some state that has been provisionally adopted as the goal.

The "fuel" feeding the growth of the system is new information. Consequently, self-developing systems must have an internal source for generating new information. In this sense, a self-developing system can be characterized as one that is developing in the informational sense, in which information is constantly generated, accumulated, renewed, and analyzed by the system itself. In the course of this analysis, the system teaches itself. The special characteristic of the process of self-development understood in this sense is the fact that the information generated must be of a nature that is new in principle.

Under conditions of rapid scientific and technical progress, the accumulation of social and economic information is demonstrated above all in the generation of new scientific and technological ideas and their subsequent embodiment in designs for new technologies, technical documentation, new products, and so on. These processes have always taken place, but at an increasing rate in recent years, and this enables us to draw the generally accepted conclusion that our society is living through a new scientific and technical revolution.

Regardless of what terms we use in this particular case, one thing is clear: qualitatively new information is being rapidly accumulated in the system. Of course, this is a controlled process that moves overall in the direction corresponding to the basic needs of social development. Likewise, there is no doubt that the process of generating new scientific and technological information is, as a matter of principle, probabilistic. The increase in the flow of this type of information is a powerful generator of uncertainty in the economic system.

This problem has long been recognized in the economy. One partial sign of it is the economic obsolescence of technological equipment. The complexity of economic decisions increases directly with the time it takes to construct and operate a potential investment project. Here uncertainty about whether the desired outcome will be achieved is a vital problem, which, as practical experience shows, is far from being solved.

It is doubtful, however, whether we should assume that the problem of uncertainty about the return to a project is wholly and entirely due to technical progress and the emergence of new technological processes and types of equipment. It would be more correct to say that here the uncertainty which in fact affects every aspect of the economy is concentrated and obvious to the naked eye. We refer to the technological and economic uncertainties affecting even production processes that have been well tested by designers and are fairly well settled into operation.

Many years of experience in implementing large-scale investment projects both at home and abroad have shown that it is more the exception than the rule to achieve the projected capacity at exactly the planned time and at the initial estimated cost. This is explained not by professional incompetence or malice on the part of designers or contractors (though for various reasons this factor may operate as well in a number of particular cases), but by the unavoidable complexity of taking account of the whole multiplicity of factors involved in the coordination of technical processes in a contemporary multistage factory, in the social and economic aspects of regional location, in the economic interrelationships with neighboring enterprises and customers, and so on. At the same time, we must bear in mind that these factors should be taken into account during the design process and that not only do they apply at the time construction is started, but they should be incorporated into forecasts covering at the very least the period up to the time when the project starts producing at its design capacity. Hence, the fact that the design or construction of a new facility does not involve technologies that are new in principle does not in itself allow one to say that uncertainty and the probabilistic element in the investment process have been eliminated.

According to data derived from an analysis of plan fulfillment in the first years of the Ninth Five-Year Plan [6], of 2,000 major units listed in the national economic plan, about 500 (25 percent) were not commissioned by the time specified and are being carried over to the next year; some of these are being

carried over a second time. According to submissions by ministries and departments of the USSR and the councils of minis-
ters of the union republics, in 1971-72 alone agreement was
reached for the USSR State Construction and State Planning
commissions to reapprove 390 projects whose cost estimates
had increased by 5.4 billion rubles. This figure included 1 billion rubles resulting from mistakes by design organizations and
0.55 billion rubles incurred through reconsideration of design
decisions and changes in the circumstances affecting construction. The initial cost estimate for the Kama River automobile
factory, a major project of national importance, was 1.7 billion
rubles, while the cost estimate when the design was worked out
exceeded 3 billion rubles.

In 1975 the USSR Central Statistical Administration investigated 978 enterprises in different sectors. It turned out that
about 60 percent of them were incurring costs substantially in
excess of those forecast at the design stage. As a result, the
economy has a shortfall of about 1 billion rubles each year.

Inaccuracies in estimating the costs of projects and the returns to be expected from them are a standard feature of large
investment projects the whole world over; in fact, this tendency
is also observed in cases where new technological ideas play a
relatively restricted role. Departures of capacity from projected levels, inaccurate estimates of the time taken to commission capacity, divergences between actual and projected
cost levels — these are all major problems that arise in carrying out investment projects.

The general nature of the phenomena we have cited prevents
us from attributing them entirely or largely to planning errors.
In our view, if we consider not the individual cases but the general trend, these facts show that indeterminacy is an organic
part of the investment process.

*   *   *

The reason we have emphasized the probabilistic character
of socioeconomic processes is that, by referring to this prob-

lem, we can most clearly explain the limitations of the purely
"engineering" approach to solving the problems of optimizing
control of the economy. This applies above all to the formulation of a national optimality criterion. In social systems, the
choice of an objective, which is a necessary condition for conscious management activity, cannot be regarded as an action
prior to and outside the operation of the socioeconomic system
as a whole. Since the economy's criterion is a reflection of
existing conceptions of socioeconomic progress, it objectively
bears the stamp of current levels of demand, the current state
of scientific and technical knowledge, the current productive
potential, the current social structure, and so on. Hence, to
argue along the chain, goals–constraints–optimal plan, necessarily impoverishes the formulation of the problem of rational-
izing economic management. There is but a small improvement in this state of affairs if we tack on to this framework
"an economic mechanism for plan implementation"; this is because we need to incorporate into the procedure not only the implementation but also the compilation of the plan (and here we mean
all stages of compilation, including the goal stage of planning).

In determinate systems, we are fully justified in linking up
the optimal plan and the process for implementing it, since the
very logic of deterministic optimization implies that the planning agency "knows everything" about the units it controls and
has at its disposal the appropriate optimization algorithms and
the necessary computer technology. Under these conditions,
the compilation of a plan seems to be the decisive factor determining everything, while the implementation mechanism is a
formal consideration. This mechanism need not even be an
economic one, but may be purely administrative. Within the
framework of a deterministic formulation of the problem, the
various ways of stimulating creativity, providing incentives,
and encouraging initiative are merely embellishments.

Essentially, what we have here is not the combination of
an optimal plan, on the one hand, and an economic mechanism,
on the other, but with an internal (and not everywhere obvious)
opposition between them; this is as shortsighted and unscien-

tific as the antithesis between "plan and market" which existed in our literature several years ago (and which has now been taken over by revisionists of all colors).

Our experience of the scientific and ideological struggle over this antithesis shows how what appears at first sight to be an unobjectionable abstraction can lead us far away from features in the development of a socioeconomic system that are of great significance if it is to be adequately described. Hence, it is particularly important to emphasize that the urgent task of developing the theory and methods of control over the planned socialist economy requires us to carry out research into the development of models that adequately reflect the true features of the system as it operates — i.e., models that incorporate elements of indeterminacy into the behavior of the components of the economic system.

An understanding of current problems encountered in modeling economic processes at the national level combined with a refusal to treat them in a strictly deterministic form must necessarily lead mathematical economists to take more interest in simulation analysis and the mathematical tools of probability theory. These approaches to formalizing economic processes in our view are consistent with the internal social nature of those processes and with the true "technology" underlying the interaction of the agents in the economy.

NOTES

1. J. M. Keynes emphasized that his theory indicates the vital importance of "establishing certain central controls in matters that are now left in the main to individual initiative.... The State will have to exercise a guiding influence on the propensity to consume partly through its scheme of taxation, partly by fixing the rate of interest, and partly, perhaps, in other ways. Furthermore, it seems unlikely that the influence of banking policy on the rate of interest will be sufficient by itself to determine an optimum rate of investment. I conceive, therefore, that a somewhat comprehensive socialization of investment will prove the only means of securing an approximation to full employment; though this need not exclude all manner of compromises and of devices by which public authority will cooperate with private initiative" [1, pp. 364-65].

2. As S. G. Strumilin wrote as long ago as 1927, "if our economic future were 100 percent predetermined by circumstances outside our control, then it

would be pointless to compile plans of any kind for the economy" [2, p. 10].

3. The indeterminacy in the system controlled reflects actual conditions. In the first place, it may be caused by the essentially random behavior of the elements in the system (we may know only the probability distributions of the corresponding random variables). Second, it arises from our comparatively limited knowledge of the control unit (and it diminishes as that knowledge increases). Third, indeterminacy may be associated with the impossibility in principle of exhaustively describing the unit in the language chosen (this may arise, for example, from the lack of criteria for evaluating some states of the unit within the framework of the chosen axioms).

REFERENCES

1. Keynes, J. M. The General Theory of Employment, Interest and Money (Russian edition). Foreign Literature Publishing House, 1949.
2. Strumilin, S. G. "Industrializatsiia SSSR i epigoni narodnichestva." Planovoe khoziaistvo, 1927, no. 7.
3. Beer, S. Cybernetics and Management (Russian edition). Moscow: Fizmatgiz, 1963.
4. Wiener, N. God and Golem (Russian edition). Moscow: "Progress" Publishers, 1966.
5. Petrakov, N. Ia. Nekotorye voprosy upravleniia sotsialisticheskoi ekonomikoi. Moscow: TsEMI AN SSSR, 1971.
6. Isaev, V. "Puti povysheniia effektivnosti kapital'nykh vlozhenii." Voprosy ekonomiki, 1973, no. 8.
7. "Kazhdomu po trudu." Pravda, July 25, 1975.

Received June 7, 1976

GOAL-RELATED PROGRAMS AND OPTIMAL LONG-TERM PLANNING

V. I. Danilov-Danil'ian

In recent years, increasing importance has been attached to the
program-goal approach as one possible way of improving national economic planning (see [1-4], for example). We cannot
say that a generally accepted definition of the concept of a
"goal-related program" has yet been found, even less that there
are reliable formal methods for devising such programs or
describing and analyzing them. There are in fact substantial
disagreements even over what should be the object (or unit) for
program-goal planning and over the limits within which this
approach can advantageously be applied in the management of
the socialist economy.

The difficulties that arise both in formalizing program-goal
concepts and in combining them with earlier systems of planning models are not accidental. They arise mainly because the
problems encountered are very unusual for mathematical economics. At the same time, the large scale of goal-related programs and their exceptional importance for the economy are
leading some researchers to put all other economic problems
in the shadow of goal-related programming; as a result, the

Russian text © 1977 by "Nauka" Publishers. "Tselevye programmy i optimal'noe perspektivnoe planirovanie," Ekonomika i matematicheskie metody,
1977, vol. 13, no. 6, 1151-63.
Presented as a formulation of the problem.

principles of this approach are implicitly or explicitly considered as dominating any decision-making process, irrespective
of its level, scale, or degree of determinacy, and regardless
of the extent to which the problem to be solved can be formalized and whether or not the information required is available.
At the same time, the principles themselves are not formulated
with sufficient clarity; instead, elementary propositions are
often advanced that apply to any kind of rational human activity.
As a natural result, the content of the program-goal approach
is eroded and the concept itself is becoming nonoperational.
The special feature of the approach is becoming indistinguish-
able, and attempts to formalize it are turning into highly simplified constructions that can lay claim neither to practical ap-
plicability nor to theoretical value.

    In order to strengthen the scientific foundations of the pro-
gram-goal approach, we must specify correctly the areas in
which it can be applied. The present article is directed chiefly
to setting out some general methodological principles with the
aim of subsequently applying them in order to incorporate the
program-goal aspect into a system of optimal long-term planning.

1. Goal-Related Programs and Their Role in the Management Structure of a Socialist Economy

    The general interest in goal-related programs at the
present time is a result of the dynamic nature of the socioeconomic development of our country under the scientific-
technological revolution and of the switch to an intensive
type of economic development. New sectors of industry arise
and grow rapidly; gigantic regional production complexes are
set up in localities that previously were scarcely exploited;
problems come to light and their solutions require the implementation of an entire complex of economic policies. Goal-
related programs in the economy are generally associated with
processes on this scale; they all lead to special management
problems which clearly go beyond the framework of the as-

sumptions underlying the traditional quantitative methods for resource allocation.

Of course, if we analyze the development of the Soviet economy over the past sixty years, we can easily identify similar problems in the 1920s and 1930s as well as in the postwar years. In the first place, however, the situation has changed greatly compared with previous decades: social and economic projects of global importance for the country have come to be numbered not singly but in dozens; the periods over which they are implemented overlap, and the plans that have to be compiled and the policies necessary to implement them must be coordinated not only with each other, but also with sectoral and regional plans. Second, the scientific and methodological basis of the system of economic management and the technical equipment it uses have become much richer, and it is desirable that their possibilities be fully exploited in practice, particularly in program-goal planning. Third, the following question arises: should any complex social process or even major policy measure be associated with a goal-related program?

In our view, it is possible to distinguish four major conditions (or properties) that should apply to a socioeconomic problem if its solution is to be sought using goal-related programs: (1) the expected outcome should be operationally determinate; (2) the resources required should actually be available; (3) the goal should be of an emergent character; (4) the objective should not be that of sustaining an existing operation but of affecting a transition in order to make possible a new activity.

Let us consider these properties in more detail. It is often said that operational determinacy of the outcome is the major distinguishing feature of a goal-related program. Normally it is assumed more or less explicitly that the outcome can be described in quantitative terms; values are assigned to some indicators reflecting production levels, or demand to be satisfied, or activity generally. However, the outcome may in principle be defined operationally not in quantitative terms but in terms of a precise structural description (through a diagram of administrative or organizational relationships, for example).

This condition is necessary because goal-related programs essentially involve devising alternative ways of achieving a goal, finding the most efficient way of doing so, identifying the separate stages of the program, and so on. These problems cannot be subjected to systems analysis and synthesized into a single goal-related program unless their outcomes can be defined operationally.

If we say that resources are immediately available in necessary (or, more precisely, sufficient) quantities to implement the program, we mean that it should be possible in principle to produce them when required or to switch them from other sectors of the economy; of course, this possibility is taken up only if the goal-related program is adopted. Mistakes in evaluating the availability of resources are not infrequent, and the following examples are very typical: exaggeration of the regional mobility of labor and of labor's ability to adapt quickly to different conditions of production resulting from new technology; underestimation of the uncertainty surrounding the resources, including time, required for research and development; inadequate consideration of the ecological consequences of economic activity — this leads to unforeseen additional costs that cannot always be met at short notice.

A substantial number of problems that can be defined in operational terms and supplied with resources, however, are traditional in nature (here we have in mind not the scale of the resources needed to overcome a problem, nor the time required to do so, but the problem's complexity from a management standpoint, and its nontraditional and nonstandard properties). Hence, it is important to define a goal-related program not only in terms of the feasibility of defining the outcome and supplying resources; it is also important to establish which element in the system is the custodian of the goal and what the nature of that goal is.

By saying that the goal of the program is an emergent one, we mean that the system as a whole is the custodian of the goal. The very concepts of emergent goal and emergent interest are controversial. They were introduced in [5, 6] to denote components of a goal that are revealed only at the level of the system as a whole, that are not held by any of the individual constituents of the system, and that cannot be inferred from the goals of those constituents. Arguments against this definition usually come down to the proposition that any goal of a system (particularly an "emergent" goal) must express the interest of at least some of the system's components. The issue, however, is not opinions in the abstract concerning the desirability or undesirability of any states of the system or development trajectories for the system or any of its separate elements. We recall that a goal is the outcome in our consciousness of ac-tivity. An emergent goal is not pursued actively through the social or economic activity of a single element in the system until it is also known at the systemwide level as well. If the necessary resources are available and the other conditions are fulfilled, a set of organizational measures is worked out and implemented; as a result, agents come into existence for whom the goal can be an internal objective of their activities. In our view, the area of operation of the program-goal principle should be those social and economic problems whose solution is intended to achieve the emergent goals of the corresponding system [7] .

Of course, a goal-related program is intended to achieve a transition, as distinct from certain other forms of control which are intended to maintain an operation that has already been established in the system to be controlled. Iu. M. Samokhin emphasizes this point: "In fact the need for programs arises where the changes in existing trends are so large that they exceed the adaptation possibilities of the existing planning system. On this basis, we can speak of a program as a planning tool that carries out a sharp realignment of trends, which could not be done within the framework of the existing methodology, technology, and organization of sectoral planning" [4, p. 239] . The view so clearly expressed in this quotation can certainly be generalized to cases where it is not methods of sectoral management or management in the economy as a whole which turn out to be inadequate, but where the inadequacy lies in bodies at other levels of socioeconomic systems that use traditional control systems. This makes clear the link between goal-related programs and problems that arise in connection with intensive growth; the latter require structural reorganization and the implementation of a whole series of transitional processes by various agencies.

Thus the four properties of goal-related programs that have been specified relate to: (a) the way in which the goal is described; (b) the feasibility of providing resources; (c) the custodian (or personification) of the goal within the system; and (d) the nature of the goal in relation to the system. We now have to see how these are affected when account is taken of the polyhierarchical nature of socioeconomic systems and of the hierarchical structure of its individual sectors. In saying that a structure is polyhierarchical, we mean that several hierarchies are combined within it [7]; [6] gives a detailed account of such a synthesis as applied to sectoral and regional aspects of the productive, institutional, and social substructures of the system.

We first note that the program-goal aspect plays two very important roles in relation to the structure of management: first, it is recognized with increasing clarity as a new perspective for centralized planning, side by side with the sectoral and regional perspectives that have long been analyzed; second, it enables us to define a principle for ordering the elements in a hierarchical structure [8] (it has this aspect, too, in common with the sectoral and regional principles). It seems to us that the analogy is not a surface one but one which reflects the fact that some important structural properties of the system are being reproduced in new form. Many studies have also identified in principle other aspects of management — social, psychological, resource, ecological, etc. — but their functions and significance in the management system are different in fundamentals from those of the sectoral, regional, and program-goal aspects. The similarity between the latter is strikingly revealed in the hierarchical nature of their respective substructures, and in the common methodological features of the coordination problems that arise in connection with each of them.

The identification of goal-related programs as a new perspective in centralized planning means first and foremost that the set of major programs forms a programmatic section in the plan and that each program generally speaking has a hierarchical internal structure. For example, a goal-related program at the national level is broken down either into separate subprograms or into regional or sectoral "fragments"; any principle for hierarchical subdivision can then be applied to each of these units in turn.

We may note that, in discussions of the problems of devising goal-related programs, the principle of subdivision into subprograms (construction of a tree of goals) is too often seen as the only possibility. This impoverishes the class of structures goal-related programs can have and distorts their actual role. If we follow this path, we break each goal-related program down into subprograms at the various levels, in such a way that finally we reach programs for producing shoes and shoelaces, although it is quite clear that programs are not required to solve such problems. Whenever our structural analysis of a program reaches a level at which it loses its special features as a program, we must use different principles of segmentation — sectoral (or technological) and regional (or territorial).

The very identification of goal-related programs may, however, operate as a principle for revealing units that can be integrated into a sectoral or a regional hierarchy. The program-goal aspect may be seen in systems of various scales; it need not necessarily be the socioeconomic system of the country as a whole, and it can also be applied in an economic region, a sector, a territorial production complex, or an economic association. In such cases the appropriate management system can (and should) create a goal-related program as one or more of its subsystems and take the requisite organizational measures. The nature of its internal structure depends on the details of the particular case. These issues are discussed in [3], which is based on an analysis of the solution of a number of practical problems.

The four characteristics of goal-related programs that we
have specified are clearly related to principles for hierarchical
organization within a structure. Whenever conditions exist in
a hierarchical or multihierarchical structure for the formulation of a goal-related program, that program must be linked
unambiguously with a specified level of the system under consideration; this is necessary because the goal in question cannot
be formulated operationally and supplied with resources at the
level of the corresponding subsystems, while in the case of the
system above the property of emergence is lacking. The final
indication of a goal-related program is that it involves changes
in the established regimes in a system (in the course of implementing the program) at the same time that the framework of
established procedures in the system above is unaltered. For
example, switching to mass production of a completely new
model (in the automobile industry, for example) involves the
implementation of a goal-related program to replace one established regime in that system by another; for the economy as a
whole, on the other hand, such a change of model is accom-
plished through established procedures. Obviously, if there is a
multiplicity of goal-related programs, implemented in overlap-
ping periods, the concept of an "established procedure" becomes
no more than an abstraction to be used for a systems analysis
of the problem under investigation.

The implementation of a goal-related program will normally
require organizational changes and the formation of new elements in the management structure. If the program is successfully implemented, these elements cease to be formal and legal
and are reflected in actual institutions; they go through a transformation as the program is implemented and may, on its completion, be integrated into the structure of the new process.
But if we analyze a goal-related program at the stage of compiling a long-term plan when the issue of whether or not to implement it is still open, then naturally no body yet exists in the
institutional structure — just as an enterprise management
does not yet exist when the question of whether to build that enterprise is only being considered and analyzed. And just as an

enterprise management is quite different from a design organization, the organization that controls the implementation of a goal-related program is generally a different body from the organization that did the work at the pre-plan stage. The issue of management structure is not dealt with in this article, but we assume that the targets associated with the implementation of the goal-related program are allocated to the same bodies in the institutional structure that existed at the time of plan formulation. At the macro level these bodies are, in addition to the center, sectors (or unionwide economic associations) and major economic regions (with union republics always distinguished) [6].

Management in a multihierarchical system contends with the major problem of coordinating decisions in the various dimensions of the structure. This problem has not yet been fully solved even in application to the two "classical" dimensions of sectors and regions and is made all the more complex with the introduction of the new program-goal dimension. The multiplicity of possible types of programs seems to rule out the possibility of a single uniform solution even at a given level of management of the economy. Solutions at different levels must be all the more varied and cannot be reduced to the mechanical replication of a previous answer.

Goal-related programs of the investment type are most closely related to long-term planning, both as it has grown up in practice and as it has been developed by researchers in recent years.[1] In fact we analyze such programs in more detail below, treating them at the level of the economy as a whole (i.e., as intended to realize the emergent interests of the socioeconomic system as a whole, as personified at that particular stage of its development by the center, which alone has the resources to realize them). Before going on to describe their position and role in optimal long-term planning, however, we find it appropriate to make some observations concerning the economic mechanism[2] — viewing the latter as one of the major elements of control in a multihierarchical structure, helping to coordinate the interests of the agents in the economic process by compiling a single centralized plan and regulating the course of its implementation.

Plans should be coordinated on the basis of an analysis of the interests of economic agents (the elements of the social structure) and of society as a whole, as those interests are actually revealed [6]. The basis for such a procedure is the long-term plan to coordinate the interests of the major economic units (regions and sectors), both with one another and with the interests of the socioeconomic system as a whole, i.e., with the program-goal aspect of centralized planning in particular. Obviously this is one way of further developing the system of optimal long-term planning described in [6]. The principle for concerting interests set out there (either by finding an equilibrium in an n-person game, with the center necessarily included as one of the participants, or by finding a fixed point in the set of operators for transforming indicators) can be applied in this case as well.

Plans should be coordinated in a way that is strictly controlled and anchored in law. Their coordination relative to some unit in the final analysis is reflected in the fact that the same indicators are used by the various management agencies and economic organizations, each with its own respective rights and powers. For example, if the plans of an economic region and a sector are to be coordinated with respect to some projected new enterprise, then both of them must either accept or reject the project simultaneously. Plans of two management agencies are coordinated if such agreement is achieved for all the units either in which those agencies have an interest or over which they exercise control. As below we consider only goal-related investment programs at the national level, we note some possible ways of coordinating sectoral and regional plans of economic regions with the program-goal aspect of the centralized plan in such a way as to satisfy this principle.

Coordination of interests, as reflected in the coordination of plans, can persist in the implementation phase if each participant has a certain margin of choice rather than a single alternative either imposed on him "from above" or forced on him by other constraints affecting his activity. The next requirement for coordination to work is that each coordinating agent have available to him ways (whether economic or administrative) of influencing his colleagues; the latter, even at the stage of compiling the plan, will be required to bear in mind their role in implementing it. This function can be fulfilled by a heterogeneous combination of indicators in physical or financial units or in value terms, provided only that they are controlled within certain limits by the corresponding planning agency.

Although some aspects of program-goal management — particularly in the area of long-term planning at the national level — have in fact been in use for a fairly long time, they do not yet have an adequate methodological foundation, nor are they adequately formulated in organizational terms. It seems that the first requirement is to find ways of meeting the two conditions specified: providing each participant in the planning process with a sufficiently wide area of choice of his plan, and finding either economic or administrative means of influencing his behavior. Obviously we are raising here a very broad range of problems dealing with improvement of the system of economic management. Without going into questions of an organizational or legal nature concerning the introduction of the program-goal principle into either planning or the management system, we merely note some ways of ensuring that this principle and certain other theoretical results are used effectively.

Freedom of choice over plan variants can be extended to the various agents in the planning process in different ways. In the case of goal-related programs of the investment type, it is important that the pre-plan stage not fix the temporal and spatial aspects of the units under construction (these should be fixed when the goal-related program is coordinated with sectoral and regional plans); for the same reasons, it is desirable that the draft of the goal-related programs be set out in terms of structure and function. Productive capacity should not be assigned in its entirety to meeting centralized sectoral targets (although finding feasible loading levels is a very complex problem, the solution to which depends on the structure of the whole system of plan indices and legal norms in the economy). If we start from the proposition that goal-related programs principally express emergent interests of the socioeconomic system and that for this reason the program-goal aspect of the long-term plan should be dominant from the standpoint of the center, then centralized plan targets should normally be set only to provide the resources necessary to carry out the policies implied by that aspect of the plan.

One major way of extending the margin of choice in sectoral plans is to strengthen the role of credit — to guarantee loans to finance all investment projects with a rate of return above the standard rate.[3] The same principle for granting credits should be used both for major economic regions (particularly union republics) and for sectors; however, it is particularly important to create special regional funds (to finance infrastructural development, the training of personnel, the protection of the environment, etc.). It is especially important to give a region the right to choose the design of large enterprises in its territory on the basis of what is best from its point of view and to put forward suggestions for coordinating the development and location of production by the sectors.

The central bodies for controlling goal-related programs at the national level, on the one hand, and at the level of sectors and regions, on the other, have various ways of influencing one another. The most obvious are the means by which the center can affect a sector or region: it can allocate credits on favorable terms to carry out measures related to goal-related programs; or it can introduce differential rates of payment into centralized funds. Among the ways in which regions can affect goal-related programs, we may cite the creation of more favorable conditions for the location and operation of enterprises (in terms of availability of labor, resources, infrastructure, etc.). Of course, it follows from this that a sector can affect centrally controlled goal-related programs by devoting to those programs (at its discretion) any productive capacity that is not required to meet centralized plan targets.

Naturally, we do not take up all the propositions set out in this section in the discussion of problems of modeling goal-related investment programs presented below; we consider only those that can be expressed formally within the framework of the system of optimal long-term planning described in [6], since it is the latter, as amended to incorporate the program-goal aspect, which is used as a basis for discussion. In all probability there may be other versions of the model of a goal-related program, oriented toward other approaches to optimizing long-term planning. These, however, should take account of the special nature of the unit in question and must avoid mechanically transferring to goal-related programs techniques that have been applied more or less successfully in other cases.

Thus in our view it is unacceptable to adopt an approach based on the degree of implementation of a program, taken to be something measurable that can vary within the interval [0; 1]. Because its outcome is operationally determinate, a program must (when the plan is compiled) be either accepted or rejected, and the methods for implementing it are also discrete. Moreover, it is questionable whether the principles of disaggregation traditionally used in balances can properly be applied here. Disaggregation in terms of output, in our view, is clearly inconsistent with the goal-related principle. It is more acceptable to use certain forms of network models, and these are adopted as a formal basis for the present article.

2. Goal-Related Programs within a System of Models for Optimal Long-Term Planning

If the program-goal perspective is to be incorporated into a system of models for optimal long-term planning, then particular attention must be paid to the problems of goal formation. It has been observed in [6, 9] that the center's goals (the emergent goals of the socioeconomic system) play an integrating role that must be reflected in various ways: through the optimality criterion in the model of the center, the constraints in that model, the structure of the whole system of models for long-term planning, and the algorithm for compiling the plan.

In [6, pp. 253-54] there is a discussion of control problems arising from the need "to carry out projects of so large a scale ... that their implementation is outside the scope of any individual economic association or region"; it was suggested that such projects can be incorporated independently into the center's model. Essentially what we had in mind was goal-related investment programs at the national level. We noted that the major complication in modeling such projects is evaluating the return; since the latter involves crossing cost "thresholds" [10], it is inappropriate to use standard methods based on shadow prices in the case of large-scale projects. The complexities of modeling goal-related investment projects and coordinating the interests of the center with those of other agents in the planning process (sectors and regions) have clearly been underestimated.

In the present article, we shall not formally describe how the model of a goal-related program of the investment type can comprise part of a system of optimal long-term planning,[4] because of the cumbersome nature of the model's construction; we limit ourselves to a discussion of the major structural properties of the model and its interrelationships with the other elements in the system.

The absence in [6] of a clear account of the program-goal aspect of planning allowed us to formulate a model of the center (in a game-type system) with a single criterion — maximization of the integral of investment over the plan period. (As noted already, other aspects of the center's objectives were reflected in other ways.) The incorporation of goal-related programs prevents us from using an approach based on a single criterion. It is doubtful, however, whether the method of vectoral optimization will help: in the case of a goal-related program, we cannot measure implementation continuously and use such a measure (possibly in conjunction with others not directly related to the program-goal aspect) as an element in the vectoral criterion. In compiling a long-term plan, it always becomes necessary to choose from the set of goal-related programs that are feasible in principle the subset which would be optimal in some sense and which overall can be furnished with the necessary resources. It is important that each goal-related program considered in the planning process not be fixed and absolutely rigid, but be flexible and capable of change; only in this way is it possible to coordinate the interests of the center (one of which is in the outcome of the program) with those of other agents in the planning process.

Hence, the program-goal aspect can be incorporated into a system of long-term planning in two stages: the first stage involves choosing from the set of goal-related programs considered in compiling the plan a subset intended for implementation; the second stage involves fixing the structure of each chosen program as part of the process of compiling a single optimal and socially balanced long-term plan.

If we follow the traditional line of mathematical economics, then it is natural for us to combine the first and second steps into a single iterative process. In fact, it might seem desirable, when the choice of a subset of programs has been made at the first stage and after the appropriate plan indices have been determined at the second, to repeat the first stage with the revised goal-related programs and then go on to the second stage, and so on. In our view, however, this procedure makes no real sense. The first stage is precisely intended to distinguish the area in which formal methods play essentially an auxiliary role in decisions (regarding the subset of goal-related programs intended for implementation) from the area in which they are important in themselves; in the terminology adopted in [6] , the problem is that of dividing the management process into a subsystem which is by-and-large nonformalized and another which is by-and-large formalized. The special feature of our case is that practically the same modeling construct is used in both subsystems. As will be seen below, the difference lies mainly in the role of the expert. At the first stage, he is interested in the intermediate results coming from the formalized part and treats them essentially as preliminary information helping in the decision-making process (rather than as feasible plan variants), whereas, at the second stage, the system of models completes the process. At the start, information about all the subsystems under consideration is fed into the system; later, only information about the subset chosen at the first stage is included.

If goal-related investment programs at the national level come under the direct control of the center, then it is necessary to change the model of the center in [6] into a system of models, including a balancing block, which assesses the summary plans of the sectors and finds shadow prices at the national level for goods, services, and resources; the system also includes models of the goal-related programs and a set of auxiliary blocks to take account of the information derived, which is transmitted to other parts of the planning system.[5]

Before discussing the question of the optimality criterion in a goal-related program, we must first define some major properties of its structure. Investment programs are a set of measures (associated with the implementation of projects for constructing new enterprises or rebuilding existing ones) embodying certain cause-and-effect relationships that operate in the time dimension. It is natural that, in very general terms, the structural framework of a goal-related program of this type should be similar to a network, in which the nodes are events signifying the installation of capacity into enterprises under construction or being rebuilt and the arcs connect pairs of events between which a cause-and-effect relationship applies. It is material that each node corresponds to a set of alternative ways of building new or rebuilding existing enterprises, which differ from one another with respect to their location, the technology adopted, the date and duration of implementation, departmental (sectoral) subordination, and so on.

It is not the main purpose of a model of a goal-related program to find values for the variables in the network that minimize the time of implementation at given cost or that minimize cost subject to a specified date of completion. Essentially we are dealing not with a network in the normal meaning of the term, but only with a general representation of a goal-related program in terms of a network. The problem lies in synthesizing the network by choosing for each node in the network diagram a possible way of performing that action — i.e., choosing a design for building a new or reconstructing an existing enterprise (conventional optimization of the network can only be used to finish off such a synthesis). Naturally, the choice of variants at each separate node should not be made in isolation from choices made at adjacent nodes; the combination of individual variants chosen must be feasible if an integrated network is to be built up.[6] It is well known that in conventional network models there are certain (sometimes very substantial) degrees of freedom both in the nodes and in the arcs. But these are practically always represented by continuous variables (for example, the start or completion date for a project may lie within certain limits).

Here, however, the degrees of freedom apply in an important sense to discrete choices, although the standard methods for computing the network are retained and are one of the components used to implement the model.

Insofar as the model of a goal-related program has the structure of a network, it is natural that we should consider using one of the optimality criteria that are normally used in such models, and minimize either time or costs. Although other criteria are also employed in network models (though rarely) and although one finds in other types of models a large number of various objective functions, it seems that in our case it is sufficient for us to limit ourselves to the alternatives mentioned (we recall that a goal-related program is characterized by having an outcome that can be defined operationally).

If costs are taken as the criterion of optimality, then the time allowed for implementing the program must be specified. It is quite feasible in principle to fix the time to be allowed if we are discussing one or more goal-related programs that are supplied with resources overall and that can be realized. But if we are considering a set of programs which by design cannot all be supplied with resources, then it becomes clearly undesirable to specify a time for implementing each of them. The point is that fixing the time allowed simultaneously establishes a lower limit for the costs of implementing the program (the latter is the optimal cost level, which has to be found through the computations) and makes the description of the program unnecessarily rigid; this prevents examination of other alternatives at lower cost but of longer duration, which is desirable in systems modeling. Moreover, goal-related programs at the national level are controlled by the center, which also controls the use of financial resources. This brings us to the other reason why it is undesirable to specify the costs of implementing the program (assuming it is not obvious, i.e., not at a minimum level known in advance). Since the center disposes of financial resources, it is natural that its choice of any particular variant for implementing a goal-related program should depend on the degree of shortage of financial resources at various times in the plan period.

These deficiencies of the cost criterion do not apply to the time criterion. It seems to us that to optimize the network determining the structural framework of a goal-related program by minimizing the time required to fulfill it fits in completely with the model's function in the system of models for long-term planning. Whatever deficiencies this criterion has when a network model is taken on its own, they do not apply when it is incorporated into a system. In fact, since the center is the custodian of emergent interests, especially as revealed in goal-related programs, it will want them to be completed as quickly as possible. Even if this does not satisfy all the interests in the socioeconomic system, this wish on the part of the center can be coordinated with the interests of other agents in the planning process in such a way that the deficiencies of the time criterion are eliminated.

Using the time criterion does not presuppose that costs are fixed. Since models for all goal-related programs are worked out in the center's subsystem, financial resources can be allocated to them on an iterative basis, to take account of their reserves in each year of the plan period according to the situation arising at the next iteration of the planning process.

What is the sense of using the time criterion in all the mod-

els of goal-related programs simultaneously at the first stage
when the program-goal aspect is incorporated into a system of
optimal long-term planning? If the set of goal-related programs considered is so broad that they could not all be provided
with resources, then, as noted above, the outcome of such a
procedure will not be a feasible plan variant; it will not be possible to achieve a synthesis of the network comprising all the
goal-related programs simultaneously because the resources
required to implement them are lacking. If, however, we assume that there is an iterative procedure for finding a plan that
does achieve such a synthesis, then it throws up information
about the feasibility of furnishing the goal-related programs
with resources and makes it easier for an expert subsequently
to decide to eliminate certain programs. In other words, even
"unsuccessful" attempts to impose a feasible plan by incorporating a complete (or even slightly reduced) set of goal-related
programs allow the expert progressively to rank them from the
point of view of their feasibility in the light of the resources
available. Of course, this does not exclude us from assessing
the degree of priority of programs on the basis of their expected
return; but at present there are no formal procedures for comparing such estimates with indices of resource scarcities, and
for this reason this task lies entirely within the sphere of com-
petence of the expert.

Of course, one can in principle visualize a complete selection
process such that, in place of the first step, the second stage is
performed for as many times as there are subsets in the set
of all the goal-related programs under examination. When the
number of these programs is fairly large, the number of elements in each subset to be supplied with resources will differ
substantially from the overall number of elements; moreover,
unless the subsets degenerate into single programs (or at most
a pair of programs), then the selection process takes on huge
dimensions and doubts arise concerning its feasibility. At the
same time, we do not assume that, as a result of the first stage,
the expert finds a single optimal and feasible subset (optimality
is understood here in an informal sense, although this does not,

of course, exclude the use of various economic, social, and political arguments to justify the decision made by the expert);
it may turn out that several subsets of goal-related programs
are chosen, and each of them in turn will be analyzed at the second and subsequent stages. It is now clear that the second stage
is essentially the concluding stage of the expert's dialogue with
the computer, in which the latter performs the computations
with the system of models, while the expert, having solved the
major problem of selecting programs, is eliminated from the
routine process of compiling the plan in detail.

We now consider in more detail the center's role in coordinating the model of goal-related programs with models of other
agents involved in the process of compiling the plan. We noted
in section 1 that the major instruments by which the center influences sectors and regions are credits and limitations on the
use of scarce materials. How these methods are used should
depend on an analysis of computations performed on the models
of goal-related programs. Operating relatively autonomously,
peripheral agents in the planning process may, if their actions
are not coordinated and guided by incentives, take decisions
that will make it impossible to construct a network which incorporates one or more goal-related programs. It is not only that
the variants chosen by the different nodes in the network may
not satisfy the network constraints. It may also turn out that
no sector (or no economic region) has an interest in carrying
out any of the projects at some node. These situations must
be brought to light when attempts are made to synthesize the
network. Computations with the model must reveal the bottlenecks in the network; i.e., they must identify the nodes at which
no alternative is chosen or at which the choice is incompatible
with decisions taken at adjoining nodes. Moreover, cases may
arise where a project chosen at a node is feasible but is not desired by the center. Of course, cases stick in the memory in
which various planning agencies incorporate mutually exclusive
alternatives in their local plans. For each such node, alternatives must be found that are desirable from the center's standpoint as well as from the standpoint of the sectors and regions

associated with them. The center's problem consists in encouraging the corresponding planning agencies to choose the alternatives that are most advantageous for it. Here it uses credits and additional allocations of scarce resources. Having found the bottlenecks in the model for a goal-related program, the center finds ways of widening them by appropriate credit policy and allocations of scarce resources. This makes it possible to perform a new iteration of the planning process, since the original information used by sectors and economic regions is changed. Changes are made, first, in the allocations of rationed inputs and, second, in the overall financial situation of the projects linked with goal-related programs, through the use of financial subsidies and nonrepayable credits. The successful synthesis of a network for each of the goal-related programs is one of the signs, together with those listed in [6] , that the planning process is completed.

In our view, it is important not to exaggerate the scope for formalizing the process of compiling a long-term plan incorporating the program-goal principle. There is no doubt, however, that the problem of maintaining balance in national economic plans — a problem which becomes even more complex when a program aspect is distinguished — can be solved only on the basis of man-machine systems operating in dialogue.

The author must express his sincere gratitude to D. G. Levchuk, B. Z. Mil'ner, V. A. Pavlikov, V. O. Toroian, A. I. Chuknov, S. S. Shatalin, and other colleagues at the All-Union Scientific Institute for Systems Research (VNIISI) of the State Committee for Science and Technology and the USSR Academy of Sciences for their help in elaborating and discussing the problems examined in the present article.

NOTES

1. Investment-type programs may be directed toward such objectives as building new sectors or sharply increasing the level of activity of existing sectors, exploiting regions rich in natural resources, or introducing machinery and capital equipment into social production on a large scale. It is easy, however, to give various examples of possible goal-related programs of a quite

different nature, for which the distinguishing feature is not investment but organizational change or research activity; examples are improving the system of controlling the economy or reforming education in schools. Some programs are mixed: these include programs for the large-scale introduction of computers into management or for the elimination of nonmechanized work in industry.

2. The economic mechanism is interpreted here in a very broad sense, to include, in particular, planning, the formation of the administrative hierarchy, the system of commercial law, and so on.

3. Naturally, the requirement to maintain a standard rate of return does not arise when prices are used to maintain balance in the plan for investment goods and services and when an optimal scale of interest rates for credit operates within the framework of complete financial independence.

4. This model was developed by V. O. Toroian.

5. A set of models of this kind (excluding models for goal-related programs) is given in [6]; however, it is described in a paragraph devoted to the process of plan compilation rather than to modeling the center's activity. Nevertheless, it does also contain a number of major points directly relevant to the center's assumed function in a system of optimal long-term planning of the economy.

6. For example, suppose that a particular node corresponds to the installation of capacity to produce some product and that there are two designs for the corresponding enterprise, each based on the use of a different raw material. The preceding nodes include one that involves the installation of capacity to provide materials of either the first or the second kind. Obviously, the choice of the projects in the two nodes must be coordinated.

REFERENCES

1. Kompleksnoe narodnokhoziaistvennoe planirovanie. Moscow: "Ekonomika" Publishers, 1974.

2. Lemeshev, M. Ia., and Panchenko, A. I. Kompleksnye programmy v planirovanii narodnogo khoziaistva. Moscow: "Ekonomika" Publishers, 1973.

3. Mil'ner, B. Z. "Problemy sistemnogo podkhoda k organizatsii upravleniia ob'edineniiami." Ekonomika i matematicheskie metody, 1976, vol. 12, no. 6.

4. Samokhin, Iu. M. "K voprosu ob ispol'zovanii programm v kompleksnom planirovanii." Ekonomika i matematicheskie metody, 1977, vol. 13, no. 2.

5. Matematika i kibernetika v ekonomike. Moscow: "Ekonomika" Publishers, 1975.

6. Danilov-Danil'ian, V. I., and Zavel'skii, M. G. Sistema optimal'nogo perspektivnogo planirovaniia narodnogo khoziaistva. Moscow: "Nauka" Publishers, 1975.

7. Danilov-Danil'ian, V. I. "Sistema modelei optimal'nogo perspektivnogo planirovaniia narodnogo khoziaistva i otsenka proektnykh reshenii." Trudy TsNIPIASS (Moscow), no. 12, 1976.

8. Pol'terovich, V. M. Optimal'nye razbieniia proizvodstvennykh sistem i kratchaishie seti. Moscow: TsEMI AN SSSR, 1968.

9. Danilov-Danil'ian, V. I., and Zavel'skii, M. G. "Sintez sistemy modelei optimal'nogo sotsial'no-ekonomicheskogo planirovaniia." In Ekonomiko-matematicheskie issledovaniia zatrat i rezul'tatov. Moscow: "Nauka" Publishers, 1976.

10. Novozhilov, V. V. Problemy izmereniia zatrat i rezul'tatov pri optimal'nom planirovanii. Moscow: "Nauka" Publishers, 1972.

Received May 28, 1977

ON MODELING ECONOMIC MECHANISMS

I. A. Vatel' and N. N. Moiseev

Recent years have seen the widespread use of mathematical models and mathematical methods to improve procedures for planning and management in the economy. First, these models, used in conjunction with computers, have helped to solve important practical problems; second, they have given a powerful impulse to the development of the theory of management of the socialist economy. The major developments in this direction have revolved around the issue of improving methods of directive planning (current planning at the enterprise or branch level, the input-output model, regional planning, etc.). Whether or not such models are successful depends to a large extent on how fully the planning agencies are informed about the background against which planning targets will be implemented and about the true potential of the organizations in the economy. The fact, however, that these matters are, for objective reasons, uncertain makes it necessary to devise special control procedures or, as they are often called, economic mechanisms — the study of which is becoming an increasingly important part of economic science.

Prominence is now being given to the problems of devising

Russian text © 1977 by "Nauka" Publishers. "O modelirovanii khoziaistvennikh mekhanizmov," Ekonomika i matematicheskie metody, 1977, vol. 13, no. 1, pp. 17-30.

mechanisms designed to allow the control agencies and other agents in the economy to operate on a financially accountable basis. At present a number of institutes are conducting research into the operational problems of these mechanisms [1-8]. In recent years these issues have also been analyzed at the Computer Center of the USSR Academy of Sciences. The present article gives a brief account of the results of this research [9-27].

The starting point for the concepts to be developed is a view of the economy (or of a particular branch or association, etc., depending on the scale of the model) as a combination of subsystems, each having economic interests or objectives that it tries to achieve within the margin of choice allowed by its plan for output and inputs; this margin of choice is either set a priori or is allotted to it as the system operates.

The literature traces a number of stages in the evolution of the concept of "an economic interest" under socialism. Fifteen years ago, the predominant type of explanation was: there is only a national interest and all agents in the economy must adhere to it. Later, articles appeared that noted the existence of local interests, and the problem was posed of making the latter compatible with the national interest. This problem is in fact extremely serious, if only because qualitatively different indicators are used to describe the operation of economic units at different levels.

As mathematical modeling of the economy developed, a national criterion began to be formulated more strictly (final consumption with a specified structure, for example); also, as a result of the design of decomposition procedures for planning, the issue was formulated in the following way: what criterion (profit, for example) should be imposed on subordinate agents for their local maximization to lead to the attainment of the national optimum [1, 3, 6]? This mathematically irreproachable formulation, which relies on a successful economic interpretation of duality theorems (the prices to which the subordinate agents react are the duals of the corresponding constraints), when combined with the use of iterative numerical algorithms to find the optimal plan through interaction (on an independent accounting basis) between a planning agency and the subsystems, has played a dominant role in many researchers' views on the control mechanism in a centralized economy.

To simplify matters somewhat, we can say that, in the discussion which followed, two planning schemes were compared, as follows: (1) At the start of the planning period, the subsystems inform the center of the parameters describing their own production possibilities; the center solves an optimization problem and issues plans to the subsystem. (2) Alternatively, the center computes a plan in advance according to some "base-line" information about the model's parameters (last year's values, for example), but it does not issue plan targets to the subsystems; instead, it communicates criteria, which the subsystems have to maximize (alternatively, the nature of the criterion is fixed, and its coefficients — prices — are transmitted); the subsystems have more precise information about the period in question, and use it to maximize the pre-specified criteria. The second scheme relies on the stability property of optimal prices in the neighborhood of the optimal plan (for small changes in the original parameters of the plan, prices do not change, and optimizing the local criteria leads to an optimum of the global criterion in the new circumstances).

When discussing procedures for optimal planning, people often assert that the second scheme is greatly to be preferred and treat it as a mechanism for coordinating national and local plans. We emphasize that we are not talking here about objectives that the subsystems actually have but about objectives that are assigned to them. Let us assume, however, that the subsystem's behavior does not correspond to the hypothesis; i.e., it does not maximize the criterion laid down for it — for example, let us assume that an enterprise maximizes gross output. At the end of the period, the center will have data on how the subsystem has performed and can compute the value of the local criterion; but, in order to verify whether it has in fact been maximized, it must process all the information, and this nullifies the advantages of the second scheme. This point has been noted before, and attempts have been made to modify the criterion to take account of the "internal interests" of the subsystems.

It seems to us that there is no contradiction in saying that subsystems have their own interests ex ante, determined by the overall economic and legal structure and the special features of the subsystem itself; however, they are not necessarily opposed to the interests of the system as a whole, as reflected by the center. Moreover, fairly flexible representations of these interests are possible (for example, they may be a combination of "social" and "personal" interest [15]). Interests (or criteria) are some function of the parameters reflecting the processes of production and distribution (levels of output, resources utilized, input coefficients, incentive funds, etc.). At the same time, the center's strategies (which in the general case are fairly complex functions of the information available) become control mechanisms, and the reaction to these strategies is forecast using some hypothesis about the structure of the subsystem's interest and the principles on which it takes decisions (we return to this subject in more detail below).

We notice at once, however, that the interests of the agents in the economic system are not in any sense rigid. They can change under the impact of external circumstances, but do so fairly slowly, since the time scale for such a change is substantially longer than that in which day-to-day measures of economic policy operate (to put it more precisely, interests are developed gradually). We shall thus assume that in the models considered the interests of the subsystems are fixed attributes with an objective existence and that they depend both on choices made by the center and on the subsystems themselves.

Of course, our view does not eliminate all the problems that arise when control procedures are formalized and investigated. It is easy to say that interests have an objective existence. The problem lies in the fact that the center does not know what they are. Recognizing the fact of their existence, however, is the foundation on which we can begin to construct a theory, particularly since the corresponding mathematical theory has already been developed for some decades. Here we mean the theory of operations research (and a part of that theory, the theory of games). In recent years, new and important developments in this theory have been made.

Before presenting a formal account of control mechanisms in the economy, we note that the classics of Marxism have given a large role to "interest" as an objective economic category. Engels declared: "The economic relations of any given society are revealed primarily as interests" (K. Marx and F. Engels, Works [Sochineniia], vol. 18, p. 271). In an analysis of the problems of management in a socialist economy, Lenin noted that giving state enterprises financial independence — a choice made necessary "by the urgent need to increase labor productivity, to reduce losses, and to raise the profitability of each state enterprise — will in view of the inevitable departmental interest and the exaggeration of departmental zeal which will be created, unavoidably generate a certain conflict of interests" (V. I. Lenin, Complete Works [Polnoe sobranie sochinenii], vol. 44, p. 343). He also declared that the masses must be brought to communism "not by enthusiasm directly, but with the help of enthusiasm generated by the great revolution and through personal interest, personal incentives, and financial accountability" (ibid., p. 151).

1. The Basic Model and a Classification of Assumptions

We first describe the basic model underlying the entire exposition that follows. We assume that a system (an economic association, for example) consists of a controlling center and n production subsystems (enterprises); we take the static case in which a decision is taken once and for all for the whole plan period and no information is received or processed at intermediate stages (we shall discuss the incorporation of dynamic elements into the basic system below). Each subsystem is characterized by a production set X_i, from which it chooses an element, vector x_i; i.e.,

$$x_i \in X_i, \quad i = 1, \ldots, n. \tag{1}$$

The controlling center tries to maximize a criterion

$$w_0 = g(x_1, \ldots, x_n, y_1, \ldots, y_n), \qquad (2)$$

which generally depends both on the outcome of the subsystems' actions, $x_i, i=1, \ldots, n$, and the center's interventions with the subsystems $y_i, i=1, \ldots, n$; the center's overall intervention belongs to some set Y; i.e.,

$$(y_1, \ldots, y_n) \in Y. \qquad (3)$$

In order to discuss the effectiveness of the center's control, we need one further element — the reaction of the x_i in each subsystem to the impact of y_i. If this reaction is specified, then we have an account of a subsystem in the spirit of the theory of automata (the link between input and output is given) or, as we say, a "reflector" account [9] — to each stimulus (or input, y_i), there corresponds an automatic or reflected reaction x_i (which may not be unique). Most simulation systems used to model planning and control procedures describe a control mechanism of this type.

Another approach is possible, however. We consider a "nonreflector" subsystem, but one that tries to maximize its own criterion:

$$w_i = f_i(x_i, y_i), \ i=1, \ldots, n. \qquad (4)$$

To switch to a model of a "reflector" subsystem, we have to adopt a number of further assumptions concerning the information held by the subsystems and the center, the sequence in which decisions are taken, the principles for choosing rational strategies under uncertainty, and so on. This approach seems more realistic to us than a direct reflector representation, since it allows us to systematize the major factors affecting the circumstances under which decisions are made and implemented and to make as complete an analysis as possible of rational behavior.

Let us consider one possible set of hypotheses that is characteristic of hierarchically organized economic systems. The center first takes a decision about the control variables $y_1, \ldots, y_n$

and communicates parts of that decision to the corresponding subsystems (using the terminology of [16], the center has the right to make the first move). After this, the outcome of each subsystem in terms of criterion (4) depends solely on that subsystem's actions, and it chooses $x_i \in X_i$ (1) to maximize (4), i.e., the subsystem is turned into a "reflector" subsystem.

Other assumptions are possible, of course. For example, if the center knows how the subsystems behave under uncertainty (averaging over the uncertainty, choosing a guaranteed payoff, and so on), then it may find it expedient not to communicate its signal y_i accurately.

After these two assumptions are specified (the sequence in which decisions are taken and the form of the subsystems' response), it might appear that our model for making decisions in a hierarchical system is now closed, in the sense that we can seek the center's best control values according to criterion (2). However, this is not so. In the first place, a subsystem may give an ambiguous response to the given control variable (the maximum of criterion f_i (4) may not be achieved at a unique point). We are faced with the problem of removing this indeterminacy.

At this stage we could, for example, assume that the subsystem is "generous," i.e., that, when confronted with a set of outcomes between which it is indifferent, it chooses the one that is best for the center. This hypothesis, however, complicates the information flows in the system. If we reject "generosity," it is only rational (to reduce risk) to adopt the principle of maximizing the guaranteed return [10]; i.e., we should pay attention to the response that is worst for the center. Moreover, we have not described the center's strategies in detail; these may take many forms and may be determined by what procedures for exchanging information between the center and the subsystems are feasible and by what possibilities there are for processing that information.

Thus it is only after we have made our assumptions about the environment in which the control mechanism will operate that we can go on to formulate a mathematical optimization problem.

To illustrate what we have said, we present a classification of some standard cases and corresponding types of mechanism in the simplest version of the basic model (1)-(4), with only one subsystem:

$$w_0 = g(x, y), \quad w = f(x, y), \quad x \in X, \quad y \in Y. \tag{5}$$

We assume that the center formulates a control mechanism in accordance with the principle of obtaining the maximum certain return evaluated by its criterion $g(x, y)$, and that the subsystem maximizes its own criterion $f(x, y)$ where the outcome depends only on its choice. The classification is by the type of strategy adopted by the center, which is determined by the amount of information it processes.

Case 1. The center does not perform computations based on information about the particular x chosen (or it cannot process this information). In this case, its control mechanism consists in specifying a particular y. This may, for example, involve the communication of certain parameters (prices, etc.), or the allocation of resources to the subsystem before production begins.

In accordance with the above, a "reflector" account of the subsystem associates a subset of responses to each $y \in Y$:

$$R^{(1)}(y) = \{x \in X \mid f(x, y) = \max_{x \in X} f(x, y)\}.$$

The maximum guaranteed return to the center is:

$$w_0^{(1)} = \max_{y \in Y} \ \min_{x \in R^{(1)}(y)} g(x, y). \tag{6}$$

Case 2. The center receives information on vector x and formulates a mechanism (or strategy) as a function of this: $\tilde{y} = y(x)$. This specifies rules for granting bonuses and penalties ("if you do x, you will get y"). Then to each function $\tilde{y}$ there corresponds a subset of responses:

$$R^{(2)}(\tilde{y}) = \{x \in X \mid f(x, y(x)) = \max_{x \in X} f(x, y(x))\}.$$

The center's maximum guaranteed return in this case is:

$$w_0^{(2)} = \max_{\widetilde{y}} \quad \min_{x \in R^{(2)}(\widetilde{y})} g(x, \widetilde{y}). \tag{7}$$

Case 3. The center receives information concerning the function $\widetilde{x} = x(y)$ (for example, $x(y)$ may be the subsystem's production function, linking output x with an allocation of resources y; the subsystem chooses this function). The center's control mechanism is a function $\widetilde{y} = y[x(y)]$ (a rule for allocating resource y in accordance with how it is used, $x(y)$). To each $\widetilde{y}$ there corresponds a subset of responses

$$R^{(3)}(\widetilde{y}) = \{x(y) \mid f(x(y), y[x(y)]) = \max_{x(y)} f(x(y), y[x(y)])\}.$$

The center's maximum guaranteed return is:

$$w_0^{(3)} = \max_{\widetilde{y}} \quad \min_{\widetilde{x} \in R^{(3)}(\widetilde{y})} g(\widetilde{x}, \widetilde{y}). \tag{8}$$

In formal terms, we could extend the recursive element in describing the mechanism indefinitely and derive very elaborate cases 4, 5, etc. As [17] shows, however, from the point of view of the outcome for the center, the possible outcomes are exhausted by the cases enumerated; in fact $w_0^{(2k)} = w_0^{(2)}$, $w_0^{(2k+1)} = w_0^{(3)}$ for all $k = 2, 3, \ldots$ and, moreover, the following relation applies:

$$w_0^{(2)} \geqslant w_0^{(3)} \geqslant w_0^{(1)}. \tag{9}$$

Formulas (6)-(8) bring home to us how complicated it is to compute the center's return, particularly for cases 2 and 3. But according to [16, 17], computing (7) and (8) reduces to a special problem in nonlinear programming, which converts the problem of forming control mechanisms to a class of conventional optimization problems (this is also true for the basic model).

Another set of assumptions would lead to a different formulation. For example, assuming generosity of the subsystem would mean that in (6)-(8) the interior operation min must be replaced by max, which would substantially simplify the problems. We note also that a flexible combination of the types of mechanism shown may occur in actual systems. For example, the resource may be allocated according to case 1 and incentives to use it rationally may operate in accordance with case 2.

The method of analysis set out is fairly standard, although it is demonstrated in the simplest example. Two conclusions can be drawn from the foregoing. First, the number of mechanisms is not as large as appears at first sight. Many mechanisms collapse into one another and can be studied by the same methods. Second, the approach developed here shifts the whole discussion into another plane. In place of arguments over what criterion to use to evaluate the enterprise's actions or how to form an incentive fund, we have to study the actual situation and define the interests (or tendencies) in subsystems as they operate — in particular, the legal aspects without which no economic system can function. When we have such a model, we can also determine the rules for forming incentive funds, the structure of sanctions, etc. The whole discussion has a well-defined scientific basis.

2. Control Mechanisms Using Prices

As an example of case 1, let us consider a control mechanism using prices as applied to our basic model (1)-(4).

We represent output of the subsystems by a production function

$$x_i = F_i(z_i, u_i), \tag{10}$$

where z_i is the vector of resources allocated to the subsystem by the center; u_i is a factor of production chosen by the subsystem (labor input, for example, or the production technique); (1) is replaced here by

$$u_i \in U_i. \tag{11}$$

We assume that the center formulates a mechanism based on financial accountability as follows: the vector of "benefits" y_i distributed to the subsystem depends on vectors of output x_i and resources utilized z_i; i.e.,

$$y_i = cx_i - pz_i, \tag{12}$$

where c is a vector of product prices and p is a vector of resource prices.

We shall assume that the subsystem's criterion makes commensurate "benefits" y_i and the "effort" (costs) associated with choosing any particular u_i; i.e.,

$$w_i = f_i(cF_i(z_i, u_i) - pz_i, u_i) = f_i^*(z_i, u_i, c, p). \tag{13}$$

The center's criterion also combines, on the one hand, the return from the outputs produced and purchased and, on the other, the "costs" of interacting with the subsystem on a financially independent basis and of supplying the subsystems with the resource:

$$w_0 = g\left(x_1, \ldots, x_n; \sum_{i=1}^{n} y_i, \sum_{i=1}^{n} z_i\right) = g^*(z_1, \ldots, z_n, u_1, \ldots, u_n, c, p). \tag{14}$$

An alternative account is possible, in which costs do not enter into the criterion but constraints on the benefits and resources are specified:

$$\sum_{i=1}^{n} y_i \leqslant Y, \quad \sum_{i=1}^{n} z_i \leqslant Z. \tag{15}$$

We thus derive the following model. The center specifies output prices and prices at which resources can be purchased. Each subsystem chooses the amount of resource z_i to be purchased and values u_i to maximize (13) subject to (11). The center's problem is to find prices c and p to maximize criterion (14) (without breaching constraints (15), if they apply); i.e., we have arrived at the formulation in case 1.

As an illustration, we consider the problem of rational prices for water and agricultural produce in land requiring irrigation [18, 19]. Assume that n collective farms are spread over a region with a common irrigation system; each farm can produce any of the m crops cultivated in the region, according to a Cobb-Douglas production function:

$$x_{ik} = a_{ik} u_{ik}^{\alpha_{ik}} v_{ik}^{\beta_{ik}} , \tag{16}$$

where x_{ik} is the yield of crop k per hectare in farm i; u_{ik}, v_{ik} are inputs per hectare of labor and water, respectively; a_{ik}, $\alpha_{ik} < 1$, $\beta_{ik} < 1$ are given parameters.

The objective function or criterion of the collective farm is, by assumption, profit:

$$w_i = \sum_{k=1}^{m} s_{ik} (c_k x_{ik} - p v_{ik} - h_{ik} u_{ik}), \tag{17}$$

where c_k is the sale price of the k-th crop; p is the price of water per cubic meter; h_{ik} is the standard wage per hour for the k-th crop; s_{ik} is the area under the k-th crop. Constraints (11) in this case are constraints on the labor force:

$$\sum_{k=1}^{m} s_{ik} u_{ik} \leqslant U_i. \tag{18}$$

We shall assume that, in accordance with the principles of program planning, the center wants to produce agricultural out- . put over the plan period in proportions determined by demand at the national level. In fact, the center attempts to procure output in given proportions $\hat{x}_1, \ldots, \hat{x}_m$, equal to the control figures of the plan. Thus the center's interest is in maximizing

$$\varphi = \min_{1 \leqslant k \leqslant m} \sum_{i=1}^{n} s_{ik} x_{ik} / \hat{x}_k. \tag{19}$$

In addition, costs (in money terms) are taken into account:

$$\psi = \sum_{i=1}^{n} \sum_{k=1}^{m} c_k s_{ik} x_{ik} + r(v) - pv, \tag{20}$$

where $v = \sum_{i=1}^{n} \sum_{k=1}^{m} s_{ik} v_{ik}$ — the total usage of water. The first

component in (20) expresses the center's expenditure on purchasing agricultural products; $r(v)$ are the costs associated
with the provision of water (a nonlinear function of total usage);
and pv is the income from the sale of water to the collective
farms.

We can assume that the center tries either to maximize criterion (19) for a given value of (20) or to maximize criterion
(20) taken with a negative sign for a given value of (19); alternatively, some combination of criteria (19) and (20) can be used
as an objective function.

Assume that the center knows parameters a_{ik}, α_{ik}, β_{ik}, s_{ik}, h_{ik}.
It designates prices $c_1, \ldots, c_m$, p; the collective farms purchase
water and allocate their labor forces to crops to maximize (19)
subject to constraints (18). The center's problem is to find
prices that maximize its guaranteed return for one of the criteria chosen. In view of the concavity of production functions
(16), criteria (17) are concave; the collective farms' responses
are unique, and there is no need in (6) for an internal minimization operation. We also assume that labor is not a limiting factor; i.e., (18) are fulfilled as strict inequalities; in this case,
the farms' responses can be found (for $\alpha_{ik} + \beta_{ik} \neq 1$) from the
necessary conditions for an unconstrained maximum of (17). In
this case, the price problem reduces to a system of transcen-
dental equations [19].

If we analyze the price problem in models incorporating financial accountability from the operations research standpoint,
we reach the following conclusion. Prices for resources in
deficit and for output are interdependent and are the control instrument in a centralized hierarchical system with a particular
fixed feedback mechanism (12). They should be determined in
such a way as to maximize the center's criterion, whatever assumptions are made about the interests and behavior of the
subsystems.

Of course, the models we are discussing only demonstrate
an analytical technique. Realistic models of the economy must
incorporate a high degree of uncertainty and require more complex assumptions both about the behavior of the elements of the

system and about the information they have about each other.

3. Models of Incentives in the Economy

We consider models falling under case 2. As stated above, the control mechanism (12) based on prices implied a particular form of strategy, the function $y_i(x_i, z_i)$; the problem was then reduced to finding constants c and p — i.e., to case 1. At the same time, the problem set out in section 2 could also have been treated as case 2, without fixing (12). In order to show the special features of this case, we consider a simple example in which the center and subsystems have the following criteria, according to which they choose reward level y and output level x, respectively:

$$w_0 = bx - y, \quad w = y - ax^2, \quad y \geqslant 0, \quad x \geqslant 0, \tag{21}$$

where a and b are constants.

We assume that, as above, the center chooses the form of its intervention with the subsystem

$$y = cx, \tag{22}$$

and the unknown is the price c for a unit of output (case 1). It is easy to see that the level of output, the reward, and the value of the center's criterion are, respectively:

$$x^{(1)} = b/4a, \quad y^{(1)} = b^2/8a, \quad w_0^{(1)} = b^2/8a. \tag{23}$$

We now consider a control system in the spirit of case 2.

$$\tilde{y} = y(x) = \begin{cases} b^2/4a + \varepsilon, & \text{if} \quad x = b/2a, \\ 0, & \text{if} \quad x \neq b/2a, \end{cases} \tag{24}$$

where $\varepsilon > 0$ is some positive small number (the sensitivity of the subsystem's objective function to an outcome in excess of the guaranteed zero outcome). It is easy to see that after strategy (24) is communicated to the subsystem the values similar to (23) are:

$$x^{(2)} = b/2a, \quad y^{(2)} = b^2/4a + \varepsilon, \quad w_0^{(2)} = b^2/4a - \varepsilon. \tag{25}$$

A comparison of (25) and (23) shows that for small ε a mechanism of the second type is practically twice as effective from the standpoint of the center $(w_0^{(2)}/w_0^{(1)}=2-O(\varepsilon))$. We would get the same outcome for the center as (25) if we used a type (22) mechanism, but with the price depending on the level of output, as follows:

$$\tilde{c}=c(x)=\begin{cases} b/2+\varepsilon, & \text{if} \quad x=b/2a, \\ 0, & \text{if} \quad x\neq b/2a. \end{cases} \tag{26}$$

Thus, extending the class of strategies open to the center normally improves its outcome (as already noticed in (9)). However, computing (7) for case 2 and looking for a corresponding optimal strategy for the center is generally a more difficult task than for the model based on control using prices [20, 21].

We now introduce an optimal strategy for one class of basic models (1)-(4), which we designate as models for giving incentives for increasing output (22); but first we indicate what we mean by "incentives."

We subdivide the process of planning into two phases: (1) compiling the plan on the basis of data on input coefficients (or on the basis of results in the previous period); (2) inducing the subsystems to expand their input of labor to obtain "above-plan" output. If the input coefficients are fairly accurate, then it would be normal for the center's plan targets formulated at the first phase to be reached. The role played by interest here is indirect (if, for example, the center raises targets without justification, then the outflow of labor may increase — a phenomenon that operates over a long time scale and is encountered only in models for long-term planning). When we are dealing with the operation of incentives, then the interrelations of the center and the subsystem can be interpreted as the latter exchanging "extra labor" in return for bonuses allocated by the center. The subsystem does, of course, have an interest in getting additional bonuses, but it is not indifferent to the extra exertions required from it. Thus, if the center is to work out soundly based incentive rules, it needs a model of the subsystem's objectives in which effort above the standard rate is in some way made commensurable with reward for that effort.

Bearing these points in mind, we introduce one possible framework for describing in formal terms how incentives work. Let x_i be the vector of indices to which bonuses are to be related (above-plan output, quality indicators, savings of materials, etc.), and let the center receive reliable information about these indicators only at the end of the plan period; let y_i be the vector of benefits distributed by the center (premiums, extra privileges, funds for social or everyday amenities, and so on). We make the following assumptions regarding the basic model (1)-(4). The functions $f_i(x_i, y_i)$ in (4) are monotonically increasing in every component of vector y_i, monotonically decreasing in every component of vector x_i, and concave in all variables; sets X_i are convex. We normalize on a vector of standard indicators and zero rewards such that:

$$f_i(0, 0) = 0. \tag{27}$$

The center's criterion increases monotonically in $x_1, \ldots, x_n$ and decreases monotonically in $y_1, \ldots, y_n$. In practical work, it is also standard to adopt a formulation in which the center's criterion depends only on above-plan output

$$w_0 = g(x_1, \ldots, x_n), \tag{28}$$

and bonuses are constrained by the size of the incentive fund

$$\sum_{i=1}^{n} y_i \leqslant Y. \tag{29}$$

As is shown in [20, 21], the optimal strategy for offering bonuses is as follows:

$$y_i(x_i) = \begin{cases} \overset{0}{y_i}, & \text{if } x_i = \overset{0}{x_i}, \\ 0, & \text{if } x_i \neq \overset{0}{x_i}, \end{cases} \quad i = 1, \ldots, n, \tag{30}$$

where $(\overset{0}{x_1}, \ldots, \overset{0}{x_n}, \overset{0}{y_1}, \ldots, \overset{0}{y_n})$ is the solution to the problem of maximizing (28) subject to (29) and the constraints

$$f_i(x_i, y_i) \geqslant \varepsilon_i, \quad i = 1, \ldots, n. \tag{31}$$

Here ε_i is the sensitivity of the subsystem's preference function to an outcome different from the guaranteed outcome according to criterion (4) — which is zero (for $x_i=0$, $y_i=0$).

We make the following observation on our result. Strategy (30) is a discontinuous function (as in the example considered at the start of this section). It promises the subsystem a fixed premium $\overset{0}{y_i}$ only if it produces a particular level of output $\overset{0}{x_i}$. Otherwise, the center sets y_i equal to zero. This part of the strategy is designated the "punishment strategy" $y_i^{\text{п}}(x_i)$ [16] (a more complex version for general models is given in [21]). At first glance, this result contradicts generally accepted views about strategies for distributing bonuses. Thus it is often assumed that the bonus function is continuous. Both this property and a number of others, however, are not based directly on a mathematical model of the phenomenon under study, but are deduced from external considerations. The strategy (30) was derived from an analysis of the mathematical model formulated above and is optimal for that model. In fact, it is often not unique, and it may be possible to adopt a continuous strategy equivalent to (30), although (30) is of a form that is characteristic for directive planning. We emphasize that the wishes of the subsystems are fully taken into account and are not ignored. The "directive nature" of strategy (30) is explained by the center's complete information about the wishes and potential of the subsystems.

4. Control When the Center Lacks Complete Information

The models set out in sections 2 and 3 are idealized in the sense that they assume that the center has precise knowledge of the criteria (4) and production possibilities (1) of the subsystems. Actual planning processes, of course, operate in different circumstances. The analysis set out above, however, is useful, first, because it sets out the problem of devising a mechanism in a clear mathematical form (the solution to which can be compared with the initial premises) and, second, because it gives an estimate of the ideal outcome for the center, which can be approximated by increasing the information available to it (this is discussed below).

We now examine possible forms of control under uncertainty. To do so, we make some changes in the basic model (1)-(4); in particular, for $i=1, \ldots, n$, let

$$w_i = f_i(x_i, \; y_i, \; \alpha_i), \quad x_i \in X_i(\beta_i), \tag{32}$$

$$\alpha_i \in A_i, \quad \beta_i \in B_i, \tag{33}$$

where the center knows only the sets A_i, B_i, but not the particular values of α_i and β_i. Since we are talking about a single operation and the center faces uncertainty, its rational behavior is to calculate for the worst case — i.e., to make decisions according to the principle of maximizing the guaranteed return.

As is shown in [23] , the type of strategy adopted by the center in model (32)-(33) is substantially more complex, and finding that strategy involves solving very difficult problems. An assumption that the subsystems are "cautious" [24] eases the position somewhat. Since we cannot give a detailed exposition of these issues here, we only present some of the qualitative conclusions as they affect our model of incentives [22] .

The center may have incomplete information about the motives and possibilities of the subsystems because, for example, the latter practice deliberate concealment. We take model (21) to illustrate what consequences this may have for the center and the subsystems.

Assume the center knows that $a^- \leqslant a \leqslant a^+$; then its minimum guaranteed outcome by criterion w_0 is $w_0^{(2)} = (b^2/4a^+) + \varepsilon$; i.e., it is less than (25). If the center knows parameter a, the subsystem receives a bonus of $(b^2/4a) + \varepsilon$, and, at the same time, must incur costs on above-plan output (the second component in criterion w (21)) equal to $b^2/4a$; i.e., on its criterion w its overall outcome is ε. In the other case, the subsystem's bonus is reduced but its costs are reduced too, and by a larger amount, so that the result for the subsystem on the basis of the criterion w (21) is now more than ε. We note too that incentive strategy $y_i(x_i)$ generally ceases to reveal property (30) (with one point,

x_i^0, y_i^0 , singled out, and with the punishment strategy operating at the other points in set X_i); the subset in which the punishment strategy is applied shrinks.

If the center is to obtain appropriate information, it must incur expenditure on acquiring and processing data. This expenditure is greater, the larger the number of subsystems the center controls. It is partly for this reason that the center, when devising some economic or legal mechanism, must start from the notion of some "average" subsystem. This means that when the center does not know the parameter α_i of subsystem i in (32), for example, it uses some average value $\bar{\alpha}$ for which it forecasts a "large system's" response to the intervention. Calculating $\bar{\alpha}$ a priori, however, may lead to large errors in estimating the outcome. It is appropriate to use a later model [25] here. The subsystems are divided into l groups with n_j in each j-th group, where all subsystems in a group have the same parameter α_j. Then

$$w_j = f_j(x_j,\ y_j,\ \alpha_j),\quad j = 1, \ldots, l, \tag{34}$$

$$w_0 = \sum_{j=1}^{l} n_j g(x_j, y_j, \alpha_j), \tag{35}$$

and the center knows values of n_j, $\displaystyle\sum_{j=1}^{l} n_j = n$. It formulates a single mechanism $y(x)$ for the whole system and, by calculating the reaction of each group, it can calculate the outcome for itself.

Model (34), (35) can also be viewed as a formalization of the control of a single subsystem of which the center has only a description in probabilistic terms. Then the distribution of parameter α specifies the n_j; and expression (35) is the mathematical expectation of the outcome for the center.

5. Control Mechanisms in Repeated Processes

The introduction of a dynamic element into planning brings

about a qualitative change in the nature of the economic mechanism. On the one hand, the dynamic element opens up new ways of influencing the subsystems, as the information held by the center is augmented; on the other hand, it also increases the possibilities for the subsystems, and this substantially raises the number of hypotheses that must be considered for a systematic study of the problem. The problems in analyzing dynamic models spring not only from the need to use a more complex mathematical apparatus but also from the fact that the principles for making decisions in dynamic systems are inadequately developed. In fact, only purely optimizing models (excluding uncertainty) have received intensive study, and investigation of multistage and differential games (basically with complete information) has only begun. At the same time, such factors as changes in the situation as the procedure operates or increases in the information available require a gradual change in the procedure's aims. Unfortunately, this very important aspect of dynamic processes has not yet been given the analysis it needs.

We limit ourselves to a single special class of dynamic models, which can be called repeated processes [27]. Assume that in the basic model (1)-(4) the center has no a priori knowledge of the criteria (4) and production possibilities (1) of the subsystems (apart from certain of their properties). If the process is repeated many times with the same model of the subsystems, then the center, on the basis of its observation of the choices realized by the subsystems, can augment its information. Thus in repeated processes the center can adapt to models of the subsystems that are imprecisely known to it and improve the outcome for itself (the minimum certain value of this outcome may be very small at the outset, as was noted in section 4).

In [27] the assumption that subsystems are "myopic" and try to maximize their criteria (4) at each round is analyzed. Moreover, the center knows the "punishment strategies" $y_i^{\text{H}}(x_i)$ (for incentive models they are always known: $y_i=0$). This assumption, together with a number of others, allows the center at some repetition of the process to "grope for" the point

$(x_1^0, \ldots, x_n^0, \ y_1^0, \ldots, y_n^0)$ that yields it the best outcome according to criterion (2). In the process of "groping," it uses a procedure that may be called "counterplanning" [27]; at the k-th process the center communicates to the i-th subsystem a set H_i^k and proposes that it choose x_i^k, and also state a desired y_i^k. If, moreover, $(x_i^k, y_i^k) \in H_i^k$, then this pair is implemented by the center; if $(x_i^k, y_i^k) \notin H_i^k$ or if the subsystem does not communicate y_i^k, the center adopts the "punishment strategy." The strategy described here is an extension of the strategy in case 2.

Algorithms have also been devised that permit the center not only to "grope for" the desired point but also to acquire the information it needs about the criteria and production possibilities of the subsystems. This is important if the center's criterion changes in the course of the repetitions. These classes of algorithm can be interpreted as processes of iterative counterplanning, the outcomes of which are optimal coordinated plans as in an input-output model, for example.

Attempts to incorporate elements of "foresight" into the subsystems lead to complex formulations of the problems. In the first place, it becomes questionable whether iterative planning is possible, since the subsystems may give distorted information at the iterations. The only correct formulations are those in which each iteration is actually feasible in production. In these cases, the center may evaluate the outcome for itself as the sum of the outcomes at each iteration (in each period). It then becomes very important to optimize the actual process of "groping." Without going into details, we note that the formulation in [27] recalls the problem of optimal search for the extremum of a unimodal function and can be reduced to calculating a sequential maximin.

"Foresight" on the part of the subsystems can also be formalized as an attempt to maximize the following criterion:

$$F_i = \sum_{k=1}^{N_i} \mu_i^k f_i(x_i^k, y_i^k, \alpha_i),$$

where μ_i^k is the weight given to the outcome at the k-th operation and N_i is the planning horizon. Reference [27] considers a problem in which the center knows μ_i^n, N_i, f_i, $i=1,\ldots,n$, but not the parameters α_i. As it turns out, it can devise strategies of the type $y_i^1(x_i^1)$, $y_i^2(\hat{x}_i^1, x_i^2)$, $y_i^3(\hat{x}_i^1, \hat{x}_i^2, x_i^3), \ldots,$ where $\hat{x}_i^1, \hat{x}_i^2, \ldots$ are actual choices made by the subsystems, which became known to the center at the respective operation of the process, such that, starting from a particular operation (which depends on the dimensions of vectors α_i), the center's result is the same as it would have been if it had known α_i.

Thus the approach to modeling control mechanisms in a centralized economy developed at the Computer Center of the USSR Academy of Sciences is based on a representation of the economic system as a set of subsystems with the property of relative independence. At the same time, we treat economic mechanisms as a means of implementing national economic programs by affecting the interests of these subsystems. In fact, control systems have a complex multilevel structure. The rational number of levels is determined by the complexity and speed of information processing (for more details, see [9]). At the same time, the controllers at each level inevitably develop their own interests, which are conditioned by their position in the overall structure. In order to determine the efficiency of any controls, we must clearly set out our assumptions concerning what information subsystems hold about each other and specify the principles on which they make decisions under conditions of unavoidable uncertainty. In our view, further research should pursue the following major directions: improvements should be made by mathematicians in analytical and computational analysis; at the same time, in conjunction with economists and sociologists, work should be done to produce a detailed and systematic account of each organization (this would include a model of the organization's objectives, the principles on which it makes decisions, and so on).

REFERENCES

1. Kantorovich, L. V. Ekonomicheskii raschet nailuchshego ispol'zovaniia resursov. Moscow: USSR Academy of Sciences Press, 1960.

2. Aganbegian, A. G.; Bagrinovskii, K. A.; and Granberg, A. G. Sistema modelei narodnokhoziaistvennogo planirovaniia. Moscow: "Mysl'" Publishers, 1975.

3. Sistema modelei optimal'nogo planirovaniia. Moscow: "Nauka" Publishers, 1975.

4. Diukalov, A. N.; Ivanov, Iu. N.; and Tokarev, V. V. "Printsipy modelirovaniia na EVM sistem ekonomicheskogo upravleniia." Parts I and II. Avtomatika i telemekhanika, 1973, no. 12; 1974, no. 1.

5. Emel'ianov, S. V., and Burkov, V. N. "Upravlenie aktivnymi sistemami." In Aktivnye sistemy. Moscow: Institut problem upravleniia, 1973.

6. Vol'konskii, V. A. Printsipy optimal'nogo planirovaniia. Moscow: "Ekonomika" Publishers, 1973.

7. Baranov, E. F.; Danilov-Danil'ian, V. I.; and Zavel'skii, M. G. "O sisteme optimal'nogo perspektivnogo planirovaniia." Ekonomika i matematicheskie metody, 1971, vol. 7, no. 3.

8. Danilov-Danil'ian, V. I., and Zavel'skii, M. G. "Sotsial'no-ekonomicheskii optimum i territorial'nye problemy narodnokhoziaistvennogo planirovaniia." Ekonomika i matematicheskie metody, 1975, vol. 11, no. 3.

9. Moiseev, N. N. Elementy teorii optimal'nykh skhem. Moscow: "Nauka" Publishers, 1975.

10. Germeier, Iu. B. Vvedenie v teoriiu issledoviia operatsii. Moscow: "Nauka" Publishers, 1975.

11. Germeier, Iu. B. Igry i neprotivopolozhnymi interesami (teoriia priniatiia reshenii pri nepolnom edinstve). Moscow: Moscow State University Press, 1972.

12. Germeier, Iu. B., and Moiseev, N. N. "O nekotorykh zadachakh teorii ierarkhicheskikh sistem upravleniia." In Problemy prikladnoi matematiki i mekhaniki. Moscow: "Nauka" Publishers, 1971.

13. Moiseev, N. N. "Ierarkhicheskie struktury i teoriia igr." Kibernetika, 1973, no. 6.

14. Vatel', I. A., and Ereshko, F. I. Matematika konflikta i sotrudnichestva. Moscow: "Znanie" Publishers, 1973, no. 8.

15. Germeier, Iu. B., and Vatel', I. A. "Igri s ierarkhicheskim vektorom interesov." Izvestiia AN SSSR, seriia tekhnicheskaia kibernetika, 1974, no. 3.

16. Germeier, Iu. B. "Ob igrakh dvukh lits s fiksirovannoi posledovatel'nostiu khodov." Doklady AN SSSR, 1971, 198, no. 5.

17. Kukushchkin, N. S. "Rol' vzaimnoi informirovannosti v igrakh dvukh lits s neprotivopolozhnymi interesami." Zhurnal vychislitel'noi matematiki i matematicheskoi fiziki, 1972, vol. 12, no. 4.

18. Vatel', I. A. "Nekotorye voprosy modelirovaniia protsessov priniatiia reshenii v zadachakh ratsional'nogo ispol'zovaniia vodnykh resursov." In Metody sistemnogo analiza v problemakh ratsional'nogo ispol'zovaniia vodnykh resursov. Vol. 1. Vienna: VTs AN SSSR, 1974.

19. Berkovitch, R. N., and Vatel', I. A. "Model' raspredeleniia vody mezhdu kolkhozami c uchetom nekotorykh printsipov khoziaistvennogo rascheta." In Metody sistemnogo analiza v problemakh ratsional'nogo ispol'zovaniia vodnykh

resursov. Vol. 2. Moscow: VTs AN SSSR, 1975.

20. Vatel', I. A.; Ereshko, F. I.; and Kononenko, A. F. "Igry s fiksirovannoi posledovatel'nost'iu khodov i ierarkhicheskie sistemy upravleniia v ekonomike." In Metody optimizatsii i ikh prilozheniia. Irkutsk: Sibirskii energeticheskii institut, 1974.

21. Kononenko, A. F. "Teoretiko-igrovoi analiz dvukhurovnevoi ierarkhicheskoi sistemy upravleniia." Zhurnal vychislitel'noi matematiki i matematicheskoi fiziki, 1974, vol. 14, no. 5.

22. Vatel', I. A. "O matematicheskikh model'iakh stimulirovaniia v ekonomike." In Planirovanie i upravlenie ekonomicheskimi tselenapravlennymi sistemami. Novosibirsk: "Nauka" Publishers, 1975.

23. Vatel', I. A., and Kukushchkin, N. S. "Optimal'noe povedenie igroka, obladaiushchego pravom pervogo khoda, pri netochnom znanii interesov partnera." Zhurnal vychislitel'noi matematiki i matematicheskoi fiziki, 1973, vol. 13, no. 2.

24. Kononenko, A. F. "Rol' informatsii o funktsii tseli protivnika v igrakh dvukh lits s fiksirovannoi posledovatel'nost'iu khodov." Zhurnal vychislitel'noi matematiki i matematicheskoi fiziki, 1973, vol. 13, no. 2.

25. Vatel', I. A. "K probleme upravleniia bol'shimi odnorodnymi kollektivami." VI Vsesoiuznoe soveshchanie po problemam upravleniya (Tezisy). Moscow, 1974.

26. Danil'chenko, T. N., and Mosevich, K. K. "Mnogoshagovye igry dvukh lits s fiksirovannoi posledovatel'nost'iu khodov." Zhurnal vychislitel'noi matematiki i matematicheskoi fiziki, 1974, vol. 14, no. 4.

27. Vatel', I. A., and Dranev, Ia. N. "Ob odnoi klasse povtoriaiushchikh igr c nepol'noi informatsiei v dvukhurovnevoi ekonomicheskoi sisteme." In Trudy mezhdunarodnoi konferentsii "Modelirovanie ekonomicheskikh protsessov." VTs AN SSSR, 1975.

Received March 9, 1976

Part 2

Planning Models

INTRODUCTION

Martin Cave

The materials presented below fall within the field of mathematical economics which has received most attention in the USSR — the construction of planning models involving some form of optimization. As Soviet economists are fond of pointing out, some of the earliest mathematical planning models were devised in the Soviet Union in the 1920s. It is only in the last two decades, however, that conditions have existed in which this early work could be developed and brought closer to practical realization (for a more general account of this process, see [1]).

Planning models in some form are now used quite widely at all levels of the economy, from aggregate models down to models for enterprise planning. Most of the developments have been in the field of long-term planning, where major strategic decisions are taken and where the planning process is not trammeled by the need to disaggregate to the level of individual plan executants. At the national level the major modeling tool used is dynamic input-output analysis (see [2]) and similar models are used for regional planning. At the ministry level, a standard investment planning model has been developed and is now widely used. At enterprise level, linear programming models are often solved in the course of the planning process.

Many Soviet economists, however, doubt the value of using

such models individually, and much effort has been devoted to building up systems of models embracing a more or less comprehensive set of planning levels and functions. Four such systems of models are described in the extracts presented below. All the systems are intended for planning over a period of ten years or so. Although they are fairly aggregative, they often rely heavily on procedures which allow the overall planning problem to be broken down into a number of smaller problems. In each case the models were prepared within research institutes but they are all intended for implementation by the state planning agencies.

The extracts below give general accounts of systems of models concerned. The labor involved in formulating, collecting data for, and programming such models is enormous, and it is not surprising that their development takes a period of time which can almost be measured in decades. Over so long a period the detailed structure of the model inevitably changes, and one of the aims of the present introduction is to give a brief account of the current status of each model. First, however, it may be useful to describe some features common to many systems of models of this type.

Assume we are compiling a long-term plan for an economy with a given objective function. The problem is clearly that of choosing the optimal development path consistent with resource availabilities and some specification of the required state of the economy in the postplan period. The latter can normally be imposed on the model from outside; the former can be found in a more or less sophisticated way through expert estimates or, in the case of labor supply, by demographic forecasting. Over a planning period of this length, the crucial variable is investment, and the planners' main task is to choose how capacity should be expanded. Because of the size of the problem, however, the planners cannot choose the optimal combination of investment projects centrally; the overall problem needs to be split up into a number of more manageable parts.

Subsections of the economy are therefore identified. These are assigned local objective functions and constraints, and solve their separate local problems. The solutions are aggregated and a check is made of whether they are consistent with one another in the overall sense. If they are not consistent, then some parameter is altered in the local objective functions or the local constraints, and the process is repeated until a consistent solution is found (see, for example [3]).

The planning procedures thus tend to share a common basis in the form of the local model for choosing investment projects, but differ with respect to (i) the principle on which the economy is decomposed, which can be sectoral or territorial, (ii) the nature of the local and global objective functions, and (iii) the form of adjustment made to the local problems in the iterative process; here the major alternatives are either to change quantities — input allocations or output targets — or to change price-type variables. Of course we have given merely the skeleton of a planning process, and the models presented below not only differ in other important respects too; they also embody further complications and elaborations.

This last point is fully illustrated by the first of the models described below, which was first formulated by Baranov, Danilov-Danil'ian, and Zavel'skii and is currently being developed by a research team in TsEMI headed by Baranov. The model is given in two versions, and in each version the economy is decomposed in two directions into branches and regions. In the first version branch plans are initially coordinated at the national level; then the regions, which have objective functions expressing the interests of their own populations, step in to make a selection from the investment projects proposed by the various branches in their regions. The sum of regional plans thus formed will normally differ from the initial national plan, and an iterative process ensues, with branch plans being recomputed on the basis of different parameters (particularly shadow prices for resources) until a plan is reached which is consistent and optimal in both sectoral and regional dimensions. In the alternative version of the process the regions first select a set of investment projects which suits their interests; then when the branches come to prepare their plans they have to

pay the regions a form of compensation for developing a production unit beyond the level envisaged in the regional plan.

As if the model were not complex enough already, it also incorporates a procedure of allocating resources to transport
products from region to region and, more unusually, a model
of the process of attaining "social balance" — interpreted here
as a balance of migration between regions in response to differences in living standards. Not surprisingly, critics have
condemned the model for being too complex, and simplifications
have had to be introduced for the purposes of practical implementation. For example, [4] describes the version of the model
used since 1974 for experimental calculations. The main differences between the experimental and the original models are:
(i) in the experimental model a different sequence of computations is adopted, as follows: the regional models are first
solved, followed by those for migration and the transportation
complex; these results are checked for consistency at the upper level and only then do the branch models come into operation; their solutions are fed into the regional models and the
cycle continues; (ii) it was not possible in the experimental
model to disaggregate down to individual enterprises; instead
a 98-sector input-output model was used to represent branch
technologies; (iii) the branches' objective function was changed
to a quadratic form, for speed of convergence; (iv) the transportation model was reformulated (for a detailed account see
[5, 6]).

Even with these simplifications, the experimental model incorporated 98 separate outputs, 16 branch complexes, 24 regions, 78 consumer goods, 33 occupational groups, and seven
types of natural resources, and the calculations covered a 10-
year period. Although the authors of the model described in
the article below propose it as a basis for Gosplan's operations,
in view of the system's complexity it is hardly surprising that
so far it has only been used within a research institute. Development continues, however; it is proposed to extend the number
of branches to 260 [7] and at present attempts are being made
to incorporate econometric relationships within it, for such

purposes as forecasting input coefficients.

The second system of models described here has also been developed within TsEMI, by a team headed by V. F. Pugachev. Two articles are devoted to it here. The first sets out the basic principle on which the system operates, which is the principle of approximating possibilities at various levels by taking linear combinations of alternative plans. This starts at enterprise level, where a number of discrete development variants are calculated. A weighted average of these specifies the branch's production possibilities, and the branch then compiles a set of plan variants based on different assumptions about the structure of demand for its output and its allocation of scarce resources. These variants are then aggregated to yield a compact formulation of the production possibilities of the whole economy, from which a provisional plan is chosen; the neighborhood of this plan is then investigated using the marginal rates of substitution between final outputs associated with the optimal plan.

Since plans are worked out at each stage in variant form, there is no need for numerous iterations. Alternatively, if iterations are possible, the variants computed at each iteration can gradually move in on the neighborhood of the optimum found at the preceding stage. For example, a version of the model might emphasize the role of the capital charge or coefficient of relative efficiency (a kind of interest rate) in balancing supply and demand for investment goods. Investment decisions are made at branch level to minimize total costs, including capital charge. Altering the capital charge affects choice of technique at branch level and thereby changes the structural parameters in the upper level model. As the procedure operates, the range of values of the capital charge contracts with each iteration. The range of variation of branch output targets will also diminish as the calculations proceed.

The Pugachev model was first used in connection with a projection over the period 1976 to 1990. More recently, Gosplan resolved to employ it for some purely experimental calculations for the plan for the 10-year period from 1981, but unfortunately only 40% of the 80 to 100 branches identified in the model were

ready to participate. It is expected that from 1983 Gosplan will
be using the system for long-term planning with a full comple-
ment of branches and in conjunction with a 260 × 260 input-output
table. A version of the model incorporating branch complexes
is now available [8].

The second article by Pugachev discusses ways of developing
the system further. These advances take a fairly predictable
form — improvements in the optimality criteria used at the
various levels, incorporation of a regional element, ensuring
of consistency between branch output levels on a less aggregated
basis, and so on. Much discussion is given to the implications
of switching to a genuinely dynamic formulation to replace the
current "quasi-static" version, which calculates the total investment required to produce the output level of the final year
of the plan, but does not break it down on a year-by-year basis.
Interestingly, however, Pugachev reports that there is little demand within Gosplan for these refinements. He also notes that
the major impediment to successful use of the model is not technical at all. It arises instead from the fact that the incentive
system at branch level does not encourage minimization of
costs, particularly capital costs. Branches thus tend to distort
the information they contribute to the process.

The third system of models discussed here, which focuses
on regional planning, was developed at the Institute for the Organization and Economics of Industrial Production at Novosibirsk. It was developed jointly by Granberg, author of the present article, Aganbegian, the institute's director, and other colleagues. The version presented here is a development of the
original model which incorporates a method for optimizing the
growth of investment. The article also discusses computational
problems, particularly procedures for eliminating certain constraints and variables and for converting the model into a form
in which it can be solved in several blocks. As with the other
two systems of models, an important distinction is drawn between products which are transportable (or tradeable) and which
can therefore be dealt with on the national level, and those which
have to be dealt with on a regional basis. Originally 16 indus-

tries and 10 regions were distinguished; these were increased to 45 and 11, respectively, in 1976.

The Novosibirsk model has not been taken over by Gosplan in the same way as the preceding model. Recently, however, Granberg has argued that some further modification of the model can be useful to the planners in various ways. At the initial stages of planning, it can investigate the impact of re- gional factors and devise an overall location policy. Subse- quently it can be used in a disaggregated version to compile a detailed interregional plan and to check for consistency between the various dimensions of planning [9].

The fifth and final extract differs from its predecessors in that the model discussed is intended for planning within a repub- lic and has been developed in detail in the Computing Center of the Lithuanian Gosplan, where it has been used to forecast the development of the economy up to 1990. In many respects the model is similar to those intended for use at the national level, except that it incorporates disaggregation down to district level, (although the procedures are not set out here). Again, the au- thors emphasize above all the benefits of getting coordinated re- sults from using the models as an interacting system, going so far as to formulate the maximization of feedback between the components of the system as an objective in model building. A recent development in the model not discussed in the present article is the extensive use of production function analysis to forecast output at branch level. The central input-output model has also been used to compute the turnpike or maximum bal- anced growth path for the republic [10].

The selections presented here describe only some of the ma- jor systems of planning models developed in the USSR. Others are omitted, either because accounts of them are readily avail- able in English (Dudkin's system of planning by iterative ag- gregation comes into this category [11]), or because they are little developed and unlikely to have an impact on planning in practice. The basic principles underlying mathematical plan- ning models — interpretation of shadow prices, decomposition, etc. — are now well understood, but the major outstanding problem is to exploit these principles in a way which either renders the models comprehensible to practitioners of planning, or tackles some of the major unresolved issues in planning, such as coordinating sectoral and territorial aspects. The models presented below go some way toward satisfying one or the other of these (possibly mutually exclusive) objectives.

Martin Cave

REFERENCES

1. Cave, M. Computers and Economic Planning, Cambridge: Cambridge University Press, 1980.

2. Birger, E. S., et al. "Experimental Construction of a Dynamic Input-Output Model." Matekon, 1979, vol. 15, no. 3, pp. 59-82.

3. Bagrinovskii, K. A., et al. "On Methods for Coordinating Sectoral Plans within a System of Models." Matekon, 1979, vol. 15, no. 3, pp. 3-12.

4. Baranov, E. F., and Matlin, I. S. "Ob eksperimental'noi realizatsii sistemy modelei optimal'nogo perspektivnogo planirovaniia." Ekonomika i matematicheskie metody, 1976, vol. 12, no. 4, pp. 627-648.

5. Kovshov, G. N. "Transport in a System of Models for Perspective Planning of the Economy." Matekon, 1978/9, vol. 15, no. 2, pp. 3-38.

6. Bedenkova, M. F. "Transportation and Commercial Relationships in a System of Models for Optimal Long-Term Planning." Matekon, 1980, vol. 16, no. 4, pp. 77-94.

7. Matlin, I. S. "An Overall Model for the Economy within a System of Models for Optimal Long-Term Planning." Matekon, 1979/80, vol. 16, no. 2, pp. 71-88.

8. Pugachev, V. F.; Martynov, G. V.; and Pitelin, A. K. "The Multibranch Complex in a Multistage System of Optimal Long-Range Planning," Matekon, 1978, vol. 14, no. 3, pp. 4-21.

9. Granberg, A. G. Modeli soglasovaniia narodnokhoziaistvennykh i regional'nykh planovykh reshenii. Novosibirsk: IEiOPP, 1979.

10. Zhemetaitaite, S. A., et al. "Construction of a Balanced Growth Model of the Economy of a Union Republic." Matekon, 1977, vol. 13, no. 1, pp. 16-29.

11. Vakhutinsky, I. Y., et al. "Iterative Aggregation — A New Approach to the Solution of Large Scale Problems." Econometrica, 1979, vol. 47, no. 4, pp. 821-841.

ON A SYSTEM OF MODELS FOR OPTIMAL
LONG-TERM PLANNING

E. F. Baranov, V. I. Danilov-Danil'ian,
and M. G. Zavel'skii

After many years of research into special aspects of mathematical modeling of the economy and optimal planning of production, the necessary conditions have been created for designing a system of optimal planning which combines national,
branch, and regional aspects and which links up the production
and social aspects of the plan. Below we set out one possible
approach to constructing such a system.[1]

1. Initial Assumptions

A system of optimal planning of the economy must be directed
toward the goal of continuously increasing the welfare of the
whole working population. The concept of "social welfare"
should not be viewed in the abstract, in relation to the "average
person." It should be related to the particular sphere of activity and place of residence of individual groups, to ensure that
their individual interests are compatible with one another and
with the general development goals of socialist society. Otherwise the needs of the "average" worker may be satisfied to the

Russian text © 1971 by "Nauka" Publishers and Ekonomika i matematicheskie
metody. "O sisteme optimal'nogo perspektivnogo planirovaniia," Ekonomika i
matematicheskie metody, 1971, vol. 7, no. 3, pp. 332-350.

maximum possible extent but there may be disparities in the satisfaction of the needs of particular groups, the significance of which cannot be determined a priori.

In the present article we limit ourselves to the upper level of the socialist economy: the economy as a whole, branches, and economic regions.[2] The branches are production complexes formed from ministries and departments on the basis of the current structure of management.[3] Regions are based on the current regional division of the territory of the USSR (union republics automatically being treated separately).

The length of the planning period is taken as being 10 to 15 years, on the basis of the typical period required to install and start using capacity embodying current scientific and technological developments. Although planning over a longer period is desirable if the socioeconomic consequences of social development are to be taken into account, this gives rise to a number of complications which reduce the reliability of the data as we get further away from the base period. However our system does incorporate planned attempts to influence factors which will improve social relations in the postplan period, and it also takes account (through a long-term forecast over 20 to 30 years) of the results of allocating resources to the development of the economy in the plan period. It is assumed that accuracy in the original data is ensured by a rolling system for computing the long-term plan and making forecasts.

The system envisages the following relationship between long-term planning on the one hand and current planning and operational control over the economy on the other. The long-term plan figures, computed in aggregate form, determine the course of current planning and operational management in the initial year of the relevant period. At the same time we assume that some economic parameters (input coefficients, prices, etc.) are determined in detail only as the economy goes into operation; these data are used through a system of rolling plans to revise the original aggregate indices once the plan period has been shifted forward by one year. The links between these aspects of economic management are shown in Figure 1.

Figure 1. The framework for rolling planning: *1* — the long-range forecast for the period after $t+T$; *2* — the optimal long-term plan for the period from t to $t+T$; *3* — the current plan for year t; *4* — the long-term forecast for the period following $t+T+1$; *5* — the optimal long-term plan for the period from $t+1$ to $t+T+1$; *6* — the current plan for year $t+1$.

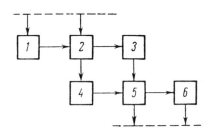

Current planning lies outside the scope of the system. This task should not be assigned to the highest level organizations of the system (no higher than the branch), and it should be organically coordinated with the widespread use of horizontal links, financial accountability, etc.

It is questionable at present whether it is possible to implement in practice all the implications which follow from our theoretical ideas. This leads us unavoidably to the conclusion that at the initial stage of experimental design certain simplifications must be adopted:

1. In the initial version of the system, the optimal plan should produce a set of indices which is similar in composition to that in current use; we thus adopt the classification of current and capital goods, services, and resources which is currently used by Gosplan USSR for the purposes of long-term planning.

2. The development of the system should rely primarily on the existing system of accounting and planning information; alternatively it should use information which is such that methods of collection can be worked out in the immediate future and the task of doing so assigned to statistical and planning bodies and design organizations.

3. The system must be oriented toward computers and programs which are already available.

4. The system of optimal planning must be consistent with the major objectives of economic policy in a socialist state (strengthening the defense capacity of the economy, meeting external political and economic obligations, ensuring full employment, and equalizing the satisfaction of the needs of indi-

vidual social groups and the economic development of individual regions).

These requirements can be satisfied by devising a structure for the system and incorporating special parameters and exogenous constraints within that structure.

2. The General Framework of the Experimental System for Optimal Planning

The system must be a single whole. This presupposes that its individual parts are organically combined on the basis of an iterative planning process which includes a regular exchange of information between different levels of the economy both from the bottom up and from the top down.

In a process of this kind, the central planning agency fixes the major socioeconomic targets, controls the use of major sources of finance, and allocates goods in short supply. Each branch, on the basis of the scientific and technical information available to it, devises draft plans for constructing, rebuilding, and using the enterprises subordinate to it and then implements whichever draft is chosen. The regions evaluate these drafts from the standpoint of how they can most effectively use the labor and natural resources at their disposal in order to solve the problems of the social development in their areas.

To get a first approximation for the plans (national, branch, or regional) we use data from balances and forecasts made using special mathematical models and expert estimates [4, 5].

The optimality criterion for each region is the total real income of that region's population over the plan period. The criterion for the upper level model is the overall return to using primary resources (labor and natural resources) in social production. The shadow prices in which this return is measured are computed jointly with the optimal plans and are in the nature of rental payments [1, 6, 7].[4] In the course of the overall planning process the criteria of the upper level model and of the regions coordinate the interests of the economic regions and of the economy as a whole in such a way as to yield an op-

timal value for the overall national criterion which turns out
to be equal to the upper level criterion computed at the completion of the process — i.e., at the optimal values for the
shadow prices of natural resources and labor in the regional
models [1]. The optimality criterion for each branch complex
is profit. This is calculated in a way which values goods and
services (capital and current) produced and used at the shadow
prices associated with the optimal plan, and which values the
labor and natural resources used at the regional shadow prices.

Under this approach, the problem of choosing the relationship between consumption and accumulation reduces to devising
a mechanism for coordinating the regional criteria with the criterion in the upper level model, subject to a given fixed loading
on the economy resulting from the major socioeconomic and
political problems facing society. This fixed loading includes
the obligation to produce current and capital goods and services
to meet the needs of defense, administration, science, and external trade, to develop the economy in the postplan period,
and to augment stocks and reserves; these obligations also impose resource constraints.[5]

The dual treatment of the economy — from the branch and
regional viewpoints — determines the special feature of the
iterative process adopted to optimize the plan. In fact, each
complete cycle of calculations (a "large" iteration in the planning process) includes several cycles of "small" iterations;
the plan is coordinated in one respect by the small iterations,
while the other aspect is "covered" by a sequence of large
iterations.[6] With this allocation of functions between large
and small iterations there are two main versions of the process. However, the nature of the unit to be modeled imposes
such strong demands that neither version is simply a re-
arrangement of the other.

Let us consider the first version of the planning process.
Each branch works out a variant of its optimal development
plan, by making a selection from the set of possible ways of
constructing, rebuilding, or operating the enterprises under
its control. Each such project is allocated to a particular lo-

cation in a particular region and is represented by a vector of inputs and outputs broken down by year of the plan period according to the classification adopted (current and capital goods, services, natural resources, and labor); each project is also costed financially. At the same time constraints governing the use of materials and finance by branches must be observed, together with constraints on major output targets and resource use established at the upper level. The branch's optimality criterion — profit — is computed in terms of national shadow prices for goods and services and regional shadow prices for natural resources and labor.

The shadow prices associated with the constraints in the branch model are transmitted upward, together with the input-output vector for the branch as a whole. A check is made at the upper level that the plans submitted by the branch complexes together make up an optimal plan (more precisely, a provisionally optimal plan, since the regional aspect has not yet been considered) which is balanced in terms of the production (or supply) of and demand for current and capital goods, natural resources, labor, and finance; this must include both the constant and the variable[7] loading on the economy. The solution to this provisionally optimal problem will show which plans should be lowered and which should be increased in order to meet social needs; upper level shadow prices for goods and resources are also computed.

If the check made using these shadow prices and the shadow prices for scarce resources derived from the branch models turns out to be unsatisfactory, or if the degree of tautness of the branch plans is unsatisfactory, then branches receive new resource allocations and output targets. In those cases where an increased return can be expected if a branch is allocated more of a particular resource, the relevant limits are increased, while branches whose output does not meet overall demand are given higher output targets. In the opposite case targets and constraints are reduced. Such changes must be mutually consistent.

Using new figures for the resource constraints, output targets, and upper level shadow prices, the branches recompile their plans. A preliminary coordination of sectoral and national plans is achieved through these small iterations. The branch plans together make up a balanced plan which yields an optimal value for the upper level criterion (they do not however take account of the opportunities or interests of the regions).

It is at this stage that work on the compilation of a single optimal national plan begins. At this stage the calculations include models to optimize regional development.

The model for each region includes any projects in that region which have been included in the branch plans; these have already been coordinated with one another and with the national plan. Moreover the model uses the shadow prices for goods and services derived at the upper level, together with levels of fixed and variable loading on the region's economy. The regional model takes account of this loading and of the natural resources and labor available, and it is used to compile a regional development plan which is balanced in terms of the supply of and demand for goods, services, and resources and in terms of the income and expenditure of the population. The plan also yields an optimal value for the regional criterion. In structural terms the production part of the plan is a selection of the projects proposed by the branches for implementation in that region. The plan also determines desirable levels of exports and imports, income levels by group of wage earner and by family type,[8] and private and social consumption of goods and services. Regional shadow prices for goods and resources are computed at the same time.

If the set of projects selected in the production section of the regional plan is not identical with the set of projects from which the choice is made, then the regional and branch aspects of the plan are not fully consistent. If an inconsistency of this kind arises, the branch plans are recomputed to take account of the new regional shadow prices for natural resources and labor; these determine the level of rental payments and thus the return to locating production in any region. Thus we revert to the previous cycle of calculations and continue the sequence of large iterations.

If the projects selected in each region are identical with those from which the selection is made — if the branch and regional plans are consistent — a calculation is made of the economy's transportation needs (based on the import requirements and export potential of all the transportation districts[9] within each region, as given by their plans). The transportation complex then compiles a plan which determines the development and operation of the transportation network. This plan is balanced in terms of the availability of and need for haulage capacity and the capacities of the segments of the network, and it incorporates any fixed loading on that network. The plan ensures that any imports required are supplied (subject to feasible regional export levels) in such a way that costs over the whole plan period are minimized. Costs are computed on the basis of the upper level shadow prices for goods and services, including credits, and on the basis of regional shadow prices for natural resources and labor.

By use of the plan for the transportation complex and the regional plans (which yield figures for personal and social consumption) the variable loading is computed for the upper level model and a check is made of how much the corresponding indices have changed from their previous values. If the changes go beyond some prespecified level (a parameter of the process) then the new figure for the variable loading is communicated to the upper level model, new regional shadow prices for labor and natural resources and new delivered prices for goods are transmitted to the branch models, and new indices for the variable loading on the regions (for transportation only) are sent to the regional models. The next large iteration of the process is then performed. If the change in the variable loading at the upper level is less than some given magnitude, the plan is deemed to be consistent in its branch, regional, and national aspects and is then checked for social balance.

We now consider the second version of the planning process. Each region compiles a draft plan for optimal development within its own boundaries. This takes account of the fixed and variable[10] loading, constraints on natural resources and labor,

and any material and financial balances affecting the region.
Each region receives from the upper level model the shadow
prices for outputs and resources computed at the previous iteration, and it gets from the branches the scales of payment from
their profits into the region's budget. Within the framework of
the regional optimization problem these funds are divided between social consumption and accumulation (decentralized regional investment).

The production section of the regional plan is found by the
region's making a selection from all the projects for constructing, rebuilding, or operating enterprises in all branches within
its territory. The regional plan also determines desirable
levels for the development of individual plants (these are max-
ima for the branches) and desired levels of exports of individual goods and resources: it also fixes money incomes by wage
group and family type, consumption levels, decentralized regional investment, a method for financing social consumption
funds from the region's resources, and regional shadow prices
for goods and resources. The shadow prices of labor and natural resources and decisions about the desired level of development for individual factories are communicated to the branch
models.

As in the first variant of the process, the branches compile
their own plans to maximize their profits. The only difference
is that together with the previously specified constraints they
must also bear in mind the maximum extent to which they can
develop each production unit in each region, as dictated by that
region's plan. If it turns out that it would be profitable for a
branch to develop a particular factory in a region beyond the
specified limit, the branch informs the region of the scale of
payments from profit it would be willing to make into the regional budget (the shadow price of the corresponding constraint).

A calculation is then made of the economy's demand for transportation, broken down by district (possible exports are given
by the total of branch plans; indispensable imports are given by the
regional plans; and imports of other products are given by the
total of branch plans). These indices and the maximum level

of exports of each product from each region (as given in its plan) are communicated to the model for the transportation complex. This complex compiles a plan for the development and operation of the transportation network using the same model as in the previous planning process, with the addition of constraints on the maximum possible level of exports from each region. These constraints have shadow prices associated with them, which are used in the same way as scales of payment into the regional budgets from the profits of other branch complexes.

A check is then made to verify the stability of the scales of payment from the profits of each branch into the regional budgets. If such stability has not been achieved, a new plan of the transportation complex is formed which fixes new values for the variable loading on the regional models. These values, together with scales of payment out of profits and limits on the imports of various products into each region, are communicated to the regional models, and new shadow prices for delivered products are communicated to the branch models. The sequence of small iterations is then resumed.

Once stable scales of payment out of profit have been found, based on plans for the regions and the transportation network which are consistent with the plans for remaining branches, a computation is made of the variable loading for the upper level model. These data, together with input-output vectors for the branches, are communicated to the upper level model, which is used as in the first version of the process. The upper level shadow prices are then checked for stability. If the outcome of the check is unsatisfactory, then the resource constraints and output targets for the branch are reviewed as in the first version. Moreover, new values for the investment constraint are computed for each region and passed to the regional model. These are based on payments made to the regions from branch funds, any credits they may receive, and financial constraints applying to social consumption funds and the state budget at Union level. The model then moves on to the next large iteration.

If the new upper level shadow prices are within a given distance of their previous values (the distance being a parameter

of the process), then the plan thus derived is deemed to be coordinated in the branch, regional, and national dimensions and
is then checked for social balance.

In the second version of the planning process the instruments
for coordinating regional and branch development plans are
payments into the regional budgets out of the profits of the
branch complexes. These payments are a means of reallocating national income between regions, insofar as national income
consists of rental payments for the use of labor, natural resources, and land. The level of payment is determined by the
shadow prices corresponding to constraints specifying the maximum quantities of particular goods which the various branches
may produce in a particular region (as given by the model of
the corresponding branch complex); in the case of the transportation complex they are given by the shadow prices associated with the constraints on the maximum level of exports from
each region (as given by the model for the transportation complex). It is much better to redistribute income between regions
via an iterative planning process than to do so in a way which
is not adequately related to planning.[11] In this way the interests of the regions are taken into account in compiling the
branch plans, and the regional plans further the goal of increasing efficiency in production.

When the regions first establish their maximum permitted
output levels, they try to ensure the most efficient structure of
output in their territory, bearing in mind their limited labor
resources.

Payments from the profits of the branch complexes add to
the regional budget in cases when it is in the national interest
for a region to specialize in a way which is disadvantageous
for the region itself. In such cases it may turn out to be advantageous for the region to reconsider its plans and make
corresponding changes in the constraints it imposes on the location of production, since the region will be able to use the
extra resources it receives to develop social consumption funds,
to finance the training of personnel, to improve the infrastructure, and to implement other measures intended to create con-

ditions which will change the structure of its economy for the better.

Thus in the first version the cycles of small iterations coordinate branch plans with national plans, while the series of large iterations links these plans up with the regional plans. In the second version the cycles of small iterations coordinate regional and branch plans, while the series of large iterations links these plans up with national plans.

The final stage in optimal planning is to ensure that the plan is balanced in its social aspects and stable in terms of the effects which it has on human behavior. Such behavior is strongly affected by the plan, but in the present state of knowledge it can only be controlled indirectly and within certain limits.[12] We have in mind particularly changes affecting such aspects as the regional, occupational, sectoral, and social breakdown of the labor force and population and the determination of demand. The special feature of this type of coordination is that it involves man's dual role in social reproduction.

On one hand, the prospects for the development and location of production hinge to a considerable extent on the allocation of labor between different spheres of activity and different branches and regions; on the other hand this allocation is itself strongly affected by changes in the scale and structure of the economy. Hence a system of optimal planning cannot treat the allocation of labor in the same way as it treats the allocation of other resources. A plan will be stable in terms of its effects on people's behavior only if the system for compiling the plan takes account of movements of the population and the labor force. Only in this case can the elements in the plan which show how far the goals of socialist economic development are achieved be made compatible with the objective interests of various groups of workers.

The breakdown of the population by family type and the composition of the labor force by sector, occupational group, and region depend on a complex set of factors — socioeconomic (such as wages, social consumption levels, working conditions, housing, etc.), demographic, climatic, and so on. In the pre-

liminary stage, values are chosen for these factors on the basis
of a forecast made with exogenous data; in the later stages of
planning their values change under the impact of the development and location of the economy and they can be computed using the relevant variant of the plan. These values are fed into
special models for forecasting the distribution of the population
by family type and the breakdown of the labor force by branch,
occupational group, and region. The results derived from these
models are first used to establish constraints on the labor force
in the upper level and regional models; later they are used to
forecast demand in each region using statistical models [8-10];
these demand forecasts help to determine the variable loading
in the upper level model.

It may turn out that at the next iteration the factors listed
above — the arguments in the forecasting models — take somewhat different values from those on which the previous forecast was based. In these circumstances the forecast should
be repeated using the new data and a check made of the differences between the new values and the previous ones. If the
differences are substantial, then the computations should be
repeated to take account of the new constraints on the labor
force and the new structure of consumer demand. But if the
difference in the constraints on labor supply and in the variable
loading (in respect of consumer demand) fall within given limits
(parameters of the process), then the plan is deemed to be socially balanced.

We should note the role played by the planning of wages at
the stage of achieving social balance. This works as follows.

The shadow prices of labor computed in the planning process are regional shadow prices for the workers in particular
occupational and educational groups employed in the various
branches. Each of these shadow prices is regarded as the sum
of the rental payment for using the particular worker and that
worker's wage. At the stage of achieving social balance a
check is made that the relationship between these two components specified in the plan (or in the first iteration, established
via a forecast or by statistical reporting) satisfies the require-

ment of stabilizing the constraints on labor [1]. If as a result of checking the plan for social balance it turns out that this requirement is not satisfied, then the wage levels are reviewed. Elements of the method of directed search are used here; wage rates are raised for categories of labor for which there is excess demand and lowered in the opposite case, although not below the wage level in the base year; the size of the change is determined in the course of the process and depends on the parameters chosen. New wage rates are communicated to the branches, and the latter make the appropriate changes in their projects for building, rebuilding, or operating subordinate enterprises.

The process of compiling the optimal plan is then repeated. If this plan is socially balanced, then the regional shadow prices for different categories of workers (and hence the rental payments for labor) will be the final ones.

In the course of the planning process it may happen that, with wages at the level used in the previous check for social balance, the shadow price of some category of workers falls below the corresponding wage rate.[13] In this case the rental payment for employing the workers will be negative, and the resources of the state budget are used to cover the difference for the branch.

Of course, ensuring equal economic development in all regions is an important part of verifying that the plan is stable with respect to patterns of behavior which are influenced by the level of development. The problem here is that, if this requirement is not satisfied in the plan period, the consequences may only be revealed in the very distant future. The level of a region's economic development can be measured by the output produced by its labor and natural resources per head of population. If a region's economic development exceeds or falls short of that of other regions, the extent of the deviation can be measured by the difference between the level of output in the region and the average level for the USSR. When the second version of the optimizing model is used, inequalities in the economic development of the regions are reflected in the regional breakdown of the payments which branches make into regional budgets out of their profits. Payments of this kind received by a region can be used as a measure of how far that region lags behind in economic terms.

In order to ensure that the plan is satisfactory in this respect, we propose a mechanism based on correcting the discount coefficients used in the upper level optimality criterion for the different regions and the different years of the plan period [1].

We propose that before the plan is compiled experts prepare a hypothetical curve giving a timetable for reducing disparities in regional economic development.[14]   It is clear that this curve should approach a horizontal asymptote monotonically from above. When a cycle of large iterations has been completed, a curve is drawn showing the implied changes in regional inequalities. This is compared with the hypothetical curve, and, if the regional inequalities exceed some specified level, a correction is made to the discount coefficients in the optimality criterion at the upper level. The coefficients are raised for those regions and those years of the plan period where the return per capita to labor and natural resources is below the average (in the first version of the planning process) or if payments are made into the regional budget from branch profits (in the second version). The extent of the correction depends on how far the region is falling behind in terms of the indicator specified.

Once the discount coefficients have been corrected the planning process is repeated. If the gap between the hypothetical curve for reducing regional inequalities and the curve drawn using the figures in the new plan is sufficiently narrow, then the plan — assuming it is socially balanced in other respects — is accepted as the final version. However this may never happen if the hypothetical curve goes beyond what is objectively possible given the level of development in the base year. This is revealed to be the case if the plan ceases to respond to changes in the discount coefficients (i.e., if changing the coefficients does not change the plan, because, for example, of the lag between allocating resources to speed up a region's development and the training of the necessary personnel). In this case the hypothetical curve must be replaced by a curve which corresponds to the final plan variant (which is the best curve given the system's initial state) and that variant is the one adopted.

Thus ensuring that the plan is socially balanced is itself an iterative procedure, and balance is achieved by incorporating forecasts and a directed search as an integral part of the optimization process.

3. Branch Models

The function of a standard branch model is to choose projects for building, rebuilding, and operating enterprises; for this reason branch models are normally discrete. However in the case of branches with a large number of comparatively homogeneous enterprises or branches which are widely dispersed (some branches of the food industry and agriculture fall into this category), continuous or only partly integer-valued models can be used.

The units to be modeled are administrative complexes of ministries and departments or, where necessary, structural subdivisions of these bodies (chief administrations, trusts, etc.). This means that the model of a branch complex will include many different outputs.

The goods and services and other outputs produced by a branch complex may include the following: goods and services from branches engaged in material production, in the form either of producer goods or consumer goods; construction activity to rebuild existing capacity or create new capacity, whether productive or nonproductive; machinery of various kinds and capital goods from material production branches; the output of trained personnel of various specialisms and qualifications; provision of free services of a nonproductive nature to the public or to enterprises, agencies, and organizations.

Some of these activities and the production of some goods and services will be concentrated in several branch complexes; but this does not prevent their production being coordinated within the framework of a single complex. For example, a complex engaged in professional and technical education may combine the production of specialists with the output of various goods; a construction branch may combine construction with the output of construction materials and the training of personnel, and so on.

The function of each branch model is to make an optimal selection of projects for constructing new and rebuilding existing enterprises within the branch, to choose production programs for all enterprises, and to set major financial targets for the branch for each year of the plan period. This is done on the basis of the branch's own capacity and the resources available to it. As noted above, a branch makes decisions in a way which maximizes its profit at the shadow prices derived at the previous iteration of the upper level and regional models.[15] Profit is defined to incorporate cash flows between the branch and the financial and credit system. These include long-term loans for expansion, rental payments, and debt servicing (or accumulation of money balances, including bank interest).

The list of projects for selection is made as follows. For existing enterprises, the range of choices consists of alternative possible input-output vectors; these need not involve redesign of the enterprise, but they may represent alternative ways of expanding the enterprise over different periods. In the case of new enterprises, the choice is made from alternative designs which differ in terms of location, capacity, date of installation, and levels of output and inputs.

When the list of projects is prepared, account is taken of the technical progress to be expected in the plan period. In extractive branches account is taken of stocks of minerals available for industrial exploitation, and attention is paid to geological forecasts. The number of projects considered should be substantially greater than the number which the branch could actually implement, as estimated from past experience or using optimistic forecasts of future development.

For each project data should be prepared for the following

variables, broken down by year of the plan period and expressed in the appropriate classification: levels of output of goods and services; current material inputs of goods and services from material production; construction work needed to carry out the project (specifying type of work required); the machinery, fixed or otherwise, required by the project; the demand for labor, broken down by occupational and educational group; the total amount of wages and other income payable to each occupational and educational group for supplying labor needed by the project; the profit expected from the project, calculated as the difference between the value of output and the cost of all the inputs listed above.

Each branch complex has to satisfy a number of constraints, broken down by year of the plan period (at the first iteration they are based on a preliminary rough forecast; at subsequent iterations they are derived from the upper level model and the models for social balance). These are: constraints on the use of scarce goods and services (including capital goods) produced by other branches; minimum output targets for certain goods and services produced by the branch (these are included both to take account of the loading and for algorithmic reasons — to control the computational process); probable limits on the employment of workers in each professional and educational group; and a limit on the credit balance for each year of the plan period.

In the second version, the regional models also impose constraints on the maximum quantities of output the branches can produce in each region.

It is assumed that data are available on the liabilities and the credit balance of the complex at the start of the period.

The branch models get some of the parameters which they use in the optimization process for each year of the plan period from the upper level model. These are shadow prices for current and capital goods and for any transferable fixed capital which they lease, and interest rates on loans or on bank deposits. They also receive shadow prices for transportation (from the model for the development of transportation),

levels of rental payments for the use of natural resources and
labor (from the regional models), and wage rates (from the
models for social balance).

By solving the optimal model for each year of the plan period
the branch chooses the projects for building, rebuilding, and
operating enterprises capacity which it wants to realize. A
calculation is made of the branch's credit balance in each year
of the plan period (this is done by subtracting interest charges
and debt repayments from any credits received); the branch's
bank balance is also computed (in the case where the complex
has not incurred debts).

Naturally, the model for any particular branch must take account of that branch's special features, and this will cause the
original model to be modified in some way. Models for transportation and construction and for branches producing goods
and services for public consumption exhibit a different structure, but it is not possible to discuss these questions in detail
in a journal article (see [1]).

4. The Upper Level Model

The upper level model shows the extent to which the projects
chosen by the branch complexes satisfy the overall constraints
and the model's optimality criterion. The structural parameters for the upper level model are aggregated input-output
vectors for the branches. These vectors are found by summing
over the projects included in the optimal plan for each branch
at the previous iteration. The aggregate vector for a branch
complex includes the following data: levels of output and of
material inputs; output of structures and equipment (transferable and nontransferable equipment being listed separately)[16]
and of demand for capital goods; output of trained personnel
and the demand for labor in various occupational and educational
categories; natural resource needs; group wage rates; the total
return to labor and natural resources used by the branch; and the
overall balance of the branch complex with the financial and credit
system (liabilities to the financial system minus credit balances).

The model incorporates the following constraints: on the
fixed loading on the economy — these consist of targets for
the output of current and capital goods and services and for
training qualified personnel, together with the constraints on
the input of goods and services, labor, natural resources, and
finance implied by these targets; on the variable loading on the
economy, expressed in terms similar to those for the fixed
loading (the variable loading includes expenditure on the development and operation of the transportation system, as given
in the plan for the transportation complex, and on consumption,
including social consumption, as given by the regional plans);
on the availability of nontransferable equipment and natural
resources at the start of the period; and on the most probable
supply of labor broken down by occupational and educational
category for each year of the plan period (derived from the
models for testing for social balance).

These indices are the structural parameters and constraints
in the national model, which incorporates balances for: current goods and services, construction activity, equipment, labor, natural resources,[17] and budgetary and credit variables.

The solution of the model yields intensities for the summary
plan vectors submitted by the branches, which maximize the
upper level optimality criterion. The intensity of a branch
vector (which cannot be negative) indicates how closely the
aggregate plan vector of that branch fits in with the optimality
criterion and constraints at the upper level. If the intensity is
less than unity, it means that the branch has proposed a plan
variant which from the national point of view is too high in respect of at least one of the kinds of goods and services produced
or used. Conversely an intensity in excess of unity means that
the branch has made some of its plan indices too low.

A balance is achieved between the national plan and the branch
plans when the top level model chooses an intensity for the aggregate plan vector of each branch complex which is either
equal to or fairly close to unity.[18]

5. The Regional Models

Although the regional development models are similar in
general terms, they differ in detail depending on which version
of the planning process is used.

In the first version, the function of a regional model is to
make an optimal choice of projects for constructing, rebuilding,
and operating the enterprises of the various branches within
that region's territory; the choice is made from the subset of
projects included in the optimal plans of the branch complexes.
In the second version, the selection is made from all projects
falling within that region.

In both cases the region starts out from its own internal
possibilities (natural resources and labor). However, in the
first version of the planning process it is assumed that other
resources (i.e., materials and finance) are available in the
quantities required. The second version incorporates constraints on the use of centrally allocated financial resources
and on imports of various goods into the region. The optimality
criterion is maximization of the real income of the region's
population over the plan period. The criteria in the regional
models do not directly incorporate discounting, since the use
of discounting at the upper level means that all the parameters
in the system are affected via the shadow prices associated
with the upper level constraints.

The following exogenous constraints are established for each
region and for each year of the plan period: minimum targets
for the region's output of certain kinds of goods and services,
as a fixed loading on the regional economy (derived from a
forecast or by expert estimates); most probable values for the
labor force (broken down by occupational and educational group)
available for employment in the various branches of the region
after allowance has been made for the fixed loading (these data
are found using the social balance models); most probably levels of exhaustible and nonexhaustible natural resources, after

subtraction for the fixed loading (these are forecast values).

In the second version, additional constraints are established covering central financing of capital investment and social consumption funds (these are derived from the upper level model) and on the inflow of goods and resources into the region (from the model of the transportation complex).

The structural parameters for each regional model are input-output vectors corresponding to projects for building, rebuilding, or operating branch enterprises. In the second version the optimization parameters passed on by the branch models to the regional models are scales of payment which branches are willing to make out of their profits into regional budgets.

These indices make up the optimality criterion and constraints in the regional model for each year of the plan period. The constraints are: balances for current goods and services; investment balances; labor balances; natural resources balances; balances covering the distribution of money incomes among families of various types; and constraints on the consumption of goods for which no charge is made.

In addition to these constraints, the second version of the planning process includes balances for the expansion and financing of social consumption, and also constraints on the maximum level of imports of various goods and services into the region.

By solving the regional model for each year of the plan period we establish which projects for building, rebuilding, or operating enterprises the region will implement within its territory. Levels of consumption, and imports and exports of goods and resources, are found for each year of the plan period. And at the same time regional shadow prices are found for natural resources and labor.

6. Models for Forecasting the Socioeconomic Consequences of Implementing the Plan

In the course of ensuring that the plan is socially balanced, forecasts are made for the following: the distribution of labor by region, sphere of activity, and occupational and educational group; the distribution of families by type; and the demand for goods and services by families of various types.

The starting point for forecasting the socioeconomic consequences of implementing the plan is a forecast of the territorial breakdown of population growth. We can use for this purpose a system of models for demographic forecasting, including a model for forecasting the breakdown of the population by age and sex, a model for calculating natural reproduction coefficients, and a model for forecasting natural reproduction and migration.[19] Data derived from these models are a starting point for forecasts for the following period. The parameters of the forecast are established from statistical processing of data for previous years, using existing methods [14, 15]. Migration is forecast as a function of economic development and of the changes in the welfare of different groups in the population, as given by the plan.

A forecast of this kind establishes the most likely breakdown of the population of each region by age and sex, including those of working age. However in order to get from these figures to data on the labor force of working age broken down by occupational and educational group, the demographic forecast must be converted into a labor supply forecast; use can be made here of statistics on the occupational and educational structure of the population of working age and on the breakdown by age and sex of the wastage of labor in different occupational and educational groups; data are also needed on shifts in the occupational, educational, and sectoral structure of the working population in the different regions.

Reference [1] describes a general framework for making long-term forecasts of the occupational and educational structure of the population of working age. The calculations can be made, as with a demographic forecast, using the method of projecting each separate age group for every category of the working age population. Persons who have not yet attained working age are allocated to a professional and occupational group numbered zero. As we progress from one year to the next we need to forecast changes in the coefficients indicating whether workers continue in employment and to project coefficients showing how people choose a particular occupational and educational group. These coefficients are forecast using statistical models.[20]

When we switch from data on the population of working age to labor supply data, we must take account of the participation rates of women of all ages and of male pensioners. These rates are also forecast using statistical models. A forecast can similarly be made for the number of persons in the various occupational and educational groups wishing to work in the various branches.

One fairly effective method of organizing the statistical information required to build this forecasting model is to construct a labor mobility balance [20].

The figures obtained from these forecasting models are used in the right-hand sides of the labor constraints in the planning models. In addition, the demographic forecasts are used to determine upper and lower levels for the provision of social consumption in each region in each year. They are also used to forecast the breakdown of the population by family type and to express consumption demand in each region as a function of family type, family incomes, and planned retail prices. These demand forecasts are used in the top level model to compute the variable loading on the economy. The reader can acquaint himself with methods for constructing such models in references [8, 9, 21]. Some of the models are at the stage of study and experimental testing and require substantial improvement.

The models described above together form the basis for a procedure for modeling the population's response to implementing the national plan. This procedure is used to ensure that the plan is balanced in social terms.

Before our system for optimal planning of the economy is installed and comes into use, it is extremely important that we resolve the following issues.

In the first place we have to solve the problem of providing the planning process with data and with computational facilities. This must be part of an overall solution of theoretical and practical problems of devising complex man–machine systems for controlling the economy. The system of models for compiling an optimal socially balanced plan for the development and location of production described above can be treated as a basis for the technical specification for designing a system of this nature (an automated system of planning calculations). An important role in such a system belongs to the human operative who will scrutinize the primary and processed data, supervise the process, and informally control it. Supervision does not necessarily mean that the experts are aware of all the values taken by the plan variables in the planning process. The expert need only have access to information on the course of the planning process in general form, although the current value of any plan indicator should in principle be accessible to human supervision. The expert can use such information as a basis for deciding when to intervene and correct the parameters in order to reduce the time taken to compile the plan or to take account of any special circumstances which may have arisen.

In view of the active role played by human operatives in the planning process, especially at the stage of preparing the original data and switching intermediate information between the various parts of the system, the question of legal control over the process becomes very important. Existing principles of economic law must be systematized, together with the sanctions for breaching them; in some cases these principles and the sanctions for breaking them must be extended and spelled out, and they must form the basis for a unified system of legislation in the economic field. Such legislation should on the one hand be directed toward preventing information's being distorted (even unintentionally) in the process of plan compilation; on the other hand it must help to ensure that the plan is implemented on time.

Economic legislation is by no means a thing unto itself: since it is based on the fundamental legal enactments of socialism, especially on social ownership of the means of production, its content is substantially determined by the structure of the planning process and system of planning and management. With this in mind we have to devise a legal basis which reflects the system's special properties.

NOTES

1) A formal exposition of this approach is given in reference [1].

2) When this system is further developed the aim should be to include long-term plans for interregional development and location which go right down to individual sites and population points [2].

3) It is assumed that foreign trade is given exogenously. This is quite acceptable as a first approximation, since foreign trade is a special sector of the economy and can to a degree be optimized independently. A model is being devised in the Central Mathematical Economics Institute (TsEMI) of the USSR Academy of Sciences which takes account of the two-way relationship between foreign trade and other sectors. This model will be incorporated in our system later [3].

4) Other versions of the criterion for the upper level model are also being investigated.

5) These indices are assumed to remain unchanged throughout the whole optimization process. They may (and probably will) be altered, but outside the process, and any important change will cause the plan to be recalculated. The fixed loading is determined before the planning process starts. The optimal planning system will incorporate calculations to optimize the fixed loading as the appropriate methods are developed.

6) The division of responsibilities between large and small iterations is mainly a convenient way of describing the optimization method. The two could be combined in the actual planning process.

7) The variable loading ensures that transportation is developed in accordance with the economy's needs, that social consumption funds are adequate, and that consumer demand is satisfied. At the first iteration the variable loading is determined on the basis of a forecast; subsequently it is computed in the course of the planning process.

8) Workers are allocated to the same wage group if their money incomes fall in the same interval of the income scale; families are allocated to the same type within a region if the breakdown of their consumption is similar.

9) The concept of a transportation district can only be developed in detail on the basis of a detailed analysis of the economy. For brevity we shall refer to a transportation district simply as a district (as opposed to an economic region, which is called a region).

10) The variable loading in a regional model incorporates constraints as follows: on centralized investment financed from the branches' own resources and by credits; on the financing of social consumption funds; and on the imports of various goods and resources into the region. It also includes targets for re-

sources required for national needs.

11) National income is at present redistributed through regional differences in the payment of turnover tax into the budgets of the republics.

12) Here we consider those social aspects of economic development which at present can be analyzed usefully at the macro-level.

13) Moreover, the shadow prices can in some circumstances be negative, since the constraints on the employment of labor in the regions are equalities.

14) In essence, choosing this curve is a way of expressing the fixed loading on the economy required to solve social problems; hitherto this has proved difficult to formalize.

15) Given that there are two ways of achieving an allocation of scarce resources between sectors — administrative allocation (setting limits on output and demand, which vary from iteration to iteration — cf. [11, 12]) or price allocation (establishing shadow prices for resources — cf. [11, 13]) — we start from the assumption that the most effective procedure must be one which combines both methods: administrative allocation for the scarcest resources, and control by the price mechanism for the rest. Throughout the optimization process the algorithm should reclassify resources into these two categories at each iteration.

16) This distinction is necessary because of differences in the way machinery can be allocated in the economy. Nonshiftable machinery is assigned to an enterprise over its whole service life, unless that enterprise is reconstructed; shiftable machinery can be transferred between enterprises (or branches) without one's having to redesign the enterprises.

17) Natural resource balances are included in the upper level model (as well as necessarily being incorporated in the regional models) in order to stabilize the computational process; labor balances are included to ensure that the economy is provided with the labor needed by the transportation complex.

18) With the top level shadow prices being stable, in the second version of the planning process.

19) The method of demographic forecasting described in reference [16] could serve as the basis for such a system. It is based on an analysis and generalization of the methods of demographic forecasting used in the Central Statistical Agency (TsSU), the Central Statistical Agency and the Chief Computer Center of Gosplan USSR, the Institute of Economics of the Siberian Division of the USSR Academy of Sciences, the Computer Center of Belorussia, and the Population Division of the UN Social Bureau.

20) Some approaches to constructing such models are set out in [17-19], together with the results of some experimental calculations.

REFERENCES

1. Baranov, E. F.; Danilov-Danil'ian, V. I.; and Zavel'skii, M. G. Problemy razrabotki sistemy optimal'nogo planirovaniia narodnogo khoziaistva, Moscow: TsEMI AN SSSR, 1970.

2. Zavel'skii, M. G., et al. Problemy i metody optimal'nogo territorial'no-proizvodstvennogo planirovaniia narodnogo khoziaistva, vols. 1 and 2. Moscow: TsEMI AN SSSR, 1968.

3. Shagalov, G. L. "Optimizatsiia vneshnetorgovogo obmena i kriterii ego effektivnosti." Ekonomika i matematicheskie metody, 1970, vol. 6, no. 2.

4. Baranov, E. F.; Klotsvog, F. N.; Kossov, V. V.; Shatalin, S. S.; and Eidel'man, M. R. "Itogi i perspektivy mezhotraslevykh issledovanii v SSSR." Ekonomika i matematicheskie metody, 1967, vol. 3, no. 5.

5. Mikhalevskii, B. N. "Sistema modelei dlia rascheta sbalansirovannogo srednesrochnogo plana." Ekonomika i matematicheskie metody, 1967, vol. 3, no. 5.

6. Katsenelinboigen, A. I.; Lakhman, I. L.; and Ovsienko, Iu. V. "Optimal'noe upravlenie i tsennostnoi mekhanizm." Ekonomika i matematicheskie metody, 1969, vol. 5, no. 4.

7. Katsenelinboigen, A. I.; Movshovich, S. M.; and Ovsienko, Iu. V "Kharakteristiki rabotnikov i ikh deiatel'nosti v modeli optimal'noi ekonomiki." Ekonomika i matematicheskie metody, 1969, vol. 5, no. 2.

8. Balansy dokhodov i potrebleniia naseleniia (voprosy metodologii i statisticheskii analiz). Moscow: "Statistika" Publishers, 1969.

9. Dokhody i pokupatel'skii spros naseleniia. Moscow: "Statistika" Publishers, 1968.

10. Statisticheskoe izuchenie sprosa i potrebleniia. Moscow: "Nauka" Publishers, 1966.

11. Danilov-Danil'ian, V. I. "Zadachi bol'shoi razmernosti i iterativnye metody optimal'nogo planirovaniia." In Sbornik programm i algoritmov dlia resheniia na EVTsM. Moscow: "Statistika" Publishers, 1967.

12. Kornai, I., and Liptak, T. "Planirovanie na dvukh urovniakh." In Primenenie matematiki v ekonomicheskikh issledovaniiakh, vol. 3. Moscow: "Mysl'" Publishers, 1965.

13. Dantzig, G., and Wolfe, P. "Algoritm razlozheniia dlia zadach lineinogo programmirovaniia." Matematika, 1964, vol. 8, no. 1.

14. Izuchenie vosproizvodstva naseleniia. Moscow: "Nauka" Publishers, 1968.

15. Pressa, R. Narodonaselenie i ego izuchenie. Moscow: "Statistika" Publishers, 1966.

16. Analiz, otsenka, prakticheskaia proverka i korrektirovka modeli territorial'nogo demograficheskogo prognozirovaniia. Kiev: VTs Gosplana Ukr. SSR, 1967.

17. Kolichestvennye metody v sotsiologii. Moscow: "Nauka" Publishers, 1966.

18. Migratsiia sel'skogo naseleniia: tseli, zadachi i metody regulirovaniia. Novosibirsk: Doklady k zasedaniiu issledovatel'skogo komiteta po sel'skoi sotsiologii, 1969.

19. Nauchnyi seminar po primeneniiu kolichestvennykh metodov v sotsiologii, nos. I, II. Novosibirsk: 1966.

20. Baranov, E. F., and Dreev, B. D. Osnovnye printsipy postroeniia balansov dvizheniia trudovykh resursov. Moscow: TsEMI AN SSSR, 1969.

21. Aivazian, S. A. "Modelirovanie semeinykh dokhodov," Ekonomika i matematicheskie metody, 1970, vol. 6, no. 2.

Received November 12, 1970

A MULTISTAGE SET OF MODELS FOR
OPTIMAL PRODUCTION PLANNING

V. F. Pugachev

1. Aspects of Optimizing the National Economy:
The Approximation Scheme

We consider here the production aspect of a system for optimal planning of the economy. A system of this kind can only be a multistage one. It must clearly determine what to produce, how to produce it, and where it produce it, and do so dynamically, over time. Consequently, if we neglect the social aspect, there are four related basic issues in output planning:

(1) structural optimization (choice of the level and composition of output);

(2) technological optimization (choice of production techniques);

(3) territorial optimization (choice of the location of production);

(4) optimization over time (choice of the best sequence of development).

We consider these aspects in turn, trying to evaluate the significance of each of them and the interrelationships between them.

Russian text © 1972 by "Nauka" Publishers. "Mnogostupenchatyi kompleks modelei optimal'nogo planirovaniia proizvodstva." Problemy optimal'nogo funktsionirovaniia sotsialisticheskoi ekonomiki, Moscow, 1972, pp. 346-358.

The structural aspect of optimization of the economy is the major element in planning. By linking the structure of output of all goods to the structure of final demand, optimization models must first ensure that plans are balanced — i.e., that they are realistic. By choosing the best composition of output to satisfy each of society's particular needs (whether concerned with production or otherwise), optimizing models must identify progressive shifts in the structure of production and control the process of replacing old products with new ones.

The technological aspect of optimization of the economy is also of the greatest importance. A system of economic planning would be of little practical interest if it were unable to choose the best variant for economic development and the best technological policy for a branch or if it were unable to define the set of projects which should be implemented.

Major questions concerning choice of technique must be solved directly; the shadow prices associated with the optimal plan can be used to decide minor issues.

There is no doubt about the importance of location problems. Much research in mathematical economics has been devoted to solving them. However we shall try here to make a careful investigation of the regional aspect and its interrelationship with structural and technological optimization.

The location of production depends upon a large number of factors, such as society's goals, overall location policy, the availability of labor and natural resources, and closeness to raw materials and consumers. The last two factors cause the greatest complications in mathematical location models. It is in consequence of them that the models have to include some form of transportation problem.

But is the transportation aspect so important that it must always be incorporated via a transportation problem? In fact this is only necessary for the 10 to 20 resources which involve particularly high transportation costs (fuel, ores, etc.). For all other products the transportation factor can be either ignored or taken into account approximately, through an average haulage radius.

This will ease the problem of optimizing the economy, since it will allow us to operate not in terms of regions themselves but in terms of the resources located in those regions. In fact when we devise a set of models for optimal planning we can either abstract totally from alternative ways of locating production (if location has no effect on the cost structure) or we can treat alternative locations as different production techniques. By this method the regional aspects of optimization are as it were "put in parentheses." They can be resolved separately after an optimal structural and technological plan has been found, rather than at the same time.

We turn finally to the temporal aspect of optimization. We do not need to demonstrate that optimal planning models should be dynamic. On the other hand it is quite clear that dynamics complicate the model.

Thus in practice the issue is not whether the temporal aspect should be incorporated; the question is rather — what artificial methods can be used to convert the model either to static or at least to quasi-static form? Such methods undoubtedly exist.

We start from the assumption that the economy and its component parts develop more or less smoothly, without any sudden jumps. This entitles us to build into the calculations some assumptions about development, or regularities in the way variables change over time (for example, we can assume a constant level of absolute increases, or a constant growth rate). By leaving open one or more of the parameters which determine the development pattern we can optimize the plan, perhaps not over the whole interval which concerns us, but in one respect at least. In this way dynamic models can be substantially simplified.

While we are using such highly simplified models to optimize the plan for any particular year, we must, of course, take account of a number of factors relating to other time periods: the prospects for producing fixed capital in the preceding years, the relationship between the capital goods produced in the year to be optimized and the demand for capital in later years, and so on. Hence the models which we get when we adopt a simplified dynamic approach are not strictly static, but rather quasi-static.

It is clearly desirable to build up a set of models for optimal economic planning in a quasi-static form, the plans being subsequently checked for balance year by year. A gradual transfer can be made to dynamic models once the quasi-static models have been mastered.

We can draw the following conclusions from our analysis of the major aspects of optimization of the economy. A set of models for optimal planning of the economy should be geared primarily to taking simultaneous account of structural and technological aspects; territorial and temporal aspects should be incorporated subsequently and in an approximate way.

In particular it follows from this that irrespective of the structure of economic management, the set of models we develop should be based on the branch principle.

The basis of our set of models for optimal planning is an approximating scheme for multistage optimization. The basic idea is as follows. A local unit at any level does not compute a single optimal plan with a given local criterion, but devises a set of plans within a larger or smaller neighborhood of the expected optimum. This set can be conveniently represented either by an approximating hyperplane or by an approximating polyhedron.

This representation allows us to aggregate information on the production possibilities of the local unit and to communicate it in this form to the superior body. There, on the basis of information supplied by all subordinate units, a set of plans can be found in the neighborhood of the expected optimum; information is thus condensed. It is therefore possible to construct an optimal plan at the economy level in terms of the aggregated information.

The process operates in reverse and detailed plans are formed using horizontal links between units at the same level. In this way detailed plans can be found for all local units.

Such a process of vertical communication and subsequent op-

timization will in principle be iterative. However in the first
place the number of vertical iterations is likely to be small,
and secondly the process can be interrupted at any iteration,
since we assume that it is possible to ensure balance in the
disaggregated plans by means of horizontal links.

The advantage of the approximation scheme lies in the fact
that it embodies the principle of optimal planning based on variants and extends it to all the intervening levels of economic
management. Clearly if each local unit gives its superiors an
intelligently constructed set of draft plans rather than a single
plan, then it is fairly easy to find the optimal plan in this set
after a comparatively small number of vertical iterations.

2. Branch Optimization Models

We go straight on to construct a set of models for optimal
economic planning. We stated above that the major role in a
multistage optimization system should be played by the branches.
Although the system can contain a number of stages in total (the
economy as a whole — multibranch complexes — subbranches),
the major distinction is between two levels of planning, the
economy and the branch.

Correspondingly we shall distinguish two classification levels — an overall level and a branch level. Both are aggregated,
but the degree of aggregation is different: each heading in the
overall classification will normally combine a substantial number of products in the branch classification.

We shall assume that the system of optimal planning does
computations down to branch level; plans are specified in further detail through horizontal ties between enterprises.

We shall set out a multistage system of quasi-static optimization models covering a single year, which can be more or
less remote from the date when the plan is compiled.

We consider some possible models for optimal branch planning, beginning with those kinds of output for which the transportation factor is not very important.

It follows from our previous discussion of the various aspects

of optimization of the economy that it is better for the branch organizations compiling plans for producing such goods to restrict
themselves to optimizing structure and technology rather than
to solve the location problem in the first instance. Each branch
should work out a set of optimal structural and technological
plans in the branch-level classification and transmit the results
to the economy level in terms of the classification used for
overall planning.

The initial information the branch must have is a mathematical representation of:

all existing enterprises, including possible ways in which they
might be expanded;

all enterprises under construction;

all plans for building new enterprises.

For concreteness we shall assume (although this is not essential) that all these variants are represented by an approximating polyhedron:

$$x^k = A^k \xi^k, \ \varepsilon \xi^k \leqslant 1, \tag{1}$$

Here x^k is a vector[1] of inputs and outputs in the branch-level
classification (outputs are positive, inputs negative);

A^k is a matrix of supporting points for the approximating
polyhedron (base-line plans);

ξ^k is a vector of the intensities with which base-line plans
are used;

ε is a unit vector.

We have to specify more precisely what we mean by a long-
run input-output vector x^k. Production in the year under consideration not only requires current inputs in that year but also
depends on previously incurred capital costs. Hence the vector
x^k must include an individual breakdown of capital investment
in all previous years (in terms of the branch-level classification used by the producers of fixed capital).

All data concerning existing enterprises and plans for new
enterprises are represented in form (1), and after preliminary
analysis and checking they are allocated to the appropriate heading in the classification used for overall national planning.

Branch agencies must evaluate the prospects for getting the scarce resources which they need to build and operate new capacity. They should do so in terms of the branch-level classification of the supplier, concentrating on all scarce resources figuring in the input side of vectors x^k (this should include fixed capital required in the earlier years and should specify a breakdown of labor inputs).

Several alternatives should be considered at this stage, based on different assumptions about the development of the economy. Depending on the particular case an appropriate allocation of scarce resources can be found for the branch and represented by a vector b^{lm} (l is the branch superscript; m the superscript of the particular variant).

At least two variants must be computed for each branch — one of them pessimistic, incorporating a poor outlook, the second optimistic, subject to a reasonable upper limit. It would be very useful to include several intermediate variants.

For each alternative allocation of resources to the branch, an estimate is also made of the most likely structure of demand for the branch's output. As a result a set of vectors S^{lm} is found, giving the most probable composition of planned output.

Of course, it is not easy to construct alternative allocations of resources and structures of output. However, to implement the approximation scheme for multistage optimization we only require rough values for these indices, since a set of plans is constructed for each branch. Branch planning bodies are in the best position to give a priori estimates of demand for their output and of their prospects for getting scarce resources.

Once vectors b^{lm} and S^{lm} have been chosen, they are put into a model to optimize the branch. This yields a particular variant for the branch's development. Such a model could, for example, involve maximizing output in a given structure:

$$\varepsilon \xi^{klm} \leqslant 1;$$
$$x^{lm} = \sum_k x^{klm} = \sum_k A^{klm} \xi^{klm} \geqslant b^{lm};$$
$$x^{lm} \geqslant \Theta S^{lm}; \quad \Theta \to \max, \tag{2}$$

where k is the index for an enterprise in branch l;

x^{lm} is an input-output vector for the branch as a whole;

Θ is the quantity of output produced in the composition determined by S^{lm}.

We note that the second groups of inequalities in problem (2) can also incorporate a balance for intermediate inputs within the branch and any other constraints which may apply.

By solving problem (2) for each (l, m) combination we can derive a variant of the plan for any branch in the form of a vector x^{lm} which incorporates both inputs and outputs.

Using these base-line plans we can also represent x^l, the set of feasible plans for branch l, in the form

$$x^l = \sum_m \alpha_{lm} x^{lm}, \tag{3}$$

where $\displaystyle\sum_m \alpha_{lm} \leqslant 1$.

Form (3) is a compact way of representing the solutions of type (2) problems for branch l.. It also shows the feasible area in terms of the classification adopted in branch planning and the relationship between the inputs and outputs of the branch.

In the course of solving problem (2) we also find the rates of substitution in production between the separate outputs of the branch, in the form of coefficients of the approximating hyperplane in the neighborhood of x^{lm}. We represent these coefficients by vector h^{lm} in the same space as x^{lm}; however, the only non-zero components in h^{lm} will be those relating to outputs.

For each (l, m) combination, the plans in the neighborhood of x^{lm} can be expressed in terms of the approximating hyperplane $h^{lm}x^l = 1$, and the production possibilties corresponding to variant m for branch l can be written as a single linear inequality: $h^{lm}x^l \leqslant 1$.

This approximation of the branch's production possibilities shows the combinations of outputs between which the branch is indifferent. It draws attention to the fact that the output structure in plan x^{lm} can be changed. However, only changes which preserve the inequality $h^{lm}x^l \leqslant 1$ are feasible, i.e., one type of output can only be replaced by another in accordance with h^{lm}, the rate of substitution in production between them.

This circumstance allows us to use these coefficients to aggregate the branch's output and thus to make an even more compact approximation of (2). This is a useful aggregation procedure for switching from the classification used in branch planning to that used in overall planning. For this purpose each branch is represented by one number, in terms of a single generalized output.

To do this, in the case of each branch we have to average the rates of substitution in production corresponding to all the variants computed for the development of the branch. After some judicious averaging we derive a single vector:

$$h^l = \bar{h}^{lm}.$$

We use this vector to combine the outputs of the branch into a single generalized product $X_l = h^l x^l$. Each development variant x^{lm} can now be represented in terms of some level X_{lm} of the generalized output.

The plans for each branch can be similarly aggregated in terms of their resource requirements. To do so we have to use coefficients for the technological substitution between inputs from the various supplying branches. As a result we can construct for each X_{lm} a fully determinate vector of inputs in the classification used in overall planning. Having performed this operation we can represent the output and inputs for each development variant in each branch by a single input-output vector X^{lm}, in the classification used for overall planning.

Instead of (3), the whole set of feasible plans X^l for branch l can now be represented in aggregated form:

$$X^l = \sum_m \alpha_{lm} X^{lm}, \tag{4}$$

where $\sum_m \alpha_{lm} \leqslant 1$.

Form (4) is the most compact form possible of representing the branch in terms of single generalized output and a single linear inequality. This makes it possible to construct a very simple model for overall planning of the economy.

The use of (4) to represent the whole set of branch plans also has certain benefits for decision taking by branch planning agencies. This is important both for the introduction of the approach set out above in individual branches, and for the operation of the overall multistage system of optimal planning.

When working with branch plans expressed in the form (4), we can immediately identify the inputs and outputs corresponding to any feasible plan for the branch. Here both outputs and inputs are expressed in terms of the overall classification in which the branch exchanges information with the central planning agency.

At the same time (3) can be used to express branch plans in terms of the branch-level classification and to correct the structure of output, using the coefficients for the rate of substitution in production h^{lm}.

We now summarize our remarks concerning branch models which do not incorporate the transportation aspect. It follows from the analysis that:

(a) a problem of type (2), solved for a number of variants for the branch's development, can be used as a mathematical model of the branch:

(b) when we solve such a branch model we do not get a unique optimal plan, but a set of plans which can be expressed in terms of (4). The principle of constructing variants of the optimal plan is thus implemented at branch level.

We note that these conclusions should only be regarded as furnishing guidance for the construction of branch models. Each branch has its own special features, as well as features common to all branches. For this reason any recommendations based on an analysis of the branch's place in a multistage optimization system cannot be exhaustive.

We now consider branches in which transportation is a decisive factor. In the case of these branches we have to devise models for the development and location of production which incorporate transportation. A standard method of formulating and solving such models has now been worked out.

As noted above, it is only desirable to use this method to decide where to produce a relatively small number of products, involving 10 to 20 types of output. Each location model can be solved on a local basis and need not incorporate in precise form any constraints on the labor and natural resources available in any region or on the capacity of the transportation network. It is enough to take these factors into account in an approximate way, using the shadow prices associated with resource constraints.

Thus the territorial location problems which have to incorporate the transportation factor are not combined to form a global location problem. The solution of the overall location problem need not in its turn involve an iterative procedure for linking up individual location problems incorporating the transportation factor.

In the approximation scheme for multistage optimization each branch's local model yields not a single optimal plan but a set of plans, expressed in form (4) in terms of the classification system used for overall planning and in form (3) for the system used by the branches. This also applies to branches where it is desirable to incorporate transportation.

A quasi-static model for such a branch should take the form of a number of problems solved for several alternative development paths of the branch. Such variants differ mainly in their estimates of the branch's prospects for getting hold of scarce resources (vector b^{lm}) and in the corresponding structure of demand (vector S^{lm}).

Location problems are generally solved using local criteria expressed in value terms, rather than maximization of output of a given composition, because it is necessary to make transportation costs commensurable with other costs.

3. The Model at the National Level and the Location of Production

We assume that each branch is represented in form (4). This

takes account not only of inputs and outputs in the year to be optimized, but also of the requirements to produce fixed capital in all the preceding years. Foreign trade opportunities are represented as a single branch. Any resources which are in limited supply for the country as a whole are aggregated to the national planning level and take the form of economy-wide constraints.

We can then formulate a quasi-static model for optimization at the overall level as follows:

$$\sum_m \alpha_{lm} \leqslant 1,$$

$$X = \sum_l X^l = \sum_{l,m} \alpha_{lm} X^{lm} \geqslant \beta, \tag{5}$$

$$U(x) \to \max.$$

The second group of inequalities in this problem includes balances for all types of resources in the classification used for overall planning, covering final consumption goods, intermediate goods, and scarce resources. This group also incorporates balances for the production of fixed capital in all preceding years, depending on the assumption made concerning the development of the corresponding production units. Vector β consists partly of lower limits on final outputs, partly of zeros, and partly of limits on the availability of scarce resources.

Problem (5) assumes that there is some national optimality criterion U to be maximized. Its arguments are the components in X which correspond to final demand.

Since we are adopting a method for finding variants of the optimal plan, we can restrict ourselves to one of a number of fairly simple criteria U. It is quite acceptable to adopt the criterion of maximizing final output in a particular composition considered the most likely. This composition might be found, for example, by aggregating the revised indents for final output submitted by all final users.

If we use vector S to denote the most likely composition of final output X in the classification used for planning at the overall level, we can rewrite model (5) in the form:

$$\sum_{m} \alpha_{lm} \leqslant 1,$$

$$X = \sum_{l,m} \alpha_{lm} X^{lm} \geqslant \beta, \qquad (6)$$

$$X \geqslant \Theta S; \quad \Theta \to \max.$$

By solving this problem we derive a plan X which corresponds to the given criterion. However since the criterion is not fully accurate, this plan may turn out to be not wholly satisfactory and to require certain corrections.

The simplest way to make such corrections would be to use the coefficients for the rate of substitution between different components of final output. For this purpose we could use the coefficients of the approximating hyperplane in the neighborhood of plan X, as derived from model (6). Finding these coefficients is fairly easy.

If we denote this vector of coefficients by H, then the whole economy can be represented in terms of a single linear inequality:

$$HX \leqslant 1. \qquad (7)$$

Using H we can make any reasonable change in the original plan X, without going outside the economy's production possibilities.

In the case of some components of final output, such corrections could even now be made using mathematical methods. This applies particularly to that part of final output which is sold through the trade network. An objective function in consumption or demand functions could be used for this purpose. In all other areas, corrections to X can be made on the basis of qualitative analysis or evaluation by experts.

By making these corrections we can replace X by a vector $\overset{\circ}{X}$, which is the optimal plan. This vector is the final outcome of our use of the principle of compiling optimal plans in variant form.

Vector $\overset{\circ}{X}$ is feasible in terms of (6), since it satisfies (7) and

lies in the region where approximation (7) is permissible (this
is so, because of the approximation method adopted). Thus if
we were to solve (6) again for $S = \overset{\circ}{X}$ we would get plan $\overset{\circ}{X}$. This
plan can be disaggregated to branch level in accordance with
the approximation for multistage optimization.

Thus:

(a) the quasi-static model (6) can be used for optimizing the
economy, since it incorporates all the variants for the development of the branches and the full classification used for planning at the overall level;

(b) the outcome from solving this model should be a set of
comprehensive economic plans, in the form of a draft plan X
for the most probable composition of final output and a vector
H of rates of substitution between the components of final
output.

4. The Model for the Location of Production

We shall now assume that the models described above have
been used to work out an optimal plan for economic development at branch level in the classification adopted by the
branches. This plan has solved all questions concerning structural and technological optimization, but there is still no general framework for the location of production.

Given the approach set out above it is logical to try to construct a mathematical model which will allow us to specify an
overall framework for the location of production once we have
found a development plan which is optimal in terms of technology and structure.

Some location problems have trivial solutions. In the first
place, some enterprises have to be located close to their
sources of raw materials; others, close to their customers.
Secondly, we have already decided which variants for rebuilding
existing enterprises or for operating those under construction
are to be included in the plan. Finally, the location issue has
already been solved for the groups of branches where the transportation factor is important. It only remains to choose sites

for those new enterprises for which the problem has not yet
been solved.

Within the classification system used for branch planning we
identify those resources which cannot be moved or cannot be
transported far (including resources previously allocated to
regions on the basis of local location problems). We denote
the availability of such resources in region n by d^n; more precisely d^n denotes resources which are available for use by enterprises whose location has not yet been chosen.

Any k-th enterprise in this category, irrespective of which
branch it belongs to, can be characterized by a vector c^k representing its demand for resources which are specific to a particular region. Obviously the sum of vectors c^k for any region
may not exceed vector d^n.

We introduce a variable η_{kn}, which measures the "intensity"
with which enterprise k is located in region n. In principle η_{kn}
is an unknown integer which can take the value of 0 or 1. Moreover,
the sum of such integers for each enterprise must be unity:

$$\sum_n \eta_{kn} = 1, \tag{8}$$

this guarantees that each enterprise is located somewhere.

The following constraints must be satisfied by the enterprises
located in each region:

$$\sum_k c^k \eta_{kn} \leqslant d^n. \tag{9}$$

The total number of these constraints is at a maximum equal
to the product of the number of resources and the number of
regions, while the total number of unknowns is the number
of enterprises to be located multiplied by the number of
regions. As a result, (9) is a very extensive system of
constraints.

We assume that there is some optimality criterion for
the location of production $V(\eta_{kn})$. As will be clear from
what follows, the choice of V should depend on the particular case. Hence without yet specifying V, we set out the
overall location model:

$$\sum_{n} \eta_{kn} = 1,$$

$$\sum_{k} c^{k} \eta_{kn} \leqslant d^{n}, \tag{10}$$

$$V(\eta_{kn}) \to \max.$$

In practice we may neglect the integrality requirement η_{kn} though we need not do so. The exposition which follows is based on the assumption that the unknowns in problem (10) are continuous, nonnegative variables.

Before discussing the choice of criterion V, we must satisfy ourselves that a solution to problem (10) does exist; i.e., we must be sure that constraints (8)-(9) are compatible.

There is in fact a reason for doubting the compatibility of these constraints. There must be sufficient resources over the country as a whole, since they are balanced in terms of the structural and technological aspects of the plan. The special "elongated" structure of constraints (8)-(9) is an indication that it is improbable that they will be incompatible. Nonetheless the regional allocation of resources may be so unsatisfactory that there is no combination of values η_{kn} which satisfies inequalities (8)-(9).

In order to analyze the constraints in problem (10), we construct an artificial linear criterion. We take a more or less arbitrary system of "measures of transportability" for resources in the form of a vector q, and write V in the form:

$$V = q \sum_{n} \left(d^{n} - \sum_{k} c^{k} \eta_{kn} \right) \to \max. \tag{11}$$

The harder it is to shift resources from one region to another, the higher is q. Consequently, when $d^{n} > \sum_{k} c^{k} \eta_{kn}$ criterion (11) requires us to avoid the need to move resources, and when $d^{n} < \sum_{k} c^{k} \eta_{kn}$, it obliges us to minimize the costs to the economy from shifting them.

When we try to solve problem (10) using criterion (11), any

incompatibilities between constraints (8) and (9) will immediately come to light. Any such incompatibility means that given the regional allocation of resources the existing plan for the composition of output and the technology of production is infeasible.

An escape from this situation can be sought in two directions — either by recasting the previous optimal plan, artificially reducing the availability of some resources, or by trying to reallocate resources between the region at the cost of additional expenditure.

The first method is an obvious one, but it should either be avoided totally or used in very rare cases. The second method can be implemented in the following way.

If we use iterative methods for solving problem (10)-(11) any incompatibility in the constraints will be reflected in the fact that the shadow price of some resources will go to infinity in some regions, while it will be zero in others. On this basis we can devise a reallocation which changes the values of d^n. Thus shadow prices are used to reallocate resources on the basis of criterion (11) — i.e., on the basis of minimizing the losses to the economy of shifting resources.

In the final analysis this reallocation process is bound to make problem (10) compatible. This is guaranteed by the fact that the optimal plan for the economy is balanced in the structural and technological senses. Comparing the new values of d^n with the old we can devise ways of reallocating resources between regions. By solving (10)-(11) repeatedly for several sets of values of q we derive alternative variants of d^n and consequently alternative ways of reallocating resources.

Having carried out a comprehensive analysis of possible reallocations, we can choose a particular variant and thus make problem (10)-(11) compatible.

We now consider the case in which the constraints (10)-(11) either were compatible in the first instance, or were made so by revising the values of d^n. In other words we assume that at least one combination of η_{kn}, or a set of such combinations, satisfies (8)-(9).

If there is only a single combination, then it will be the solution to problem (10) for any criterion V. We can use criterion (11), for example, to find this solution.

If however there is a set of combinations which satisfies constraints (8)-(9), then this gives us some freedom in solving the location problem, and this freedom can be used to achieve goals which go beyond the structural and technological plan. It is a sign that such a possibility exists if a number of the shadow prices associated with the constraints in problem (10)-(11) are zero.

We note that when we compiled the structural and technological plan we could have incorporated lower values for the availability of scarce resources than the total of the regional figures. This would be to the detriment of the optimal national plan, but it would also create an opportunity to achieve certain additional goals. Only experiments and practical experience can show whether this method should be generally adopted, and to what degree.

Thus assume there is some "slack" in constraints (8)-(9). Should we use the purely artificial criterion (11) in this case? Clearly it is desirable to replace it by some alternative which whether formally or informally reflects the additional aims of location policy.

We could achieve these aims informally by analyzing possible ways of reallocating enterprises from region to region while ensuring that all the constraints are satisfied.

Formal methods require the specification of a mathematical criterion. For example, if particular factories have to work in conjunction with one another, then this interdependence can be expressed in maximizing the function

$$V_1(\eta_{kn}, \ \eta_{k'n}) = \eta_{kn}\eta_{k'n}V_1(k, \ k', \ n).$$

Social priorities — to locate enterprise k in region n for example — can be incorporated by using an objective function $V_2(\eta_{kn})$, and so on.

By devising such partial criteria and incorporating them in model (10) we can compute and analyze the required number of location variants. If we then formulate some combined criterion V by weighting all the partial criteria, we get the final version of the location plan.

It is thus desirable to use model (10) as a model for finding the overall location of production once an optimal structural and technological plan has been devised. A particular version of the location plan can be chosen on the basis of a comprehensive analysis of feasible solutions to the model — i.e., using the variant method of optimal planning.

The above is a general account of a set of models for optimal planning of the economy which satisfies as far as possible the requirements formulated at the outset. We must continue our theoretical and experimental research into problems of multistage optimization of the economy and continue to analyze the set of models. We must develop a clear conception of the structure of our set of models and of the information it requires; this should take account both of the model's theoretical basis and of the existing system of planning.

NOTE

1) Here and below vectors, as distinct from scalars, are written without subscripts.

REFERENCES

1. Pugachev, V. F. Optimizatsiia planirovaniia (teoreticheskie problemy). Moscow: "Ekonomika" Publishers, 1968.

2. Martynov, G. V, and Pitelin, A. K. "Eksperimental'nye issledovaniia approksimatsionnoi skhemy mnogostupenchatoi optimizatsii." Ekonomika i matematicheskie metody, 1969, vol. 5, no. 5.

ON IMPROVING THE MULTISTAGE
SYSTEM FOR OPTIMIZING
LONG-TERM ECONOMIC PLANS

V. F. Pugachev

Over the past fifteen years, research organizations and planning agencies in our country have accumulated much experience
of using a number of models for long-term planning — macroeconomic models, models of consumer demand, input-output
models, branch models, etc. However, when computations
based on mathematical models are made in an uncoordinated
way, it is impossible to optimize the development of the economy on a broad enough scale. Hence a gradual shift is taking
place away from the use of individual models toward integrated
and coordinated work in mathematical economics.

In this connection we must acknowledge the work of the teams
led by A. G. Aganbegian, A. I. Anchishkin, E. F. Baranov, and
others. It is not my aim to make a survey or analysis of all
types of integrated modeling of the economy. The present article is devoted to questions of improving a multistage (or
multilevel) system of models developed in connection with the
long-term plan for the development of the Soviet economy over
the period 1976 to 1990 [1, 2]. This system of models was con-

Russian text © 1978 by "Nauka" Publishers and Ekonomika i matematicheskie
metody. "O sovershenstvovanii mnogostupenchatoi sistemy optimizatsii perspektivnykh narodnokhoziaistvennykh planov," Ekonomika i matematicheskie metody,
1978, vol. 14, no. 6, pp. 1082-1090.

structed in accordance with an approximation scheme for multi-stage optimization [3, 4] and includes three levels: branches, multibranch complexes, and the economy as a whole. The full-est account of the model is contained in [5].

The system is designed for practical implementation; it uses well-known and tried-and-tested models; and it does not impose excessive demands in terms of computation or optimization techniques. But the price for such practicality is a number of simplifications in its construction.

In the first place, we found it necessary to restrict ourselves to a static model which optimizes the plan for the final year of each five-year period. This enabled us to optimize at all levels of planning while restricting the problems to be solved to an acceptable size. Optimality criteria were chosen in such a way as to retain the linear formulation of the problem. As a national criterion we used maximization of final output with fixed pro-portions between branches. We envisaged, however, that these proportions would be specified in variant form and could be changed as the plan was reviewed. As a local criterion for the branches and multibranch complexes we used total costs (in-cluding capital charge) of producing and delivering output. At the same time the level of output and required rate of return to investment were chosen in several variants and made pro-gressively more accurate in the course of the multistage op-timization process.

It is a serious drawback to almost all the optimal branch models in current use that they do not disaggregate the labor, capital, and material inputs in the plan which they yield. Hence it is impossible for a multilevel optimization system to balance branch production levels directly by calculating the orders which branches place with one another. We have instead to co-ordinate branch plans using an input-output model in physical and financial units. This method is less accurate, since the parameters of the input-output model are established on the basis of prior projections of the branches' development. Also, it only coordinates branches at the aggregate level in terms of the classification used in the input-output model, rather than in the more detailed classification used in branch planning.

In the multistage system the territorial aspect only figures in the branch models and in the multibranch complexes and is not represented at the overall level; hence the problem of coordinating branch plans on a territorial basis (outside the confines of the multibranch complexes) is, so to speak, assigned to an informal coordination process. This gap could be filled by any model for coordination on a territorial basis; but this would require substantial additional information which it would be difficult to provide.

All these simplifying assumptions characterize the multistage system as a system of approximate optimization. It is intended to calculate long-term economic plans that are substantially better than plans which are simply balanced, but which could at the same time be optimized at a deeper level.

Does the multistage system use all the possibilities now available? As far as its simplifying assumptions go, they are the minimum necessary. Abandoning even one of them would make the system infeasible.

It has been obvious for a long time that there is a need for some version of the multistage optimization system which we have developed. However the increasing complexity of the economy, recent developments in planning at the theoretical and practical levels, and progress in information and computer technology are setting mathematical modeling new tasks and opening up new possibilities. It is becoming increasingly necessary to improve the multistage optimization system and to modify it further.

There is a need for theoretical and experimental work on a number of problems: on the operation of the system as a whole; on the construction of national and local criteria; and on the design of new mathematical models which give a fuller and more realistic representation of actual economic processes. At the same time we must start from the experience we have accumulated and from the requirements and possibilities revealed by use of the system in practice.

What developments can we expect to see in the foreseeable

future as far as practical implementation of the multistage
system is concerned? In the first place we should undoubtedly
expect a substantial increase in computational possibilities.
This is a most important factor affecting further progress in
the area of mathematical modeling of the economy. We can be
far less confident of a significant improvement in the immediate future in the information used for optimization. The current system of information for planning is a long way short of
fully meeting the requirements of optimization at the branch or
interbranch level. The original data are prepared independently
by research or design organizations working on individual problems, and this is a very labor-intensive task.

These two factors — the growth of computational possibilities
and problems of providing information — will determine the
prospects for the next stage in the development of the multistage system for optimizing long-term economic plans. In order to identify the nature of this stage, we consider some possible ways of improving the system.

1. Branch plans could be balanced directly (by summing the
orders branches place with one another), but only provided that
the breakdown of labor, capital, and material costs is specified
in detail for each alternative method of building or rebuilding
enterprises considered at the branch level. Since it is improbable that an adequate system of collecting such primary data
will be developed in the immediate future for all branches, it
is not yet possible to coordinate long-term branch plans directly. Input-output tables will still be the only realistic means
of coordination.

2. It is also impossible to coordinate branch plans on a regional basis without information on the cost breakdown of alternative ways of constructing or reconstructing enterprises.
The variants chosen in the optimal plans for one branch also
fix the territorial distribution of demand for other branches.
Without a detailed cost breakdown it is impossible to follow up
these interrelations between branches.

In our view it is questionable whether we can compensate
for the lack of primary cost data by using regional input-output

tables. A fairly disaggregated regional planning input-output table (especially in incremental terms) is much more sensitive to particular planning decisions than a table for the USSR as a whole. It is determined by the totality of projects for building or rebuilding enterprises chosen for the region, and these choices cannot be made in advance of the national plan.

Thus coordinating branch plans on a territorial basis hinges on the same problem as linking them up directly: the need to know the structure of costs at the stage of preparing primary information.

3. Switching from static to dynamic models causes both computational and informational problems. The former arise from the increase in the size of the problems to be solved and from the qualitative change in their complexity; these may be overcome. The informational problems concern the "dynamization" of all the initial data and spring from the need to switch from a static to a dynamic description of: (a) all possible ways of developing enterprises; (b) all constraints — sectoral, regional, or of the input-output type; and (c) all the components in the national and local optimality criteria.

The most difficult task is preparing basic data in dynamic form at the enterprise level. It is improbable that this could be found directly, on the basis of design documents. However, simpler approaches are feasible, such as converting originally static data into dynamic form on the computer, using normal rates for the annual installation of capacity and assimilation of capital. Moreover, each static variant for constructing or reconstructing an enterprise can be converted into a set of dynamic variants, differing in the dates at which construction starts and finishes, the time taken to install capacity, and the way in which that capacity is utilized.

In exactly the same way the computer can perform the additional calculations required to dynamize other types of primary data. The overall informational problem can be reduced simply to additional computer processing of the information prepared for static models. This data processing can be incorporated into the software for optimization used at the branch level.

This approach is feasible because dynamization does not require information which is qualitatively different, and the problem can be solved by interpolation between the final years of the five-year periods. Thus it is quite realistic to develop the multistage system of models for long-term planning along the lines of converting it into a dynamic system.

4. An improvement in the overall optimality criterion will enable the needs of society to be reflected more completely and precisely. Here we should distinguish two aspects of the problem: the mathematical formulation of the criterion and the information required to use that formulation.

The increase in computational possibilities which we can expect in the immediate future will allow us to switch to more complex forms of the overall criterion — from linear to nonlinear forms and from static to dynamic representations. Society's needs can adequately be expressed with the overall criterion described in [3, Ch. 2]. Here a nonlinear objective function makes it possible to take account of the interdependence between quantities demanded and prices. By weighting (discounting) static objective functions over time, we can make present and future needs commensurable.

There are, however, serious difficulties in making the improvements in the informational base which are necessary if a global optimality criterion is to be devised. We do not always have direct access to the information needed to determine the parameters of that criterion, and some of them must be found using artificial methods. For example, even before the plan is compiled, we know on the basis of forecasts of the social and economic development of the country the rough quantities and prices of the goods which make up final demand. These forecast prices can then be used as the linear components of the coefficients in an objective function in consumption, and the quadratic elements can be interpreted as "penalties" for departing from the desired consumption levels; it seems that higher order components can safely be disregarded [3, Ch. 2].

Household budgets surveys, retail sales data, and other sources can furnish expenditure elasticities for a number of components of final demand. In such cases the coefficients in quadratic terms can be computed in a more satisfactory way.

The weighting function in the global optimality criterion can be chosen on the basis of the results of preliminary aggregative calculations [3, Ch. 2]. Estimates for the postplan period can be made on the basis of an asymptotic description or extrapolation of trends observed in the plan period.

We recognize that a global optimality criterion constructed in this way cannot give an exhaustive and absolutely precise representation of society's preferences. It will be necessary to alter the parameters of the criterion within a certain range and to make them more precise in the course of the calculations. Thus even in the future the multistage optimization system must be oriented not toward compiling a single, definitive optimal long-term plan but toward devising a series of alternative drafts requiring further review. The attention given to the drafts, their number, and the operational usefulness of the calculations will depend directly on how the multistage system develops.

5. Improvements in the local optimality criterion will enable the national interest to be reflected more precisely at the level of branches and multibranch complexes. The growth of computational facilities will enable us to switch from the linear forms of the local criterion used today to modifications which are more general [6, 7].

A dynamic quadratic local criterion is both satisfactory in theoretical terms and practicable. The initial choice of parameters can be made in the same way as for the national criterion — on the basis of a forecast of quantities and prices. The parameters can be made more precise in the course of an iterative multistage optimization process as described in references [8, 9].

The principle of setting alternative values for the parameters of the criterion and of devising alternative drafts of the plan should certainly be extended to the local levels of the system. This is necessary if the system is to give an approximation of the prospects for the development of the branches and multibranch complexes.

6. The prospects for improving the models at different levels in the multistage system follow from what has been said above. The crucial factors here are the growth in computational facilities and the development of new techniques for solving problems.

At branch level we shall use a dynamic multiproduct model for optimizing the development and location of production embodying linear constraints and a quadratic criterion and incorporating both continuous and partially integer-valued variables. Models (or system of models) of this type will be used at the multibranch complex level, though the latter will be broken down into separate branches.

The overall optimization model will be a dynamic one, with linear constraints and a quadratic criterion: it will contain (at the classification used in the input-output model) all the alternatives computed for the development of branches and multibranch complexes.

If all these models are to be used in practice, uniform software must be developed along the lines of that available for static optimization at the branch level [5, Ch. 5]. This will minimize the labor required to prepare the computations, to perform them, and to get out the results.

7. Methods for linking up the computations with the models will be changed in the appropriate ways. The approximation scheme for multistage optimization should be used in its dynamic version. Local units would be represented by dynamic polyhedra, the supporting points of which are characteristic trajectories for the units' development over the whole plan period. After aggregation of outputs (approximation by a hyperplane), these trajectories are incorporated into the overall model as dynamic variants for the development of branches and multibranch complexes.

Since it is questionable whether so many trajectories could be computed at once, there will clearly be more global iterations than in the static case [8, 9]. However the speedy convergence of the process should be preserved.

Let us summarize the foregoing. The coming stage of development of the multistage system for optimizing long-term national plans is likely to involve dynamizing the model with appropriate modifications in the forms of the criteria, in the models used at different levels, in techniques for linking them up, and in the software used in the computations. For the reasons specified above the problem of linking up the optimized branch plans directly in the input-output or the regional sense will still remain unsolved.

When a multistage system of dynamic models is in use, long-term optimal plans will be found on a pattern which differs somewhat from the pattern of the static models described in references [1, 2, 4, 5].

The compilation of a perspective plan — either a long-term or a five-year plan — always starts with preplan studies: these include demographic forecasts, an analysis of demand, forecasts based on macro-models, calculations with small dynamic input-output models, and preparation of a detailed input-output table. As a result, possible alternatives can be found for capital and labor inputs, rates of growth, the time path of net and gross output, and the discount factor. This makes it possible to identify alternative ways of developing branches and to derive reliable "brackets" for their major variables.

The first stage in compiling a long-term plan is to decide the principal direction in which the economy will develop — the control figures. This begins from below, from enterprises, associations, and branches. When dynamic optimization models come into use at the branch level this stage can be organized as follows. Enterprises, associations, and design and research organizations in each branch prepare preliminary information concerning possible ways of constructing new enterprises or expanding existing ones, just as they do with the static models. The computer center used by the branch then processes each static variant for developing or rebuilding an enterprise into one or more dynamic variants. These new basic data are further processed in the computer for the optimization algorithm which is to be used.

The flow of information reaching the branch model from below — on possible ways of constructing or expanding enterprises — must be complemented by information from above — concerning possible values of demand for the branch's output. The branch can estimate alternative levels of demand on the basis of the data produced at the preplan stage. Each such variant is disaggregated to the branch classification and broken down by time and space over the whole plan period. On the basis of this information and price data, the branch can formulate alternative versions of its objective function.

Depending on computational possibilities, the branch optimization problem can be solved in a larger or smaller number of variants which differ in various ways: in the time path of growth of output, the discount factor (or standard rate of return to investment), the assumptions made in disaggregating demand or in breaking it down over space and time, and so on. The most important factors are the first two.

The next tier in the multistage optimization system consists of multibranch complexes. The problems of incorporating these complexes in a multistage system of static models are considered in references [5, Ch. 6; 10]. The difficulty of linking the complexes up with the overall input-output model are overcome in reference [10] by combining two approximation methods — based on a polyhedron and a hyperplane. This method can also be used for dynamic optimization of multibranch complexes. A "dynamic polyhedron" can be constructed for each complex in the same way as for a branch. Each supporting trajectory of this polyhedron enables us to alter the structure of output within the limits permitted by hyperplane approximation. At the same time the overall input-output model can link up the computations made for the complexes.

When optimizing calculations have been performed for the branches and the multibranch complexes in several variants, we can represent the major development alternatives for the economy in input-output terms. A dynamic optimizing input-output model can be used for this purpose, since it produces results at the level of aggregation adopted in the detailed input-output table.

While performing the overall calculations we may find it nec-

essary to go back to the branches for further development variants. Coordinating branch plans in a dynamic context involves
the use of a far larger number of balances than in the static
case, and this cannot be compensated for by a corresponding
increase in the number of alternative branch plans prepared at
the outset. Thus with a dynamic system for multistage optimization, rather than the static model, we may have to perform
independent computations with individual models.

Thus new and stricter requirements must be imposed on the
organization of the whole optimization process. If in the static
framework it is more or less a matter of indifference where
and how the sectoral variants are devised, the dynamic system
must operate with a single technology and within a system of
linked computer centers. All the original branch data must be
stored continuously in the computer memory and must be available for additional calculations.

When an aggregative dynamic input-output model is used to
identify the major directions in which the economy will develop,
this should be done in variant form. Depending on computational
possibilities, a larger or smaller number of variants can be
computed, differing from one another in terms of time path of
the relative shares of consumption and investment in national
income, the relationship between personal and social consumption, the structure of the latter, the regional breakdown of output, and so on.

Having found alternative variants for the overall development
path of the economy we can approximate economic possibilities
in the plan period using a single "dynamic polyhedron." As distinct from those found at the lower levels, this polyhedron cannot be incorporated in any higher-order model. Hence it must
be used for informal analysis of the situation and for making a
final choice of the particular variant of economic development
(which can either be one of the variants already calculated, or
some compromise combination of those variants). Such a choice
can be made in the course of a discussion of major directions
in which the economy might be developed.

Choosing a particular development variant is the final stage of determining the major directions of change and is at the same time the start of the succeeding stage of compiling a detailed long-term national plan. The aim of this stage is not to analyze alternative development paths but to develop the variant already chosen with the necessary accuracy and detail.

We should begin the process of compiling a detailed plan by recomputing the dynamic branch models and the models for the multibranch complexes. However, there is no need now to compute a large number of variants, since the major variables in the branch plans and the discount factor are determined as soon as the overall model is finally solved. However, as at the stage of choosing major directions for development, we may need to go back to the branch models in the course of constructing an overall plan.

Further calculations at the lower levels of the system allow us to furnish the overall dynamic input-output model with new information and to recompute the overall plan to make it more accurate. By using such an iterative process we can perform all the calculations needed to compile a disaggregated economic development plan of the required detail and accuracy. If the plan as a whole covers a period of 15 to 20 years, then the greatest detail and accuracy is needed for the first 5 years, and within that for the first 1 or 2 years. In this way an organic link can be formed between long-term, five-year, and annual planning.

A dynamic system for multistage optimization of long-term economic plans is much more complex than a static system. If we are to have such a system we must first carry out a series of studies. In particular, we must:

(i) continue with our theoretical work concerned with national and local optimality criteria (discounting, evaluation of the post-plan period, etc.), methods for aggregation and disaggregation, and techniques for optimization at all levels;

(ii) perform a large number of computer simulations with small artificial systems of dynamic models, in order to analyze how quickly potential optimization methods converge in practice and to choose the best one, and also in order to choose parameter values and get experience in constructing and using systems of dynamic models;

(iii) carry out research into better ways of formulating the primary information required for branch optimization in dynamic terms, improve our techniques for getting primary data for dynamic branch models, and develop them into a system of programs;

(iv) devise a uniform dynamic model for sectoral optimization and a uniform system of software for it, and also organize the development of algorithms for optimizing dynamic sectoral models, which take account in an efficient way of their special structural features;

(v) perform actual calculations for a number of branches using uniform dynamic models;

(vi) devise standard dynamic models for optimizing multibranch complexes; these should include software and efficient algorithms for incorporating indices for the branches within the complex;

(vii) perform actual calculations on one or two multibranch complexes using standard dynamic models;

(viii) choose the best variant of the overall dynamic input-output model, devise efficient solution algorithms which take account of the special features in its structure, and carry out experimental calculations with a realistically sized model;

(ix) use the overall dynamic input-output model to prepare long-term and five-year plans for the development of the economy on the basis of the primary data available;

(x) link up all the components in the dynamic optimization system on an experimental basis, using models of actual size.

To round off all this theoretical and experimental research it will be necessary to prepare methodological materials describing the dynamic system for multistage optimization of long-term plans and the unified system of software.

The next stage will consist in further theoretical work on the problems of dynamic multistage optimization and in the construction and investigation of experimental models [11].

REFERENCES

1. Kossov, V. V., and Pugachev, V. F. "Mnogostupenchataia sistema optimizatsionnykh raschetov perspektivnykh narodnokhoziaistvennykh planov." Planovoe khoziaistvo, 1974, no. 10.

2. Pugachev, V. F. "Ekonomiko-matematicheskaia razrabotka perspektivnykh narodnokhoziaistvennykh planov." Kommunist, 1975, no. 9.

3. Pugachev, V. F. Optimizatsiia planirovaniia (teoreticheskie problemy). Moscow: "Ekonomika" Publishers, 1968.

4. Pugachev, V. F. Problemy mnogostupenchatoi optimizatsii narodnokhoziaistvennogo planirovaniia. Moscow: "Statistika" Publishers, 1975.

5. Sistema modelei optimal'nogo planirovaniia. Moscow: "Nauka" Publishers, 1975.

6. Pugachev, V. F. "Novye aspekty matematicheskogo analiza problemy lokal'nogo kriteriia." Ekonomika i matematicheskie metody, 1969, vol. 5, no. 6.

7. Pugachev, V. F. "Prilozheniia obshchei formy lokal'nogo kriteriia narodnokhoziaistvennoi effektivnosti." Ekonomika i matematicheskie metody, 1970, vol. 6, no. 2.

8. Pugachev, V. F.; Martynov, G. V.; Mednitskii, V. G.; and Pitelin, A. K. "Mnogostupenchataia optimizatsiia c lokal'nym kriteriem obshchego vida." Ekonomika i matematicheskie metody, 1972, vol. 8, no. 5.

9. Pugachev, V. F.; Martynov, G. V.; Mednitskii, V. G.; and Pitelin, A. K. "Mnogostupenchataia optimizatsiia c konkretnymi formami lokal'nogo kriteriia." Ekonomika i matematicheskie metody, 1973, vol. 9, no. 2.

10. Pugachev, V. F.; Martynov, G. V.; and Pitelin, A. K. "Mnogootraslevoi kompleks v mnogostupenchatoi sisteme optimizatsii perspektivnogo planirovaniia." Ekonomika i matematicheskie metody, 1977, vol. 13, no. 2.

11. Graborov, S. V. "Dinamicheskaia dvukhstupenchataia sistema optimizatsii perspektivnykh narodokhoziaistvennykh planov." Ekonomika i matematicheskie metody, 1978, vol. 14, no. 6.

Received January 31, 1978

A MODIFIED VERSION OF THE OPTIMAL
MULTISECTORAL INTERREGIONAL MODEL

A. G. Granberg

The present article discusses some modifications to the optimal multisectoral interregional model (OMIM), which has been used for a number of years on an experimental basis to calculate the optimal development and location of production in the USSR in terms of an aggregated classification of branches and regions [1, 2].

The first version of the model was made deliberately simple. We are switching to better models as we solve the special modeling problems involved (such as those concerning transport, the relationship between regions, or socioeconomic problems relating to work and consumption) and as we collect data and improve the software. It will take substantial resources to implement models which either incorporate additional relationships or use more disaggregated indices. For this reason it is important to develop the model in a way which does not require the use of qualitatively different information or more powerful computational equipment. The modifications to the OMIM considered below fall into this category.

At the present stage of research, the components of the

Russian text © 1974 by "Nauka" Publishers and Ekonomika i matematicheskie metody. "Modifikatsii optimizatsionnoi mnogootraslevoi mezhraionnoi modeli," Ekonomika i matematicheskie metody, 1974, vol. 10, no. 1, pp. 22-35.

model are classified as follows:

(A) By the method through which production and transportation aspects are coordinated: (1) some regional product balances incorporate all shipments between regions (an example is the model set out in [1]); (2) other balances used in the first step of the calculations only incorporate the net balance of trade between regions; (3) yet other balances (for tradeable products) are given for the country as a whole, the technique of production being chosen on a regional basis.

(B) By the method in which regional growth paths are calculated: (1) the major indices (production and consumption, interregional flows) can be calculated for the last year of the plan period, subject to constraints on total investment (capital accumulation) over the plan period and subject to a specified share of capital expenditure in the final year of the plan; (2) the major indices can also be calculated for the final year on the assumption of a given growth rate for investment or fixed capital; in this case absolute values for capital are not specified for the whole plan period. Both modifications exhibit backward recursiveness. They can be used to determine the time path for the growth of and location of the productive forces year by year, from the final year back to the start of the plan period.

1. A New Account of the Original Model

The unknowns are as follows: $\overset{\circ}{x}_i{}^r$ is the level of output in branch i in region r, produced in the final year using capacity operating at the start of the plan period (branches are numbered so that the last ones in the sequence, starting from $k+1$, are branches producing investment goods); $\bar{x}_i{}^r$ is the increase in output of branch i in region r resulting from expansion of capacity; $x_\tau{}^r$ is the level of transportation activity in region r; $x_i{}^{rs}$ is the shipment of product i from region r to neighboring region s (only trade between adjoining regions is taken into account directly); z is the overall level of consumption in the country.

The parameters are as follows: N_i^r is the output of branch i in region r which can be produced in the final year of the plan period from capacity in operation at the start of the plan period; q_i^r is the fixed component of final demand for output of branch i in region r; H_i is the limit on net investment of the i-th kind for the country as a whole over the plan period; F_l^r is the constraint on the use of resource l (such as labor or natural resources) in region r; $\bar{d}_j^r$ is the maximum growth of output of branch j in region r; d_j^r is the minimum growth of output of branch j in region r; δ_{ij} is an element in an identity matrix ($\delta_{ij}=1$ for $i=j$, $\delta_{ij}=0$ for $i\neq j$); $\overset{\circ}{a}_{ij}^r$ is the input of goods from branch i per unit of output of branch j in region r, using capacity in operation at the start of the plan period ("old" capacity); a_{ij}^r is the input of goods from branch i per unit of output of branch j produced on capacity installed during the plan period ("new" capacity); h_{ij}^r is the capital of type i required per unit of output of branch j produced in region r on new capacity; b_{ij}^r is the capital input of type i in the final year per unit of output of branch j in region r, using new capacity; $\overset{\circ}{f}_{lj}^r$ is the input of resource l per unit of output of branch j in region r, produced on old capacity; f_{lj}^r is the input of resource l per unit of output of branch j in region r, produced on new capacity; $a_{i\tau}^r$ is the input of goods from branch i per unit of transportation activity in region r; $f_{l\tau}^r$ is the input of resource l per unit of transportation activity in region r; $a_{\tau j}^{rr}$ is the cost of shipping a unit of output of branch j within region r; $a_{\tau j}^{rs}$ is the cost of shipping a unit of output of branch j from region r to region s; α_i^r is the percentage of total consumption in the economy going on the output of branch i in region r (we assume that output of all branches is expressed in value terms, so that

$$\sum_{i,r} \alpha_i^r = 1\bigg).$$

With the exception of H_i and h_{ij}^r, all the unknowns and parameters refer to the final year of the plan period. To simplify the notation and the account of the model, here and subsequently we do not specify the variables and parameters for the import and export of goods or for transmission of electricity. All forms of transportation are aggregated together.

When all transformations have been made, the model can be written as follows:

$$\sum_{r,j} h_{ij}^r x_j^r \leq H_i, \quad i = k+1, \ldots, n, \tag{1}$$

$$\sum_{j} (\delta_{ij} - \mathring{a}_{ij}^r) \mathring{x}_j^r + \sum_{j} (\delta_{ij} - a_{ij}^r - b_{ij}^r) \bar{x}_j^r - a_{i\tau} x_\tau^r -$$

$$- a_i^r z - \sum_{s \neq r} x_i^{rs} + \sum_{s \neq r} x_i^{sr} \geq q_i^r, \quad i = 1, \ldots, n, \; r = 1, \ldots, m, \tag{2}$$

$$- \sum_{j} a_{\tau j}^{rr} \mathring{x}_j^r - \sum_{j} a_{\tau j}^{rr} \bar{x}_j^r + x_\tau^r - \sum_{s \neq r, j} (a_{\tau j}^{rs} - a_{\tau j}^{rr}) x_j^{rs} - \tag{3}$$

$$\sum_{s \neq r, j} a_{\tau j}^{rr} x_j^{sr} \geq 0, \quad r = 1, \ldots, m,$$

$$\sum_{j} f_{lj}^r \mathring{x}_j^r + \sum_{j} f_{lj}^r \bar{x}_j^r + f_{l\tau}^r x_\tau^r \leq F_l^r, \quad l = 1, \ldots, \bar{l}, \; r = 1, \ldots, m, \tag{4}$$

$$\mathring{x}_j^r \leq N_j^r, \tag{5}$$

$$\underline{d}_j^r \leq \bar{x}_j^r \leq \bar{d}_j^r \text{(for some } j, \, r), \tag{6}$$

$$\mathring{x}_j^r, \quad \bar{x}_j^r, \quad x_\tau^r, \quad x_j^{rs} \geq 0, \tag{7}$$

$$z \to \max. \tag{8}$$

The differences between this model and the model set out in [1] are as follows.

In the first version, the total level of output x_j^r was represented as an algebraic sum: $x_j^r = N_j^r + \bar{x}_j^r - \underline{x}_j^r$, where $\underline{x}_j^r$ was interpreted as the decline in output from capacity in operation at the start of the plan period. Now $x_j^r = \mathring{x}_j^r + \bar{x}_j^r$. Thus $\underline{x}_j^r = N_j^r - \mathring{x}_j^r$. The switch to new variables has certain advantages in putting data on the computer and in mathematical analysis of the optimal variants.

The breakdown of output between new and old capacity does not create any special difficulties in getting the appropriate information. At the same time it creates a valuable opportunity to determine some important parameters of technical progress within regions (such as the speed at which old techniques are replaced). The first experimental calculations incorporated only a single general-purpose resource in each region — labor. Constraints (4) are more general. The model can also incorporate certain additional constraints which complicate its structure (such as constraints on the levels of some interregional flows, etc.). If we assume that the old capacity is fully utilized in the optimal plan (i.e., $\overset{\circ}{x}{}_j^r = N_j^r$), then constraints (5) are eliminated and (2)–(4) are simplified (relationships involving $\overset{\circ}{x}{}_j^r$ are eliminated).

The model (1)-(8) can be developed at the cost of including additional factors, altering the relationships between them, or extending the range from which variants for the development and location of production are chosen — i.e., by incorporating new information of a technical, socioeconomic, or other kind. However, it is possible to improve the quality of the results even within the framework of the model's basic structure, by using that structure more flexibly. We illustrate this with two examples.

It was assumed in the original model that labor supply in each region is given by a forecast of natural reproduction and migration, irrespective of the location of production. This is clearly a deficiency. It would, however, make the model far more complex if we incorporated conditions for switching labor from region to region, and an alternative method of improving the model's results is preferable. After the model has been solved for the first time, an analysis is made of the shadow price of labor in each region (i.e., of the extent of labor shortages). Then, using information on costs of controlled migration, we work out recommendations for reallocating labor between regions, and these are used at the second stage of the calculations [2, pp. 123-125].

It is a further significant simplification that the structure of consumption (coefficients α_i^r) is specified exogenously. But the original structure can be modified on the basis of a comparison of the ratio of the shadow price of a commodity to the utility derived from consuming it [2, pp. 117-120]. Alternatively, coefficients α_i^r can be viewed in another way. If the consumption level achieved at the start of the plan period is taken as being q_i^r, then α_i^r has to be interpreted as incremental consumption (compared with the previous level). In this case the structure of total consumption, which depends on z, will be found on the basis of calculations with the model as a whole.

2. A Model for Optimizing Investment

There are a number of disadvantages in the method adopted in the original model to incorporate the time path of development and investment in the regions. Specifying constraints on investment over the plan period complicates the problem of finding the optimal relationship between consumption and investment for the country as a whole. Although the level of investment can be derived within the framework of the global model of the economy, we have to correct it when we come to optimize the relative rate of development in each region. This correction can in principle be made by computing several optimal variants for different investment levels. However, it takes too long to calculate such variants. Another disadvantage of the original model concerns the method for calculating coefficients b_{ij}^r. On average these coefficients are λ_i^r times less than coefficients h_{ij}^r, where the λ_i^r depend on the assumptions made about the growth of investment by region in the course of the plan period; however, the level of capacity utilized,

$$\sum_j h_{ij}^r \bar{x}_j^r,$$ obtained from the optimizing problem, will only ac-

cidentally correspond with the proposed rates of growth of investment. Hence after a first solution to the problem has been found it is necessary to change the coefficients and recompute the whole problem, and so on.

In the model as modified here, changes are made to the constraints on investment (1) and to the output balance equations (2).

Let u_i^{tr} be the level of expenditure on productive investment of the i-th kind in region r at time t (the plan period is T

years). The regional output balance equations for the final
year of the plan (for branches making investment goods) incorporate the values u_i^{Tr}, while the regional investment balances incorporate productive investment over the whole plan
period $\sum_{t=1}^{T} u_i^{tr}$. In the modified model in place of (1) and (2)
we have regional balances for investment and output which are
mutually consistent:

$$\sum_j h_{ij}^r x_j^r - \sum_{t=1}^{T} u_i^{tr} \leq 0, \quad i = k+1, \ldots, n, \; r = 1, \ldots, m, \quad (9)$$

$$\sum_j (\delta_{ij} - \mathring{a}_{ij}^r) \mathring{x}_j^r + \sum_j (\delta_{ij} - a_{ij}^r) \bar{x}_j^r - u_i^{Tr} - a_{i\tau}^r x_\tau^r - a_i^r z - \quad (10)$$

$$\sum_{s \neq r} x_i^{rs} + \sum_{s \neq r} x_i^{sr} \geq q_i^r, \quad i = 1, \ldots, n, \; r = 1, \ldots, m.$$

Conditions (3)-(8) are retained. To complete the model we
have to link u_i^{Tr} and $\sum_{t=1}^{T} u_i^{tr}$. If we assume a particular law
for the growth of investment over the plan period, then invest-
ment in the final year of the plan and total investment over all
years can be expressed as functions of the known level of investment in the base year u_i^{0r} and the unknown parameters for
the growth of investment ρ_i^r.

If investment grows <u>linearly</u> (i.e., if the <u>absolute</u> increase
is the same each year), then

$$u_i^{Tr} = u_i^{0r} + T\rho_i^r, \quad (11)$$

$$\sum_{t=1}^{T} u_i^{tr} = T u_i^{0r} + \frac{T(T+1)}{2} \rho_i^r. \quad (12)$$

If we substitute these expressions into (9) and (10) the linearity of the model is retained, which is an important benefit.

We used the model with a linear increase in investment to
perform experimental calculations for the optimal development
and location of production for 16 branches of material produc-

tion and 10 economic zones of the USSR over a 10-year period. The solution obtained differs significantly from the optimal variant in the original model (although the data were identical). Consumption in the final year increased by 4.7%; gross social product was up 10.6%, and investment over the whole period was up 20.9%.

It is well known that if an <u>absolute increase</u> is constant, the <u>annual rate of growth</u> declines monotonically. In the new optimal variant, the rate of growth of investment for the country as a whole fell from 17.3% in the first year to 6.8% in the tenth year. It may be desirable from the standpoint of maximizing consumption in the final year to phase investment in this way, but it is questionable whether it is acceptable from the point of view of ensuring a continuous increase in living standards. The assumption of a constant absolute increase is only justified for regions which develop slowly. But the decline in growth rate exhibited by most regions between the first and the tenth years (from 31.2% to 8.2% in the Volga region, for example) is too large. Hence it is desirable when deciding the question of the optimal development and location of production to adopt an alternative assumption concerning the growth of investment.

In the case of a developing economy it is most natural to assume that investment grows in accordance with a power function, i.e., with a constant annual rate of growth:

$$u_i^{Tr} = (1 + \rho_i^r)^T u_i^{0r}, \tag{13}$$

$$\sum_{t=1}^{T} u_i^{tr} = \frac{(1 + \rho_i^r)[(1 + \rho_i^r)^T - 1]}{\rho_i^r} u_i^{0r}. \tag{14}$$

Incorporating (13) and (14) into (8) and (9) makes the problem one of nonlinear programming. However, by making a piecewise linear approximation of (13) and (14) we can turn it into a linear programming problem with side constraints. Because of the special features of (13) and (14) a <u>single</u> solution of the linear programming problem will solve the original nonlinear programming problem to any desired level of accuracy. This property is associated with the fact that the function $\varphi=(1+\rho)^T$ increases more quickly than the function $\chi=(1+\rho)[(1+\rho)^T-1]/\rho$. For example, as ρ goes up from 0.06 to 0.07 the ratio of the increase in χ to the increase in φ is 4.612; when ρ changes from 0.07 to 0.08 the ratio is 4.491, and it subsequently declines monotonically, for $\Delta\rho=0.01$, as follows: 4.391, 4.286, 4.194, etc. In analytical terms this property of the functions χ and φ is reflected in the fact that $(\chi'/\varphi')'<0$.[1]

Let ε be some approximation interval, and let μ be the number associated with that interval. Functions (13) and (14) are replaced by the following piecewise linear functions (for simplicity we omit regional and branch subscripts):

$$u^T = u^0 \sum_{\mu} a_{\mu}\Delta\rho_{\mu}, \qquad (13')$$

$$\sum_{t=1}^{T} u^t = u^0 \sum_{\mu} b_{\mu}\Delta\rho_{\mu}, \qquad (14')$$

Where $a_{\mu}=(1+\mu\varepsilon)^T-[1+(\mu-1)\varepsilon]^T$,

$$b_{\mu} =$$

$$\frac{(1+\mu\varepsilon)[(1+\mu\varepsilon)^T-1]}{\mu\varepsilon} - \frac{[1+(\mu-1)\varepsilon]\{[1+(\mu-1)\varepsilon]^T-1\}}{(\mu-1)\varepsilon}.$$

Moreover,

$$0\leqslant\Delta\rho_{\mu}\leqslant\varepsilon. \qquad (15)$$

Clearly $b_{\mu}/a_{\mu}=\Delta\chi/\Delta\varphi$ for $\rho\in[(\mu-1)\varepsilon, \mu\varepsilon]$. In the limit as ($\varepsilon\to0$), $b_{\mu}/a_{\mu}=\chi'/\varphi'$. As noted above, $(b_{\mu}/a_{\mu})'<0$. Let $\hat{\mu}$ be the largest number for which $\Delta\rho_{\mu}>0$. Then the unknown value of ρ is found by formula:

$$\rho=(\hat{\mu}-1)\varepsilon+\Delta\rho_{\hat{\mu}}. \qquad (16)$$

We now introduce notation for the dual of problem (3)-(10): v is the shadow price of output — corresponding to (10); w is the shadow price of investment — corresponding to (9); y_{μ} is the shadow price associated with constraint (15). All these shadow prices are nonnegative.

We show that this method of approximation allows us to solve the original nonlinear problem in one step to any degree of accuracy specified by the value of ε. For this purpose it is sufficient to prove that the optimal plan in the linear programming problem only includes variables $\Delta\rho_\mu$ with sequential numbers, starting with $\mu=1$.

Proof. We shall begin from the standard properties of the $\overline{\text{OMIM}}$: (1) optimal solutions to the primal and the dual problem exist and are unique; (2) the shadow prices v and w are strictly positive. We focus our attention on three qualitatively different cases, when the optimal $\Delta\rho_\mu$ falls either at one of the ends or in the interior of interval $[0, \varepsilon]$.

1. If $0<\Delta\rho_\mu<\varepsilon$, then $\Delta\rho_{\mu-\eta}=\varepsilon$, $\Delta\rho_{\mu+\theta}=0$ (η and θ are positive integers, where $\eta<\mu$). From the constraint in the dual problem corresponding to the variable $\Delta\rho_\mu$, we get: $u^0 b_\mu w - u^0 a_\mu v = 0$, from which $v/w = b_\mu/a_\mu$. We assume that $\Delta\rho_{\mu-\eta}<\varepsilon$. Then from the corresponding condition in the dual problem we find $v/w = b_{\mu-\eta}/a_{\mu-\eta}$. But this is impossible, since $b_\mu/a_\mu < b_{\mu-\eta}/a_{\mu-\eta}$. We assume then that $\Delta\rho_{\mu+\theta}>0$. Then $u^0 b_{\mu+\theta} w - u^0 a_{\mu+\theta} v - y_{\mu+\theta} = 0$, from which $v/w \leqslant b_{\mu+\theta}/a_{\mu+\theta}$, which is also impossible since $b_{\mu+\theta}/a_{\mu+\theta} < b_\mu/a_\mu$.

2. If $\Delta\rho_\mu=0$, then $\Delta\rho_{\mu+\theta}=0$. Otherwise we get two incompatible inequalities from the constraints in the dual problem: $v/w \geqslant b_\mu/a_\mu$ and $v/w \leqslant b_{\mu+\theta}/a_{\mu+\theta}$.

3. If $\Delta\rho_\mu=\varepsilon$, then $\Delta\rho_{\mu-\eta}=\varepsilon$. We assume that $\Delta\rho_{\mu-\eta}<\varepsilon$. Then $y_{\mu-\eta}=0$ and we get incompatible inequalities from the constraints in the dual problem: $v/w \leqslant b_\mu/a_\mu$ and $v/w \geqslant b_{\mu-\eta}/a_{\mu-\eta}$.

Another way of linearizing functions (13) and (14) has been suggested in reference [3]. The following formula is adopted:

$$u_i^{tr} = u_i^{0r}(1 + \Delta_i^{tr}\sigma_i^r), \qquad (17)$$

where Δ_i^{tr} is the relative increase in investment in t and σ_i^r is the unknown growth rate for investment. In other words, it is assumed that investment grows at annual rates the ratios between which are fixed in advance. The growth rates to be expected are not always accurate and hence it may be necessary to solve the problem repeatedly. Moreover, experimental testing of this method of linearization shows that setting the coefficients Δ_i^{tr} in accordance with the optimal ρ_i^r does not guarantee an optimal plan with those growth rates. There is a consistent tendency toward a variant with constant absolute increases in investment, which is "most suitable" from the standpoint of maximizing consumption in the final year of the plan period.

The linearity of the model can also be preserved by assuming that investment grows in accordance with a second-order parabola [4]. Let $u_i^{0r} - u_i^{-1r} = \Delta_i^r$ (the known rate at which investment grows in the base year); $u_i^{1r} - u_i^{0r} = \rho_i^r$, where ρ_i^r is the unknown investment growth parameter. By the formula for a second-order parabola

$$u_i^{Tr} = u_i^{0r} + \frac{T(T+1)}{2}\rho_i^r - \frac{(T-1)T}{2}\Delta_i^r, \qquad (18)$$

$$\sum_{t=1}^{T} u_i^{tr} = Tu_i^{0r} + \frac{T(T+1)(T+2)}{6}\rho_i^r - \frac{(T-1)T(T+1)}{6}\Delta_i^r. \qquad (19)$$

A second-order parabola exhibits a time path of investment with growing absolute increments but a declining rate of growth. The feasibility of using formulae (18) and (19) for at least some regions can only be evaluated on the basis of an analysis of investment statistics.

3. Using the Special Features of the Branches to Reduce the Size of the Problem

The size problem is very important in practical applications of the OMIM. As well as designing a rational system for the classification of branches and regions, we have to make use of any opportunities for reducing the size of the problem by transforming the model itself. One such possibility is to eliminate certain balance relationships by making substitutions. In order to do this, two conditions must be satisfied: (1) the inequality which is eliminated must be strictly fulfilled in the optimal plan; (2) a variable in the constraint to be eliminated must be expressible as a linear combination of the remaining variables with nonnegative coefficients. The first condition is satisfied (as a normal property of an optimal plan) in the case of balances for output and transportation. The second condition guarantees nonnegativity of the excluded variable. Both conditions are satisfied for transportation balances and for output balances which do not involve interregional flows $(x_i^{rs}, x_i^{sr}=0)$. Thus we can eliminate from the OMIM any balances and the corresponding variables which relate to transportation and nontradeable goods.

From (3) we have:

$$x_\tau^r = \sum_j a_{\tau j}^{rr} \dot{x}_j^r + \sum_j a_{\tau j}^{rr} \bar{x}_j^r + \sum_{s,j} a_{\tau j}^{rr} x_j^{sr} + \sum_{s,j} (a_{\tau j}^{rs} - a_{\tau j}^{rr}) x_j^{rs}.$$

It is natural to assume that $a_{\tau j}^{rs} \geqslant a_{\tau j}^{rr}$. We substitute the values of x_τ^r into (10) and (4). As a result of these transformations we derive the following expressions:

$$\sum_j (\delta_{ij} - \mathring{\hat{a}}_{ij}^r) \dot{x}_j^r + \sum_j (\delta_{ij} - \hat{a}_{ij}^r) \bar{x}_j^r - u_i^{Tr} - a_i^r z -$$

$$\sum_{s,j} (\delta_{ij} + a_{ij}^{rs}) x_j^{rs} + \sum_{s,j} (\delta_{ij} - a_{ij}^{rr}) x_j^{sr} \geqslant q_i^r, \qquad (20)$$

$$\sum_j \mathring{\hat{f}}_{ij}^r \dot{x}_j^r + \sum_j \hat{f}_{ij}^r \bar{x}_j^r + \sum_{s,j} f_{ij}^{rr} x_j^{sr} + \sum_{s,j} f_{ij}^{rs} x_j^{rs} \leqslant F_i^r, \qquad (21)$$

where $\mathring{\hat{a}}_{ij}^r = \mathring{a}_{ij}^r + a_{i\tau}^r a_{\tau j}^{rr}$, $\hat{a}_{ij}^r = a_{ij}^r + a_{i\tau}^r a_{\tau j}^{rr}$, $a_{ij}^{rs} = a_{i\tau}^r (a_{\tau j}^{rs} - a_{\tau j}^{rr})$, $a_{ij}^{rr} = a_{i\tau}^r a_{\tau j}^{rr}$, $\mathring{\hat{f}}_{ij}^r = \mathring{f}_{ij}^r + f_{i\tau}^r a_{\tau j}^{rr}$, $\hat{f}_{ij}^r = f_{ij}^r + f_{i\tau}^r a_{\tau j}^{rr}$, $f_{ij}^{rr} = f_{i\tau}^r a_{\tau j}^{rr}$, $f_{ij}^{rs} = f_{i\tau}^r (a_{\tau j}^{rs} - a_{\tau j}^{rr})$.

From product balances (10) which do not involve interregional trade, we get: $\bar{x}_i^r = \dfrac{1}{1 - a_{ii}^r} \left(-\dot{x}_i^r + \sum_j \mathring{a}_{ij}^r \dot{x}_j^r + \right.$ $\sum_{j \neq i} a_{ij}^r \bar{x}_j^r + u_i^{Tr} + a_{i\tau}^r x_\tau^r + a_i^r z + q_i^r \Big)$. $\dot{x}_i^r$ features on the right-hand side of this equation with a negative sign. Hence we cannot assume that the nonnegativity condition for $\bar{x}_i^r \geqslant 0$ is fulfilled, whatever values are taken by all the variables in the problem. However we recall that $\dot{x}_i^r$ is bounded from above

$(\overset{\circ}{x_i^r} \leqslant N_i^r)$, while the relation $\sum \overset{\circ}{a_{ij}^r} \overset{\circ}{x_j^r} + \sum_{j \neq i} a_{ij}^r \bar{x}_j^r + u_i^{Tr} + a_{i\tau}^r x_\tau^r +$ $a_i^r z + q_i^r \geqslant \overset{\circ}{x_i^r}$ corresponds to the actual situation in a developing economy, when demand for nontradeable product i increases in each region. In some cases $q_i^r \geqslant \overset{\circ}{x_i^r}$, which is a sufficient condition for the nonnegativity of $\bar{x}_i^r$. Making substitutions for the eliminated variables $\bar{x}_i^r$ introduces changes in the balances for investment, output, and resources.

In modeling the location of production it is particularly important to take account of the fact that branches differ in the extent to which their output can be moved or traded. On this criterion branches can be divided into three groups: (1) those with tradeable output but substantial transportation costs; (2) those with tradeable output and insignificant transportation costs; (3) those with nontradeable output.

In the case of branches in the first group, it is convenient to compile balances for the production and distribution of output for each region, as in the modified OMIM set out above. By identifying the third of the groups above (region-based branches) we can eliminate the corresponding product balances from the main problem. Identifying the second group of sectors is the major source of reduction in the size of the problem. In the case of these sectors, the regional output balances can be replaced by a single country-wide balance which incorporates regional techniques of production:

$$\sum_{r,j} (\delta_{ij} - \overset{\circ}{a}_{ij}^r) \overset{\circ}{x}_j^r + \sum_{r,j} (\delta_{ij} - a_{ij}^r) \bar{x}_j^r -- \sum_r u_i^{Tr} - \sum_r a_{i\tau}^r x_\tau^r - a_{iz} z \geqslant q_i,$$
$$i = 1, ..., n_1, \tag{22}$$

where n_1 is the number of branches in which the transportation factor is weak and

$$a_i = \sum_r a_i^r.$$

It is an indication that product balances for the various regions can profitably be amalgamated if the shadow prices of a branch's output are approximately equal in all regions. In particular, the experimental calculations we have performed showed that the variation between the highest and lowest shadow prices for the output of light industry in the 10 zones of the USSR was 0.004 rubles [2, p. 115]. It is obvious that regional balances can be amalgamated for this branch without a perceptible loss of accuracy. (For comparison we note that the variations in the shadow prices for other branches were as follows: 0.032 for the food industry; 0.145 for the engineering industry; 0.836 for electricity; and 1.168 for the fuel industry.)

The dividing lines between these three groups are provisional and depend upon the criteria for judging whether transportation costs are significant and the way in which the economic regions are identified. Thus products which are definitely nontradeable are relatively few, but for the purposes of practical calculations they can be augmented by products which for economic reasons cannot profitably be moved between major regions. The number of products in the second category could be expanded if we could devise methods to take indirect account of transportation by using the cost coefficients of the transportation branch and thereby link up the production and transportation aspects iteratively as parts of a single problem.

The classification of branches in three major groups should be based (1) on an analysis of statistics showing the share of transportation costs in total costs for different products and the different costs of transportation to different destinations; regional transportation balances for output should also be examined; (2) on experience gained in the course of optimal branch planning of classifying goods and branches on the basis of the importance of the transportation factor; and (3) on an analysis using the methods of mathematical economics of existing solutions to optimal development and location problems.

4. Incorporating Techniques of Production into the Model

Incorporating regional techniques of production into the model substantially extends the area from which optimal decisions can be chosen and allows regional conditions to be taken into account more fully and accurately.

Production techniques in the OMIM are divided into two basic types: (1) technological and organizational techniques ψ (which take account of differences in technology, organizational methods, use of substitutable inputs, ways of extending capacity, and so on) and (2) area-specific techniques γ (which take account of the location of production within a region).

Breaking down output by the organizational form and tech- nology adopted does not complicate the structure of the OMIM; it only increases the number of variables involved and the number of constraints on those variables. It is a more significant departure if the problem incorporates techniques of production which use scarce regional inputs (electricity generation in the national grid, for example) or production techniques which exhibit considerable regional differences in their input coefficients for resources with different marginal products or degrees of shortage, such as fuel and energy, labor, or investment resources. It is worth noting that the fact that output produced on old and new capacity is shown separately in the OMIM makes it possible to take account of many regional differences in production conditions. In particular it allows us in some degree to reduce the harmful consequences of aggregation of output. If information on production with old capacity is based on past differences in the composition of output, then when input coefficients are being found for new capacity, we can start from a comparable (and more homogeneous) structure of output.

A linear programming model imposes very strong constraints on the mathematical representation of production processes. In particular it is assumed (a) that the scale of production can be varied continuously; (b) that inputs increase proportionately with output for each technique; and (c) that the output of one good is independent of output of another. As the classification of branches becomes finer, these assumptions become more and more unrealistic.

Incorporating nonlinear relationships between inputs and outputs (if such are known) presents no particular difficulty

provided that there are decreasing returns to scale, as is the
case for many enterprises in extractive industries. In this
case the method of piecewise linear approximation set out in
Section 2 can be adopted. The situation is much more complex
in the case of algorithms for solving problems incorporating
functions with increasing returns (as occur, for example, when
production units in processing industries are combined).

It is well known that many production units and plants are by
nature indivisible. In order to represent their operations
mathematically, we have to use integer programming methods.
In such cases the plant's production possibilities and use of
resources can be described in terms of alternative development variants. The relevant variable will be $x_{l\varphi}^r$ – the intensity at which variant φ is used to develop enterprise k in region r. The following constraints are imposed on the variable $x_{h\varphi}^r$

$$x_{k\varphi}^r = \begin{cases} 1 \\ 0 \end{cases}, \quad \sum_{\varphi} x_{k\varphi}^r \leq 1.$$ In our view it will be possible in the im-

mediate future for the OMIM to compute plan variants incorporating major enterprises which, in the nature of their technologies, are integer-valued (hydroelectric stations, metal-
lurgical combines, oil processing plants, main-line transportation routes, etc.).

Including area-specific production techniques within the
OMIM substantially extends the scope of the model. Area-
specific techniques indicate the output produced and resources
used at the level of the finer territorial units that make up the
major regions which figure in the basic classification of the
interregional problem. For example, within the Baltic economic region, the Latvian, Lithuanian, and Estonian union republics can be distinguished, together with the Kaliningrad
oblast'. Incorporating area-specific techniques allows the
OMIM to solve certain major problems of locating production
within a region in a way which takes account of differences in
the costs and location of natural resources, labor, and productive capacity. Within each area techniques of production can
be differentiated in terms of the organizational methods and
technology employed.

The majority of the constraints in OMIM are only insignificantly modified by the incorporation of alternative organizational methods and technologies. In investment and product balances, there is only an increase in the number of coefficients and unknowns characterizing each production technique. If output of some branches is not shiftable between subregions, then the problem can incorporate special balances for the production and distribution of output by subregion.

It is clearly desirable that the regional transportation balances should use differentiated cost coefficients for shipments within a region. However as a first approximation the model might use the following formulation:

$$-\sum_j a_{\tau j}^{rr} \sum_{\gamma,\psi} \overset{\circ}{x}_{j\psi}^{r\gamma} - \sum_j a_{\tau j}^{rr} \sum_{\gamma,\psi} \bar{x}_{j\psi}^{r\gamma} + x_\tau^r - \sum_{s,j}(a_{\tau j}^{rs} - a_{\tau j}^{rr})x_j^{rs} -$$
$$\sum_{s,j} a_{\tau j}^{rr} x_j^{sr} \geqslant 0, \quad r = 1, \ldots, m. \tag{23}$$

Constraint (23) can be eliminated by substitution. Resource constraints are established for each area (subregion); these will take account of the fact that some resources are allocated for transportation throughout the region as a whole.

Thus incorporating area-specific production techniques in the OMIM enables us to make our analysis much more detailed without substantially increasing the size of the problem to be solved. Hence even for computations to be made in the immediate future we can use a classification of regions and subregions which includes all the union republics and the major economic regions in the RSFSR.

5. Block Programming Models

Although the modifications we have made to the OMIM differ in important ways, they all exhibit a standard structure: regional blocks are linked by a set of constraints which are common to a number of regions. This gives rise to the idea of transforming the OMIM into a block programming problem.

By using block programming methods we can make the branch and regional classifications much finer and reduce the difficulty of the computations. Another factor is of equal importance. Block programming methods often provide a basis for devising frameworks for the optimal planning and operation of a socialist economy which combine the centralized and decentralized principles of taking decisions and which link directive planning with self-regulation of the economy.

The special feature of a two-stage production and transportation model lies in the fact that an overall problem for the development and location of production is broken down into two stages: (1) the development and location of production is first calculated, together with the trade balance between regions — the transportation factor being taken into account only approximately; (2) interregional trade flows are then found, and the transport costs used in the first stage of the model are revised. The idea of solving the location and transportation problems sequentially was first put into effect in reference [5]. However the major defect of that model is that it takes no account of the impact of the transportation aspect on the location of production; as a consequence, the optimal solution derived is unrealistic [6]. The two-stage production and transportation models for optimal branch planning which have been widely used in practice share the same property [7].

In the model discussed below, the interdependence between location and transportation decisions is not eliminated but transformed in such a way as to yield a "good" structure for the first stage of the model. The first stage, in addition to the modifications to the OMIM considered above, incorporates balances for interregional trade for the country as a whole and equations linking consumption in the whole country and in the regions.

We introduce some additional notation. Let $v_i{}^r$ be the trade balance for region r in the output of branch i. Since $v_i{}^r$ can take any sign, in order to use standard linear programming algorithms we replace this magnitude by the difference between two nonnegative numbers: $v_i{}^r = {}^+v_i{}^r - {}^-v_i{}^r$; z^r is the consumption level in region r, $\sum_r z^r = z$; λ^r is the share of region r in total consumption, $\sum_r \lambda^r = 1$; $\bar{a}_i^r$ is the proportion of output of branch i allocated to consumption in region r, $\sum_r \bar{a}_i^r = 1$; $\bar{a}_{\tau j}^{rs}$ is the cost of transporting output of branch j from region r (this coefficient is altered once the second stage of the problem has been solved). All the modification to the OMIM can be incorporated in the two-stage model, but in order to illustrate its principal features we take as a basis the model set out in Section 2.

The first stage. The first group of constraints refers to all regions. These constraints form the coordinating part of the block programming problem. They comprise:
Export and import balances for the branches

$$\sum_r {}^+v_i^r - \sum_r {}^-v_i^r \geqslant 0, \quad i = 1, \ldots, n_1. \tag{24}$$

Equations for regional consumption

$$z^r - \lambda^r z \geqslant 0, r = 1, \ldots, m. \tag{25}$$

All the other constraints are regional and form nonoverlapping sets within the overall problem. They are:
Product balances

$$\sum_j (\delta_{ij} - \mathring{a}_{ij}^r) \mathring{x}_j^r + \sum_j (\delta_{ij} - a_{ij}^r) x_j^r - \tag{26}$$

$$u_i^{Tr} - a_{i\tau}^r x_\tau^r - \bar{a}_i^r z - {}^+v_i^r + {}^-v_i^r \geqslant q_i^r.$$

In terms of the new variables, the resources needed to transport goods within the region are given by
$\sum_j a_{\tau j}^{rr} (\mathring{x}_j^r + x_j^r + {}^-v_j^r - {}^+v_j^r)$. It is suggested that the following method be used to calculate the resources needed to make shipments between regions: they should include the cost of

shipping the positive component of the trade balance $\left(\sum_j \bar{a}_{\tau j}^{rs+} v_j^r\right)$

and the cost of shipping goods in transit (q_τ^r); the latter figures should be revised on an iterative basis. Overall, the transportation balances will read as follows:

$$-\sum_j a_{\tau j}^{rr\circ} x_j^r - \sum_j a_{\tau j}^{rr} x_j^r + x_\tau^r - \sum_j (\bar{a}_{\tau j}^{rs} - a_{\tau j}^{rr})^+ v_j^r - \sum_j a_{\tau j}^{rr-} v_j^r \geqslant q_\tau^r. \tag{27}$$

The constraints on investment and resource balances are unaltered.

The principal advantage of structuring the model in this way is that it can be interpreted as a synthesis of regional models (a generalization of the "East-West" problem to the case of a multiregional system).

Using a procedure for allocating centralized resources, we then decompose the overall territorial planning problem into m regional problems. An import-export balance is specified for each region for all tradeable commodities. Thus each regional problem includes constraints on central resources as well as purely regional constraints. The center has to allocate each homogeneous resource between regions in such a way that its shadow price is the same in each region [8].

The second stage (determining interregional trade). This model reduces to various modified versions of a multiproduct transportation problem. In simplest form (in the absence of constraints on the transportation network) the second stage decomposes into a number of independent transportation problems (depending on the number of transportable products). The main difficulties in refining the two-stage model (for experimental testing) are: (1) incorporating transit shipments in the first stage; (2) choosing optimality criteria for the second stage; (3) devising techniques for linking up the two stages by revising transportation costs and the interregional trade balance.

The OMIM can be transformed into a block programming problem without any loss of precision in the calculations. However, there is the problem of reducing the size of the overall (coordinating) part of the problem.

The OMIM can be converted into a block programming problem by means of certain identity transformations. As in the two-stage problem, let

$$\sum_{s \neq r} x_i^{rs} - \sum_{s \neq r} x_i^{sr} = {}^+v_i^r - {}^-v_i^r. \tag{28}$$

These conditions ($n_1 m$ in all), together with the equations for regional consumption and the transportation balances, form the coordinating part of the model. The regional blocks include the product and investment balances. The large number of type (28) constraints makes it difficult to use the resulting block programming approach in practice.

An alternative approach is based on use of the duality principle. To any problem of finding an optimal plan for the development and location of production (which is the basis for any modification of the OMIM) there will necessarily correspond a dual problem which determines a system of shadow prices associated with the optimal plan. This dual problem is a standard one in block programming [9]. The coordinating part of the dual problem contains constraints on the relationships between the shadow prices of goods in adjoining regions. The number of such constraints may actually be very large. Hence from a computational standpoint there are no obvious advantages in switching to a block programming problem of this form. Special algorithms are at present being developed which exploit the special structure of the overall (coordinating) part of the block programming problem formulated here.

NOTES

1)

$$\varphi' = T(1+\rho)^{T-1}, \quad \chi' = \left[\sum_{t=1}^{T} (1+\rho)^t \right]' = \sum_{t=1}^{T} t(1+\rho)^{t-1},$$

$$\frac{\chi'}{\varphi'} = \sum_{t=1}^{T} \frac{t}{T} (1+\rho)^{t-T}, \quad \left(\frac{\chi'}{\varphi'} \right)' = \sum_{t=1}^{T} (t-T) \frac{t}{T} (1+\rho)^{t-T-1} < 0.$$

REFERENCES

1. Granberg, A. G. "Mnogootraslevaia model' optimal'nogo razvitiia i raz-meshcheniia proizvodstva v planovo-ekonomicheskikh raschetakh)," Ekonomika i matematicheskie metody, 1970, vol. 6, no. 3.

2. Granberg, A. G. "Eksperimental'nye raschety optimal'nogo razvitiia i raz-meshcheniia proizvoditel'nykh sil SSSR." In Metody i modeli territorial'nogo planirovaniia, no. 1. Novosibirsk: AN SSSR, Sibirskoe Otdelenie, IEiOPP, 1971.

3. Smekhov, B. M. Perspektivnoe narodnokhoziaistvennoe planirovanie. Moscow: "Ekonomika" Publishers, 1968.

4. Konius, A. A. "Perspektivnoe planirovanie pri predpolozhenii ravnomernogo rosta kapitalovlozhenii." In Planirovanie i ekonomiko-matematicheskie metody. Moscow: "Nauka" Publishers, 1964.

5. Kossov, V. V. "K voprosu ob optimal'nom planirovanii razvitiia raionov." In Problemy optimal'nogo planirovaniia, proektirovaniia i upravleniia proizvod-stvom. Moscow: Izdatel'stvo MGU, 1963.

6. Achelashvili, K. V. "Ekonomiko-matematicheskii analiz nekotorykh optimi-zatsionnykh mezhraionnykh modelei." In Metody i modeli territorial'nogo plan-irovaniia, no. 2. Novosibirsk: AN SSSR, Sibirskoe Otdelenie, IEiOPP, 1971.

7. Metodicheskie polozheniia po optimal'nomu otraslevomu planirovaniiu v promyshlennosti. Novosibirsk: "Nauka" Publishers, 1967.

8. Granberg, A. G., and Chernyshev, A. A. "Zadacha optimal'nogo territorial'-nogo planirovaniia 'Zapad-Vostok.'" Izvestiia Sibirskogo Otdeleniia AN SSSR, 1970, no. 6, Seriia obshchestv. nauk, no. 2.

9. Optimal'noe territorial'no-proizvodstvennoe planirovanie. Novosibirsk: "Nauka" Publishers, 1969.

Received December 25, 1971

INTEGRATED SETS
OF MACROECONOMIC MODELS

V. S. Dadaian and R. L. Raiatskas

If we are going to make further progress in analyzing and, especially, applying mathematical models of the economy, this
will involve a switch from the analysis of individual macroeconomic aggregates to the development of integrated sets of
models. This approach is a logical step in the evolution of research in mathematical economics and is the product of a substantial amount of knowledge and practical experience of working with macroeconomic models. It is understandable that the
attention of Soviet economists has been directed to the need to
construct such sets of models since as long ago as the 1960s
(see, for example, [1-3]).

In our view, it is symptomatic that the most interesting
models of the developed capitalist economies, particularly
those intended for government development planning, are also
oriented toward synthesizing models of various kinds (or,
rather, of various levels) [4]. Particular attention should be
paid to the work which has been undertaken in a number of foreign countries since the start of the 1970s to analyze and make
long-term forecasts of the world economy. The tools used in

Russian text © 1976 by "Nauka" Publishers and Ekonomika i matematicheskie
metody. "Integrirovannye makromodel'nye kompleksy," Ekonomika i matematicheskie metody, 1976, vol. 12, no. 2, pp. 256-267.

such work are systems of models which are linked up with one another in such a way that the output from one model serves as an input into others [5-7].

In general terms, integrated sets of models are the product of combining the principles of systems analysis with those of mathematical modeling of the economy. In a narrower sense, each set of models involves in some degree an attempt to construct a model which is approximately closed. The latter aspect is most important for our argument that the general approach proposed is a new stage in the development of economic modeling. Hitherto, models of individual economic units (however large they are, since we are talking about fairly realistic representations of reality) have been open models; this means that the results derived from them are to a large extent predetermined by the values chosen for the exogenous variables. If, however, the exogenous variables in their turn can be derived from another model, then it is logical to combine both models. The number of exogenous variables is then reduced by the number of variables which are transferred from one submodel to another. If we develop this argument, bearing in mind that in the real world subsystems in the economy are not only linked directly, but also by feedbacks, it is easy to go on to the idea of constructing a set of models which combines individual submodels "recursively." The property of such a set of models which gives it its special qualitative features vis-à-vis its own constituent parts is that the exogenous inputs into the autonomous submodels are endogenized to the maximum possible extent and replaced by outputs from other submodels in the set. In this way the total number of exogenous variables is reduced to a minimum.

For example, in a dynamic input-output model the structure of consumption can be taken as given while the physical composition of investment is found as the solution to the problem. However in a combined model not only the level of consumption but also its structure will be determined in a way which depends upon the level and distribution of incomes, which in their turn are affected by the time path of accumulation. As well as making a radical change in the ratio of exogenous and endogenous variables in the calculations, a set of models has a further important property: it incorporates not only relationships between blocks but also indirect relationships between qualitatively dissimilar subsystems. A signal from one block to a neighboring one produces a diminishing chain reaction throughout the set as a whole, and the system automatically takes account of the side effects, however small they may be.

The presence of these side effects of varying strengths means that the control parameters in the economic subsystems take a narrower range of values than those in the isolated models. The threshold values for the controls can be established in precisely the same way as one evaluates the economic consequences of specifying particular numerical values for any control variables.

In its completed form, a set of macro-models is a man-machine system, the cross section of which looks like this. Firstly, at the man-machine interface there is a facility for "keying" inputs into the set of models. This permits the researcher to select any combination of control variables within the permitted range and any exogenous structural variables. Secondly, there is a level of operation within the computer in which two independent components work in parallel: a set of models which has been programmed and translated into an algorithmic language, and a data bank in machine-readable form, which stores information and provides the appropriate software. Thirdly, at the man-machine interface there is a system for displaying the results in a form suitable for analysis.

On the basis of research into the general properties of "supermodels" of this type and some experience of constructing and using them in practice, we can formulate some general principles for their design.

The principle of two-dimensional integration means that not only should models at the same level be combined in a single complex but also that each submodel should be disaggregated vertically by specifying the relationships within that submodel, in theory down to any level of detail.

Maximization of the amount of feedback between submodels essentially ensures that the set of models is integrated and unified as a system, and not merely the sum of its parts. This principle can be used as a measure of how good a set of models is (in fact it is for this reason that it is formulated as a maximand).

A level of abstraction appropriate to the goal means that we should devise a system of models at each level which corresponds to the analytical, planning, or management work performed at that level. In a sense this principle controls the operation of the other two, since we could specify an individual submodel, or the feedback between submodels, to any desired level of detail.

All these principles are independent of one another and of equal force. If we satisfy each of them we have created the necessary and sufficient conditions for converting heterogeneous models into a single complex which satisfies the definition of a system [8, p. 495; 9, p. 322; 10].

For economic calculations at the highest level of aggregation, the planning and statistical agencies use an aggregated classification of the major branches of the economy which is as follows: (1) industry; (2) construction; (3) agriculture; (4) transport and communications; and (5) trade, supply, and procurement. Models are currently available for making long-run, goal-related forecasts for economic development in these major sectors [11]. Reference [12] evaluates some attempts to combine these models with models of the revenue and expenditure sides of the state budget, of income and expenditure of the population, and of the growth of the population and of labor supply. However, the models are such that the system we get from combining them is much the same as what we would get by treating them individually with given exogenous variables. This happens because the high level of aggregation (and perhaps loss) of information eliminates the very rich variety of feedbacks which actually occur in real economic process. Thus in the first place, the revenue of the state budget and household income only have a weak and gradual impact on the structure of the economy in terms of major branches. These changes cannot be uneven, since the level of sectoral aggrega-tion described above only deals with the major components of social production. Secondly, even a substantial shift in the level and composition of money incomes has an almost imper-ceptible effect on the structure of consumption, if the latter is viewed in terms of such "superaggregates" as industrial goods or agricultural goods.

If we satisfy the principle of two-dimensional integration it automatically means that there are several horizontal levels in the set of models. However it is not necessary for all the upper-level blocks to be disaggregated to the same extent. It is quite permissible for disaggregation to be limited to any one block in the system. In this case the problem is reduced to that of ensuring convergence of an iterative process for disaggre-gating higher level information within that block (see, for ex-ample, [13]), while the interrelations of that block with other elements in the complex are dealt with as before at the upper level.

However, a single disaggregated block which is only linked with its aggregated equivalent is an isolated and foreign ele-ment in a set of models. If we are to observe the principle of maximizing feedback it must mean precisely that we have to construct a whole system of disaggregated blocks to be linked up at the next informational level.

The principle that the level of abstraction (or the extent to which information is aggregated, which in this case is the same thing) should be appropriate to the objective of the modeling process means that information must be assigned to a level of the hierarchy of economic data appropriate to the analytical, planning, or forecasting problem which the model is to solve.

An outline of the upper level of a set of models is shown in Figure 1. Obviously, such a flow diagram cannot express the nature of interrelationships between the various economic vari-ables nor the size either of the problem or of its individual components; however, it does allow us to follow the direction of the functional relationships in the system; also (and this is

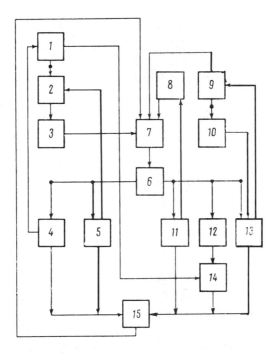

Figure 1. A flow diagram of the upper level of an integrated set of models. Blocks of calculations are denoted as follows. (1) The size and structure of the population; (2) education; (3) labor resources; (4) expenditure on health; (5) expenditure on culture, education, and training of personnel; (6) national income; (7) total social output; (8) natural resources; (9) fixed capital; (10) depreciation; (11) expenditure on prospecting for and exploiting mineral deposits and maintaining the environment; (12) money incomes; (13) capital investment; (14) consumption; (15) final social product.

particularly important) it clearly shows how closed the system is. The points at which the controls are applied (illustrated in Figure 1 by black dots) do not, of course, show all the possible ways of controlling the system; to describe these fully we need to move on to the next level of description — to the models themselves.

As an example, we shall consider the integrated set of macromodels which has been devised and used in the State Planning Commission (Gosplan) of the Lithuanian Soviet Socialist Republic; it is intended for long-term forecasting and for overall and regional planning within the republic [14]. The three functional subsystems in the complex are constructed in such a way that, the shorter the period for which the corresponding subsystem is intended, the more detailed the information it contains. The links between the three subsystems are shown in the diagram.

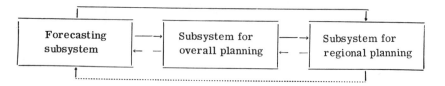

The links between subsystems in the integrated set of models for a republic.

The best developed component in the set is the subsystem for overall planning, which consists of eleven blocks, including forecasts for (1) population and (2) labor supply; and computations of (3) money income and expenditure; (4) personal consumption; (5) social consumption; (6) real incomes; (7) capital investment; (8) final consumption; (9) social product and national income; (10) resource requirements; and (11) a balance of the economy. The interrelationships between the blocks in the subsystem for overall planning are shown in Figure 2.

Long-term population forecasting is done by the components method; migration is also taken into account. This method allows us to compute the change in the age structure of the population, which is very important when the rate of reproduction varies from age group to age group and when there is a constant increase in the urban population as a proportion of the total population. Since the components method allows us to find the breakdown of the population by age and sex, it simultaneously solves the problem of computing the following age groups: infants; preschool population; school population; population of working age; and retired population.

The size of the population broken down by age and type at the end of year N^{t+1} is given by formula:

$$_0N^{t+1} = E_n(_0N^t \otimes H_i^t) + e_1(n^t \otimes h_0) + (N_m^{t+1} + N_v^{t+1}), \tag{1}$$

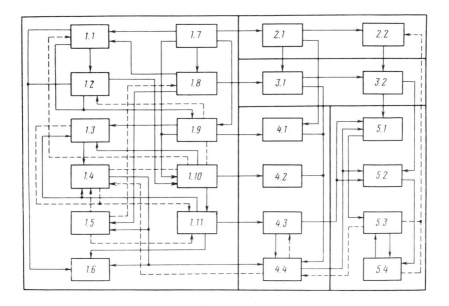

Figure 2. Interrelationships between blocks in the subsystem for overall planning. The numbers denote the following activities: 1.1 calculating money income and expenditure; 1.2 calculating real incomes; 1.3 determining final consumption; 1.4 calculating social product and national income; 1.5 balancing the demand for and supply of resources; 1.6 calculating the balance of the economy; 1.7 population forecasting; 1.8 forecasting labor supply; 1.9 determining personal consumption; 1.10 calculating social funds and public consumption; 1.11 fixing capital investment; 2.1 forecasting population by district [raion]; 2.2 forecasting the urban and rural populations by district; 3.1 identifying labor supply by district; 3.2 identifying urban and rural labor supply by district; 4.1 calculating personal consumption by district; 4.2 calculating social consumption by district; 4.3 allocating investment by district; 4.4 determining branch production levels in each district; 5.1 identifying constraints on the location of production units; 5.2 identifying constraints on the location of nonproductive organizations; 5.3 locating units involved in material production; 5.4 locating units involved in nonmaterial production.

where $_0N^t$ is a matrix of the size of the population by age and type at the start of the plan year (101 age groups are distinguished and four population types: urban males, urban females, rural males, and rural females): H_i^t is a matrix of survival factors by age and population type; n^t is a vector of births (by population type); h_0 is a vector of survival factors for infants up to a year old (by population type); N_m^{t+1}, N_v^{t+1} are matrices of, respectively, intrarepublican and extrarepublican migration; E_n is an auxiliary matrix for switching from the i-th age group to the $(i+1)$-th[1]; e_1 is the unit vector and $\otimes$ is the symbol for multiplication element by element.

The vector n^t of births by population type is computed using the formula:

$$n^t = \left[\frac{1}{2} \sum_{i=15}^{49} \sigma_i^t \otimes ({}_0N_i^t + {}_0N_{i-1}^t \otimes H_{i-1}^t) \right] C_\eta^t, \qquad (2)$$

where σ_i^t is a matrix of birth rates by population type (the elements in columns 1 and 3 of the matrix are zero, as are rows 1-15 and 50-101 in columns 2 and 4); C_η^t is an auxiliary matrix for distributing births by population type.

The third component in formula (1) takes account firstly of net intrarepublican migration, caused by a redistribution of the population between town and country, secondly of extrarepublican migration, and thirdly of the increases in urban population caused by administrative reclassification of rural areas as urban and suburban (the model aggregates this with intrarepublican migration). The average population over the year is taken as the arithmetic mean of the numbers of the start of the year and at year end.

This information enables us to determine the supply of labor. In order to find how labor is allocated by branch and by sphere of activity in the plan period, we first have to identify the factors which affect this allocation.

Factors tending to increase the supply of labor are: an increase in the number of entrants to the work force from general schools, professional and technical colleges, and universities; arrivals from other republics; and reductions in the number of persons occupied with domestic or private work. Factors tending to reduce labor supply are deaths and emigration to other republics.

Some modifications have been made in the Central Mathematical Economics Institute of the USSR Academy of Sciences

(TsEMI) to a demographic model based on the idea of combining demographic balances and multiple regression equations. A matrix of transitional probabilities has been introduced into the model, which makes it possible to base the calculations on migration flows broken down by age group rather than the data from a migration balance. The birth rates for the age groups used in the modified version of the model are not based on expert assessment but on multiple regression equations. This procedure automatically opens up further possibilities for incorporating this block in a system of interrelationships with other submodels.

Labor supply is calculated using the "personnel" model. For simplicity a number of submodels are distinguished, corresponding to the following aspects: (1) preschool institutions; (2) eight-year general schools; (3) general middle schools; (4) technical schools; (5) specialized secondary schools; (6) higher educational institutions; (7) employment.

The basic information used in the calculations is in the form of structural matrices M_k^t, corresponding to the aspects cited above; here k is an index for the organization, which gives the actual breakdown of the persons engaged in each activity (i) by year of education and age group ($k=2, 3, 4, 5, 6$); (ii) by age group ($k=1$); and (iii) by sector and age group ($k=7$).

By formalizing the relationship between these submodels we can switch from an initial vector of labor demand L_1^{t+1} to a vector L_2^{t+1} which takes account of the reallocation of labor among sectors within the republic.

The way in which we get from L_1^{t+1} to L_2^{t+1} can be described in simplified terms as follows. Suppose we have a number of matrices M_k^t, showing the distribution of students in the k-th type of educational institution by year of study and by age at time t. As we move a year forward in the model for population forecasting (i.e., as we switch to $t+1$) we replace matrices M_k^t with matrices M_k^{t+1}. By making this switch the model reveals how the number of pupils and students changes by age and year of education (taking acccount of the dropout rate from the particular educational institution); how graduates from general schools are allocated to other types of educational institutions and the various sectors in the republic's economy; how dropouts from one school are distributed among other educational institutes and the branches of the economy; we also learn the breakdown of the pupils and students in their first year of education.

Our model of the movements of labor between branches is based on two major assumptions. Firstly, the major factor regulating the mobility of labor is demand for labor in the branches. It is assumed that demand for labor in branch l in year t affects the supply of labor in year $t+1$. Secondly, we introduce an elasticity of the supply of labor with respect to the demand for labor. A vector $\bar{L}_n^{t+1}$ shows how the supply of labor to branches in the republic in year $t+1$ is affected by the demand for labor; it is given by the expression: [2]

$$\bar{L}_n^{t+1} = L_2^{t+1} + (\hat{L}_p{}^t \hat{L}_p^{t-1} - E)\hat{e}_p^{t+1} L_2^{t+1}, \tag{3}$$

Here L_p^{t-1} and $L_p{}^t$ are respectively vectors of the branches' demand for labor in the two previous years, as given by the block of calculations dealing with the demand for labor; and e_p^{t+1} is a vector of forecast values of the elasticity of the supply of labor with respect to demand in year $t+1$, as found by time series analysis.

These labor supply calculations give us the allocation of labor to the branches in the republic in each year.

The information derived from the demographic and employment forecasts is subsequently used to calculate indices of the growth of welfare. The data contained in a differentiated balance of income and expenditure can be used to evaluate living standards [15].

The process of constructing and using a differentiated balance involves the following stages. We first verify that the average per capita income of manual workers, office workers, and collective farmers is distributed log-normally. This is done by analyzing the standardized mean absolute deviation from the arithmetic mean of the logarithm of incomes and standardized central third- and fourth-order moments. If there is no significant difference between the sample estimates and the theoretical values, then we can assume that the distribution is normal.

In the second stage we use the log-normal model to compute a theoretical distribution of per capita income based on the general properties of the distribution we seek: the logarithm of average per capita income (as calculated from aggregate national income data) and its variance as given by budget survey data. The parameters of the log-normal distribution are found by the formula:

$$\overline{\ln x} = \ln \overline{x} - \frac{1}{2} \sigma_{\ln x}^{2}, \tag{4}$$

where x is the annual per capita income and σ is the standard deviation of its logarithm. We compute the probability distribution by taking the difference between successive values of the cumulative frequency of the normal distribution; this shows the relative size of the population group with a particular per capita income. By multiplying these percentages by the total population we find the distribution by per capita income.

At the third stage we check how close the sample distribution is to the estimated distribution, using Pearson's criterion. In the fourth and final stage the values of the individual indices in the differentiated balance are computed with the help of matrices showing the structure of money income and expenditure in homogeneous socioeconomic groups. The construction of the matrices is based on an assumption concerning the homogeneity of consumers. By this assumption, one can use budget studies to identify a specific structure of income and expenditure for each socioeconomic group. As incomes increase, some families are shifted from lower income groups to higher ones. Thus frequencies decline in the lower and rise in the higher intervals. Consequently, the structure of expenditure can be viewed as a function of the distribution of consumers by per capita income.

The most important item in personal expenditure is the purchase of goods through state and cooperative trade. If this item is to be disentangled, we have to forecast the level and structure of demand. For long-term calculations the structure of the model is geared toward the use of physiological or rational norms for the consumption of individual commodities.

In modeling demand in the medium term, the following factors are taken into account: the level of per capita income; the retail price of particular commodities; the share of income in kind in total consumption of particular foodstuffs; and a time trend. In longer term calculations account is taken of the change in the ratio of the rural to the urban population in the republic.

The estimate of social consumption over the plan period should be coordinated with figures for consumption as a whole and for final output by branch of material production.

Since we have not yet developed a normative method for determining the structure of expenditure in nonmaterial production sectors, we can use the sample surveys carried out when input-output tables are compiled for the republic. Such inquiries are highly representative.

Using data in the second quadrant of the ex post input-output table, we construct a matrix $A_v{}^t$ of the structure of material inputs used in nonmaterial production. The rows of matrix $A_v{}^t$ correspond to pure material production branches, and the columns correspond to branches involved in nonmaterial production. Thus the vector of social consumption for the plan period is given by:

$$V^t = A_v{}^t V_i{}^t, \tag{5}$$

where $V_i{}^t$ is a vector of material inputs in branches involved in nonmaterial production over the plan period.

Further work in the area of modeling the operation of the nonproductive sphere is being carried out jointly by the Research Institute for Economics and Planning (NIIEP) attached to the State Planning Commission of the Lithuanian Soviet Socialist Republic and by TsEMI. In these studies the nonproductive sphere is broken down into major branches, and a value is found for demand for the services of each branch and for employment, investment, and material inputs in each branch. Special indices are used to calculate demand for services (for example — the number of visits to the doctor per person per year, or the number of pupils by type of education, etc.); the figures are found using regression equations.

To model investment, branches are differentiated in accordance with their lag structure, in order to take account of the time taken to construct plants and the breakdown of capital expenditure by year. First, a calculation is made of how output will grow over the period equaling the longest construction time — i.e., over the period equal to the longest lag. A vector of increases in gross output levels is found from the input-output equation:

$$\Delta q(t) = [E - (E - \hat{m}_1)A - (E - \hat{m}_1)\hat{W}_1]^{-1}(E - \hat{m}_1)\Delta y(t), \qquad (6)$$

Here $\Delta y(t)$ is the increment in final output in year t ; m_1 is a vector of the proportions of imports to total resources; W_i is a vector of the proportion of exports in output; and A is a matrix of direct input coefficients.

Using a branch specialization matrix C_x , we can switch to a vector of gross outputs by administrative branch $\Delta x(t)$:

$$\Delta x(t) = C_x^{-1}(E - \hat{h}_{75})\Delta q(t), \qquad (7)$$

where h_{75} is a vector of the percentage rate of turnover tax on the gross output of the pure sectors. A calculation is then made of the fixed productive investment $f_i(t)$ needed to sustain the increase in gross output $\Delta x(t)$

$$f_\cdot(t) = (E - \hat{h}_{72})\hat{Z}(E - h_{76})\Delta x(t) + \hat{h}_{72}f_3(t-1), \qquad (8)$$

Here h_{76} is a vector indicating what proportion of the increase in output is obtained by increasing labor productivity without further investment; h_{72} is a vector of depreciation coefficients for fixed capita; Z is a vector of branch capital-output ratios; and f_3 is a vector of the average level of fixed capital over the year.

Using vector $h_{77}(t)$ (the elements of which show how much of the overall value of capital installed in each branch in year

t is the result of investment made in the plan year), we can find the vector of productive investment required in the plan year by using the formula:

$$s_1 = \hat{C}_3^{-1} \sum_{t=1}^{\Gamma} h_{77}(t) f_4(t),$$
(9)

Here C_3 is a vector of coefficients for adjusting data for the actual installation of fixed productive capital by administrative branch into average figures for the year.

Having determined capital investment, we next move on to the block covering changes in fixed capital. However, we do not give a description of this block here.[3]

The vector of final demand is found by summing its individual components (ignoring the interrepublican trade balance):

$$y = C_y l + v + s_1 + s_2 + \sigma + \sigma_3,$$
(10)

Here σ_3 is a vector of changes in working capital and stocks over the plan year; C_y is a conversion matrix, translating personal consumption from a commodity classification to a classification in terms of pure branches (the number of rows in the matrix corresponds to the number of pure branches distinguished, and the number of columns to the number of commodities; the sum of the elements in each column is one — i.e., each commodity is fully allocated to the pure branches); l is a vector of retail turnover, classified by commodity; [v is a vector of social consumption;] σ is a vector for repairs to fixed capital; s_1 and s_2 are respectively vectors of capital investment in the productive and nonproductive sectors.

Knowing the vector of final demand we can go on to determine a vector of gross output by branch.

Output levels by administrative branch (vector q) are computed as:

$$q = [E - (E - \hat{m}_1) A - (E - \hat{m}_1) \hat{W}_1]^{-1} [E - \hat{m}_1 (y + W_2)],$$
(11)

where W_2 is a vector of "obligatory" exports. Bearing in mind that under the existing system of planning and control of the economy of a union republic there are three forms of subordination — (1) Union, (2) Union-republican, and (3) republican — equation (11) can be rewritten as follows (for any q_i where $i=1, 2, 3$):

$$q_i=[E-(E-\hat{m}_i)A_i-(E-\hat{m}_i)\hat{W}_i]^{-1}\Big\{ (E-\hat{m}_i)(y+W_2)-$$
$$\sum_{j\neq i} [E-(E-\hat{m}_i)A_j-(E-\hat{m}_i)\hat{W}_i]q_j\Big\}. \tag{12}$$

Having found the major variables for the development of the branches involved in material and nonmaterial production, we can move on to compute the distribution of national income. National income produced is given by:

$$\gamma=I'(E-A)q-I'\sigma_4, \tag{13}$$

where I' is a unit row vector and σ_4 is a vector of depreciation. We compute national income utilized in the republic by deducting the balance of trade ω from γ :

$$\beta=\gamma-\omega. \tag{14}$$

For a given share of accumulation α, the following condition must be observed:

$$\alpha\beta+I'\sigma_4=I'(s_1+s_2+\sigma+\sigma_3), \tag{15}$$

from which it follows that:

$$\alpha=[I'(s_1+s_2+\sigma+\sigma_3-\sigma_4)]\beta^{-1}, \tag{16}$$

where s_1 is a vector of productive investment; s_2 is a vector of nonproductive investment; σ is a vector of repairs to fixed capital; and σ_3 is a vector of increases in working capital and stocks.

On the other hand accumulation G is determined by the change in fixed capital and in unfinished construction:

$$G=I'\Delta f_1+I'\Delta f_2+I'\sigma_5, \tag{17}$$

where Δf_1 is a vector of fixed capital accumulation in the productive sphere; Δf_2 is a vector of capital accumulation in the nonproductive sphere; and σ_5 is a vector expressing the change in unfinished construction.

By calculating the same variable by two different methods, we can devise a procedure for choosing the final value via an iterative process, and this eliminates one of the exogenous elements in the set of models. The model is closed overall by the supply of labor, since one cannot reallocate labor between regions in the same way as one can shift fuel or raw materials or investment. At the current stage of readiness of the integrated set of models, the role of closing the model is performed by a modified production function. But at the same time both the Scientific Research Institute for Economics and Planning attached to the State Planning Commission in Lithuania and TsEMI are working intensively on experimental methods for closing the model iteratively. The preliminary results of this work justify our hopes that a fully closed set of models constructed on the basis of the principles set out above will become a reality in the near future.

NOTES

1) In the case of the age group 99, E_n also adds in survivors in age group 100.
2) The symbol $\wedge$ indicates that the corresponding vector is transformed into a diagonal matrix.
3) The level of nonproductive investment is determined in a simplified way as a proportion of the level of productive investment.

REFERENCES

1. Aganbegian, A. G. "Sistema ekonomiko-matematicheskikh modelei optimal'nogo territorial'no-proizvodstvennogo planirovaniia na perspektivu." In Problemy narodnokhoziaistvennogo optimuma. Novosibirsk: 1968.

2. Aganbegian, A. G., and Bagrinovskii, K. A. "Postanovka lokal'nykh zadach c fondirovaniem global'nykh resursov." In Matematicheskie metody v ekonomike. Novosibirsk: 1968.

3. Problemy optimal'nogo funktsionirovaniia sotsialisticheskoi ekonomiki. Moscow: "Nauka" Publishers, 1972.

4. Econometric Methods for the Medium-Term Economic Plan 1964-8. A Report by the Committee on Econometric Methods, Economic Planning Agency, Government of Japan, August 1965.

5. Forrester, J. W. World Dynamics. Cambridge: 1971.

6. Meadows, D. The Limits to Growth. New York: 1971.
7. Mesarovic, M., and Pestel, E. The Population Model. Multilevel Model Project. Technical University, Hanover, April 1974.
8. Matematika i kibernetika v ekonomike. Slovar'-spravochnik. Moscow: "Ekonomika" Publishers, 1975.
9. Filosofskii slovar'. Moscow: "Politizdat" Publishers, 1968.
10. Issledovaniia po obshchei teorii sistem. Moscow: "Progress" Publishers, 1969.
11. Dadaian, V. S, and Kiseleva, V. V. "Metodologicheskie printsipy razrabotki dolgosrochnogo ekonomicheskogo prognoza v svodnykh pokazateliakh." In Problemy planirovaniia i prognozirovaniia. Moscow: "Nauka" Publishers, 1974.
12. Sharikadze, V. A., and Basalaeva, N. A. Obshchee opisanie integrirovannogo kompleksa modelei analiza reshenii v masshtabakh soiuznoi respubliki, preprint. Moscow: TsEMI AN SSSR, 1974.
13. Dudkin, L. M., and Ershov, E. B. "Mezhotraslevoi balans i material'nye balansy otdel'nykh productov." Planovoe khoziaistvo, 1965, no. 5.
14. Raiatskas, R. L., and Zhemaitaitite, S. A. Informatsiia-Prognoz-Plan. Moscow: "Ekonomika" Publishers, 1972.
15. Dokhody i pokupatel'skii spros naseleniia. Moscow: "Statistika" Publishers, 1968.

Received November 20, 1975

Part 3

The Analysis of
Consumer Behavior

INTRODUCTION

Alastair McAuley

The study of consumer demand in the Soviet Union, both empirical and theoretical, has come about largely in the last twenty years. During that period, however, the topic has attracted considerable attention, and a voluminous literature now exists. The current selection includes four recent contributions to the field; in these introductory paragraphs, we shall provide a brief survey of the area as a whole. A more detailed assessment can be found in [3] .

Studies of empirical demand in the USSR have been intended, in the first instance, to serve as an adjunct to traditional methods of planning. The reasons for a revival of interest in this topic can therefore be found in the evolution of the economy after 1955 and in the emergence of more formal theorizing about the nature of planning and the role the state should play in it. Since these antecedents have influenced the character of the work that has been undertaken, it is worth examining them in slightly greater detail.

Under Stalin the central authorities had no difficulty in disposing of the consumer goods that were produced (the problem was rather one of producing enough to satisfy demand). Empirical studies of consumer behavior were unnecessary, and the issue of consumer sovereignty (choice) received little attention in Stalinist economic theory. Increases in per capita incomes after 1953, however, together with a significant expansion in the quantity and variety of consumer goods produced, made Soviet consumers more particular. The early 1960s witnessed the emergence of a number of problems in the marketing of consumer goods: there were substantial increases in the inventories of some goods, while others continued to be in short supply, and savings deposits began to increase.

In response to these (and other) economic problems, first Khrushchev and then Kosygin called for the development of economic theory and the introduction of more scientific methods of planning. The revival of interest in the study of demand was a response to this call and to the underlying problems that prompted it. At the same time, its specifically empirical character also owed something to the growing availability of computers in the USSR. As a result, it became possible to undertake, as a matter of routine, calculations that previously would have been embarked upon only by the most dedicated investigator.

In a Soviet-type economy, the composition of output is determined largely by the plan; it is the central planners who bear the responsibility for ensuring that demand and supply are in equilibrium. Once it is accepted that the income elasticity of demand for different categories of consumption may differ, increases in per capita income (or changes in the distribution of income) imply changes in the composition of consumer demand. These changes must be met by adjustments in the pattern of output or prices if market equilibrium is to be maintained. The accumulation of inventories and the persistence of shortages mentioned above have been almost universally attributed to the planners' inability to predict these changes in demand, and it is this problem that has attracted the attention of major research teams. One of the contributions included here (Maier and Ershov) is a description of the forecasting model used by Gosplan in the preparation of the 1971-75 plan. It presumably represents the best currently feasible solution to the problem. On the whole, it is unimpressive, and below I suggest reasons for this.

The demand-forecasting problem that the Gosplan model is

intended to solve requires the estimation of a consistent set of
equations — where, by consistency, I mean that the sum of predicted expenditures should equal total predicted expenditure.
This calls for the estimation of large numbers of parameters
from a limited amount of data. In such circumstances, Western
economists have used restrictions drawn from the assumption
of utility maximization (together with the so-called Slutsky hypothesis that the market as a whole acts as if it maximized a
utility function) to improve the efficiency of estimation. The
result has been complete systems of demand equations derived,
for example, from the linear expenditure system or the Rotterdam model. (Unfortunately, the restrictions of demand theory
are usually rejected in such exercises — that is, the resultant
equations do not fit the data very well. This should probably be
taken to imply that the Slutsky hypothesis is false and that alternative aggregation procedures should be employed.) The
traditional Soviet analysis of demand rejects the hypothesis of
utility maximization but fails to provide a rigorous formal development of any alternative. As a consequence, Soviet econo-
metricians have not managed to generate alternative restrictions that would improve the efficiency of estimation. Nor have
they published estimates of a complete system of demand equations based on Soviet data. This failure can be attributed only
partly to the shortcomings of Soviet theory, however. Economists are certainly aware of both the LES and Rotterdam models, and the former has been used to analyze consumer demand
in the United States [5, 8].

A second factor that has almost certainly contributed to the
shortcomings of various Gosplan forecasting models is the nature of the data available for their estimation. (Data problems
have also undermined the validity of more academic inquiries,
as Mikhalevskii and Solov'ev point out in their study.) In principle, there are two approaches that may be adopted in estimating demand equations: either they may be derived from
time series on retail trade expenditures, or they may be based
on cross-sectional (survey) data on family expenditures at a
given point in time. Western economists have shown a slight

predilection for the former approach, since it usually ensures greater variability in relative prices. Both sorts of data exist in the USSR and both have been used by Gosplan for demand-forecasting purposes. (In the preparation of the 1966-70 plan, the time-series approach was used, whereas Maier and Ershov rely on family-budget survey materials.) It is claimed, however, that both sorts of data suffer from serious shortcomings.

In view of the inadequacies of the demand-function approach to generating forecasts of the structure of consumers' expenditures in future years, economists at Gosplan have continued to work on the "rational norms" approach as well. In essence, this involves specification by a panel of experts of a pattern of purchases that they regard as rational for any given level of income (expenditure). This was the procedure used to plan consumption before 1965 — and its weaknesses did much to prompt the revival of interest in the empirical study of demand reviewed here. This approach is described in more detail in [4] and [6]. It appears that the forecasts of demand used in the most recent five-year plans have been derived by some combination of expert assessment and empirical projection [8, p. 65]. Expert assessment still provides the only procedure for generating demand forecasts to be included in long-term (ten- or twenty-year) plans.

The market disequilibria that emerged in the USSR in the early 1960s were particularly troublesome in the field of consumers' durables, and factors influencing the demand for these have been a subject of special study since the mid-1960s. The nature of the problem can perhaps best be indicated by an account of the difficulties encountered in the production and marketing of one such item. When sewing machines for sale to the general public were put into mass production in the 1950s, planners had little idea of the extent of demand for them; indeed, they had only the most rudimentary conception of the factors that might influence it. Consequently (and in line with general planning procedures of the day), they based future output plans on current sales without making any allowance for stocks in the hands of the public. The result was that inven-

tories of unsold machines built up. In response, output was reduced and factories were reequipped to produce other goods.
But once again the planners were caught out. They had failed
to allow for replacement demand. In the mid-1960s, sewing
machines were again in short supply and capacity had to be re-
converted to their production. (For more detail on these developments, see [3, section V] and the sources cited there.)

It is clear from this account that a knowledge of the demand
function for sewing machines would have enabled the planners
to avoid some of their mistakes. A number of Soviet economists
have published estimates of demand functions for analogous
durables in the past ten or fifteen years. One example of this
genre is included here (Chitashvili). As Chitashvili points out,
a knowledge of the demand function for a particular consumer
durable allows the planners to do more than avoid production
scheduling errors. Given a knowledge of the time form of demand, as well as data on the costs of various investment programs, planners can calculate the costs (welfare losses) of al-
lowing excess demand to persist for a greater or shorter period. That is, they can attempt to devise an optimal investment
program.

A knowledge of the scale and structure of demand is desirable
not only for central planners. There is scope for what may be
called market research by individual manufacturers and retail
stores. Many of the books and articles on demand analysis that
have been published in the USSR in the past twenty years either
have been intended to provide managers with a basic tool kit for
conducting such inquiries (explaining the concept of a demand
function, defining price and income elasticities, and describing
how they can be calculated) or have themselves been reports
of such investigations. The bulk of Soviet work in this genre
has shown little sophistication, either in the derivation or in
the estimation of relationships. No examples of it are included
here, although this category probably includes a majority of the
titles that have been published.

The three sorts of empirical demand study described so far
have been limited in scope and practical in intent. But the em-

pirical study of demand has also been undertaken by those with more academic interests, and it is from this class that the remaining two contributions included here are taken. The revival of economics as a discipline in the 1960s led to the emergence of a Soviet school of mathematical economics. Among the questions workers in this field set themselves was that of which criteria were or should be used by planners in determining the composition of output or the directions of development for the economy as a whole. This issue of optimal planning or the optimal functioning of a planned economy raises the question of the existence and specification of a social welfare function. This latter topic is one of the most fundamental in welfare economics, and it is clearly impossible to do justice to the range of Soviet thinking about it here. But one of the solutions proposed might be described as the "revealed preference approach." It is to this school that the Mikhalevskii and Solov'ev study included here belongs. Very crudely, the argument runs as follows: the social welfare function should incorporate the welfare of individuals, which in turn derives from their preferences; consumers' behavior in the market can be used to infer properties of their preferences, which can then be incorporated into the social welfare function and thus used by planners. There are serious logical difficulties involved in this argument, but it has resulted in a number of suggestive demand studies. (A more extended discussion of the conceptual and practical problems associated with Soviet work on optimal planning can be found in [7] and [1]. For a recent Soviet assessment of these questions, see [2].)

The last selection included here is rather different. The problem posed by Aivazian, Bezhaeva, and Makarchuk is as follows: given information about the consumption behavior of individual households, is it possible to classify them into mutually exclusive categories (i.e., can one suggest that they are maximizing different utility functions)? Second, on the basis of other, possibly socioeconomic, data on these households, is it possible to derive an algorithm that will assign them to one or another consumption class? The results of this inquiry (as given in the book from which the excerpt included here is taken) are meager. But the formulation of the problem and the analysis developed are thought provoking. For example, they provide one possible way of modifying the Slutsky hypothesis. Even if the market as a whole does not react to changes in income and prices as if it were maximizing a collective utility function, it is possible that one will be able to describe the behavior of more homogeneous groups of consumers in this way. The second stage may provide an operational procedure for predicting how the relative importance of these subgroups changes. That is, a solution to the Aivazian problem may improve the quality of demand-function estimation in a variety of environments.

In this introduction, I have described the different types of work on demand that have been undertaken in the USSR in the past two decades. In general, I would suggest that the level of sophistication has not been high, in either analysis or estimation. But much of the work has been competent. Surely it has contributed to the effectiveness of planning. At its best, however, it has provided insight and understanding. This is borne out by the contributions published here.

Alastair McAuley

References

1. Despres, Laure. "Politique économique et fonction objectif de plan." In Marie Lavigne (ed.), Economie politique de la planification en système socialiste. Paris, 1978, pp. 38-61.
2. Gavrilets, N. Iu. "The Measurement of Utility and the Concept of Optimality." Matekon, Spring 1980, pp. 82-109.
3. McAuley, A. "The Empirical Study of Demand in the Soviet Union." Jahrbuch der Wirtschaft Osteuropas, 1980.
4. Maier, V. F., and Suvorov, V. V. "Some Aspects of Using Rational Consumption Budgets." Matekon, Fall 1980.
5. Mekler, S. G. "Prognoz potrebitelskogo sprosa po sisteme funktsii tipa Stouna." Ekonomika i matematicheskie metody, 1972, vol. 8, no. 2, pp. 276-82.
6. Raitsin, V. Ia. Planning the Standard of Living according to Consumption Norms. New York: International Arts and Sciences Press, 1969.

7. Seurot, F. "La fonction d'utilité sociale en système socialiste." In Marie Lavigne (ed.), Economie politique de la planification en système socialiste. Paris, 1978, pp. 15-37.

8. Solov'ev, Iu. P., and Druker, S. G. "Methodological Problems in Analyzing and Forecasting Consumer Demand." Matekon, Fall 1979, pp. 43-66.

FORECASTING THE STRUCTURE OF PERSONAL CONSUMPTION

V. F. Maier and E. B. Ershov

The theoretical basis for forecasting the structure of consumption is the idea that the structure of consumption depends on the level of consumption. The structure of consumption thus can always be expressed as a function of its level. Within the framework of commodity-money relations, this implies that the structure of consumption depends upon the level of income.

Both formulations are particular reflections of the dependence of the level and structure of consumption on production, since the higher the level of development of production, the broader the range of people's needs and the greater the possibilities for their fuller satisfaction; also, the higher the level of actual consumption and the higher the degree of satisfaction of both total and individual needs.

The structure of consumption is also influenced by a number of other factors, both economic and noneconomic. The most important of these must also be taken into account in plan projections and forecasting exercises.

As noted above, the methodological basis of short- and medium-term forecasts of the structure of personal consumption

Russian text © 1971 by "Mysl'" Publishers, Moscow. "Prognoz struktury individual'nogo potrebleniia," in Nauchnye osnovy ekonomicheskogo prognoza, pp. 358-74.

is the so-called behavioral approach. Under this approach, we formulate the forecasting problem as follows: how will the population behave in economic terms at a given income level and with given objective conditions influencing the structure of consumption over the plan period? In other words, in the short and medium terms, forecasting of the structure of that part of consumption sustained by personal income reduces to forecasting of the structure of consumer demand.[1]

The relationship between the factors influencing the structure of consumption (or demand) can be identified, estimated quantitatively, and embodied in a model of some kind, normally a mathematical model. The ability to express the relationships that interest us in quantitative terms and to construct the corresponding models forms the methodological basis for short-term and medium-term forecasting of the structure of consumption.

A large variety of models of consumption are described in the literature. The prospects for using most of them in practice are very doubtful, both because of their complexity and because the data are lacking. Hence, when the matters at issue are not abstract concepts but the concrete needs of planning in practice, one must go from the simple to the complex, starting by using the simplest models that are suitable for practical application.

One may distinguish two types of models of consumption (or demand): dynamic models and structural models. For the most part, we have designed structural models, into which we progressively incorporate time trends. Thus, we have sought to combine the merits and advantages of both types of model. This work is based on differentiated balances of incomes and consumption of the population.

At the Scientific Research Institute for Economics (NIEI) of USSR Gosplan, a method has been devised for constructing a differentiated balance of incomes and consumption, based on the notion of combining data from family budget surveys with data from the balances of the national economy covering incomes and consumption. As a result, it has been possible to construct differentiated balances for a number of accounting and plan

years. The major elements in the differentiated balances prepared at Gosplan's Scientific Research Institute for Economics
are the model of the distribution of income described above
[not included here — editor], models for the structure of income and the structure of consumption, differentiated by social
groups and income class, and also a model for family size and
composition.

The demand model in the differentiated balance can be represented as a balance table of the matrix type, and also as a sum of
demand functions, each of which shows analytically how the demand for each group of consumer goods or services depends
on total expenditure (or income):

$$y_i = f_i(x) \quad (i = 1,2, \ldots, n)$$

and

$$\sum_{i=1}^{n} y_i = \sum_{i=1}^{n} f_i(x),$$

where y_i is the consumption of the given commodity, or commodity group; x is expenditure on all goods (the level of income); and n is the number of commodity groups.

Formally, the demand functions given above only relate the
structure of consumption to the level of income. In fact, however, as will be shown in more detail below, they also take into
account a number of other factors affecting the structure of
demand.

If we assume that the demand functions are unchanged over
time, then, if we have data from the plan on the average income
of the population both as a whole and broken down by social
groups, if we have data on the size of these groups, and if we
also have a forecast of the distribution of the population by income level in the plan year, we can construct a differentiated
model of consumption setting out the structure of consumer demand in the plan year. The first calculations of this type, for
1970, were made in 1965-66, using data first for 1964, then for
1965.

The parameters in demand functions, however, change gradually over time. From among the factors that cause a change in the structure of consumption and thus affect the parameters of the demand functions, it is possible to identify, first, changes in the age-sex composition of the population and, second, long-run tendencies that change the pattern of consumption. Within the second group, we can distinguish improvements in the structure of consumption occurring as a result of increases in output, rise in cultural level, and changes in family size. Since the changes in family size in our country are all in one direction, under the particular circumstances of our economy there is no need in practice to distinguish among the influence of these factors when forecasting the structure of consumption.

The remaining factors are random in nature; their influence on the structure of consumption is quite insignificant.

We should at this juncture emphasize the fact that forecasts of the structure of consumption made on the basis of a differentiated balance of incomes and consumption are macroeconomic in character. They can be used to determine the rate of growth of social production, the structure of development, and the overall breakdown of production and investment. The forecast is made in aggregate terms (broken down into 25 to 30 categories of consumption goods and services for which the population pays) and does not tackle the issue of changes in the detailed composition of individual goods or commodity groups. Hence, we can limit ourselves to taking account of the influences on the structure of consumption enumerated above.

When the scientific materials were being prepared for the draft of the Major Directions for the Development of the USSR Economy in 1971-75, an attempt was made to incorporate time factors into the models, i.e., to incorporate factors that change the structure of consumption at a given level of real income, or (what amounts to the same thing) to incorporate factors changing the parameters of the demand functions over time.

The starting point for the calculations is a given level (or increase) in total real incomes, both for the population as a whole and for individual social groups. Having calculated real incomes, we determine nominal personal income, which corresponds to the overall total of personal consumption and expenditure of the population.

We then calculate the distribution of the population by per capita nominal income in the base years, an intermediate year, and the planned year. For practical calculations with the model described here, 1965 and 1966 were taken as base years, 1970 was adopted as the intermediate year (plan data were used), and 1975 was the plan year, for which the structure of consumption corresponding to demand was to be determined.

In order to find regression equations that express mathematically the quantitative relationship between the level of income and consumption (or expenditure) in the base years, the physical composition of total personal consumption (expenditures) was calculated, and separate models of consumption by workers, other state employees, and peasants were estimated.

As a basis for the forecasts, we used regression equations constructed by averaging the parameters of the regression equations for the two base years. The averaging was done to eliminate from the forecast the random fluctuations in the structure of consumption and in the quantitative relationships between consumption and income that can occur if one uses data for a single year.

In order to take account of changes in the age-sex composition of the population in the accounting period (i.e., the period between the base years and the intermediate year) and in the plan period, we identify coefficients showing the impact of the age-sex composition of the population on the structure of demand.

For this purpose, age-sex coefficients for each income group were weighted by the size of each group and coefficients were

Table 1

	Consumption coefficients for each age-sex grouping			
	Of working age		Of both sexes	
Consumer good	Men	Women	Children	Elderly
Milk	1.0	1.71	2.29	1.04

found for workers, employees, and peasants; after weighting these by the share of each social group, we found consumption coefficients for any commodity for the population as a whole.

As a result, we obtain information in the following form[2] (see Table 1).

By weighting these coefficients by the share of each group in the total population in the base and plan years, we get for each year an average coefficient for consumption of that product by the total population. Thus, for milk the corresponding coefficient was 1.63 for the base year and 1.56 for the intermediate year.

By dividing the averaged coefficient for consumption of milk in the intermediate year by the corresponding coefficient for the base year, we get a correction coefficient for milk consumption in the intermediate year. This is 1.56/1.63 = 0.9571.

Coefficients to correct for changes in the impact of the age-sex structure on consumption are introduced into the model by making the appropriate corrections to the parameters of the regression equations.

Using the corrected regression equation for the base years and data on the average level and distribution of income, we compute differentiated models of consumption (or demand) for the intermediate year, and we then find the level and structure of personal consumption (expenditure) for that year which corresponds to demand. The results are a forecast of the structure of consumption (or demand) in the intermediate year, on the assumption that the relationships between the level of income and consumption that have operated in the base years vary only in accordance with changes in the age-sex structure of the population. The forecast of the structure of demand in the intermediate year is compared with the actual structure of personal consumption in that year, and coefficients are thus found that reflect how the structure of consumption changes over time under the impact of all other factors (those not incorporated into the model) and long-term trends.

Regression equations are calculated for the intermediate year to match the actual structure of consumption in that year.

Starting from the assumption that the time trends in the structure of consumption revealed in the period between the base and the intermediate years are also maintained in the plan period, we adjust the parameters in the regression equations for the intermediate year. The parameters thus derived are then corrected to take account of changes in the age-sex composition of the population that will occur in the plan period. As a result, we get regression equations for the plan period (or the end of the plan period).

Using these regression equations for the plan year and data for the level and distribution of income in that year, we compute differentiated models of consumption (or demand) and then find the level and structure of personal consumption (or demand) in the plan year.

The structure of consumption (or demand) we have derived incorporates the following factors: the growth of average income both for the population as a whole and for each social group; the change in the social structure of the population; income distribution (broken down by social group) and the age-sex structure of the population; and changes over time in the structure of consumption at a fixed real income in the direction and at the rate shown in the period between the base and intermediate years.

By using coefficients from an (aggregated) input-output model giving the relationship between net and gross output for each product in the plan year, we determine levels of output for agriculture and for the major sectors of industry producing consumer goods; these are needed to ensure that the composition of demand we have identified is feasible.

Starting from the overall structure of consumption and assuming that payments in kind continue at the same level and structure as in the intermediate year, an approximate estimate can be made of the level and structure of turnover in state and cooperative trade.

If, in the course of further work on drafting the plan, it is discovered that output cannot meet the desired composition of demand, we can calculate how much retail prices must change and in what direction to allow demand and supply to be brought into correspondence.

Before we used the system and procedure set out above, we performed a final test. We projected the structure of consumption for 1966 on the basis of data for 1961 (i.e., a retrospective forecast). For this purpose, we constructed a differentiated consumption model for 1961 and computed regression equations showing how consumption depended on income, first in current prices, then in 1966 prices. The parameters of the regression equations were then corrected for the change in the age-sex structure of the population in 1961-66, and the consumption structure for 1966 was computed using these equations.

For the major categories — all food products, nonfood products, and beverages — the forecast was fairly accurate. It was somewhat low for services and somewhat high for taxes, subscriptions, and savings. The latter is explained in part by the fact that the model was not able to take account of measures introduced during the period under consideration for the gradual abolition and reduction of taxes.

Time trends can be incorporated more fully into the differentiated model for the structure of consumption. The accounting data required to make this possible (in particular, differentiated models of consumption) have been prepared for a number of years.

Using the demand functions for each year, we calculate per capita consumption (consumption normatives) of each good for each income group (separately for workers, employees, and peasants) at a specified level of income (the same for each year).[3]

Per capita consumption normatives for each good and each income class (at predetermined levels of income) are regressed against time for each social group separately. The resultant equations for the per capita consumption normatives for each good and each income group are then extrapolated to the plan year.

Using the values of the per capita consumption norms derived from the third stage, we compute intermediate demand functions for each good broken down by social group, and we calculate an auxiliary differentiated model of consumption for the plan year. Using the method described above, we correct the differentiated consumption model for the plan year to take account of changes in the age-sex structure of the population.

Actual demand functions are computed using the differentiated consumption model thus revised.

One model, which is a modified version of that described above, does not forecast changes in per capita consumption normatives directly but forecasts the change over time in expenditure on any group of consumer goods per ruble of income; this is done separately for each income class within each social group. In practice, this model has been used mostly to forecast the internal structure of demand for individual commodity groups, including paid services (i.e., those for which charges are made); in order to do this, we used the corresponding demand functions to calculate coefficients of expenditure on services per ruble of annual income over the accounting period, making the calculation separately for each group in the population and each type of service.

Similar coefficients were also calculated for all paid services. Income in each group was fixed for all years at a level corresponding to the average in each interval. Thus, in the group with an annual income of 900-1,200 rubles per capita, the coefficient of expenditure on all paid services ranged from 0.0889 in the first year of the base period to 0.0941 in the eighth year.

The coefficients of relative expenditure by each group on paid services as a whole and on each kind of service separately were regressed against time, using a linear function.

Thus, taking household services as an example, we derived the following parameters (see Table 2).

The regression equation parameters shown in the table were found by processing eight years' data. In order to find the coefficient of expenditure by each group in the population and on each type of service separately (and also for paid services as a whole) under the conditions assumed for the plan year, we used

Table 2

Parameters	Income class		
	Lowest	Middle	Highest
"A" (constant)	0.0081	0.0041	0.0027
"B" (coefficient of the independent variable)	0.0006	0.0001	0.0003

the following formula: $y = a + nb$, where n is the number of years from the start of the accounting period to the end of the plan period.

Thus, for household services, coefficients b were found as follows:

for the lowest income group: 0.0018
for the middle income group: 0.0055
for the highest income group: 0.0073

The coefficients for expenditure on paid services show that, as income rises, the consumer spends an ever-increasing proportion of each additional ruble on services. The exception is expenditure on housing and municipal services. In this case, the expenditure coefficients fall from low income groups to high ones. This means that workers and employees spend relatively less on rent and municipal services, the higher their income. Whereas the lowest income group spends an average of 4.27 kopecks of each ruble for these purposes, the highest income group spends only 2.88 kopecks.

Using these coefficients, and data on the breakdown of the population into groups with different per capita income levels, we determine indices of average per capita expenditure on services by each group. By multiplying these indices by the numbers in the corresponding group, we calculate the level of paid services required in the plan year.

In another kind of differentiated model of the structure of consumption, the time factor is incorporated by forecasting the change in the parameters of the demand functions; as a result, the demand functions for the plan year are fixed directly. The original data for the calculations — as in the preceding model

— are differentiated models of consumption for the economy, developed over a number of years and expressed in the form of demand functions. A necessary condition for the use of this model is that the demand functions for each good be of the same form for each year of the base period. When we devised special models for the structure of consumption (or demand) showing the internal breakdown of particular commodity groups, we obtained reassuring results with this method.

USSR Gosplan's Scientific Research Institute for Economics has devised and tested in a number of practical calculations an original dynamic model for forecasting the level and structure of demand, using data prepared in a regional breakdown over a number of years.

We can illustrate the principle on which the model is based and the way it works by taking household services as an example. The original data for constructing the model were accounts covering actual expenditure by the population in the USSR as a whole and by union republic over ten years, data on the balance of money incomes and expenditure of the population (like the other indices, these were put in per capita form), and also data on the proportion of urban dwellers in the total population.

Using this information, we established how expenditure on services depended on the level of money income and the proportion of urban dwellers in the population as a whole. The dependence was expressed in the form of a linear multiple regression equation of the form:

$$y = a + bx_1 + cx_2,$$

where y is average per capita expenditure on household services; x_1 is money income (per capita); and x_2 is the proportion of urban dwellers in the population as a whole.

Using data for each republic, we employed a computer to estimate separate equations for productive and nonproductive services for each year of the period under consideration. Thus, for productive services for 1968 the parameters were as follows:

$a = -0.8772; \quad b = 0.0322; \quad c = 0.2255.$

Using unionwide data on per capita money income and the

share of urban dwellers in the total population of the USSR and employing the regression coefficients we had found, we derived estimates of what the population of the USSR would spend on household services (productive and nonproductive) for each year of the period under investigation.

Having identified the deviations between actual expenditure on household services over the accounting period and the indices as calculated, we corrected the regression equations we had used.

Indices calculated using regression equations naturally diverge somewhat from actual data. The parameters a were corrected in accordance with the size of the deviation.

Subsequently, all parameters were regressed against time. The regression equations derived as a result of this exercise show how the parameters a, b, and c change over time.

Below, we show these equations for productive services:

$$a = -1.3788 + 0.0182t;$$
$$b = 0.0088 + 0.0023t;$$
$$c = 0.0277 + 0.0218t.$$

By using these equations, we can derive the parameters in the original multiple regression equation for any year of the plan period.

On the basis of this equation, and starting from the average per capita income level in the plan year envisaged by the plan and the possible share of urban dwellers in the population of the USSR, we calculated average per capita expenditure on household services and, using the assumed population level, we calculated the demand for household services, productive and nonproductive.

We view this model as a very promising one. It can be used to determine the possible breakdown of monetary expenditure of the population (with applications for forecasting the balance of money incomes and expenditures of the population) and to forecast the structure of demand for products sold by the state and cooperative trade network, both for the USSR as a whole and for the union republics. In the latter case, data broken down by province or major town could be used as a starting point.

We stated above that, other things being equal, the structure of demand depends upon the age-sex composition of the population and that a change in the latter can be incorporated into forecasts of consumption (or demand); this can be done by including in the model correction factors showing how the consumption coefficients depend on the age and sex of the consumer.

The following method of finding the age-sex coefficients in the consumption of particular goods was developed on the basis of a general statistical method proposed by A. Ia. Boiarskii. This method was modified for use in processing data from budget studies.

The basis for finding the coefficients is a multiple regression equation, associating consumption of a particular good (or service) with the number of adults in a family, the proportion of children, and the per capita income level. In general form, the equation is:

$$y = a_0 + a_1 x_1 + a_2 x_2 + a_3 x_3,$$

where y is consumption per capita (in rubles); x_1 is the proportion of adults; x_2 is the proportion of children; and x_3 is per capita income.

After calculating partial correlation coefficients on the basis of budget data, we use them to determine a partial multiple regression equation; then the value of x_1 taken from the data can be inserted; x_2 is set equal to zero, which corresponds to assuming that there are no children in the group; and x_3 (group income) is fixed at the actual level. Thus, from the first step in the calculations, we derive estimates of consumption normatives for adults.

These normatives are subsequently broken down into consumption of an adult male and of an adult female. For this purpose, we used a multiple regression equation of the kind described above; y in the function is now the estimated standard consumption of an adult consumer, and the independent variables (x_1, x_2, x_3) are the proportions of men and women and the level of per capita income.

The resulting equation (as distinct from that considered earlier) is used to determine consumption norms for men and women. For these purposes, the magnitudes x_1 and x_2 are set consecutively at levels of 100 percent and 0 percent, and x_3 is set at the average per capita income of the group.

Consumption norms for the elderly were also obtained. For this, estimated consumption for men, women, and children was subtracted from total consumption of each specific good and the balance was divided by the number of elderly persons in the group.

In this way, we are able to derive consumption normatives for the most important goods and services and their values relative to the consumption of an adult male (i.e., age-sex consumption coefficients) both for the population as a whole broken down by social group and for income groups. The results of the calculation for the population as a whole are given in Table 3.

If we have consumption coefficients by age and sex and if we also know the age-sex composition of the population for each income and social group for both the accounting and the plan periods, our model for planning consumption can incorporate the changes in consumption per capita caused by changes in the age-sex composition of the population.

In order to resolve the many questions that arise if we are to raise national welfare, it is important that we have information on family size and composition together with data on the incomes of particular social groups. Such information can be derived by combining census materials with budget data.

Budget data are used as a starting point to model the size and composition of families grouped on the basis of per capita incomes. But if budget survey data are to be used for planning, they must be adjusted to take account of the corresponding values for the economy as a whole.

Table 3

	Consumption by			
	Man	Woman	Child	Elderly person
Food	1	0.968	0.469	0.915
Clothing	1	1.788	0.682	0.300
Drink	1	0.257	–	0.304
Services	1	1.566	0.544	0.871

There is an inverse relationship between per capita income and family size: the higher the income, the smaller the family. Empirical regression lines showing how family size depends on per capita income over a long period indicate that the relationship has been stable and invariant for all years examined.

Calculations have shown that an exponential curve gives the best approximation to the empirical data. In actual fact, we estimated for one year the following regression equations, showing the relationship between per capita income and family size:

for workers and other state employees: $lgy = 2.8014 - 0.7927lgx$;
for collective farm workers: $lgy = 2.5725 - 0.7258lgx$.

By substituting national data on income distribution by social group into these equations, which are estimated from budget studies, we determine the number and size of families in each group.

The results of calculations by social group are compared with demographic data for the corresponding year. These calculations are based on census materials with corrections applied to the original indices.

Census data on family size also require some modification. For this purpose, we have to augment the number of family members of a particular social group living together with the number of family members living apart and single people. We then divide the resulting number of family members by the total number of families and single people. As a result, we get the average family size in each social group, which corresponds to our concept of family size in the model.

In order to shift from ex post models to forecasting models, we have to incorporate into the model of family size a correction to take account of the fact that incomes grow while family size is constant. The correction is necessary because incomes grow comparatively fast, while average family size changes very slowly.

In order to retain the previous average family size of the base year in the plan period, when the relation between social groups is changing and incomes are increasing, we have to maintain the base year family size weights in the plan year. We note that, in the base year, the family size weights will also be the weights of families with different per capita incomes.

The expected population in the plan year, broken down by social group, is then divided by the average coefficient for family membership in the base year. The result is the overall number of families in the plan year. Using the base year weights, we find the number of families in each group of the population. But in the plan year these groups will not be income groups as well, since there is a change in the weighting of each group. Hence, the resulting distribution must be transformed in accordance with the distribution of income among families.

For this purpose, we have to multiply the number of families in each group by the coefficient of family size of that group. We derive a new series that, on the one hand, gives the number of families of a particular family size in each group and, on the other, specifies the number of persons in each group. From this series, we have to get to a series showing the number of people at each income level. By doing this recalculation and dividing all the new components of the series by the coefficient of family size for the group to which they belong, we derive new figures for the number of families in each group at each income level.

By dividing the number of family members in each group by the number of families, we derive new plan coefficients of family size for each social group at each income level. As a rule, for the same average family size they turn out to be higher than the base figures. This increase in the group average coefficients of family size occurs because families with a large coefficient of family size are mixed in with groups with a high per capita income; this is due to the fast growth of incomes.

Two separate approaches to the modeling of family composition can be adopted.

In the first, family composition is seen from the standpoint of income receivers. In this case, income receivers should be divided up, irrespective of sex or age, into workers, employees, collective farm workers, pensioners, receivers of grants, miscellaneous, and dependents.

These models are based on grouped family budget data. These data are also related to per capita income, and this allows us to link up the indices of family composition as a whole with the consumption models. When we model family composition in terms of employment, we again start by constructing empirical regression lines. We first construct regression lines for income receivers and dependents. The empirical line for income receivers takes the form of a convex broken line, which can be modeled either by a parabola or by another curve close to a parabola. In our calculations, we used a second-order parabola.

The relationship for dependents is different. Here, as for family size, we observe an inverse relationship. Calculations with grouped data on workers in the USSR have shown that a hyperbolic equation of the type $y = a + b/x$ gives the best fit.

When we performed the calculations in practice, we derived equations (for families of workers) as follows: for income receivers, $y = 1.9527 + 0.0126x - 0.0078x^2$; for dependents $y = -1.17 + 1976.31/x$.

In both cases, y is the number of workers or dependents in the family and x is income.

By a similar method, we chose regression equations for other categories of family members (in particular, dependents are broken down into children and the elderly, and different categories of income receivers are also distinguished).

Since the calculations for different types of family members are carried out using different regression equations, overall they differ somewhat from those for family size. This has to be corrected. Moreover, the regression equations for family composition, as described, are based on budget studies. But it was shown above that budget data on family size are different from those for the economy as a whole. Hence, the results must be corrected to take account of family size and composition as shown by demographic data.

Intermediate indices based on budget studies are therefore adjusted to take account of national data in the way described above in connection with family size. The calculations for the plan year are made in the same way, the only difference being that the data for the base year are treated as data from budget studies, while indices for the plan year play the role of national data.

Models of family size and composition and of the age-sex breakdown of the population are used both to forecast the structure of consumption and to identify appropriate measures to increase the living standards of the population. In particular, calculations performed in USSR Gosplan's Scientific Research Institute for Economics using the models described above were employed in working out the program of measures to increase the living standards of the population of the USSR in 1971-75.

NOTES

1. We distinguish between effective demand for goods and paid services and total consumers' demand for individually consumable goods (and services), irrespective of whether they are purchased or are available for direct consumption in natural form.

2. As an illustration, we show the data for milk.

3. For this income level, we could take the average of each interval in the grouped income data, or any other level.

SOME ISSUES IN MODELING
THE TIME PATH OF DEMAND
FOR CONSUMER DURABLES

L. G. Chitashvili

The present article gives a qualitative analysis of linear and nonlinear dynamic models of the demand for consumer durables; it also contains illustrations of demand forecasts for certain major types of goods, considers models incorporating the appearance of higher quality goods, and discusses the problems of linking demand with the time path of production.

The basic data on the consumption of consumer durables are contained in information about the sales of consumer durables to the population. To give a quantitative account of the laws reflected in these data, we may consider choosing approximating curves and estimating their parameters statistically, with the aim of using these curves afterward to analyze and forecast the consumption process. Even if we have selected a curve that, on estimation, fits the data of the observation period quite well, however, it still remains problematical to forecast on the basis of extrapolation of the curve. Indeed, we can in principle find a fairly large number of parametric curves (different combinations of elementary functions) that fit the empirical data satisfactorily yet nonetheless diverge substantially in the interval

Russian text ©1980 by "Nauka" Publishers. "Nekotorye voprosy modelirovaniia dinamiki potrebleniia predmetov dlitel'nogo pol'zovaniia," Ekonomika i matematicheskie metody, 1980, vol. 16, no. 3, pp. 449-61.

following the base period. Moreover, formal approximations prevent us from interpreting the various special features of the empirical curves (changes in the rate of growth, the appearance of regions of satiation, etc.) in terms of a mathematical model. We should recognize that the typical features of empirical curves are all reflections of special elements in the demand and consumption process, such as the customer's attitude toward acquiring a particular good. This depends on his knowledge of it, the impact of the level of the family budget on ability to pay, the desire to replace a worn-out or outdated good, the impact of new, higher quality goods on this desire, and so on.

Studies of the time path of demand for consumer durables carried out with mathematical models are designed to lay a stronger foundation for an analytical account of the empirical data expressing the process under study.

We do not start the process of constructing a dynamic model by directly choosing an approximating curve for the time series; on the contrary, using a mathematical model of the process, we seek a type of curve that corresponds to the assumptions of the model. The starting point in this process is a mathematical model of the local operation of the process; i.e., an analysis of it over some time period. Hence, we derive in the normal way some relations or equations that characterize the curves we seek; depending on the accuracy of local analysis of this kind, we derive curves that describe with greater or lesser accuracy the regularities observable in the actual data.

Since this approach does not lead directly to a specification of the theoretical demand curves, but to an equation for them, we have to make a qualitative analysis of possible solutions of these equations, for if we unthinkingly estimate the parameters of a dynamic model and then use these estimates continuously to make forecasts, we may not get reliable results. An analysis of the solutions and of how they fit typical data for actual purchases of goods may reveal connections missing in the model's original assumptions and indicate ways of improvement.

We illustrate these propositions through an investigation of the Stone-Rowe model [1], the logistic model as interpreted by Bass [2], and a generalization of the latter [3]. Later in the article, we study the relationship between our model of demand and the general framework of "production-supply-demand," and analyze a model of demand for several substitutes; this model incorporates properties that characteristically arise when the quality of the consumer durables supplied to the customer rises over time.

The simplest dynamic model of the demand for and consumption of durable goods is that of Stone and Rowe [1, 4] (see also the survey article [5]). It is based on the assumption that first-time purchases per year are proportional to the gap between the saturation level and the current stock of the good in question, and that replacement purchases are proportional to the existing stock. If we denote stock in year t by s_t, the saturation level by $\bar{s}$, first-time purchases in year t by v_t, replacement purchases in year t by u_t, and total purchases by q_t, then the model can be represented by the following equations:

$$s_{t+1}-s_t=v_t, \quad v_t=p(\bar{s}-s_t), \quad u_t=\alpha s_t, \quad q_t=u_t+v_t. \tag{1}$$

The incorporation of equations linking later levels of stocks with earlier ones is characteristic of all dynamic models of demand and consumption, for, though the process itself is not directly observable (we have only particular stock estimates for a few years based on surveys of the population's ownership of a particular good), the model uses these values to describe purchasing policy. The simplest interpretation of the model is that, if the total number of purchasers is $\bar{s}$, then $\bar{s}-s_t$ is the potential number of sales, p is the probability of purchase, and α is the probability of scrapping and replacement ($1/\alpha$ is the average service life). To solve (1) we use the fact that the linear recursive equation $x_{t+1}=ax_t+b_t$ has as its solution the function

$$x_t=\sum_{s=0}^{t-1} a^{t-1-s}b_s+a^t x_0.$$

Using this formula, we derive

$$s_t = \bar{s}(1-(1-p)^t), \quad u_t = \alpha\bar{s}(1-(1-p)^t), \tag{2}$$
$$v_t = p\bar{s}(1-p)^t, \quad q_t = \alpha\bar{s}+(p-\alpha)\bar{s}(1-p)^t.$$

The sequence of total purchases q_t that we observe is characterized by a curve which declines or increases depending on whether $p \geq \alpha$ or $p \leq \alpha$ (i.e., on the ratio between the probabilities of first-time and replacement purchases) up to a stationary level $\alpha\bar{s}$, corresponding to replacement purchases at the saturation stock level, i.e., when $s_t \sim \bar{s}$. It follows from the expression for q_t and typical graphs of it that the assumptions underlying this model lead to very simple forms of the time path of sales.

But in the very typical case of sales of sewing machines (this example is particularly interesting because demand for and consumption of this good have nearly reached the final saturation stage), the sales curve shows first a rising segment and then a segment that declines to some stationary level (Figure 1).

In the Stone-Rowe model, the saturation level $\bar{s}$ is generally assumed to be variable and to be increasing in some specified way, i.e., $\bar{s}_t = \bar{s}(1+b)^t$, where by assumption the parameters $\bar{s}$ and b are related to the dynamic properties of prices and incomes. Thus, the value $\bar{s}_t - s_t$ is now interpreted as an index of potential purchasing capacity in year t, and its upper limit increases geometrically.

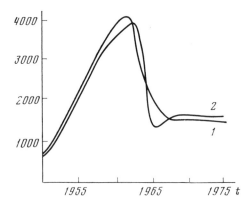

Figure 1. Curves showing the actual production and sales of sewing machines in the USSR (in thousands of units).

Substituting $\bar{s}_t$ in the stocks equation (1) and solving, we get an expression for stocks as follows:

$$s_t = \bar{s}\frac{p}{b+p}[(1+b)^t - (1-p)^t].$$

We use this formula to derive total purchases, q_t:

$$q_t = \frac{p\bar{s}}{b+p}[(1+b)^t(b+\alpha) + (1-p)^t(p-\alpha)].$$

Equations (2) follow naturally from this expression when $b=0$. It is obvious from the formula we have derived that, if the probability of first-time purchase p substantially exceeds the probability of scrapping (the minimum point

$$t^* = \ln\frac{\ln(1-p)(\alpha-p)}{\ln(1+b)(b+\alpha)}\frac{1}{\ln(1+b)-\ln(1-p)}$$

must be positive), then the sales curve declines to a given minimum as a result of the decline in the number of potential purchases; however, as distinct from the situation where $\bar{s}_t$ is constant, we may observe a range in which q_t increases as a result of a reduction in the price of the good. In the opposite case ($t^* < 0$), the probability of replacement purchases is high, and they prevent the sales curve from declining.

Of course, this may occur in actual practice with purchases of particular products; but, as stated above, the framework of the Stone-Rowe model excludes a typical situation such as that observed in the sale of sewing machines. The position is the same if we consider other variants and generalizations of the Stone-Rowe model.

An alternative approach might be based on a breakdown of owners of consumer durables in a given year by the service life of their goods; in other words, we should consider more general forms of probability distributions for the service life of the good than that adopted in the Stone-Rowe model (which assumes a constant scrapping rate α). As far as we know, no systematic research has been carried out regarding the way in which the form of the demand curve depends on the distribution of service lives. This is due to fairly substantial analytical difficulties. To do so, we have to break down stocks s_t into a series of variables $s_t = s_t^{(1)} + s_t^{(2)} + \ldots$, where s_t^i is the stock of the good that has been in service for i years.

It can be shown analytically that, if we model the general case in which the probability of scrapping a good depends on its service life i, so that $\alpha = \alpha_i$ (this includes the most interesting special case in which that probability increases with the period of service life, i.e., α_i increases in i), then we get a delay in the start of the sharp growth in the demand curve, but do not generally find a period of decline emerging later.

It is clear from the above analysis that, if the model is to be extended to include standard curves similar to those found in the case of sales of sewing machines, the extension should be in another direction than taking account of changes in incomes or prices or investigating more general distributions of the service lives of durables.

In the Stone-Rowe model p, the probability of first-time purchase, was assumed constant over time, i.e., it was assumed that the number of first-time purchases is proportional to the number of potential purchases, $\bar{s} - \bar{s}_t$. In other words, a very simple assumption was made about the buyer's strategy; irrespective of whether the good has just appeared on the market or is already widely diffused, the buyer's attitude is the same. We may wish to assume, however, that, as a good is widely sold, interest in it grows. One way of incorporating this assumption is by adopting the hypothesis that the probability p increases with the stocks of the good held by the population, in the very simple form $p_t = p + \pi s_t$. Bass's interpretation [2] of such an assumption is that first-time buyers are divided into two classes: "innovators" and "imitators." The innovators' propensity to buy, p, is not affected by how widely the good is diffused and is constant, while among the imitators the propensity is proportional to stocks, i.e., it is πs_t, where π is a parameter that can be interpreted as the probability of an additional sale per unit of ownership of the good. Hence, in order to identify the time path of stocks s_t , we have to solve a non-linear finite difference equation

$$s_{t+1} - s_t = p(\bar{s} - s_t) + \pi s_t(\bar{s} - s_t). \tag{3}$$

To simplify the exposition, we consider models in continuous time, but we also make some observations concerning the transition to the discrete case, for although on the natural time scale we should consider the process under investigation as taking place continuously, the special features of the empirical data oblige us to adopt discrete analogues of the models. The analogue of equation (3), $(d/dt)s_t = p(\bar{s} - s_t) + \pi s_t(\bar{s} - s_t)$, is converted to linear form using a transformation to the variable $1/(\bar{s} - s_t)$, and its solution is the logistic curve

$$s_t = \bar{s} - \left[\left(\frac{1}{\bar{s} - s_0} - \frac{\pi}{p + \bar{s}\pi} \right) e^{(p + \bar{s}\pi)t} + \frac{\pi}{p + \bar{s}\pi} \right]^{-1}. \tag{4}$$

Using this expression for the stock, we can also work out sales to innovators $v_t^{(1)} = p(\bar{s} - s_t)$, to imitators $v_t^{(2)} = \pi s_t(\bar{s} - s_t)$, and to repeat buyers $u_t = \alpha s_t$, as well as total sales q_t. It is clear from the corresponding diagrams that purchases by innovators decline, while those of repeat buyers increase, and the sales curve of imitators reaches a maximum. It is not difficult to compute the maximum of q_t in its graph. Differentiating the expression for q_t, we get

$$\frac{d}{dt} q_t = \frac{d}{dt} [p(\bar{s} - s_t) + \pi s_t(\bar{s} - s_t) + \alpha s_t] = [\pi(\bar{s} - s_t) - \pi s_t - p + \alpha] \frac{ds_t}{dt},$$

from which we find the value of stocks at maximum point t^* and then, using (4),

$$t^* = \frac{1}{p + \pi\bar{s}} \ln \left[\frac{(\pi\bar{s} + p + \alpha)\pi\bar{s}}{(\pi\bar{s} + p - \alpha)p} \right].$$

The role of $v_t^{(1)}$ — purchases by innovators — is interesting. It seems from empirical estimates of the parameter p for various durables that in the majority of cases their number is very small; however, they have an important influence on the process as a whole (estimates of the parameters of the logistic model for certain durables are given at the end of the article).

In fact it is easy, if we start from the formulas for $v_t^{(1)}$, $v_t^{(2)}$, u_t, and q_t, to appreciate that, as p falls, $v_t^{(1)}$ becomes an insignificant part of q_t, but at the same time the maximum on the graph moves to the right (t^* increases, if p declines): the role of innovators thus basically consists in altering the lag after which the intensive sales begin.

The operation of the logistic model can be described qualitatively as follows. When the good first appears on the market, innovators begin to make purchases in small quantities; then the appearance of stocks encourages purchases by imitators, whose numbers quickly grow and whose share in total purchases becomes dominant while the number of innovators declines sharply. Imitators' purchases reach a maximum, but replacement demand appearing at this time postpones the phase in which total purchases fall for a period; then (unless the condition $\alpha > \pi\bar{s} + p$ is fulfilled) this phase comes into operation; purchases made by imitators fall as potential buyers are exhausted, and the major share of purchases are repeat purchases, which approximate to their equilibrium level $\alpha\bar{s}$ (Figure 2). The time path of sales of sewing machines is a very typical example of this process.

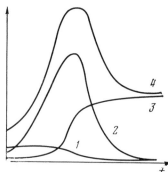

Figure 2. Curves indicating demand by first-time buyers (innovators (1) and imitators (2)), repeat buyers (3), and total purchases (4) in the logistic model.

The fact that the position of the graph of q_t depends on the magnitude p is an indication of the special importance played by measures to disseminate information about the quality of a good; this will encourage some potential purchasers to buy a newly available product.

What we have studied up to now is essentially not sales, but demand. The function q_t will in fact express purchases only if output is able to match demand. Using the logistic model for a demand function, we now examine the basic relationships that arise between output, supply, and demand in the case of a single good taken in isolation.

Π_t denotes the level of output of the good in year t; I_t, supply; $\tilde{q}_t$, the level of sales; $\tilde{v}_t$, first-time purchases; and $\tilde{u}_t$, repeat purchases. Obviously, the time path of I_t is given by the relation $I_{t+1}=I_t-\tilde{q}_t+\Pi_t$; i.e., supply in year $t+1$ is the unsold part of output accumulated over the previous years, plus output in the current year. The overall system of equations expressing demand and supply functions for consumption and for stocks takes the form

$$s_{t+1}-s_t=v_t, \quad \tilde{v}_t=\min{(I_t, v_t)},$$
$$v_t=p(\bar{s}-s_t)+\pi s_t(\bar{s}-s_t), \quad u_{t+1}=\alpha s_{t+1}+$$
$$+(u_t-\tilde{u}_t), \quad I_{t+1}=I_t-\tilde{q}_t+\Pi_t,$$
$$\tilde{q}_t=\tilde{v}_t+\min{(u_t, I_t-\tilde{v}_t)}=\tilde{v}_t+\tilde{u}_t,$$

(5)

i.e., demand from first-time buyers v_t is first calculated from the level of stocks and the volume of sales to first-time buyers, and $\tilde{v}_t$ is then found; levels of repeat demand and of repeat sales are recalculated, and then stock levels and supplies for the following year are determined.

In this model, the parameter Π_t enters exogenously, and the "output-supply-demand-consumption" system becomes a closed one if we fix some policy for production. Unless there have been shortages $(q_t \leqslant I_t)$, then, when no unsold output is accumulated $(\Pi_t=q_t)$, in view of the nature of the demand curve q_t from the logistic model, the level of output of the good should fall after q_t reaches its maximum and as demand falls; this naturally involves certain costs. Costs of another kind are associated with the appearance of unsold output.

Thus, the choice of a rational policy for production has to take account of both kinds of costs, and the outcome will depend to a large extent both on the estimate made of the relative size of these costs and on profits forgone when the level of output is low and substantial shortages persist over a long period. As an example, we consider three policies for the control of production:

1) the direct linkage of output and demand: $\Pi_t = q_t$;

2) the halting of output growth before curve q_t reaches its peak; subsequently, output is linked to demand as the latter falls;

3) a policy similar to the second except that, before being halted, output growth exceeds demand.

The solutions for $\tilde{q}_t$ from system (5) are shown in Figure 3 for policies 1-3. In the first case, losses are defined as the

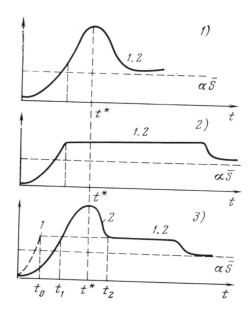

Figure 3. Output curves (1) and sales curves (2) in the logistic model with various production policies.

costs resulting from the reduction in output from level q_t to $\alpha \bar{s}$; in the second case, output needs to be cut much less sharply, but the sales process is more lengthy; a similar reduction also takes place in the third case; the sales curve is much higher, but we have to resign ourselves to the loss of some parts of unsold output over the period (t_0, t_1). Of course, it is no easy task to establish the relationship between these losses, and qualitative criteria must be sensitive to the rate at which future profits are discounted. There are also particular difficulties caused by indeterminacy of the goal of retooling production. This circumstance is related to the fact that a model of production and sale of a single good in isolation cannot, in principle, be a closed model.

The picture becomes clearer only when we have laid the necessary basis for analyzing situations where two goods are supplied that are substitutes. Let us consider the situation that arises in natural analogues of the Stone-Rowe and logistic models when a new good (of higher quality) becomes available. We must also note that we have to analyze multiproduct dynamic models of demand and consumption even when studying a single kind of consumer durable. In fact, data on the sales of goods such as watches, since they reflect changes in the technology of manufacture and the quality of output, are essentially aggregative data on the sale of different durable goods that are substitutes for one another.

Let us consider initially the time path of overall demand for two goods, using the Stone-Rowe framework and assuming, as before, that supply matches demand.

Assume that $\bar{s}$ individuals (or families) are offered two goods, and that these are complete substitutes in the sense that, at any one time, an individual will possess only one of them. Let p_1 and p_2 be the probabilities of a first-time purchase of the first and second goods; α_1 and α_2 are the scrapping probabilities; and β is the probability of the purchase of the second good by an individual currently owning the first good. The fact that an owner of the second good does not, when he scraps it, buy the first good should be interpreted as an indication that the second good is of higher quality. We assume that prior to the appearance of the second good in the market the parameters of the model for the first good were p and α. In this case, the equations determining stocks $s_t^{(1)}$ and first-time and repeat purchases, $v_t^{(1)}$ and $u_t^{(1)}$ of the first good are given by the one-good Stone-Rowe model:

$$(d/dt)\,s_t^{(1)} = p\,(\bar{s}-s_t^{(1)}), \qquad q_t^{(1)} = v_t^{(1)} + u_t^{(1)} = \alpha s_t^{(1)} + p\,(\bar{s}-s_t^{(1)}).$$

Assume that the second good appears on the market at time t_0. These equations follow from the assumptions made above:

$$s_t = s_t^{(1)} + s_t^{(2)}, \ t \geqslant t_0, \ \frac{d}{dt}\,s_t = (p_1+p_2)\,(\bar{s}-s_t), \ \frac{d}{dt}\,s_t^{(1)} = p_1\,(\bar{s}-s_t) - \beta s_t^{(1)}$$

$$\frac{d}{dt} = s_t^{(2)} = p_2\,(\bar{s}-s_t) + \beta s_t^{(1)},$$

$$v_t^{(1)} = p_1\,(\bar{s}-s_t),\ v_t^{(2)} = p_2\,(\bar{s}-s_t) + \beta s_t^{(1)},\ u_t^{(1)} = \alpha_1 s_t^{(1)},\ u_t^{(2)} = \alpha_2 s_t^{(2)}. \quad (6)$$

A solution to system (6) for $t \geqslant t_0$ can be found without difficulty. We write expressions for $q_t^{(1)}$ and $q_t^{(2)}$ — the total volumes of sales of the first and second goods:

$$q_t^{(1)} = \alpha_1 A e^{-\beta(t-t_0)} + B_1 e^{-(p_1+p_2)(t-t_0)},$$

$$q_t^{(2)} = \alpha_2 \bar{s} + (\beta-\alpha_2)\,A e^{-\beta(t-t_0)} + B_2 e^{-(p_1+p_2)(t-t_0)}, \quad (7)$$

where

$$A = s_{t_0}^{(1)} - \frac{p_1\,(\bar{s}-s_{t_0}')}{\beta-p_1-p_2}, \qquad B_1 = (\bar{s}-s_{t_0}^{(1)})\left[p_1 + \frac{\alpha_1 p_1}{\beta-p_1-p_2}\right],$$

$$B_2 = (\bar{s}-s_{t_0}')\left[p_2-\alpha_2 + \frac{(\beta-\alpha_2)\,p_1}{\beta-p_1-p_2}\right]$$

If we make the natural assumption that $\beta+\alpha_1 \geqslant \alpha$ (i.e., that sales rise after a new good, or a higher quality good, appears), then the graphs of these curves are as shown in Figure 4.1.

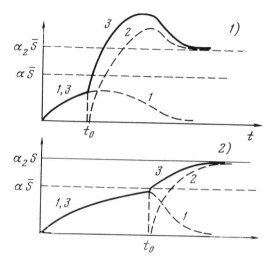

Figure 4. Demand curves for the first good (1), the second good (2), and total demand (3) in a two-good linear model of the Stone-Rowe type; the figure illustrates how the shape of the curves depends on the time when the second good becomes available.

The qualitative interpretation of (7) is as follows. Generally speaking, stocks of the first good continue to increase for some time (until the expression $p_i(\bar{s}-s_t)+\beta s_t^{(1)}$ becomes negative); then they begin to fall as owners of the first good switch to the second. Stocks of the second good, on the other hand, will obviously rise after t_0 up to level $\bar{s}$. Purchases of the first good will also fall, since naturally those replacing the first good with the second include some former repeat buyers of the first good ($\alpha_1<\alpha<\alpha_2$, $p_i\leqslant p$). Of course, as purchases of the second good grow, they may exceed the stationary level $\alpha_2\bar{s}$ in view of the fact that the magnitude $\beta s_t^{(1)}$ (additional purchases) may increase for some time.

If the second, improved product appears when stocks of the first product are approaching the saturation level soon after t_0, then

$$q_t^{(1)} \sim \alpha_1\bar{s}e^{-\beta(t-t_0)}, \qquad q_t^{(2)} \sim \alpha_2\bar{s}+(\beta-\alpha_2)\bar{s}e^{-\beta(t-t_0)}; \qquad (8)$$

this is shown in the total sales curve as a transition from a lower level, $\alpha\bar{s}$, to a higher level (Figure 4.2).

We now consider how this situation is reflected in production policy — in fact, we examine the simplest case (8). We must now consider two types of output, $\Pi_t^{(1)}$ and $\Pi_t^{(2)}$. If prior to t_0 output matched demand $\Pi_t^{(1)}=q_t^{(1)}$, $t \leqslant t_0$, then maintenance of a precise correspondence after t_0 (i.e., $\Pi_t^{(1)}=q_t^{(1)}$, $\Pi_t^{(2)}=q_t^{(2)}$) involves certain costs associated both with expanding production and with reconstructing capacity designed to produce the first product, part of which $(q_{t_0}-q_t)/q_{t_0}=(1-(\alpha_t/\alpha)e^{-\beta(t-t_0)})$ has to be progressively adapted to produce the second good; otherwise, there will be unsold output of one good. Hence, from this point of view, it may be a mistake to encourage sales of the second product (to raise β) too much.

We may adopt the wholly realistic assumption that if the second product is in short supply, some owners of the first product will, as a last resort, buy identical replacements for them (we denote this proportion of the group of owners as a whole by α). In this case, if the decision to retool is as late as it is assumed in (8), then the outcome will be a deliberate decision to allow the shortages of the second good to persist for some time to reduce losses associated with unsold output of the first good.

Formally, if supply meets demand and $\Pi_t^{(1)} \geqslant q_t^{(1)}$, then in the period (t_0, t_1) there is an accumulation of unsold output of the first type in the amount $\int_{t_0}^{t_1} (\Pi_t^{(1)}-\alpha_1\bar{s}e^{-\beta(t-t_0)})\,dt$. In the case where $\Pi_t^{(2)}<\beta s_t^{(1)}$ (a shortage of the second product is assumed), we have $\tilde{q}_t^{(2)}=\Pi_t^{(2)}$, $\tilde{q}_t^{(1)}=\alpha\left[\bar{s}-\int_{t_0}^{t_1}\Pi_s^{(2)}\,ds\right]$, and the level of unsold output of the first product $\int_{t_0}^{t_1}(\Pi_t^{(1)}-\tilde{q}_t^{(1)})\,dt$ is reduced — at the cost, it is true, of a reduction in total sales (a lower level of output). This position should be maintained until production of the first good, $\Pi_t^{(1)}$, is sufficiently reduced. But within the framework of the (narrow) Stone-Rowe model (or its analogue (6) for two substitutes), it is impossible to account for the appearance of successive declines and increases in purchases that are typical of situations where reaction to a decline in demand is delayed. This specific feature of the time path of demand, however, is captured by the logistic model of demand; this guarantees the appearance of a peak and a subsequent monotonic decline in demand to its equilibrium level, and it is this that is responsible for the occurrence of fluctuations.

In the logistic model, the system of equations for stocks of and demand for two substitute products is as follows (for $t \geqslant t_0$):

$$\frac{d}{dt} s_t = (p_1 + p_2)(\bar{s} - s_t) + \pi s_t(\bar{s} - s_t), \qquad s_t = s_t^{(1)} + s_t^{(2)},$$

$$\frac{d}{dt} s_t^{(1)} = p_1(\bar{s} - s_t) + \pi s_t^{(1)}(\bar{s} - s_t) - \beta s_t^{(1)} s_t^{(2)},$$

$$\frac{d}{dt} s_t^{(2)} = p_2(\bar{s} - s_t) + \pi s_t^{(2)}(\bar{s} - s_t) + \beta s_t^{(1)} s_t^{(2)},$$

$$q_t^{(1)} = p_1(\bar{s} - s_t) + \pi s_t^{(1)}(\bar{s} - s_t) \beta s_t^{(1)} s_t^{(2)} + \alpha_1 s_t^{(1)},$$

$$q_t^{(2)} = p_2(\bar{s} - s_t) + \pi s_t^{(2)}(\bar{s} - s_t) + \beta s_t^{(1)} s_t^{(2)} + \alpha_2 s_t^{(2)}.$$

Here the ratio of purchasers — innovators and imitators — is given by $s_t^{(1)}/s_t^{(2)}$, i.e., by the relative diffusion of the first and second products. Moreover, as distinct from the Stone-Rowe model, the probability that an owner of the first good will purchase the second is also proportional to the diffusion of the latter, $\beta s_t^{(2)}$.

To simplify matters, we show the solution to this system when $p_1 = p_2 = 0$ for initial stock levels $s_{t_0}^{(1)} = s_0^{(1)}$ and $s_{t_0}^{(2)} = s_0^{(2)}$; we express stocks $s_t^{(1)}$ and $s_t^{(2)}$ in terms of s_t, which has the same form as in the one-good model.

$$s_t^{(1)} = s_t \left[1 + \frac{s_0^{(2)}}{s_0^{(1)}} \left(\frac{\bar{s} - s_0}{\bar{s} - s_t} \right)^{-\frac{\beta}{\pi}} \right]^{-1}, \quad s_t^{(2)} = s_t \left[1 + \frac{s_0^{(1)}}{s_0^{(2)}} \left(\frac{\bar{s} - s_0}{\bar{s} - s_t} \right)^{-\frac{\beta}{\pi}} \right]^{-1}$$

The demand curves $q_t^{(1)}$ and $q_t^{(2)}$ are illustrated in Figure 5. Their shape depends on when t_0 occurs in relation to the maximum of the original sales curve $q_t^{(1)}$.

Reference [6] introduces a linear model that generalizes the Stone-Rowe model to the multiproduct case and presents a solution. [7] studies the process of first-time purchases of substitutes on the assumption that individuals' purchasing strategy is determined solely by the number of items already purchased. A sequential method is proposed in [3] for estimating the parameters of the logistic model statistically; a discrete variant is adopted for the finite difference equation of the form $s_{t+1} - s_t = p(\bar{s} - s_t) + \pi s_{t+1}(\bar{s} - s_t)$. It can be shown that the solution of this equation is the logistic curve, as distinct from the direct discrete system (3) presented in [8]. Of course, both πs_{t+1} and πs_t can equally well be used to reflect the level of diffusion

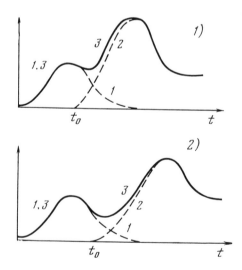

Figure 5. Demand curves for first good (1), second good (2), and total demand (3) in a two-good logistic model depending on the time the second good becomes available.

Table 1

Forecasting Demand for Refrigerators

t	Π_t	q_t	$\hat{q}_t$	$\hat{u}_t$	d_t	$\hat{s}_t$
1	359	340	280	55	82	910
2	367	425	390	75	86	1,240
3	529	518	490	100	89	1,670
4	497	680	650	133	91	2,220
5	583	805	820	175	93	2,910
6	910	780	1,050	227	95	3,790
7	1,134	971	1,320	293	96	4,890
8	1,675	1,458	1,640	374	97	6,240
9	2,205	1,948	2,010	473	97	7,890
10	2,697	2,388	2,440	591	98	9,850
11	3,155	2,886	2,890	729	98	12,150
12	3,701	3,305	3,359	887	98	14,780
13	4,140	3,756	3,810	1,062	98	17,700
14	4,557	4,202	4,200	1,250	99	20,800
15	5,030	4,497	4,520	1,450	99	24,100
16	5,423	4,912	4,750	1,640	99	27,400
17	5,426	4,743	4,820	1,835	99	30,600
18		4,823	4,810	2,010		33,580
19			4,770	2,180		36,350
20			4,650	2,330		38,800
21			4,420	2,450		40,900
22			4,215	2,560		42,700
23			3,990	2,640		44,100
24			3,830	2,710		45,200
25			3,670	2,770		46,250
26			3,535	2,820		47,000
27			3,420	2,850		47,600
28			3,325	2,885		48,100
29			3,250	2,900		48,400
30			3,190	2,925		48,700
31			3,140	2,940		48,900

of the product in the interval $(t, t+1)$.

When we use the method of least squares to estimate all the parameters affecting q_t, the following difficulty is encountered. One component in the system of nonlinear regression equations, s_t (the population's stock of durables), is not observable, and hence a special sequential search algorithm must be used to estimate it. Estimates of the parameters π, p, $\bar{s}$, and s_0 are sought in the following way. For a given value of α and s_0, a sequence s_t^α is constructed from the recursive equation $s_{t+1}^\alpha = (1-\alpha)s_t^\alpha + q_t$; then estimates of the linear parameters $x = p\bar{s}/(1-\pi\bar{s})$, $y = (1-p)/(1-\pi\bar{s})$, $z = -\pi/(1-\pi\bar{s})$, are obtained by least squares from the regression equation $s_{t+1}^\alpha = x + ys_t^\alpha + zs_{t+1}^\alpha s_t^\alpha$; this is an amended form of equation (4) for stocks s_t. Then, using the estimated parameters x, y, and z, we construct

Table 2

Forecasting Demand for Washing Machines

t	Π_t	q_t	$\hat{q}_t$	$\hat{u}_t$	$\hat{s}_t$
1	463	518	310	40	610
2	647	714	540	70	850
3	895	907	760	110	1,500
4	1,285	1,253	1,080	145	1,820
5	1,787	1,734	1,440	210	2,650
6	2,282	2,108	2,010	310	3,820
7	2,860	2,586	2,430	430	5,370
8	3,430	3,141	3,070	580	7,390
9	3,869	3,561	3,680	795	9,920
10	4,324	3,897	4,170	1,024	12,850
11	4,700	4,242	4,380	1,280	16,070
12	5,153	4,517	4,440	1,505	18,800
13	5,243	4,135	4,320	1,760	22,010
14	4,052	3,688	3,960	1,940	24,330
15	3,001	3,133	3,640	2,080	26,500
16	2,987	3,078	3,360	2,250	28,270
17	3,075	3,124	3,130	2,340	29,360
18		3,241	3,040	2,410	30,140
19		3,309	2,910	2,450	30,700
20			2,780	2,480	31,140
21			2,670	2,510	31,460
22			2,650	2,525	31,580
23			2,630	2,540	31,750
24			2,610	2,560	31,820

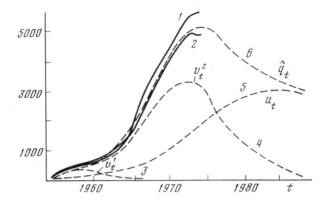

Figure 6. Actual curves for output (1) and sales (2) of refrigerators in the USSR (in thousands of units) and estimated curves for first-time demand (from innovators — 3, and imitators — 4), for repeat demand (5), and for total demand (6), according to the logistic model.

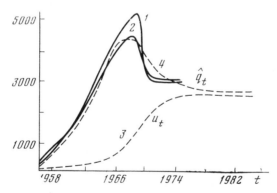

Figure 7. Actual curves for output (1) and sales (2) of washing machines in the USSR (in thousands of units), and estimated curves for repeat (3) and total (4) demand, according to the logistic model.

a theoretical (logistic) curve $\tilde{s}_t^{\alpha}$ sequentially from $\tilde{s}_{t+1}^{\alpha} = (x+y\tilde{s}_t^{\alpha})/(1-z\tilde{s}_t^{\alpha})$, $\tilde{s}_0=s_0$. We then find the mean square deviation of the observed q_t from its theoretical estimate, $q_t^{\alpha}=\tilde{s}_{t+1}^{\alpha} -\tilde{s}_t^{\alpha}+\alpha\tilde{s}_t^{\alpha}$. This procedure is repeated for various values of α, and s_0, and the chosen combination of estimates for all parameters is that which minimizes the divergence between

q_t and q_t^α. Forecasts of q_t are made by forecasting stocks from the appropriate equation.

We show in Tables 1 and 2 the results of using the logistic model to forecast demand for refrigerators and washing machines.

Tables 1 and 2 give annual values for the following indices: Π_t is the output of the durable in the USSR in thousands of units; q_t is sales through state or cooperative trade (in thousands of units [9]); $\hat{q}_t$ is the theoretical demand curve calculated from the model using parameter estimates; $\hat{u}_t$ is the theoretical value for repeat buying; ($\hat{q}_t = \hat{v}_t + \hat{u}_t$, where $\hat{v}_t$ is first-time demand); d_t is the percentage of total first-time demand accounted for by imitators (where $d_t \sim 1$ the value is not given); $\hat{s}_t$ is the estimate of stock levels.

Parameter estimates for refrigerators are: $\alpha = 0.06$, $\bar{s} = 49,700$, $\pi\bar{s} = 232$, $p = 0.002$; the residual mean square deviation $\sigma_\varepsilon = 120$, the mean of the residuals $m_\varepsilon = -36$; and the residual correlation $\hat{r}_\varepsilon = 0.46$. For washing machines, $\alpha = 0.08$, $\bar{s} = 32,000$, $\pi\bar{s} = 40$, $p \sim 0$, $\sigma_\varepsilon = 250$, $m_\varepsilon = -20$, and $r_\varepsilon = 0.36$. With 19 observations, we can assume the (theoretical) mean residuals to be zero, and the empirical correlations do not go beyond the acceptable limits:

$$\left| \frac{m_\varepsilon \sqrt{19}}{\sigma_\varepsilon} \right| < 3, \quad \left| \frac{\sqrt{18}\, r}{\sqrt{1-r^2}} \right| < 3.$$

Figures 6 and 7 graph the empirical data (as shown in Tables 1 and 2) for production and sales of refrigerators and washing machines; they also indicate theoretical forecasts made with the logistic model.

REFERENCES

1. Stone, R., and Rowe, D. "The Market Demand for Durable Goods." Econometrica, 1957, vol. 25, no. 3.

2. Bass, F. "A New Product Growth Model for Consumer Durables." Management Science, 1969, vol. 15, no. 5.

3. Chitashvili, L. G. "Logisticheskaia model' sprosa i potrebleniia predmetov dlitel'nogo pol'zovaniia." Soobshcheniia AN Gruzinskoi SSSR, 1977, vol. 87, no. 2.

4. Stone, R., and Rowe, D. "The Durability of Consumers' Durable Goods." Econometrica, 1960, vol. 28, no. 1.

5. Solov'ev, Iu. P., and Druker, S. G. "Modelirovanie potrebitel'skogo sprosa." Ekonomika i matematicheskie metody, 1975, vol. XI, no. 1.

6. Chitashvili, L. G. "Ob odnoi dinamicheskoi ekonomicheskoi modeli." Soobshcheniia AN Gruzinskoi SSSR, 1976, vol. 83, no. 2.

7. Pyatt, F. G. Priority Patterns and the Demand for Household Durable Goods. Cambridge, 1964.

8. Nash, J. C. "A Discrete Alternative to the Logistic Growth Function." Applied Statistics, 1977, vol. 26, no. 1.

9. Narodnoe khoziaistvo SSSR v 1965-76 gody. Moscow: "Statistika" Publishers, 1966-77.

Received July 5, 1978

METHODOLOGICAL PROBLEMS
IN ESTIMATING PRICE ELASTICITIES
OF DEMAND

B. N. Mikhalevskii and Iu. P. Solov'ev

The theoretical and practical problems of measuring social benefit and its associated marginal indices are becoming more and more important. This is due not only to the importance of the problem in theoretical political economy, but also to the practical needs of the present moment (see [1]).

Contemporary economic science cannot yet furnish a complete answer to all the highly complex problems associated with the nature and measurement of social benefit. Some critics conclude from this fact that nothing at all constructive can be said or done in this connection.

In our view, it does not always follow from the absence of a general answer to all questions that it is impossible to get partial, but still fairly important, answers whose accumulation may, in conjunction with work on the problem as a whole, lead in the end to a general solution. In order to find the more partial answers, it is sufficient in the meantime to apply the notion of quantitative returns at the highest level of the economy; i.e., to choose the path of aggregation and statistical estimation.

Benefits can be evaluated quantitatively without making any

Russian text © 1970 by "Nauka" Publishers and Ekonomika i matematicheskie metody. "Metodologicheskie problemy otsenki elastichnostei potrebleniia ot tsen." Ekonomika i matematicheskie metody, 1970, vol. 6, no. 1, pp. 17-29.
Presented as a formulation of the problem.

assumptions about the existence of subjective utility, by relying on the Weber-Fechner law of subjective probability as used in von Neumann and Morgenstern's measurement of utility (although the prospects for the latter method are by no means yet clear).

It seems to us that even today we can obtain quantitative results that, though preliminary, can still be used to solve the following problems:

1) What are the numerical values of the inverse of the elasticity of the marginal utility of income — the flexibility parameter ($\hat{\omega}$) — at the level of the economy as a whole and for particular, more detailed commodity groups?

At the level of the economy, this presupposes answers to the following questions: 1) what is the percentage increase or decrease in the benefit derived from consumption if the share of all components of final demand (investment, defense, the balance of payments) goes up or down by 1 percent? 2) What is the percentage increase in the benefit derived from per capita consumption if the latter increases by 1 percent? The value of $\hat{\omega}$ gives a quantitative answer to both these questions. Similarly, for the case of particular goods and services, we would then be in a position to answer the question: By how much will the welfare of the population change in response to a 1 percent change in the share of that good, and how many units of utility are gained by a 1 percent increase in per capita consumption of that good? Both properties are given by group and individual values of $\hat{\omega}$.

Obviously, quantitative answers of this kind give a clear view of the consequences of decisions at the macro level concerning the distribution of national income and final output between consumption and other uses, and the return to a particular growth rate of consumption per capita. At the level of particular commodity groups, we get a quantitative estimate of the ranking of demand, on the one hand, and a further clear outline of the economic consequences of structural shifts or shortages of particular commodity groups and the benefits resulting from alternative growth rates of per capita consumption of each good, on the other.

2) What is the value at the macro level of the long-run rate of return to resources used to finance extended reproduction?

3) How can we use numerical estimates of marginal utility to calculate a matrix of long-term price elasticities? If we have a set of such matrices over several years, together with tables showing the impact on own-price elasticities of the scale of price changes, we can draw quantitatively well founded conclusions concerning the impact of a change in the retail price of a particular good on demand for all goods and services; i.e., we can simultaneously estimate the direct and indirect consequence of a change in retail prices.

The aim of the present article is precisely to give a preliminary quantitative answer to these questions.

1. A Computational Scheme for Estimating the Elasticity of the Marginal Utility of Income, the Standard Rate of Return to Expenditure in the Long Term at the Macro Level, and the Matrix of Price Elasticities

In what follows, per capita income is equated with per capita expenditure on goods and services on all outlets for the consumption fund (i.e., excluding savings and windfalls), and the following notation is used: $i_1 = 1, \ldots, k$, is an index for groups of commodities and services; $i, j = 1, \ldots, m$, is an index for a good or service; ε_i is the expenditure elasticity for the i-th good or service; e_{ii} is the own-price elasticity of the i-th good or service; e_{ij} is the cross-price elasticity; α_i is the share of the m-th good in total expenditure; $\omega \equiv -(1/\eta)$ is the inverse of the elasticity of the marginal utility of income expressed negatively; $\hat{\omega}^* \equiv \hat{\omega} \pm \hat{\sigma_\omega}$; C_i is demand for a good or service; C is total expenditure per capita; P_i is the relative price of a good; $Q(C_i)$ is the utility function; σ, v, t^*, r_1, d, and R are, respectively, the mean square error, the coefficient of variation, the t statistic, the first-order autocorrelation coefficient, the Durbin-Watson statistic, and the correlation coefficient; y is the final output; k is the capital stock; r is the long-term rate of interest; r^* is the deterministic equivalent of the long-run rate of interest; $\sigma_{\partial y/\partial h}$ is the risk premium; $r = r^* + 0.5\sigma_r^2$ (see [2]); g is the rate of growth of final output; ρ is the stochastic rate of return to expenditure at the macro level.

Starting at the end of the twenties, Ragnar Frisch made estimates of $\hat{\omega}$ on the basis of demand functions calculated from family budget data and developed ways of computing cross-price elasticities with a known value of $\hat{\omega}$. It was he who made the first estimates of this parameter [3-5].

Later, L. Johansen and A. Amundsen calculated the parameter $\hat{\omega}$ ($\hat{\omega} \approx -2$) and, using this estimate, derived matrices of cross-price elasticities for Norway. They first used budget data and later budget surveys and time series assuming exogenous values for long-term income elasticities and at least two own-price elasticities calculated from statistical demand functions. The initial calculations yielded $\hat{\omega} \approx -2$, and the later ones gave a range from -3 to -5 [3, 4, 6, 7].

All the studies in this group were based on the following major assumptions: (a) there is a numerical utility function; (b) the whole market for goods and services can be represented fairly well by a typical consumer (the Slutsky hypothesis); and (c) the function $Q(C)$ is strongly additive — i.e., groups of commodities and services are independent of one another in terms of preferences (this does not mean demand independence, since demand for all goods and services is limited by the budget constraint).

From a formal point of view, preference independence means that

$$\frac{\partial Q_i}{\partial C_i} = \frac{\partial Q_j}{\partial C_j}, \tag{1}$$

i.e., indifference curves are assumed to have no curvature. In other words, an additive utility function is assumed, with a maximum subject to budgetary and price constraints, at market equilibrium. Frisch concludes from this that the elasticity of the marginal utility of income must be constant for any price configuration — that is, the same for all commodity groups and constant over time. Pearce, however, has shown [8, 9] that Frisch's assumptions can be removed by a more general approach to the definition of preference independence: condition (1) can be replaced by a condition

$$\frac{\partial(Q_i/Q_p)}{\partial C_j} = 0, \quad j \neq i, p, \tag{2}$$

which guarantees invariance subject to a monotonic transformation (it does not require a special assumption that there is a particular numerical representation of the utility function) and allows curvature of the indifference curves to be incorporated. From this Pearce draws the conclusion that the elasticity of the marginal utility of income must necessarily be constant within a group of commodities that are preference independent (see his theorem 1b in [8]), but need not be the same for the different commodity groups and, consequently, will not be constant over time. At the same time, calculations using actual British data led him to the same quantitative conclusions as those reached by Frisch and Johansen on the assumption of full additivity.

The next important step forward was made in the studies by Barten [10, 12] and Theil [13, 14]. Barten devised a method for simultaneously estimating a single flexibility parameter and price elasticities on the basis of statistical demand functions found using both time series data and data from sample budget surveys.

Barten's methods have the following major advantages: 1) they are based on the assumption either of almost strict additivity, which allows the substitution effect to be taken into account more fully, or of strict additivity, but with random perturbations in the utility function; 2) they compute a single flexibility parameter and income elasticity and the complete system price elasticities simultaneously, so that it is not the case that certain own-price elasticities have to be given exogenously, as in Frisch's method; 3) a random component can be incorporated as an important element in the analysis of consumer demand while the assumption of preference independence is retained. This leads to a system of equations that is nonlinear with respect to its parameters; although under certain conditions this gives the best linear unbiased estimate through an iterative procedure, at the same time it significantly increases the unreliability of the estimate. The latter, in turn, has an important impact on the estimates of the own-price elasticities and, through these (and directly), on the cross-elasticities (the estimate in [10] is that $\hat{\omega} \approx -2.12$ and in [12] that $\hat{\omega} \approx -3.125$ ($\sigma_\omega = -0.888$)).

Comparison of the methods of Frisch and Barten [10] in [15] showed that assuming not complete additivity but almost complete additivity and using the corresponding estimating procedure based on a system of linear stochastic equations with a priori information makes no substantial revisions in the estimates of the marginal utility of income and the system of elasticities as a whole, although the process of estimation is itself more rigorous and elegant. This justifies the use of a numerical utility function with strict additivity as a rough approximation.

H. Theil supplemented these results with an analysis from the standpoint of information theory. He treated budget shares as stochastic variables but maintained the assumption of strict additivity of the utility function.

Our choice of methods for estimating $\hat{\omega}$ and the matrix e_{ij} for the USSR is determined by the special circumstances in which the consumption fund is formed and the special way in which the data about it are collected.

To summarize, these circumstances are as follows: 1) the market for goods and services for personal consumption is not completely free and has certain special supply features; 2) the market is not based on a price mechanism of the kind assumed in the schemes set out above; consequently, the price and income elasticities are purely statistical parameters characterizing only the overall outcome of the interaction of demand and supply; 3) the determination of income per capita embraces the total of social consumption and consumption in kind; this certainly does not satisfy Slutsky's hypothesis; 4) the distribution of income is fairly equal; 5) price data given in price lists and data on retail turnover in constant prices are not sufficiently reliable. As a consequence, the estimates of α_i, ε_i, e_{ii}, a, and therefore of $\hat{\omega}_i$ and e_{ij} are biased. A comparison of the estimate of $\hat{\omega}$ at the level of the economy, made using a more accurate cost of living index [16] with the estimate derived by simple aggregation of the disaggregated estimates based on the less reliable data mentioned above, shows the latter estimate of $\hat{\omega}$ to be biased downward by at least one-third. In other words, because of the unreliability of the data, the disaggregated estimates presented below are primarily of methodological interest.

All these features apply to our estimates of the nature and size of $\hat{\omega}$ and of the elasticities ε_j and e_{ij}, but they operate with different force at different levels of aggregation. Whereas the assumption of a single parameter for the elasticity of the marginal utility of income can be sustained for the economy as a whole, it is certainly not justified for a more disaggregated classification of goods and services. As a result, it becomes necessary to introduce group values for the elasticity of the marginal utility of income with different numerical values for different commodity groups — i.e., to switch to Pearce's assumption. If we adopt this more realistic hypothesis, it is impossible for us to make direct use of the Barten-Theil methods outside the confines of a particular commodity group, so that the only remaining alternative is a modification of Frisch's scheme incorporating group values for $\hat{\omega}$ and a stability analysis.

We are thus led to adopt the following computational framework.

I. Point estimates of ω_{i_1} and e_{ij}

1) We use the Frisch model to estimate for a highly aggregated classification of commodities

$$\hat{\omega}_{i_1} = \frac{\varepsilon_{i_1}(1 - \alpha_{i_1}\varepsilon_{i_1})}{e_{i_1 i_1} + \alpha_{i_1}\varepsilon_{i_1}} \qquad i_1 \leqslant m, \tag{3}$$

where estimates for ε_{i_1} and $e_{i_1i_1}$ are found directly from regression equations.

If the right-hand side of (3) is approximately the same for several large commodity groups, we can treat it as an estimate of the elasticity of the marginal utility of income.

2) We next compute values of $\hat{\omega}_{i_1}$ for more disaggregated commodity groups, using (3).

3) Using $\hat{\omega}_{i_1}$ we compute the square matrix of cross-price elasticities in the full classification for a particular group of goods and services. This cycle can also include a partial reconsideration of the own-price elasticities from the regression equations (because of the great sensitivity of the e_{ii} to changes in $\hat{\omega}_{i_1}$, this should be done only when absolutely necessary):

$$e_{ii} = -\varepsilon_j\left(a_j - \frac{1 - a_j\varepsilon_j}{\hat{\omega}_{i_1}}\right), \quad i = j = 1, \ldots, k, \qquad (4)$$

$$e_{ij} = -\varepsilon_j a_i\left(1 + \frac{\varepsilon_i}{\hat{\omega}_{i_1}}\right), \quad \begin{array}{l} i = j = 1, \ldots, k \\ i \neq j. \end{array} \qquad (5)$$

4) Pearce's hypothesis is also applied outside the confines of a particular group of goods and services. This involves an estimate of $\hat{\omega}_{ij}$ for all $j = i > k$

$$\hat{\omega}_{ij} = \frac{\hat{\omega}_{i_1}a_{i_1}\varepsilon_{i_1} + \hat{\omega}_j a_j e_j}{a_{i_1}\varepsilon_{i_1} + a_j e_j} \quad j > k \qquad (6)$$

and the use of $\hat{\omega}_{ij}$ instead of $\hat{\omega}_{i_1}$ in (6) for all $i = j > k$; i.e., it involves calculation of the complete matrix e_{ij}.

5) Stability analysis is done by computing the derivatives (see [15])

$$\frac{\partial e_{ii}}{\partial \hat{\omega}_{i_1}} = -\frac{\varepsilon_i(1 - a_i\varepsilon_i)}{\hat{\omega}_{i_1}{}^2} \qquad (7)$$

$$\frac{\partial e_{ij}}{\partial \hat{\omega}_{i_1}} = \frac{a_i\varepsilon_i\varepsilon_j}{\hat{\omega}_{i_1}{}^2} \quad j = k; \quad \frac{\partial e_{ij}}{\partial \hat{\omega}_{ij}} = \frac{a_i\varepsilon_i\varepsilon_j}{\hat{\omega}_{ij}{}^2} \quad j > k, \qquad (8)$$

i.e., the sensitivity is inversely proportional to the values of

$\hat{\omega}_{i_1}$ and increases very quickly for $\hat{\omega}_{i_1} < 2$ and falls sharply for $\hat{\omega}_{i_1} > 2$.

II. Estimating the range of variation of $\hat{\omega}_{i_1}$ and e_{ij}

6) We calculate weighted mean square errors of $\hat{\omega}_{i_1}$ for the groups:

$$\sigma_{\hat{\omega}_{i_1}} = \sqrt{\frac{\Sigma(\omega_i - \hat{\omega}_{i_1})^2 \alpha_i \varepsilon_i}{(i-1)\sum_i \alpha_i \varepsilon_i}}, \tag{9}$$

and the range of variation of $\hat{\omega}_{i_1}$:

$$\hat{\omega}_{i_1}^* = \hat{\omega}_{i_1} \pm \sigma_{\hat{\omega}_{i_1}} \tag{10}$$

7) The $\hat{\omega}_{j_1}^*$ from (10) are used in (6) in place of $\hat{\omega}_{i_1}$ and in the general case confidence intervals are found for the estimates of ε_{i_1} and ε_j; as a result values for $\hat{\omega}_{ij}^*$ are found.

8) Cycle 6 is performed for the economywide estimate $\hat{\omega}$:

$$\sigma_{\hat{\omega}} = \frac{\Sigma \hat{\omega}_{i_1} \cdot \alpha_{i_1} \varepsilon_{i_1}}{\Sigma \alpha_{i_1} \varepsilon_{i_1}}, \tag{11}$$

$$\hat{\omega}^* = \hat{\omega} \pm \sigma_{\hat{\omega}}. \tag{12}$$

9) The confidence intervals of ε_j and ε_i and the values of $\hat{\omega}_i^*$ and $\hat{\omega}_{ij}^*$ are used to estimate matrices e_{ij}^*.

10) The stability analysis using (7)-(8) is supplemented by calculating the absolute and relative errors in matrix e_{ij}:

$$e_{ii} - e_{ii}^* = \frac{-\varepsilon_i(1 - \alpha_i \varepsilon_i)(\hat{\omega}_{i_1} - \hat{\omega}_{i_1}^*)}{\hat{\omega}_{i_1}\omega_{i_1}^*}, \tag{13}$$

$$e_{ij} - e_{ij}^* = \frac{\alpha_j \varepsilon_i \varepsilon_j (\hat{\omega}_{i_1} - \hat{\omega}_{i_1}^*)}{\hat{\omega}_{ij}\hat{\omega}_{ij}^*} \tag{14}$$

$$\gamma = \frac{\alpha_i \varepsilon_i - 1}{\alpha_j \varepsilon_j}. \tag{15}$$

It follows from (13)-(15) that: 1) the errors in estimating e_{ii} and e_{ij} have opposite signs; 2) since, moreover, it is possible to show that $\sum\limits_{i=1}^{m} (e_{ii} - e_{ii}{}^*) = \sum\limits_{i=1}^{m} \sum\limits_{j=1}^{m} (e_{ij} - e_{ij}{}^*)$ (see [15]), then, if the estimate of $\hat{\omega}_{i_1}$ is incorrect, the resulting error in estimating the own-price elasticity given by (14) is equal to the sum of the errors in all the cross-elasticities in the block plus a weighted sum of the errors in the estimates of the cross-elasticities outside the block.

III. Incorporating the impact of the scale of price changes

11) We introduce a scale effect into the own-price elasticities; this causes them to change in a way that depends on the range of variation of relative prices:

$$e_{i_1}{}^* = e_{i_1 i_1} + f_{i_1} \frac{d(p_{i_1}/p)}{p_{i_1}/\hat{p}_{\omega_{i_1}}}, \quad i_1 \ll i. \tag{16}$$

12) $\hat{\omega}_{i_1}$ is recalculated from (3) and then from (10); cycle 7 is done again, followed by cycle 9; then cycles 5 and 10 are repeated.

An alternative method estimates only the parameter for the economy as a whole.

This method is based, on the one hand, on a relationship between the long-run stochastic rate of return for the economy as a whole, the growth rate of the economy, parameter $\hat{\omega}$, and the long-run interest rate (see [2])

$$\rho_t = \hat{\omega}_{t+1} g_{t+1} e^{-r}, \tag{17}$$

and, on the other, on the structure of the rate of return

$$\rho = \frac{\partial y}{\partial k} + r^* + 0.5\sigma_{\partial y/\partial k}^2. \tag{18}$$

In (18) the long-run rate of return in the economy is given as the sum of the partial derivative of a macroeconomic production function and the long-run interest rate. The latter is the minimum level of guaranteed return to inputs in inelastic supply which generate income over an infinite time horizon with no foresight. The former magnitude is the standard rate of return to substitutable inputs over a finite time period with partial foresight. Hence, it can be interpreted as the deterministic equivalent of the long-run rate of return or as a risk premium. $\partial y \, / \, \partial k$ can be decomposed still further, by excluding the standard tax rate, so that the residual comprises the rate of return to investment in the strict sense of the word. In its turn, the interest rate can be represented as the sum of two magnitudes — the certainty equivalent interest rate and a risk premium.

This breakdown shows that ρ is in fact a standard rate of return for the economy, since it ensures the process of expanded reproduction in all its forms, by including all forms of surplus value in prices. But as distinct from traditional models of general equilibrium, which are based on inadequate economic assumptions, it has a single function — it cannot simultaneously fulfill the function of allocating resources and providing incentives for production. The two latter functions fall upon the long-term rate of interest and the standard long-term rate of return to investment in the pure sense of the term.

Formulas (17)-(18) can also be interpreted directly; if we know the rate of growth of final output and the long-term interest rate, then when we have estimated $\hat{\omega}$ using the scheme set out above, we can compute ρ and the certainty equivalent of the long-run rate of return, i.e., $\partial y \, / \, \partial k$.

In the following section, these questions are considered in concrete terms.

2. Evaluating the Elasticity of the Marginal Utility of Income in the USSR for the Economy as a Whole and for Commodity Groups

We have estimated the value of the elasticity of the marginal utility of income at the economy level by three methods. The first two treat the economy as a whole and incorporate all kinds

of price changes, while the third estimate uses very detailed
data but includes only retail purchases and is based only on
price-list prices and associated data for turnover.

1. The first method is described in [16]; it is based on a
direct application of Frisch's scheme to two aggregated groups
("foods" and "manufactured goods"), which are then combined
using appropriate weights. All estimates were made using
time-series data from 1951 to 1963.

The resulting point estimates for $\hat{\omega}$ were the following: for
foods, $\hat{\omega} \approx -3.255$; for manufactured goods, $\hat{\omega} \approx -3.170$; and
$\hat{\omega} \approx -3.228$ for the economy as a whole.

2. The second method uses formulas (17)-(18). The rate of
growth of final output was calculated specially, and the components of ρ were derived as follows. $\partial y / \partial k$ was found from a
macroeconomic production function estimated on 1951-65 data
in the form:

$$\lg Y_t = -0.524219 + 1.111363 (0.58804 \lg L_t + 0.33151 \lg K_t +$$
$$+ 0.08045 \lg N_t + 0.004894t),$$

$$\sigma = 0.008497, \quad v = 0.020, \quad r_1 = 0.4588, \quad d^* = 1.026. \quad (19)$$

(for details, see [17-18]). From this the value of $\partial y / \partial k$ was
0.1646 on average over 1951-65 and 0.1464 in 1965. For r^* we
may use the standard capital charge, which is 6 percent. This
procedure is not fully justified, of course, since it is difficult
to distinguish the extent to which the 6 percent charge is an interest rate and the extent to which it is a form of direct taxa-
tion. For $\sigma^2_{\partial y/\partial k}$ we took the dispersion of rates of profit in the
branches of industry in the period 1960-65, which was 0.026.
As a result, we get

$$\hat{\omega}_{1951-1965} = -3.60, \quad \hat{\omega}_{1965} = -4.29,$$

$$\frac{\partial y}{\partial k}(1951 - 1965) = 0.1646, \quad \frac{\partial y}{\partial k}(1965) = 0.1464, \quad (20)$$

$$\overset{\bullet}{\rho}_{1951-1965} = 0.1644, \quad r = 0.0730,$$
$$\rho_{1951-1965} = 0.2376, \quad \rho_{1965} = 0.2194.$$

3. Because the data underlying it are collected in a special way, the last method is solely of methodological interest, although it gives a quantitative representation of the overall scale of priorities in demand.[1] The Appendix gives the elasticities that formed the basis for these estimates of $\hat{\omega}_{i_1}$; the estimates are based on time-series data for retail trade turnover from 1953-65/6 and are given together with their statistical properties (the $t^*_{e_{i_1 i_2}}$ values clearly show the inadequacy of the underlying data). The overall scale of demand priorities is given in Table 1 (which gives point estimates of $\hat{\omega}_{i_1}$ and the range of variation of $\hat{\omega}_{i_1}^*$).

These results allow us to draw the following conclusions.

a) At present, an increase (decrease) of 1 percent in the share of consumption in final output and a 1 percent increase (decrease) in per capita consumption would increase (reduce) the utility the population derives from consumption by approximately 4.3 percent. This figure is very important for economic policy, as it shows how carefully we must approach the problem of allocating final output and evaluating alternative rates of change of the standard of living.

b) The largest increase in the social return from consumption (in descending order) would come from increases in per capita consumption of sausage, vegetables, furniture, electrical goods, meat and poultry, butter, eggs, and clothing. In other words, it would be most efficient to expand output and investment in these branches, if we wanted to improve the structure of personal consumption.

c) The standard social rate of return to expenditure of resources, as can be seen from (20), is made up as follows: approximately 30 percent is a fiscal element; of the remaining 70 percent, about 44 percent is an interest charge.

d) Aggregated values of $\hat{\omega}$ clearly exhibit substantial stability. Thus, if we eliminate printed goods, musical instruments, and toys, the value of $\hat{\omega}$ for retail turnover increases only to -2.2958, and the elimination of "fruit and vegetables" raises it only to -2.30035.

Table 1

Group Values for $\hat{\omega}_{i_1}$ (1953-1965/6)

	Commodity group	$\hat{\omega}_{i_1}$	$\hat{\omega}_{i_1}^{*}$
1	Meat, sausage, canned meat, lard;	−3.505	−2.727, −4.283
	Of which, sausage,	−5.770	−
	meat and poultry	−3.890	−
2	Furniture, electrical goods, radios,		
	bicycles and motorcycles;	−3.358	−2.635, −4.085
	Of which, furniture	−4.700	−
	electrical goods	−4.600	−
3	Clothing (knitwear, haberdashery,		
	socks and stockings, furs)	−3.100	−2.140, −4.060
4	Footwear (leather, combination,		
	rubber, and felt)	−2.300	−1.714, −2.904
5	Fruit, vegetables, potatoes,		
	canned vegetables;	−2.242	−
	Of which, vegetables	−5.059	−
6	Vodka, wine, beer	−1.800	−1.419, −2.181
7	Butter, milk, cheese, eggs;	−1.560	−0.836, −2.284
	Of which, butter and eggs	−3.218	−
8	Perfumes, soap	−1.400	−1.025, −1.775
9	Bread, flour, semolina, macaroni,		
	confectionery	−0.960	−0.782, −1.138
10	Tobacco, matches	−0.780	−0.733, −0.827
	Average for retail sales	−2.221	

We now estimate the matrix of cross-price elasticities.

3. Estimating the Matrix of Cross-Price Elasticities and Its Stability

The estimation was done for retail trade over the period 1953-65/66 by the method described in section 1 and using data on price-list prices and the associated retail turnover. Because of this, as noted above, the matrix is only of illustrative value (Table 2).

Table 2

Price Elasticities for Retail Trade Turnover (1953-65)

Commodity group	e_{ii}	Σe_{ij}	$e_{ii}/\Sigma e_{ij}$	ε_i
Bicycles	−0.71355	−0.79328	0.89949	1.77616
Meat	−0.58847	−1.043521	0.56393	1.96519
Sausage	−0.40639	−0.87552	0.46417	1.36148
Canned food	−0.65810	−0.6874638	0.95729	2.29793
Lard	−0.34152	−0.535021	0.63833	1.17393
Butter	−0.71004	−1.0374	0.68444	1.09787
Milk	−1.74764	−1.07749	1.62195	2.89762
Cheese		0.045175		1.50632
Eggs	−0.94463	−0.992976	0.95131	1.47310
Bread	−0.42339	−3.52184	0.12022	0.41499
Flour	−0.42012	−0.98792	0.4253	0.35504
Semolina	−0.70655	−1.01608	0.69537	0.67145
Macaroni	−0.46464	−0.64645	0.71876	0.44472
Confectionery	−0.84740	−1.43101	0.59217	0.80862
Vodka	−0.71031	−2.937401	0.31747	1.28881
Wine	−0.98997	−1.165565	0.84935	1.78069
Beer	−0.39598	−0.82374	0.48071	0.70115
Furs	−0.39218	−0.47761	0.82113	1.20570
Stockings	−0.46283	−0.62707	0.73808	1.41810
Haberdashery	−0.48735	−0.85679	0.56881	1.46383
Knitwear	−0.59696	−0.94857	0.62933	1.73758
Leather footwear	−0.50610	−0.79807	0.63415	4.11395
Rubber boots	−0.02665	−0.32927	0.08094	0.06023
Felt boots	−0.18447	−0.32177	0.57330	0.42174
Perfumes	−0.69220	−0.79792	0.86751	0.96695
Soap powder	−0.51084	−0.63865	0.80214	0.71282
Toilet soap	−0.45426	−0.50479	0.8999	0.63509
Tobacco	−0.82895	−1.34524	0.61759	0.64491
Matches	−0.00955	−0.07466	0.12791	0.00744
Furniture	−0.59778	−0.71667	0.8341	2.72623
Electrical goods	−0.63024	−0.66941	0.94149	2.87478
Radios	−1.36669	−1.43328	0.95354	2.88782

Analysis of the matrix reveals the following.

1) The penultimate column in the table shows what proportion of the variation in demand in the retail network is due to an own-price change. The shortfall from one in each case shows the contribution of indirect effects (the exception is milk and milk products, the results for which are quite unreliable).

These data show that, in a number of cases, the indirect effects of a change in the price of any good are even more powerful than the direct effect.

Thus, a 1 percent increase in the price of meat reduces sales of meat by 0.59 percent. But, at the same time, a 1 percent increase in meat prices reduces sales of sausages by 0.02 percent, of canned food by 0.03 percent, of butter by 0.01 percent, and of milk, cheese, and eggs by 0.02 percent. The effect of the increase is also very noticeable on sales of manufactured goods, which are reduced as follows: furs, stockings, haberdashery, and knitwear by 0.02 percent; furniture and electrical goods by 0.04 percent; bicycles by 0.02 percent; radios by 0.03 percent. In total, indirect changes of this kind lead to a further reduction in sales of 0.45 percent.

A change of 1 percent in the price of leather footwear causes a direct change in demand of 0.5 percent. But, at the same time, there are changes in the demand for meat and meat products of 0.05 percent; for milk of 0.04 percent; for sausage, cheese, eggs, and wine of 0.03 percent; and for vodka of 0.02 percent. The indirect effect on the market for manufactured goods leads to the following changes: 0.06 percent in sales of furniture and radios; 0.04 percent in electrical goods and bicycles; 0.02 percent in perfumes; and so on. In all, the indirect effects alter demand in the opposite direction by 0.3 percent; that is, they represent about three-fifths of the direct effect.

2) If we compare the sum of price elasticities with the income elasticities, we see that the standard relationship in the theory of consumer equilibrium $(- \sum_{j=1}^{m} e_{ij} = \varepsilon_i)$ is not satisfied in a single case. The original data, however, are not reliable enough for us to be able to attribute the divergence totally to the existence of elements of structural disequilibrium in the behavior of consumers and in the relationship between supply and demand; clearly, we can say only that the result does reflect to some degree the existence of these phenomena.

For the stability analysis, we first computed the matrix of

Table 3

$de_{ij}/d\hat{\omega}_{i_1}$ for Retail Sales, 1953-65/66

Commodity group	$\partial e_{ii}/\partial \omega_{i_1}$	$\sum_i \frac{\partial e_{ij}}{\partial \omega_{i_1}}$	Commodity group	$\partial e_{ii}/\partial \omega_{i_1}$	$\sum_i \frac{\partial e_{ij}}{\partial \omega_{i_1}}$
Meat	−0.1504	+0.07403	Bread	−0.4383	+0.04039
Sausage	−0.1076	+0.02313	Vodka	−0.3291	+1.02435
Canned			Knitwear	−0.1736	+0.04167
goods	−0.1857	−0.12799	Leather		
Lard	−0.0946	−0.03424	footwear	−0.2001	−0.12835
Butter	−0.4416	−0.22660	Furniture	−0.2315	−0.06755
Milk	−1.1203	−0.48087	Electrical		
Cheese	−0.6155	−0.51379	goods	−0.2513	−0.16654
Eggs	−0.6011	−0.49239	Radios	−0.2503	−0.13923

partial derivatives (7)-(8) using retail sales estimates. The diagonal elements and overall totals of row changes are shown for some cases in Table 3.

It is obvious from comparing Tables 2 and 3 that the proportionate change in e_{ij} with respect to $\hat{\omega}_{i_1}$ is at least 25 percent, when we employ the downwardly biased estimates for ω_{i_1} obtained using retail sales data. We can see from the following example how this artificially decreases the stability of the estimates. If we assume that the downward bias of $\hat{\omega}$ for meat goods is as large as the bias in the overall estimate for retail sales (found by comparing it with the more precise estimate for the economy of $\hat{\omega} = -3.60$), then $\hat{\omega}_1 = -4.90$ for the meat goods group and $\partial e_{ii} / \partial \hat{\omega}_1 = 0.0770$ instead of 0.1504.

Thus, the accuracy of the estimates of $\hat{\omega}_{i_1}$ is obviously a vital factor in the stability analysis.

The table also shows the compensating effects of $\dfrac{\partial e_{ii}}{\partial \hat{\omega}_{i_1}}$ and $\partial e_{ij}/\partial \hat{\omega}_{i_1}$, which have opposite signs.

We reach a similar conclusion if we analyze the absolute deviations (13)-(14) with the point estimates of ε_{i_1}, and interval values of $\hat{\omega}_{i_1}^{*}$. But for reasons of space we do not show our results in detail.

4. Conclusions

1. At present, the only feasible and practical way to get a partial and approximate measure of utility and of the associated marginal indices that are so important for economic policy is to adopt the notion of a numerical utility function and to use statistical methods of estimation.

2. Before we use this tool, however, we must make further empirical tests of the assumptions that underlie a numerical utility function. This, in turn, requires a radical improvement in the quality of the statistical data, since without such an improvement we cannot go beyond numerical illustrations.

3. Moving over to a complete measure of social welfare as a criterion for the economy presupposes:

a) that we can evaluate the benefits measured by our partial criteria by a switch from a vectoral to a scalar form. Generally, even for this we need a numerical estimate of the quadratic preference functions of the major types of agents in the socio-economic process with respect to each partial criterion. The general notion of a numerical utility function combined with statistical processing of the results of specially designed interviews might serve as a starting point;

b) that we have an estimate of a quadratic preference function that combines the scalar values of the partial criteria;

c) that we can develop special branches of sociology and social psychology and thus achieve a clearer understanding of the role of nonquantifiable variables in the partial or overall criteria, and that we can devise specialized methods for performing surveys and processing their results.

Each of these tasks is extremely complex. Solving them requires a long program of research by a whole group of specialized institutes and state organizations.

REFERENCES

1. Rumiantsev, A. M. "Printsip demokraticheskogo tsentralizma, ekonomicheskaia reforma i opyt matematicheskogo analiza problem soglasovannogo khoziaistvovaniia." Ekonomika i matematicheskie metody, 1968, vol. 4, no. 5.

282   The Analysis of Consumer Behavior

2. Mikhalevskii, B. N. "Odnosektornaia dinamicheskaia model' i otsenka normy effektivnosti kapitalovlozhenii." Ekonomika i matematicheskie metody, 1965, vol. 1, no. 2.

3. Frisch, R. "Dynamic Utility." Econometrica, 1964, vol. 32, no. 3.

4. Frisch, R. "A Complete Scheme for Computing All Direct and Cross Demand Elasticities in a Model with Many Sectors." Econometrica, 1959, vol. 27, no. 2.

5. Frisch, R. New Methods of Measuring Marginal Utility. Tübingen, 1931.

6. Johansen, L. A Multisectoral Model of Economic Growth. Amsterdam: North-Holland Publishing Company, 1960.

7. Johansen, L. "Explorations in Long-Term Projections for the Norwegian Economy." Economics of Planning, 1968, vol. 8, nos. 1-2.

8. Pearce, I. "An Exact Method for Consumer Demand Analysis." Econometrica, 1961, vol. 29, no. 4.

9. Pearce, I. A Contribution to Demand Analysis. Oxford, 1964.

10. Barten, A. "Consumer Demand Functions under Conditions of Almost Additive Preferences." Econometrica, 1964, vol. 32, nos. 1-2.

11. Barten, A. "Family Composition, Prices and Expenditure Patterns." In Sixteenth Symposium of the Colston Research Society. London, 1964.

12. Barten, A. "Estimating Demand Equations." Econometrica, 1968, vol. 36, no. 2.

13. Theil, H. "The Information Approach to Demand Theory." Econometrica, 1965, vol. 33, no. 1.

14. Theil, H. Economics and Information Theory. Amsterdam: North-Holland Publishing Company, 1967.

15. Ayanian, R. "A Comparison of Barten's Estimated Demand Elasticities with Those Obtained Using Frisch's Method." Econometrica, 1969, vol. 37, no. 1.

16. Mikhalevskii, B. N. "Koeffitsienty elastichnosti ot dokhoda i tsen i otsenka parametra zameshcheniia." In Statisticheskoe izuchenie sprosa i potrebleniia. Moscow: "Nauka" Publishers, 1966.

17. Mikhalevskii, B. N., and Solov'ev, Iu. P. "Proizvodstvennaia funktsiia narodnogo khoziaistva SSSR v 1951-63 gody." Ekonomika i matematicheskie metody, 1966, vol. 2, no. 6.

18. Mikhalevskii, B. N. "Odnosektornaia dinamicheskaia model' i raschet global'nykh pokazatelei srednesrochnogo plana." Ekonomika i matematicheskie metody, 1968, vol. 4, no. 1.

19. Konius, A. A. "Teoreticheskii indeks tsen potrebleniia i ego primenenie v planirovanii platezhesposobnogo sprosa." In Ekonomika i matematicheskie metody, vol. 1. Moscow: USSR Academy of Sciences Press, 1963.

20. Volkonskii, V. A. "Ob ob'ektivnoi matematicheskoi kharakteristike narodnogo potrebleniia." In [19].

21. Otto, K. "Indeksnyi metod analiza udovletvoreniia potrebnostei i peremeshcheniia sprosa." In Statisticheskoe izuchenie sprosa potrebleniia. Moscow: "Nauka" Publishers, 1966.

Received October 7, 1969

Appendix

Table 4

Statistical Properties of the Elasticities Calculated Using Estimates
of $\hat{w}$ for Commodity Groups

Commodity group	ε_{i_1}	$e_{i_1 i_1}$	$t_{\varepsilon_{i_1}}$	$t_{e_{i_1 i_1}}$	R (independent variables)	r_1	d
Meat, sausage, canned goods, lard	1.61281	−0.51628	24.243	−3.673	−0.0547	0.0960	1.9410
Fruit, vegetables, potatoes, canned vegetables	2.00511	−0.90137	18.184	−3.404	0.4786	0.1958	1.8499
Butter, milk, cheese, eggs	2.04320	−1.28091	18.139	−4.018	0.0606	0.0885	1.7558
Socks and stockings	1.41210	−0.46287	7.846	−1.026	−0.4420	0.1664	1.4814
Haberdashery	1.46385	−0.46735	5.894	−0.351	−0.8922	0.2303	1.4079
Tobacco	0.64491	−0.82895	6.036	−0.449	−0.1835	0.2194	1.5204
Furniture	2.72623	−0.59773	18.481	−0.450	−0.2227	0.0551	1.7616
Electrical goods	2.87478	−0.63024	7.413	−0.479	−0.2886	0.2740	1.3823
Radios	2.88782	−1.36669	10.464	−1.993	−0.6284	0.2762	1.2599
Bicycles and motorcycles	1.77616	−0.71355	34.697	−2.036	−0.4431	−0.1552	2.2443

MATHEMATICAL AND COMPUTATIONAL ASPECTS OF A METHOD FOR ANALYZING AND FORECASTING THE DIFFERENTIATION OF HOUSEHOLD CONSUMPTION

S. A. Aivazian, Z. I. Bezhaeva, and N. I. Makarchuk

The previous chapter [not translated here — Ed.] was devoted to a discussion of socioeconomic categories, formulation of the major aim and methods of our research, and a description of the problems it involves. In particular, sections 1-3 of chapter 1 give a more or less clear informal account of the major initial hypotheses (or assumptions) on which the authors base their research.

This chapter is devoted to formalizing major concepts and assumptions and formulating the problems to be analyzed; we also give an account of the mathematical methods, algorithms, and procedures by which these problems will be solved.

1. A Formal Account of the General Concepts and Principal Assumptions Underlying the Study

When, in the previous chapter, we analyzed the two major approaches to defining needs — the national-normative approach and the behavioral approach — we reached the following conclusion (see chapter 1, section 1).

(A) Hypothesis concerning the consumption unit: the primary

Russian text © 1978 by "Nauka" Publishers. Tipologiia potrebleniia, ed. by S. A. Aivazian and N. M. Rimashevskaia. Ch. 2, sections 1-2, pp. 45-85.

social unit in which actual needs are shaped is the household, for it is here that people's preferences, desires, and attitudes are molded.

Starting from this assumption, we have to analyze consumption behavior and its associated determinants (circumstances), both of all households together and of each family separately. In particular, let O_i be the i-th consumer unit (household) under study; $i = 1, 2, \ldots, n$, where n is the total number of households to be analyzed. For simplicity, we call $O = \{O_i, \ i = 1, 2, \ldots, n\}$ the set of households under investigation.

When we study the circumstances (or determinants) affecting household O_i we are actually fixing the values of a certain number (p) of indices $x_i^{(1)}, x_i^{(2)}, \ldots, x_i^{(p)}$ reflecting the state of the i-th household; these p indices (or markers) can be either quantitative (income, total number of family members, size of accommodation, rate of growth, etc.), or qualitative and categorized (quality of life, etc.), or classificatory (showing the occupation of household members, the sector in which the head of the household works, the form of ownership of the dwelling in which the household resides, etc.). Thus, each family has a p-dimensional vector (or a p-dimensional observation)

$$
X_i = \begin{pmatrix} x_i^{(1)} \\ x_i^{(2)} \\ \vdots \\ x_i^{(p)} \end{pmatrix},
$$

which is assumed to lie in a space X of determinants (i.e., $X_i \in X$, $i = 1, 2, \ldots, n$).

Similarly, when we study the consumption behavior (i.e., the actual consumption structure) of household O_i, we choose a number (m) of indices of consumption behavior $y_i^{(1)}, y_i^{(2)}, \ldots,$ $y_i^{(m)}$, where by $y_i^{(v)}$ ($v = 1, 2, \ldots, m$) we mean consumption of the v-th product (including goods, services, or savings) per member of the i-th family in the base period (a year), expressed in either physical or monetary terms.

Thus, associated with each family O_i there is a vector X_i as well as an m-dimensional vector (m-dimensional observation)

$$Y_i = \begin{pmatrix} y_i^{(1)} \\ y_i^{(2)} \\ \vdots \\ y_i^{(m)} \end{pmatrix},$$

which is assumed to lie in the corresponding space of consumption behavior Y (i.e., $Y_i \in Y$, $i = 1, 2, \ldots, n$).

In order to implement the algorithm we intend to use, we have to make X and Y metric spaces or, in other words, impose a metric on them (i.e., choose a way of measuring the distance between any two elements in space X or in space Y). We postpone the choice of a measure for these spaces, however, until section 2.

To get to the underlying mathematical concepts that we need in order to formalize the socioeconomic categories we are studying and to formulate the problem to be solved, we must at this stage express more clearly certain ideas mentioned in sections 1-3 of chapter 1 and partly analyzed and explained there.

(B) <u>Our hypothesis concerning the stratification of behavioral space Y</u> postulates the existence of a relatively small number N of types of consumption behavior $S_Y^{(1)}, S_Y^{(2)}, \ldots, S_Y^{(N)}$, such that any differences in the consumption patterns of families of the same type $S_Y^{(k)}$ are random (i.e., subject to a number of random influences that cannot be controlled or taken into account) and insignificant compared with the differences in consumption behavior between households of different types $S_Y^{(k_1)}$ and $S_Y^{(k_2)}$.

Interpreted geometrically, assumption (B) means that there is a metric $\rho_Y(O_i, O_j)$ in space Y that takes account of the interrelationships of individual aspects of consumer behavior and of their relative importance in differentiating the consumption structure, so that the whole set of "multidimensional points" O under study can be divided in a natural way into a comparatively small number of "clots" or clusters $S_Y^{(1)}, S_Y^{(2)}, \ldots, S_Y^{(N)}$; these clusters are some distance apart (in the sense of metric ρ_Y) but their elements are not themselves too widely dispersed.

(B*) A stronger hypothesis concerning the stratification of the space differs from hypothesis (B) in that it also assumes that the random dispersion of multidimensional points corresponding to households exhibiting consumption behavior $Y_i(k)$ belonging to any given (type k) $S_Y^{(k)}$ has an m-dimensional normal probability distribution. In other words, if $Y(k)$ is a random vector for the consumption pattern of a household chosen randomly from a homogeneous set $S_Y^{(k)}$ of type k households, then the density function for the probability distribution is given by[1]

$$f_k(Y) = \frac{1}{(2\pi)^{\frac{m}{2}} \, |\Sigma(k)|} \, e^{-\frac{1}{2}(Y-Y_0(k))'\Sigma^{-1}(k)(Y-Y_0(k))} \tag{1}$$

In this expression, vector

$$Y_0(k) = \begin{pmatrix} y_0^{(1)}(k) \\ y_0^{(2)}(k) \\ \vdots \\ y_0^{(m)}(k) \end{pmatrix} \tag{2}$$

is the mean (and also the modal) consumption pattern for all possible households of type k and matrix

$$\Sigma(k) = \begin{pmatrix} \sigma_{11}(k), & \sigma_{12}(k), & \dots, & \sigma_{1m}(k) \\ \sigma_{21}(k), & \sigma_{22}(k), & \dots, & \sigma_{2m}(k) \\ \multicolumn{4}{c}{\dots \dots \dots \dots \dots} \\ \sigma_{m1}(k), & \sigma_{m2}(k), & \dots, & \sigma_{mm}(k) \end{pmatrix} \tag{3}$$

is defined by the so-called covariances of the components in the consumption pattern of type k households; i.e.,

$$\sigma_{ql}(k) = \sigma_{lq}(k) = \text{cov}(y^{(l)}(k), y^{(q)}(k)) =$$
$$= M\{(y^{(l)}(k) - y_0^{(l)}(k))(y^{(q)}(k) - y_0^{(q)}(k))\}. \tag{4}$$

At the same time, the distribution of the random vector $Y(k)$ is assumed to be nondegenerate.

The sample (or empirical) analogues of the theoretical magnitudes $y_0^{(l)}(k)$ and $\sigma_{ql}(k)$ will be, respectively,

$$\hat{y}_0^{(l)}(k) = \frac{1}{n_k} \sum_{i=1}^{n_k} y_i^{(l)}(k) \quad (l = 1, 2, \ldots, m) \qquad (2')$$

and

$$\hat{\sigma}_{ql}(k) = \frac{1}{n_k} \sum_{i=1}^{n_k} (y_i^{(l)}(k) - \hat{y}_0^{(l)}(k))(y_i^{(q)}(k) - \hat{y}_0^{(q)}(k)) \qquad (4')$$

$$(q, l = 1, 2, \ldots, m),$$

where n_k is the total number of households exhibiting a consumption pattern of type k and $y_i^{(l)}(k)$ is the value of the l-th component of the consumption pattern registered by the i-th household of type k.

It is appropriate to note here the following interesting property of a multidimensional normal distribution, since we shall use it below to get fairly general results from the framework we shall set out. Assume that rationing or shortages of some goods $y^{(q_1)}$, $y^{(q_2)}$, . . ., $y^{(q_I)}(I < m)$ impose <u>a priori</u> constraints on these components:

$$y^{(q_\nu)} = c_{q_\nu}, \quad \nu = 1, 2, \ldots, I, \qquad (5)$$

where c_{q_ν} is the specified consumption level for good $y^{(q_\nu)}$. Assume, moreover, that we are interested only in the distribution (the form of random variation) of the consumption vector $Y(k)$ of families with a fixed per capita income s, i.e., that constraints (5) are supplemented by a constraint

$$\sum_{l=1}^{m} p^{(l)} y^{(l)}(k) = s, \qquad (6)$$

in which $p^{(1)}$, $p^{(2)}$, . . ., $p^{(m)}$ are retail prices of, respectively, $y^{(1)}$, $y^{(2)}$, . . ., $y^{(m)}$.[2]

It turns out (the result can be taken directly from [8, pp. 346-47], for example) that the conditional distribution of vector $Y(k)$ subject to constraints of type (5) and (6) is still a multi-

dimensional normal one, though its dimensionality is reduced
to $m - I - 1$, and of the vector of means $Y_0 (k)$ and the correlation matrix $\Sigma (k)$ have to be recomputed.

(C) The optimality assumption: here we briefly state our assumption that underlying each (k-th) type of household consumption behavior there is a criterion of optimality, or rationality,
that can naturally be expressed in mathematical form by a so-
called utility function or objective function of consumption,
$u^{(k)} (Y)$ (see, for example, [15, 6, 18]). This function allows
us to measure quantitatively the degree of preference (or rationality) associated with any given form of consumption behavior Y; only families of the same kind follow the same convention
for calculating utility (i.e., share a particular utility function),
and the function changes from one type of family to another.

(D) The hypothesis that optimality is shown in a statistical
sense is a natural development of the optimality assumption (C).
It postulates that the actual consumption pattern Y of a randomly selected household of type k is the outcome of the operation of objective laws of which the family is, as a rule, either
unaware or aware only at an intuitive level; these allow us to
evaluate and compare alternative feasible variants of Y in
terms of their degree of rationality. At the same time, the information each household actually possesses and the distorting
influence of the random variables prevent it from achieving the
precise optimal structure $Y_{ОПТ} (k)$; however, there is an objective tendency for all homogeneous households (of the same type)
to satisfy their needs in an optimal way (with given constraints
on income and perhaps on particular components $y^{(l)}(k)$ which
are rationed or in short supply), and this is reflected in the fact
that, by the law of large numbers $Y_{mod}(k)$, the actual modal consumption pattern of type k families (i.e., the one most frequently observed — and in a broad number of cases this is the
same as the statistical mean) is exactly the optimal one; i.e.,

$$Y_{ОПТ} (k) = Y_{mod} (k),$$

or, what is the same thing,

$$u^{(k)}(Y_{\mathrm{mod}}(k)) = \max_{Y} u^{(k)}(Y) \qquad (7)$$

subject to constraints of types (5) and (6).

(E) The assumption that there exist indices which classify households up to a confidence level of $(1 - \beta)$. This hypothesis postulates that, from among the vector of factors characterizing a household's circumstances, it is possible to distinguish a sub-vector

$$\tilde{X} = \begin{pmatrix} x^{(j_1)} \\ x^{(j_2)} \\ \vdots \\ x^{(j_{p'})} \end{pmatrix} = \begin{pmatrix} \tilde{x}^{(1)} \\ \tilde{x}^{(2)} \\ \vdots \\ \tilde{x}^{(p')} \end{pmatrix}, \quad p' < p \qquad (8)$$

and to choose a metric $\rho_{\tilde{X}}(O_i, O_j)$ in the corresponding space $\tilde{X}$ such that in this metric space we can find nonintersecting regions $S_{\tilde{X}}^{(1)}, S_{\tilde{X}}^{(2)}, \ldots, S_{\tilde{X}}^{(N)}$ to which the following proposition applies: for any type of consumption behavior $S_Y^{(k)}$ we can find a corresponding set of values of classifying indices $S_{\tilde{X}}^{t(k)}$ such that

$$P\{Y \in S_Y^{(k)} \mid X \in S_{\tilde{X}}^{t(k)}\} \geqslant 1 - \beta, \quad k = 1, 2, \ldots, N. \qquad (9)^3$$

We should note here that, if relation (9) is satisfied, we can derive an estimate of the accuracy of our method for determining a household's consumption type by the value of its classifying index. Indeed, suppose that after establishing correspondences of type $k \leftrightarrow t(k)$ between each consumption pattern $S_Y^{(k)}$ and the associated set of values of the classifying indices $S_{\tilde{X}}^{t(k)}$ we identify the type of consumption behavior of a randomly chosen household O^* by following the rule: "if

$$\tilde{X}(O^*) \in S_{\tilde{X}}^{t(k)}$$

then

$$Y(O^*) \in S_Y^{(k)}.\text{"}$$

Then it is easy to see from (9) that, with this rule, the proportion of misclassified households cannot exceed β.

2. The Overall Mathematical and Methodological Framework of the Study and a Mathematical Formulation of the Major Problems

Our analysis of the general logical framework of the study, as described in section 4 of chapter 1, together with the formal concepts and assumptions introduced in the previous section, allows us to set down the overall mathematical and methodological framework of the study and to formulate in mathematical terms the major problems encountered.

It follows from step 1 [collection of the original data and their preliminary statistical analysis — Ed.] and the special features of the original data array $\{X_i, Y_i\}, i = \overline{1, n}$ that, when we begin to process the raw data statistically, we are faced with the following two major problems.

Problem 1. This problem involves the choice of a metric in space Y; i.e., the problem of adopting a rule (or algorithm) for computing the distance between any two baskets of consumption goods Y_i and Y_j.

The success of the whole enterprise depends upon finding a solution to this problem, but we must also take into account the consequences of the substantial multidimensionality of $Y' = (y^{(1)}, y^{(2)}, \ldots, y^{(m)})$, the set of behavioral indices under study. We show this by an example, which for purposes of illustration we simplify by reducing the dimensions of the vector of consumption behavior to two (i.e., we set $Y' = (y^{(1)}, y^{(2)})$, where $y^{(1)}$ and $y^{(2)}$ are per capita consumption of "food products" and "nonfood products and services," respectively. We record the values of $(y^{(1)}, y^{(2)})$ for households in two different sets, where households of "group I" differ from those of "group II" with respect to a number of important factors affecting their daily lives (income, geographical location, social and demographic structure). The results are shown (on an artificial scale) in Figure 1, where observations of group I families are represented on the graph by a cross ($\times$) and those of group II families by a circle ($\circ$). $\hat{y}_0^{(1)}$ (I) and $\hat{y}_0^{(1)}$ (II) are, respectively, sample means of expenditure of group I and group II families on "food prod-

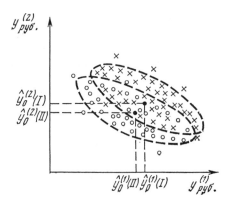

Figure 1. A graphical representation of expenditure on food products $(y^{(1)})$ and nonfood products and services $(y^{(2)})$ by families of the two groups.

ucts and $\hat{y}_0^{(2)}$ (I) and $\hat{y}_0^{(2)}$ (II) are mean levels of expenditure on "nonfood products and other services."

Statistical analysis showed that, component by component, the divergences in the means, $\Delta_1 = |\hat{y}_0^{(1)}$ (I) $- \hat{y}_0^{(1)}$ (II)$|$ and $\Delta_2 = |\hat{y}_0^{(2)}$ (I) $- \hat{y}_0^{(2)}$ (II)$|$ are not statistically significant, nor is the total divergence between means $\Delta_1 + \Delta_2$. In other words, if we look at divergences Δ_1 and Δ_2 component by component without taking account of the links between them, we are not able to demonstrate any difference in the consumption behavior of the families in the two groups under study. There is a difference, however, and it does become obvious if we use a metric that takes account of the nature of the interrelationships between the components under analysis.

In particular, if we start by adopting the strong hypothesis concerning stratification in the space of consumption behavior Y (see hypothesis (B*) above), and if we adopt the natural hypothesis that the nature of the interrelationships between components $y^{(l)}(k)$ and $y^{(q)}(k)$ (i.e., the covariance matrix $\Sigma(k)$) is the same as we move from one type of consumption to another, i.e.,

$$\Sigma (1) = \Sigma (2) = \ldots = \Sigma (N) = \Sigma,$$

then the most natural metric, as is well known (see [3, p. 80]; [7, p. 368]; [2, p. 52]) is a distance of the Mahalanobis type:

$$\rho_Y(O_i, O_j) = [(Y_i - Y_j)' \Sigma^{-1} (Y_i - Y_j)]^{1/2}. \tag{10}$$

We shall in fact use this metric in space Y, the more so since it is easy to see that, in the special cases of diagonal covariance matrices of type

$$\Sigma = \begin{pmatrix} \sigma_{11} & & & 0 \\ & \sigma_{22} & & \\ & & \ddots & \\ 0 & & & \sigma_{mm} \end{pmatrix}, \tag{11}$$

(which correspond to the case where components $y^{(1)}$, $y^{(2)}$, . . ., $y^{(m)}$ are not mutually intercorrelated, but have variances σ_{11}, σ_{22}, . . ., σ_{mm}) or of type

$$\Sigma = \begin{pmatrix} \sigma & & & 0 \\ & \sigma & & \\ & & \ddots & \\ 0 & & & \sigma \end{pmatrix}, \tag{11'}$$

(which correspond to the case where the components $y^{(1)}$, $y^{(2)}$, . . ., $y^{(m)}$ are not intercorrelated and have the same variance σ), the metric reduces, in the first case, to a weighted Euclidean metric

$$\tilde{\rho}_Y(O_i, O_j) = \left[\sum_{l=1}^{m} \frac{1}{\sigma_{ll}} (y_i^{(l)} - y_j^{(l)})^2 \right]^{1/2} \tag{10'}$$

and, in the second, to the standard Euclidean metric

$$\tilde{\tilde{\rho}}_Y(O_i, O_j) = \left[\sum_{l=1}^{m} (y_i^{(l)} - y_j^{(l)})^2 \right]^{1/2}. \tag{10''}$$

Problem 2. This problem involves reducing the dimensions of space Y, i.e., switching from an m-dimensional vector Y of original characteristics of consumption behavior to a vector $\tilde{Y}$ of substantially smaller size, $\tilde{m}$ ($\tilde{m} \ll m$), where the components $y^{(l)}$ of the latter are both based on the original properties $y^{(1)}$, $y^{(2)}$, . . ., $y^{(m)}$ (this includes the case in which $\tilde{y}^{(l)}$ can replicate particular components of vector Y) and also provide the maximum information from the standpoint of revealing the nature of the differentiation of household consumption behavior.

In formal terms, the general problem of reducing dimensions can be described as follows.

We first determine in some way a measure of the informativeness $I_m(Y)$ of an m-dimensional random variable Y. The actual choice of the functional $I_m(Y)$[4] depends on the nature of the requirements we impose on the system of indices under analysis (see, for example, [9, chs. I and II]; [2, ch. IV]; [1, pp. 21-22]). Let

$$\widetilde{Y} = \begin{pmatrix} \varphi^{(1)}(Y) \\ \varphi^{(2)}(Y) \\ \vdots \\ \varphi^{(\widetilde{m})}(Y) \end{pmatrix}$$

be the outcome of transforming the original system of indices, as a result of which we switch from a system of indices Y to a new system of indices $\widetilde{Y}$, where $\widetilde{m} \ll m$. Using for convenience of exposition the $\widetilde{m}$-dimensional vector function

$$\varphi(\cdot) = \begin{pmatrix} \varphi^{(1)}(\cdot) \\ \varphi^{(2)}(\cdot) \\ \vdots \\ \varphi^{(\widetilde{m})}(\cdot) \end{pmatrix},$$

we get

$$\widetilde{Y} = \varphi(Y).$$

Then, if Φ is the set (for definiteness, a closed set) of possible transformations in which we seek our solution, the problem of constructing the most informative system of indices $\widetilde{Y}$ of specified (and comparatively small) size $\widetilde{m}$ reduces to finding the vectoral transformation $\widetilde{\varphi}$ from set Φ, such that

$$I_{\widetilde{m}}(\widetilde{\varphi}(Y)) = \max_{\varphi \in \Phi} I_{\widetilde{m}}(\varphi(Y)). \tag{12}$$

A substantive analysis of the problem of reducing the dimen-

sions of the space **Y** of consumption behavior was made in section 6 of chapter 1. Here we recall only that, for the purposes
of our research — i.e., in a study intended to reveal groups
(types) of households differing in their consumption behavior —
we naturally regard as most informative those indices which
underline differences in consumption expenditure, that is, those
which vary the most and show the greatest change as we switch
from one household type to another.

From this point of view, the most appropriate measure of quantity of information carried in the class of normed and noninterre-
lated linear combinations of **Y**, i.e., in the class of functions

$$\Phi = \left\{ \begin{array}{l} \varphi^{(l)}\,(\mathbf{Y}) = b_{lp} + b_{l1}y^{(1)} + b_{l2}y^{(2)} + \ldots + b_{lm}y^{(m)} \\[4pt] \text{subject to:} \quad \sum_{q=1}^{m} b_{lq}^2 = 1; \\[4pt] \mathrm{cov}\,(\varphi^{(l_1)}\,(\mathbf{Y}), \quad \varphi^{(l_2)}\,(\mathbf{Y})) = 0 \\[4pt] \text{for} \quad l_1 \neq l_2 \end{array} \right\}_{l=\overline{1,\,m}} \tag{13}$$

is given by

$$I_{\widetilde{m}}\,(\varphi\,(\mathbf{Y})) = \frac{D\varphi^{(1)}\,(\mathbf{Y}) + \ldots + D\varphi^{(\widetilde{m})}\,(\mathbf{Y})}{Dy^{(1)} + \ldots + Dy^{(m)}}. \tag{14}$$

But, as we know (see, for example, [2], pp. 134-47), functional (14) reaches its maximum in the class of functions (13)
in the first $\widetilde{m}$ main components of random vector **Y**. This
means, in particular, that the indices $\widetilde{\varphi}^{(1)}\,(\mathbf{Y})$, $\widetilde{\varphi}^{(2)}\,(\mathbf{Y})$, $\ldots$,
$\widetilde{\varphi}^{(\widetilde{m})}\,(\mathbf{Y})$, which are optimal in the sense (12)-(14), are given
by equations

$$\widetilde{\varphi}^{(l)}\,(\mathbf{Y}) = \widetilde{b}_{l1}\,(y^{(1)} - y_0^{(1)}) + \ldots + \widetilde{b}_{lm}\,(y^{(m)} - y_0^{(m)}) \tag{15}$$
$$(l = 1, 2, \ldots, \widetilde{m}),$$

in which vectors $\widetilde{B}_l = (\widetilde{b}_{l1}, \widetilde{b}_{l2}, \ldots, \widetilde{b}_{lm})'$ are defined as normal-

ized $\left(\sum_{q=1}^{m} b_{lm}^2 = 1 \right)$ solutions of the system of equations

$$(\Sigma - \lambda_l E)\,\widetilde{B}_l = O \quad (l = 1, 2, \ldots, \widetilde{m}), \tag{16}$$

where λ_l is the l-th largest root of the equation

$$| \Sigma - \lambda E | = 0,$$

E is a unit matrix of dimension $m \times m$, and O is an m-dimensional column vector of zeros.

Obviously, the approach to solving problem 2 described here is related to a possible formal method of aggregating a set of original indices. We shall combine it with methods of aggregation and selection of individual most informative indices based on substantive (socioeconomic) analysis. Unfortunately, at this initial stage of our research (i.e., in the course of stage 1), we cannot use to any great extent the most effective method of choosing the indices that carry the most information — methods based on the use of so-called teaching samples (see, for example, [2, pp. 199-205]). If we intended to exploit the possibilities of such methods, then, before making a formal analysis of indices of households' consumption behavior, we would have to have at least several fairly representative "batches" of households, each of them known in advance to contain households that were homogeneous in terms of their consumption behavior, but each exhibiting different types of behavior. However, attempts to derive such "teaching samples" using specially chosen experts have not, unfortunately, given stable or reproducible results. There are no other possible ways of obtaining "teaching samples" in this situation, and hence we have had to restrict ourselves to methods of choosing and identifying the most informative indices that do not involve the use of "teaching."

As a final remark in connection with problem 2, we note that, to simplify the presentation, we shall henceforth denote by vector Y the set of indices for household consumption behavior derived by solving in some way the problem of reducing the dimensions of Y, the original space of indices.

The nature and purposes of step 2 [identification of basic consumption types by subdividing observations on Y into subclasses — Ed.] require us to solve two major problems, as follows.

Problem 3. This problem involves subdividing the set of households under study into an (unknown) number of classes in such a way that households belonging to the same class exhibit relatively similar consumption behavior. Mathematically, the problem is formulated as follows. There is a set of multi-dimensional points $\{Y_i\}_{i=1,n}$ in a space; in addition, a metric ρ_Y has been specified for this space (using equation (10)). Basing ourselves on assumption (B) (or (B*)) concerning the stratification of set $\{Y_i\}_{i=1,n}$, we have to find a way of breaking down this set S_Y into an unknown number N of nonintersecting classes $S_Y^{(1)}, S_Y^{(2)}, \ldots, S_Y^{(N)}$ in a way that in some sense reproduces the underlying stratification as accurately as possible.

Obviously, such a formulation has to be made more precise; in particular, we must show in what sense we are seeking to reproduce as precisely as possible the unknown stratification of the set of households under investigation.

We introduce here two ways of adding precision to the formulation of problem 3, the difference between them being whether we base our investigation on assumption (B) or on assumption (B*).

Variant A. Here we adopt hypothesis (B). We shall take a parametric family $\mathfrak{M}$ (θ) of classification algorithms S (θ), where the multidimensional parameter θ can generally take values from some closed region Θ. The nature of region Θ depends on the particular form of the algorithm considered. Thus, in different types of algorithms the parameter θ (which we shall call a structural parameter) may define: (a) the choice of weights in specifying the distance ρ_Y between points in the space under study (see (10) above), and in this case $\theta = (\sigma_{11}^{-1}, \sigma_{22}^{-1}, \ldots, \sigma_{mm}^{-1})$; (b) the choice of parameter r in the formula for the generalized distance (in the sense of Kolmogorov) between classes

$$\rho^{(r)}\left(S^{(k_1)}(\theta), S^{(k_2)}(\theta)\right) = \left[\frac{1}{n_{k_1} n_{k_2}} \sum_{Y_i \in S^{(k_1)}_{(\theta)}} \sum_{Y_j \in S^{(k_2)}_{(\theta)}} \rho_Y^r(Y_i, Y_j)\right]^{1/r}$$

(see [2, p. 83]); in this case, $\theta = r$; (c) the choice of threshold values in so-called threshold algorithms (see [2, p. 105] , on the interpretation of φ_0 and ψ_0), in particular the choice of the values for radius R in Forel-type algorithms (see below, and also [2, pp. 109-10]); (d) the choice of measures for coarsening and refinement in MacQueen type algorithms (see below, and also [2, p. 120]).

Thus, the nature of algorithm S (θ) and its outcome depend on the value of structural parameter θ. In particular, θ influences the number of classes N (or the mean number of classes $\bar{N}$, if N in the algorithm is random) into which the algorithm breaks down the set of units O; i.e., $N = N$ (θ) (or $\bar{N} = \bar{N}$ (θ)). Thus, having fixed the value of the parameter θ at θ_0, we essentially fix the number of classes N (θ_0) (or the average number of classes $\bar{N}$ (θ_0)) and we consider the set $\mathfrak{M}$ (θ_0) of algorithms S (θ_0) that decompose the set under study into a previously specified number of classes N (θ_0) (or, if N (θ_0) is random, then, after repeated applications of an algorithm S (θ_0) taken from set $\mathfrak{M}$ (θ_0) to a set of units, the mean value of $\bar{N}$ (θ) will tend, in a probabilistic sense, to a previously determined number $\bar{N}$ (θ_0)).

The requirements we are imposing on the unknown "most precise" breakdown $\widetilde{S}_Y(\theta_0) = \{\widetilde{S}_Y^{(1)}$ (θ_0), $\widetilde{S}_Y^{(2)}$ (θ_0), . . . , $\widetilde{S}_Y^{(N(\theta_0))}$ (θ_0)\} of set O into homogeneous classes (or strata) $\widetilde{S}_Y^{(k)}$ (θ_0) ($k = 1$, $2, \ldots, N$ (θ_0)) lead us to adopt a two-stage procedure in devising an algorithm.

In the first stage, for each fixed value of θ, and consequently for any previously specified number of classes N (θ), we find the breakdown $\widetilde{S}_Y$ (θ) = $\{\widetilde{S}_Y^{(1)}$ (θ), . . . , $\widetilde{S}_Y^{(N(\theta))}$ (θ)\} whose classificatory structure has the least interspersion of classes; i.e.,

$$\sum_{k=1}^{N(\theta)} \sum_{Y_i \in \widetilde{S}_Y^{(k)}(\theta)} \rho_Y^2 (Y_i, O^{(k)}(\widetilde{S}(\theta))) =$$

$$= \min_{S_Y(\theta) \in \mathfrak{m}(\theta)} \sum_{k=1}^{N(\theta)} \sum_{Y_i \in S_Y(\theta)} \rho_Y^2 (Y_i, O^{(k)}(S(\theta))) \qquad (17)$$

(in this equation, $O^{(k)}$ (S (θ)) means the "center of gravity" of class $S_Y^{(k)}$ (θ) in breakdown S (θ)).

In the second stage, we choose from the parametric family of breakdowns $\{\widetilde{S}_Y$ (θ)\}$_{\theta \in \Theta}$ defined by (17) the one that is in some sense most stable, $\widetilde{S}_Y(\theta_0)$.

An informal approach to finding the value of parameter θ_0 that yields $\widetilde{S}_Y(\theta_0)$, the most stable breakdown (the most stable stratification), requires a scrupulous and difficult (and not always feasible!) socioeconomic analysis of the "best" breakdowns (in the sense of (17)), $\widetilde{S}_Y(\theta_1), \widetilde{S}_Y(\theta_2), \ldots, \widetilde{S}_Y(\theta_T)$ based on different values of the structural parameter θ.

The idea underlying the formal method of finding the most stable breakdown is as follows. Suppose that θ_0 is the value of the structural parameter that ensures that the corresponding classification algorithm $\widetilde{S}_Y(\theta_0)$ gives a breakdown which is the same as or close to the actual structure S of the set to be analyzed; the latter is not known to us, but by assumption (B) it is fairly clearly defined (!). In this case, even if we alter parameter θ (within certain limits) in the neighborhood of point θ_0, the algorithms of the kind $\widetilde{S}_Y(\theta_0 \pm \Delta\theta)$ will yield practically the same breakdown as $\widetilde{S}_Y(\theta_0)$ (see [1, 13]). In order to make this precise, we have to introduce a number of concepts.

(a) We introduce a metric $d(S_Y(\theta'), S_Y(\theta''))$ in the space of breakdowns $S_Y(\theta)$. This can be done using a Kemeny-Snell type distance measure (see [2, p. 214]):

$$d_1(S_Y(\theta'), S_Y(\theta'')) = \frac{1}{n(n-1)} \sum_{i,j=1}^{n} |s_{ij}(\theta') - s_{ij}(\theta'')|, \qquad (18)$$

where $s_{ij}(\theta) = 1$ if units O_i and O_j are in the same class in breakdown $S_Y(\theta)$ and $s_{ij}(\theta) = 0$ if units O_i and O_j are in a different class.

It can easily be shown that the distance $d(S_Y(\theta'), S_Y(\theta''))$ defined by formula (18) can vary from zero (when $S_Y(\theta')$ and $S_Y(\theta'')$ are identical) to one (when one of the algorithms breaks the set O under investigation down into n single-point classes, while the other assigns all the units in set O to a single class).

In addition to the Kemeny-Snell distance measure, we can also consider a measure that is essentially equivalent but more suitable in some situations (see [12]). This is the Tanimoto distance measure

$$d_2\left(S_Y\left(\theta'\right), S_Y\left(\theta''\right)\right) =$$

$$= \frac{1}{n} \sum_{i=1}^{n} \frac{n^{(\theta')}\left(O_i\right) + n^{(\theta'')}\left(O_i\right) - 2n^{(\theta', \theta'')}\left(O_i\right)}{n^{(\theta')}\left(O_i\right) + n^{(\theta'')}\left(O_i\right) - n^{(\theta', \theta'')}\left(O_i\right)}, \qquad (18')$$

where $n^{(\theta')}(O_i)$, $n^{(\theta'')}(O_i)$ and $n^{(\theta', \theta'')}(O_i)$ are, respectively, the number of units assigned under breakdown $S_Y(\theta')$ to the class containing O_i; the number of units assigned under breakdown $S_Y(\theta'')$ to the class containing O_i; and the number of units that appear in both these classes simultaneously. It can be shown that the distance measure $d_2(S_Y(\theta'), S_Y(\theta''))$ defined by (18') can vary from 0 to $1-1/n$, and that it takes its extreme values at the same breakdowns $S_Y(\theta')$ and $S_Y(\theta'')$ as the Kemeny-Snell measure.

(b) We introduce the concept of the "ε-stability" of breakdown $S_Y(\theta)$. We shall say, given any previously specificed positive value of ε, that breakdown $S_Y(\theta)$ is ε-stable if a nonempty neighborhood $\Omega_\varepsilon(\theta) \in \Theta$ of point θ can be found (i.e., one containing at least one point $\theta' \in \Theta$ as well as θ), such that

$$\sup_{\theta', \theta'' \in \Omega_\varepsilon(\theta)} d\left(S\left(\theta'\right), S\left(\theta''\right)\right) \leqslant \varepsilon. \qquad (19)$$

It is natural here to call the neighborhood $\Omega_\varepsilon(\theta)$ the region of ε-stability of breakdown $S_Y(\theta)$, since, if we were to extend it, we would breach inequality (19).

(c) We shall say that breakdown $S_Y(\theta_0(\varepsilon))$ is most highly ε-stable, or that it has the maximum region of ε-stability, if

$$V\left\{\Omega_\varepsilon\left(\theta_0\left(\varepsilon\right)\right)\right\} = \max_{\theta \in \Theta} V\left\{\Omega_\varepsilon\left(\theta\right)\right\}, \qquad (20)$$

where $V\{\Omega\}$ is the volume of the multidimensional region Ω (defined as the corresponding multidimensional integral in space Θ with respect to region Ω), and $\Omega_\varepsilon(\theta)$ are the corresponding regions of ε-stability.

(d) Breakdown (classification) $S_Y(\theta_0(\varepsilon^*))$ is defined as being the most stable one if

$$\frac{\varepsilon^*}{V\left\{S_Y\left(\theta_0\left(\varepsilon^*\right)\right)\right\}} = \min_{\varepsilon \in (0, \varepsilon_0)} \frac{\varepsilon}{V\left\{S_Y\left(\theta_0\left(\varepsilon\right)\right)\right\}}. \qquad (21)$$

At this juncture, though, we should note the following. As-

sumption (B) postulates the existence of a clearly defined classification of a set of points $\{Y_i\}_{i=\overline{1,n}}$, i.e., of a fairly concentrated spread in space Y of the individual clusters (or classes)
of these points. As both experience and previous studies show,
such a structure guarantees (for a wide class of algorithms
$S(\theta)$) that the most stable breakdown is independent of ε; i.e.,
it guarantees the existence of a θ_0, independent of ε, such that
the optimization equation (20) is fulfilled for all $\varepsilon \in [0, \varepsilon_0]$
simultaneously.[5]

We shall demonstrate this stability property using a simple
example. Assume that the points $\{Y_i\}_{i=\overline{1,n}}$ to be analyzed are
two-dimensional (i.e., $Y_i' = (y_i^{(1)}, y_i^{(2)})$). The set is shown geometrically in Figure 2. In the figure, we see a clear classification of the set under investigation (hypothesis (B) is clearly
satisfied); this is shown by the four clusters — classes — that
can be seen to be fairly widely dispersed geometrically.

We shall show how a particular type of classification algorithm $S_Y(\theta)$ (which depends on structural parameter θ) works
in this space, taking "Forel"-type algorithms as our example.
As is well known (see, for example [2, pp. 109-10]), these algorithms are constructed as follows. The structural parameter

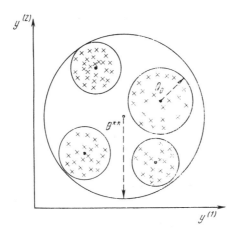

Figure 2. An example in which the classification in space Y of the set of units
under investigation is clearly shown (i.e., the figure illustrates assumption (B)
that the behavioral space is stratified).

θ is a scalar — the radius of some auxiliary hypersphere, assumed to be in space Y (hence, in our example, θ is the radius of a circle in the plane $y^{(1)}y^{(2)}$ — see Figure 2), where θ is chosen in a range between $\theta^{k} = \min_{i, j} \rho_Y(Y_i, Y_j)$ and θ^{**}, the radius of the smallest hypersphere that can "straddle" $\{Y_i\}_{i=\overline{1, n}}$, the whole set of points under investigation. Consequently, $\Theta = [\theta^{k}, \theta^{**}]$. One of the points under investigation, Y_{i_0}, is then chosen at random and a hypersphere $C_1(\theta, i_0)$ of radius θ is centered on it. We then find the coordinates of the center of gravity $\overline{Y}_{i_0}^{(1)}$ of the set of points lying in that hypersphere, and the center of the hypersphere is switched to that center of gravity. As a result of these transfers, we get another hypersphere $C_2(\theta, i_0)$ of the same radius. But the points in the hypersphere $C_2(\theta, i_0)$ may be different from those in the previous hypersphere $C_1(\theta, i_0)$. We calculate the coordinates of $\overline{Y}_{i_0}^{(2)}$, the center of gravity of this revised set of points, and transfer the center of our "roaming" hypersphere to $\overline{Y}_{i_0}^{(2)}$, and so on. We continue this "groping" movement with a hypersphere of given radius θ in space Y until, when we next recalculate the coordinates of the center of gravity of the points in set $\{Y_i\}_{i=\overline{1, n}}$ within the hypersphere, we get the same answer as at the preceding stage; i.e., until our "roaming" hypersphere stays still. When the hypersphere stops moving, we define all the points it contains as class $S_Y^{(1)}(\theta)$, and repeat the same procedure for the set of points $\{Y_i\}_{i=\overline{1, n}}$ outside $S_Y^{(1)}(\theta)$, and so on until all the points in the set $\{Y_i\}_{i=\overline{1, n}}$ under investigation are allocated to classes.

Obviously, the outcome of this algorithm — and, in particular, the number of classes it yields — depends heavily on the choice of radius θ. Thus, for $\theta = \theta^*$ it is easy to see that we get a breakdown of set O into n single-point classes (i.e., $N(\theta^*) = n$), while for a sufficiently large radius $(\theta \geqslant \theta^{**})$ the algorithm assigns the whole set under investigation to a single class (i.e., $N(\theta) = 1$). Figure 3 shows how θ affects the number of classes into which the points in Figure 2 are allocated when we use a

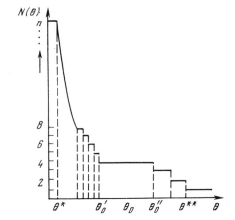

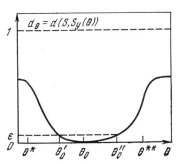

Figure 3. An illustration of how the number of classes in the breakdown depends on radius θ when we use the Forel algorithm.

Figure 4. An illustration of how the distance between the true breakdown S and the breakdown found using algorithm S_y (θ) depends on the value of the structural parameter θ.

Forel algorithm. The "plateau" (or constant region) in the curve illustrated in Figure 3 shows that there is a region of values of θ (a neighborhood $[\theta_0', \theta_0'']$ of the point θ_0) where changing θ does not affect the number of classes in the breakdown.

If we use metric $d(.,.)$ in the space of breakdowns (see formulas (18) and (18') above for distance measures d_1 and d_2) and if we introduce the classification S of the set O under investigation, which is the true one but unknown to us, we can use Figure 4 to show where the parametric family of decomposition algorithms $\{S_Y(\theta_0)\}$ is stable. Comparing Figures 3 and 4, we see that the neighborhood $[\theta_0', \theta_0'']$ of point Θ_0 defined in Figure 3 as the region in which the true number of classes $N(\theta) = 4$ is constant, corresponds in Figure 4 to the maximum region of ε-stability in the parametric family of breakdowns $\{S_Y(\theta)\}_{\theta \in [\theta^*, \theta^{**}]}$.

To conclude our account of variant (A) for giving precision to the formulation of problem 3, we note that it would be more convenient computationally and more correct theoretically if we used a parametric family of classification algorithms $\{S_Y(\theta)\}_{\theta \in \Theta}$ of the MacQueen type (or the к-means type) to solve this problem.[6]

The point is that if n, the number of units to be classified, is large enough, then it is impossible in practice to use computers to implement iterative classification procedures in which all available observations are used simultaneously at each stage of the procedure. (Forel-type procedures belong to this class.) In these cases, we have to use so-called sequential classificatory procedures, i.e., iterative procedures (or iterative algorithms) at each stage of which only a small number of the original observations are taken in turn. These algorithms are also attractive since their properties can conveniently be analyzed in the asymptote as $n \to \infty$. In fact, the к-means classification procedure belongs to this class. Research into asymptotic properties of this algorithm has so far shown (see [19]) that, in a fairly general situation when a fairly large number of observations have to be classified into a fixed number of classes, this algorithm produces a breakdown that is close to the optimal one in the sense of (17). This justifies us in choosing a class of these algorithms in the parametric family $\{\widetilde{S}_Y(\theta)\}_{\theta \in \Theta}$ that breaks down the set in a way which satisfies the first step requirement — optimization equation (17).

We recall how algorithms of this class are constructed. In this case, the structural parameter θ is a two-dimensional vector $(\theta^{(1)}, \theta^{(2)})$, the first component of which, $\theta^{(1)}$, we shall call (following [2]) a "coarsening" measure, and the second, $\theta^{(2)}$, a "refinement" measure. At step 0 of the iteration we choose any initial number of classes N_0 $(2 \leqslant N_0 \leqslant n)$. We choose at random N_0 points $Y_{i_1}, Y_{i_2}, \ldots, Y_{i_{N_0}}$ from set $\{Y_i\}_{i=\overline{1,n}}$ and (temporarily) call them base points, or the centers of N_0 unknown classes. At the same time, we assign a weight equal to one to each point in the set under investigation. Then we carry out a procedure for "coarsening" the base points. For this purpose, we calculate the distance ρ_Y between two neighboring base points and compare it with our given "coarseness" measure $\theta^{(1)}$.

If this minimum distance is less than $\theta^{(1)}$, then the associated pair of base points is replaced by a weighted average, with a weight equal to the sum of the weights of the two points. Then the next shortest distance between any two base points is found, and so on, until the distance between any two base points is more than or equal to $\theta^{(1)}$. Here the coarsening procedure (and the first step of the iteration) stops, and we switch to the second step, analysis of the next $(N_0 + 1)$-th point $Y_{i_{N_0+1}}$, which is chosen at random from the remaining points in O, the set under study.

In this step, numbered 1, we compute the distance between $Y_{i_{N_0+1}}$ and the base point nearest to it. If this distance exceeds the refinement measure $\theta^{(2)}$, then $Y_{i_{N_0+1}}$ is called a new (the $(N_0 + 1)$-th) base point and we repeat the coarsening procedure. But if this minimum distance is less than $\theta^{(2)}$, then the base point nearest to $Y_{i_{N_0+1}}$ is replaced by a base point found as the center of gravity of the old base point and point $Y_{i_{N_0+1}}$, which is combined with it. For this purpose, the weight of point $Y_{i_{N_0+1}}$, as noted above, is taken to be equal to one, and the weight of the new base point is equal to the sum of the weights of the points being combined (the old base point and $Y_{i_{N_0+1}}$). After this, we must go back to the process of coarsening all the base points available at that stage; then we advance to the next step of the iteration (step 2) — a similar "insertion" of the next $(N_0 + 2)$-th randomly chosen point $Y_{i_{N_0+2}}$, and so on, until we have analyzed all n points in this way. By performing these $n - N_0$ iterations, we get a particular set of $N (\theta^{(1)}, \theta^{(2)})$ base points, which for sufficiently large values of n should (according to the properties of the algorithm proved in [18]) be fully stable before step $n - N_0$ is reached; i.e., the base points should not change as we move from one step to the next. Then we make a final breakdown of set O into classes by sequentially computing the distance between each of the initial points Y_i $(i = 1, 2, \ldots, n)$ and each of the base points obtained in the course of the $(n - N_0)$ iterations, allocating each point to the class with the closest base point.

Obviously, the outcome of using this kind of classification procedure — and, in particular, the number N of classes obtained (here N is random) — depends on the particular choice of values for the coarsening and refinement parameters $\theta^{(1)}$ and $\theta^{(2)}$, i.e., on the value of vectoral parameter θ.[7]

The choice of an optimal value of structural parameter θ naturally can be based on a stability criterion for a breakdown of type (20) or (21).

Finally, we note that the к-means classification procedure can be modified somewhat and rendered in some sense more accurate and flexible by making the "threshold" values $\theta^{(1)}$ and $\theta^{(2)}$ variables that change by some rule as we move from one iteration to the next (for a version of this modification, see [2, pp. 51-56]).

<u>Variant B.</u> We give a precise formulation of the assumption in problem 3 that the stronger hypothesis (hypothesis (B*)) applies to the stratification of the behavioral space **Y**. In accordance with this assumption, the probability distribution of the multidimensional points **Y** relating to the whole collection of families **O** is a mixture of normal distributions, each of which relates to the consumption behavior of families of a particular type. In other words, if f (**Y**) is the probability density of a multidimensional random variable describing the consumption pattern of a household randomly chosen from **O**, then by (B*)

$$f(\mathbf{Y}) = \sum_{k=1}^{N} \pi_k f_k (\mathbf{Y}), \tag{22}$$

where f_k (**Y**) is the density of the m-dimensional normal distribution for the consumption structure of type k (see (1)) and π_k is the share (or weight) of households exhibiting type k consumption behavior in **O**, the whole set of households under investigation.

Obviously, we are here formalizing the concept of a homogeneous class (or type) of consumption behavior (a "stratum") using the concept of a multidimensional normal general set, and the problem of finding the best subdivision of set **O** into nonin-

tersecting classes $S_Y^{(1)}$, $S_Y^{(2)}$, ..., $S_Y^{(N)}$ reduces to that of the best
statistical estimation of parameters N, π_k, $Y_0(k)$ and $\Sigma(k)$
($k = 1, 2, \ldots, N$) in equations (1) and (22). In actual fact, if we
know N, π_k, $Y_0(k)$, and $\Sigma(k)$, then, bearing in mind (1) and (22),
we have exhaustive information on the nature of each type of
household separately and on how representative they are of the
whole set of households O.

Reference [2] contains a description of algorithms for solving
the problem of estimating statistically the parameters of a "mixed
normal" distribution (for a given N). N. N. Aprausheva has devised a program for use on a BESM-6 computer and has modified the algorithms in some ways (see [4]). An estimate is
made of N, the unknown number of classes, by a combination of
mathematical statistics and heuristic methods (for criteria for
testing hypotheses concerning the number of components in the
fusion, see [4]), on the one hand, and a substantive socioeconomic analysis of alternative variants of the subdivision corresponding to different values of N, on the other. As far as the
heuristic measures go, here the basic reason for choosing a
particular value of N^* is that the observed value of interclass
dispersion (17) falls relatively sharply as we switch from
$N^* - 1$ to N^k classes.

This completes our account of problem 3, which is the key
element in the overall problem of identifying the basis on which
consumption behavior is differentiated, forecasting that differentiation, and partly controlling it.

Problem 4. This problem concerns the use of family budget
studies to find the objective function underlying consumers'
behavior.

The methodology adopted in this study, as we have noted more
than once, is intended chiefly: (a) to identify the essential features of the differentiation of consumer behavior; (b) to devise
methods for analyzing and forecasting this differentiation; and
(c) to design models giving us partial control over the structure
of consumer demand. If we confined ourselves to the first two
objectives, then in order to justify the use of the methods proposed here it would be sufficient to adopt as our initial assump-

tions hypotheses (A), (B) (or B*)), and (E). But if we wish to employ methods of socioeconomic modeling that allow us to control the structure of consumer demand, then one of our instruments is retail prices and, in particular, knowledge of how they affect demand. As is well known [14, 11, 5], the most complete account of the relationship between $y^{(l)}$, the quantities consumed (or demanded) of the various goods, their retail prices $p^{(l)}$, and income s is based on objective functions for consumers' behavior $u^{(k)}$ (Y) ($k = 1, 2, \ldots, N$). The latter specify (up to a monotonic transformation) a numerical measure of the utility derived by the k-th type of household from any given basket of goods Y (see our formulation of assumption (C) above). In spite of the availability of interesting and profound theoretical and methodological analyses of utility functions (see [14, 17, 5, 6]), however, previous attempts to construct them in concrete terms on the basis of statistical data have not been successful. The chief reason for this has obviously been the unsatisfactory and unrealistic nature of the major assumptions on which the methods have been based (see, for example, Frisch's work [17], which assumes separable preferences — that the utility derived from one good is independent of consumption of another). In our view, the most promising approach at the applied level is that of Volkonskii, which is based on the so-called homogeneity assumption (see [5]). Attempts to implement it statistically for all consumers, however, have, as one would have expected, proved unsuccessful — and for one simple reason: the assumption of homogeneity essentially requires the fulfillment of our assumptions (A), (B), (C), and (D) (although this is obvious, it is not mentioned in [5], which may have resulted subsequently in improper attempts to implement this approach); but it is easy to see that these assumptions can be realistic only for a group of households whose consumption behavior is homogeneous. Hence, the statement in [5] that the models described there "in principle may also be applied to particular classes of households chosen in any way from the original set" (cited on p. 622) seems to us somewhat misleading. It is not the case that they "may be applied," but that they must only be applied to particular groups of families, and not to groups "chosen in any way" but to groups chosen according to the specific criterion of homogeneity of consumption behavior. Thus, we conclude that for purposes of solving the overall problem of identifying a typology of consumption and, in particular, of identifying special groups of consumers, we can on certain conditions make constructive use of what is, from our point of view, the most effective method of constructing the objective functions underlying consumer behavior from household budget data.

We shall briefly describe this method, basically following [5] but introducing some modifications arising from the observations we have just made.

We begin by adopting assumptions (A), (B), (C), and (D). Our initial statistical data are the household budgets of the k-th type of consumer $\{Y_i(k)\}_{i=\overline{1, n_k}}$ ($k = 1, 2, \ldots, N$), so that we are assuming that problem 3 — that of subdividing the whole set of households O into classes with similar consumption patterns — has already been solved. $Y^{(k)}(m)$ denotes the overall set of type k households (i.e., the total conceivable set, not only those to be analyzed experimentally).

The fact that both assumptions (B*) and (D) are fulfilled guarantees, first, that the mean consumption pattern of each (k-th) household type is optimal, i.e., that

$$u^{(k)}(Y_0(k)) = u^{(k)}(Y_{\text{опт}}(k)) = \max_{Y \in Y^{(k)}(m)} u^{(k)}(Y), \qquad (7')$$

and, second, that the random deviation of the consumption vectors $Y(k)$ are normally distributed not only for the whole set $Y^{(k)}(m)$ of type k households (i.e., not only in the m-dimensional space Y) but also for the narrower grouping of households $Y^{(k)}(m - I - 1)$, chosen from $Y^{(k)}(m)$ in accordance with rationing or shortage constraints (5) or the income constraint (6). This means, in particular, that

$$u^{(k)}(Y_{0.\ \text{усл}}(k)) = u^{(k)}(Y_{\text{опт. усл}}(k)) = \max_{Y \in Y^{(k)}(m-I-1)} u^{(k)}(Y), \qquad (7'')$$

where $Y_{\text{о. усл}}(k) = M\left(Y(k)\middle|\sum_{l=1}^{m} p^{(l)}y^{(l)}=s; y^{(q_\nu)}=c_{q_\nu}, \quad \nu=1,2,\ldots,I\right),$

is the conditional mathematical expectation of the random vector $Y(k)$ calculated subject to (5) and (6), and $Y_{\text{опт.усл}}(k)$ is the solution of an extremal problem of the form

$$
\begin{cases}
u^{(k)}(Y) \to \max_{Y \in Y^{(k)}(m)} \\
\sum_{l=1}^{m} p^{(l)}y^{(l)} = s; \\
y^{(q_\nu)}(k) = c_{q_\nu}, \quad \nu = 1, 2, \ldots, I,
\end{cases}
\tag{23}
$$

or, equivalently,

$$
u^{(k)}(Y) \to \max_{Y \in Y^{(k)}(m-I-1)}
\tag{23'}
$$

We note that $Y^{(k)}(m)$ is a set in m-dimensional space Y, while set $Y^{(k)}(m - I - 1)$, since it is the intersection of $(m-1)$-dimensional hyperplanes of the form $y^{(q_\nu)} = c_{q_\nu}$ ($\nu = 1,$ $2, \ldots, I$) and an m-dimensional hyperplane $\sum_{l=1}^{m} p^{(l)}y^{(l)}(k) = s,$ is a set in the corresponding $(m - I - 1)$-dimensional space.

Under the circumstances we have described (i.e., assuming (A), (B*), (C), and (D)), we can adopt a theoretical result proved in [6] (see the lemma on p. 532) as a basis for finding a quadratic approximation of the unknown function $u^{(k)}(Y)$ using family budget data. As applied to the framework of our inquiry, this result can be formulated as follows.

If the random variation in the consumption pattern $Y(k)$ of type k households can be described adequately by a nondegenerate m-dimensional normal distribution (see assumption (B*), formula (1)) and if, moreover, $Y_{\text{mod}}(k)$, the pattern most observed frequently in families of this type (with a symmetric distribution such as the normal one, this is the same as the mean $Y_0(k)$), is also optimal in the sense of (7) — and, indeed, with a normal distribution, in the sense of (7') as well (see assumption (D)) — then the objective function we seek, $u^{(k)}$ (Y), in the hyperplane (i.e., subject to) $\sum_{l=1}^{m} p^{(l)} y^{(l)}(k) = s$ is given, up to a monotonic transformation, by the density function f_k (Y) and in particular

$$u^{(k)} (Y) = a_k(s) \cdot \psi_k (Y) + b_k(s), \tag{24}$$

where

$$\psi_k (Y) = -\frac{1}{2} (Y - Y_0 (k))' \Sigma^{-1} (k) (Y - Y_0 (k)), \tag{25}$$

and the constants (for a given income s) $a_k(s)$ and $b_k(s)$ are functions of s.

In particular, it follows directly from this that, within the whole set $Y^{(k)}$ (m) (i.e., in the absence of income constraints), the objective function underlying the consumption behavior of type k families is a function of the two variables ψ_k (Y) and s, i.e.,

$$u^{(k)} (Y) = F (\psi_k (Y), s), \tag{26}$$

where $F (\psi_k, s)$ is some function increasing in ψ_k.

To get a quadratic approximation of $u^{(k)}$ (Y), we write it a second-order Taylor series in the neighborhood of Y_0 (k), using (26), the rule for differentiating a complex function, and the fact that

$$\frac{\partial \psi_k}{\partial y^{(l)}} \bigg|_{Y_0(k)} = 0, \qquad \frac{\partial^2 s}{\partial y^{(l)} \partial y^{(q)}} = 0 \qquad (l, q = 1, 2, \ldots, m).$$

As a result, we get (accurate up to a constant term and constant positive multiple):

$$u^{(k)} (Y) = P' (Y - Y_0 (k)) - A_k [P' (Y - Y_0 (k))]^2 - \\ - B_k (Y - Y_0 (k))' \Sigma^{-1} (k) (Y - Y_0 (k)). \tag{27}$$

In this equation, $P' = (p^{(1)}, p^{(2)}, \ldots, p^{(m)})$, the vector of retail prices,[8] and constants A_k and B_k are determined on the basis of further considerations, which we now discuss.

To determine the unknown constants A_k and B_k, we use a combination of several approaches, as follows:

(a) We use information on constants A_k and B_k, derived from the postulate of "preference independence" (see [17]). Mathematically, this postulate as applied to goods $y^{(l)}$ and $y^{(q)}$ can be expressed as

$$\frac{\partial^2 u^{(k)}(Y)}{\partial y^{(l)} \partial y^{(q)}} = 0; \tag{28}$$

this means that the marginal utility of $y^{(l)}$ is independent of consumption of $y^{(q)}$ (but not that demand for $y^{(l)}$ is independent of purchases of $y^{(q)}$, since demand for all goods is interdependent in view of the income constraint). It would be wrong to apply this assumption to all the components of vector Y (even at a fairly high level of aggregation) in order to construct a utility function $u^{(k)}(Y)$ (see [17]), since in this form the assumption is clearly unrealistic.

It is quite realistic, however, to choose one or several pairs of components of vector Y

$$(y^{(i_1)}, y^{(j_1)}), \quad (y^{(i_2)}, y^{(j_2)}), \quad , \ldots, \quad (y^{(i_T)}, y^{(j_T)})$$

(or pairs of magnitudes found by appropriate aggregation of the intial components) such that the assumption of "preference independence" is approximately satisfied for each of them; i.e.,

$$\frac{\partial^2 u^{(k)}(Y)}{\partial y^{(i_t)} \partial y^{(j_t)}} = 0, \quad t = 1, 2, \ldots, T. \tag{29}$$

Taking $u^{(k)}(Y)$ in form (27), introducing matrix $\Gamma(k) = (\gamma_{l_q}(k))_{l,\,q=\overline{1,\,m}} = \Sigma^{-1}(k)$, and assuming for definiteness that components of vector Y are expressed in money terms, we derive from (29) the system of equations

$$A_k + B_k \gamma_{i_t j_t}(k) = 0, \quad t = 1, 2, \ldots, T. \tag{30}$$

If we solve this system by the method of least squares, i.e., minimizing

$$\sum_{t=1}^{T} (A_k + B_k \gamma_{i_t j_t})^2,$$

we are able to estimate the ratio $\tau = A_k/B_k$. This estimate is

$$\hat{\tau} = -\frac{\sum_{t=1}^{T} \gamma_{i_t j_t} (k)}{T}. \tag{31}$$

(b) Information on constants A and B contained in income elasticities of demand. By $e_l(k)$, the income elasticity of the l-th good $y^{(l)}$ (for the k-th type of family), we shall mean the simple (not the logarithmic) derivative of $y^{(l)}$ with respect to s, i.e.,

$$e_l(k) = \frac{\partial y^{(l)}(k)}{\partial s},$$

the actual value of which can be found, for example, from demand functions (Engel's curves — see [5]); this is quite feasible statistically.

By simple operations involving differentiation of the utility function $u^{(k)}(Y)$, we reach the following system of equations for constants A and B:

$$\varepsilon(k) = (U^{-1}(A_k, B_k) \cdot 1_m \cdot 1_m')^{-1} (U^{-1}(A_k, B_k) \cdot 1_m), \tag{32}$$

where $\varepsilon(k) = (e_1(k), e_2(k), \ldots, e_m(k))'$, a column vector of elasticities,

$$U(A_k, B_k) = -A_k \begin{pmatrix} 1 & 1 \ldots 1 \\ 1 & 1 \ldots 1 \\ & \cdots \\ 1 & 1 \ldots 1 \end{pmatrix} - B_k \Gamma(k)$$

an $m \times m$ matrix, and $1_m = (1, 1, \ldots, 1)'$, an m-dimensional unit column vector. Unfortunately, solving system (32) numerically is complex and requires iterative procedures that can be performed only on a computer.

As noted at the start of our account of problem 4, we consider one of the more practical advantages of utility functions $u^{(k)}$ (Y) to be the fact that we can derive from them relationships between demand and retail prices — relationships reflected in the corresponding price elasticities of demand (which are also very hard to find statistically!). We must realize, however, that when we interpret these elasticities complications may arise because of the possible appearance of shortages of particular goods and services. Obviously, where demand for a good or service clearly exceeds supply, then for the purposes of the model it should be included as one of the components $y^{(\tau v)}$ ($v = 1, 2, \ldots, I$), the value of which is specified in advance.

(c) The aims and purpose of step 3 is to allow us to solve the following two major problems.

Problem 5. This problem involves choosing the most informative classifying indices in space X.

This problem is similar to problem 2, which involved identifying the indices in behavioral space Y that were the most informative from the standpoint of defining differentiation in household consumption behavior. Problem 5, however, is different in two important respects. First, the p-dimensional indices X in space X that we are to analyze are heterogeneous, i.e., the components of vector X include quantitative, qualitative, and classificatory indices. In the final analysis, this does not alter the overall formulation of the problem in principle; it only adds some further technical complications to those that arise in implementing the logical framework for solving problem 2. (For example, we have to devise and use a special technique that allows us to employ the tools of factor analysis, particularly the method of principal components, on nonquantitative indices — see, for example, [10, 12, 16] .) The second difference between problems 5 and 2 is one of principle: indeed, it allows us to change the overall formulation of the problem in such a way that we can use much more efficient methods for choosing the most informative indices than we used in problem 2. We refer to methods based on the availability of so-called teaching samples; in problem 5 — and here it differs from problem 2 — the investigator knows the breakdown of the units (households) under consideration into homogeneous classes (consumption groups) $S_Y^{(1)}$, $S_Y^{(2)}, \ldots, S_Y^{(N)}$ before analyzing the set of indices. Hence, when analyzing the behavior of different components of vector X in different classes $S_Y^{(k)}$, one would naturally identify as most informative those combinations that vary sharply from one class $(S_Y^{(k_1)})$ to another $(S_Y^{(k_2)})$.

Before demonstrating this proposition, we formulate the problem mathematically. Assume that initially we have a p-dimensional index $X = (x^{(1)}, x^{(2)}, \ldots, x^{(p)})$ of varied composition. In order to present a unified algorithm for processing all the components of vector X simultaneously, each component $x^{(l)}$ $(l = 1, 2, \ldots, p)$ can take a finite set of possible values (or gradations) $x^{(l)}$ (1), $x^{(l)}$ (2), $\ldots, x^{(l)}$ (m_l). Moreover, if $x^{(l)}$ is a quantitative index, then $x^{(l)}$ (ν) is the average value for the ν-th group, assuming that in some way the whole range of possible values of the random variable $x^{(l)}$ has been divided into groups; if $x^{(l)}$ is a qualitative index, then $x^{(l)}$ (ν) = ν is the number of gradations expressing the level (or sequence) of that property or quality; if $x^{(l)}$ is an index of classification (a nominal index), then $x^{(l)}$ (ν) = ν is the number of the class to which the unit can be assigned. It can easily be shown that the total number of possible values for index X is given by the product $m_1 \cdot m_2 \ldots \ldots m_p$.

As a preliminary to solving problem 5, we switch to auxiliary variables $\varphi(X) = (\varphi^{(1)}(X), \varphi^{(2)}(X), \ldots, \varphi^{(p)}(X))$ found by aggregating the original variables $x^{(1)}, x^{(2)}, \ldots, x^{(p)}$; the aim of doing so is the same as that of the corresponding stage in the solution of problem 2 (see equations (12)-(16)) where we sought to maximize a particular measure of informativeness. For this purpose, we may profitably use methods of factor analysis (principal components) intended for Boolean variables (taking the value 0 or 1) — see, for example, [10, 12, 16]). It is true that, to do so, we must replace each component $x^{(l)}$ of vector X by an m_l-dimensional vector $(x^{(l,1)}, x^{(l,2)}, \ldots, x^{(l,m_l)})$, where coordinate $x^{(l,\nu)} = 1$ if $x^{(l)} = x^{(l)}$ (ν) and $x^{(l,\nu)} = 0$ if $x^{(l)} \neq x^{(l)}$ (ν). Correspondingly, the size of the multidimensional index increases in

p up to $p^* = \sum_{l=1}^{p} m_l$.

In what follows, we shall assume that the transformation $\varphi(X)$ has been made and, as before, we shall for simplicity denote the p^*-dimensional system of indices $\varphi(X)$ thus derived by X.

To give a formal account of how random variable X changes when we switch from one class of households $(S_Y^{(k_1)})$ to another $(S_Y^{(k_2)})$, we have to introduce a quantitative measure of how the index varies between classes.

The most satisfactory measures of the difference between general sets — measures of the informational distance between distributions[9] (Kul'bak distances, see [9, pp. 16, 33]) — turn out to be inapplicable in our case, not so much because of the heterogeneous nature of the index X as from the fact that there is a clear breach of the property of absolute joint continuity in the probability measures $P_1(X)$, $P_2(X)$, . . ., $P_N(X)$ which give the probability distributions for the random variable X in the first, second, and N-th classes, respectively (here $P_k(X)$ is the probability that a household randomly selected from the k-th class will have a multidimensional index X, and the two probability measures P_{k_1} and P_{k_2} are said to show absolute joint continuity if the sets of possible values of X in which each of them is significantly positive are identical).

After analyzing the sets observed in space X both in terms of their substance and experimentally, we were led finally to adopt as the most convenient and informative measure of the difference between general sets of households numbered k_1 and k_2 the so-called variational distance, given by

$$\Delta(k_1, k_2; X) = \frac{1}{2} \sum_{X} | P_{k_1}(X) - P_{k_2}(X) |, \qquad (33)$$

where the summation is over all $m_1 \cdot m_2 \ldots m_p$ possible values of the index X under study.

It can easily be verified that the "distance" measure (33) has been constructed so that it is always nonnegative and never exceeds unity, and $\Delta (k_1, k_2) = 0$ if and only if $\mathbf{P}_{k_1} (X) \equiv \mathbf{P}_{k_2} (X)$, i.e., if the probability distributions of index X for classes k_1 and k_2 are identical.

It is obvious that in experiments we shall have to use experimental analogues of the magnitudes in (33), i.e.,

$$\hat{\Delta} (k_1, k_2; X) = \frac{1}{2} \sum_X | \hat{\mathbf{P}}_{k_1} (X) - \hat{\mathbf{P}}_{k_2} (X) | , \qquad (33')$$

where $\hat{\mathbf{P}}_k (X)$ is the relative frequency (or proportion) of k-type households in the total number of households the value of whose index is X, and the summation is done over all the values of X registered in the appropriate sets.

Subsequently, we calculate for each given dimensionality of $p' = 1, 2, \ldots, p - 1$ or for each set of components $X (p') = (x^{(j_1)}, x^{(j_2)}, \ldots, x^{(j_{p'})})'$ (the number of different combinations of given size p' is obviously equal to the number of possible combinations of p' elements from p, i.e., $C_p^{p'}$) the value of $\hat{\Delta} (k_1, k_2; X (p')) (k_1, k_2 = 1, 2, \ldots, N; k_1 \neq k_2)$ and we identify the most informative combination $\tilde{X} (p')$ of given size p' from condition

$$\hat{\Delta}_{cp} (\tilde{X} (p')) = \max_{X(p')} \hat{\Delta}_{cp} (X (p')) \qquad (34)$$

or from condition

$$\hat{\Delta}_{min} (\tilde{X} (p')) = \max_{X(p')} \hat{\Delta}_{min} (X (p')). \qquad (34')$$

In equations (34) and (34'),

$$\hat{\Delta}_{min} (X) = \min_{(k_1, k_2)} \hat{\Delta} (k_1, k_2; X), \qquad (35)$$

while

$$\hat{\Delta}_{cp} (X) = \sum_{\substack{k_1, k_2 = 1 \\ k_1 \neq k_2}}^{N} \omega_{k_1 k_2} \cdot \hat{\Delta} (k_1, k_2; X), \qquad (36)$$

where the "weights" of pairs of classes (k_1, k_2) are given by the formula

$$\omega_{k_1 k_2} = \frac{n_{k_1} + n_{k_2}}{\sum\limits_{\substack{l,\,j=1 \\ i \neq j}}^{N} (n_i + n_j)} = \frac{n_{k_1} + n_{k_2}}{(N-1) \cdot n} \qquad (37)$$

(here as before, n_k is the number of households allocated in the solution to problem 3 to the k-th consumption class).

We assume that the dimension of the most informative index of all indices $\widetilde{X}(p')$ $(p' = 1, 2, \ldots, p)$ satisfying (34) or (34') is chosen on the basis of considerations of a substantive or socio-economic nature. At the same time, it is desirable to see how $\hat{\Delta}_{\mathrm{cp}} (\widetilde{X}(p'))$ (or $\hat{\Delta}_{\mathrm{min}} (\widetilde{X}(p'))$) change with p', and in the first instance, to choose values of p' at which we observe substantial discontinuities in the first differences

$$\hat{\Delta} (\widetilde{X}(p')) - \widetilde{\Delta} (\widetilde{X}(p'-1)).$$

Thus, in solving problem 5, we have fixed upon a p'-dimensional index $\widetilde{X} = (\tilde{x}^{(1)}, \tilde{x}^{(2)}, \ldots, \tilde{x}^{(p')})'$ the components of which are either chosen from among the components of the original index X, or are functions of the latter. This index $\widetilde{X}$ can be regarded as an experimental approximation to some classifying index that is not known to us a priori, but whose existence is postulated in assumption (E). In the end, it will help us to determine (and to forecast) the nature of a household's consumption behavior on the basis of the values of its determinant factors.

Problem 6. This problem involves choosing the best metric for the space of classifying indices $\widetilde{X}$ and, on this basis, breaking down the set O of households as far as possible in terms of homogeneity of consumption behavior.

As we noted in chapter 1, the way in which we break down the set of households $O = \{O_i\}_{i=\overline{1,\,n}}$ into nonintersecting classes $S_{\widetilde{X}}^{(1)}, S_{\widetilde{X}}^{(2)}, \ldots, S_{\widetilde{X}}^{(N)}$ in space $\widetilde{X}$ depends not only on the components of vector $\widetilde{X}$ of classifying indices but also on how we compute the distance $\rho_{\widetilde{X}} (O_i, O_j)$ between two households in this space.

We introduce the notion of the distance between units characterized by a multidimensional index of mixed composition. By
the gradation of index $\tilde{x}^{(l)}$ we shall mean: (i) in the case of a
quantitative index, one of the group intervals into which the values of that index are divided; (ii) in the case of a qualitative index, one of the qualitative categories to which the unit may belong; (iii) in the case of a classification index, one of the homogeneous groups (or classes) to which the units under investigation are assigned. Let m_l be the overall number of possible
gradations for index $\tilde{x}^{(l)}$. Then each "observation" — the
result of measuring the value of index $\tilde{x}^{(l)}$ taken by O_i —
can conveniently be represented by a binary vector $\tilde{X}_i^{(l)} =$
$(\tilde{x}_i^{(l.1)}, \tilde{x}_i^{(l.2)}, \ldots, \tilde{x}_i^{(l.m_l)})'$, all the components of which (apart from
one) are equal to zero. At the same time, the number of the in-
dividual component $v^{(l)}$ (O_i) of vector $\tilde{x}_i^{(l)}$ equal to one shows the
gradation of the index to which unit O_i belongs. We shall as-
sume that we have a method of computing a distance measure
$\delta^{(l)}(v_1, v_2)$ between the $v_1^{(l)}$-th and the $v_2^{(l)}$-th gradation of index
$\tilde{x}^{(l)}$ $(v_1^{(l)}, v_2^{(l)} = 1, 2, \ldots, m_l)$. If the group intervals and qualitative measures are ranked in terms of quantitative and quali-
tative indices, it would be natural to adopt the following distance measure:

$$\delta^{(l)}(v_1^{(l)}, v_2^{(l)}) = c_l \cdot |v_1^{(l)} - v_2^{(l)}|, \qquad (\#)$$

where c_l is some proportionality multiplier. In the case of
classificatory indices, the procedure for implementing this distance measure is normally specified by experts. If there are
no substantive considerations on the basis of which we might
compare the differences between the various gradations, then
for classificatory components of $\tilde{x}^{(l)}$ we might, for example, set

$$\delta^{(l)}(v_1, v_2) = \begin{cases} 0, & \text{if} \quad v_1 = v_2 \\ c_l, & \text{if} \quad v_1 \neq v_2. \end{cases} \qquad (*)$$

Then the distance between any two units O_i and O_j with
multidimensional observations $\tilde{X}_i$ and $\tilde{X}_j$ can naturally be
specified by the relation

$$\rho_{\tilde{X}}^{(W)}(O_i, O_j) = \sum_{l=1}^{p'} w^{(l)} \cdot \delta^{(l)}(v^{(l)}(O_i), v^{(l)}(O_j)), \qquad (38)$$

where the weights w^l determining the relative importance of the separate components in $\tilde{x}^{(l)}$ $\left(w^{(l)} \geqslant 0, \sum_{l=1}^{p'} w^{(l)} = 1 \right)$ are unknown magnitudes that must be chosen optimally in some sense, and the distance between the gradations $\delta^{(l)}(v^{(l)}(O_i), v^{(l)}(O_j))$ to which O_i and O_j belong in terms of index $\tilde{x}^{(l)}$ is measured using either (#) or (*) (whether we use (#) or (*), we can without loss of generality set $c_l = 1$, since the proportionality multipliers c_l are essentially the weights $w^{(l)}$ we are looking for). We note in this connection that, if $\delta^{(l)}$ are given by rule (*), the values $\delta^{(l)}$ $(v^{(l)}(O_i), v^{(l)}(O_j))$ can be computed by the formula:

$$\delta^{(l)}(v^{(l)}(O_i), v^{(')}(O_j)) = \frac{1}{2} \sum_{q_l=1}^{m_l} |\tilde{x}_i^{(l \cdot q_l)} - \tilde{x}_j^{(l \cdot q_l)}| =$$

$$= \begin{cases} 0, & \text{if } v^{(l)}(O_i) = v^{(l)}(O_j) \\ 1, & \text{if } v^{(l)}(O_i) \neq v^{(l)}(O_j). \end{cases}$$

The problem lies in finding a vector of weights $\tilde{W} = (\tilde{w}^{(1)}, \tilde{w}^{(2)}, \ldots, \tilde{w}^{(p)})'$ such that the distance between breakdowns S_Y and $S_{\tilde{X}}(\tilde{W})$, as measured in the Tanimoto metric (see (18')) or the Kemeny-Snell metric (see (18)) are at a minimum; i.e.,

$$d(S_Y, S_{\tilde{X}}(\tilde{W})) = \min_W d(S_Y, S_{\tilde{X}}(W)). \qquad (39)$$

In (39), S_Y is the outcome of solving problem 3; i.e., classification S_Y stratifies the set of families O under investigation into $S_Y^{(1)}, S_Y^{(2)}, \ldots, S_Y^{(N)}$ on the basis of the homogeneity of their consumption behavior; subdivision $S_{\tilde{X}}(W)$ is the outcome (stable in the terms of the approach adopted in variant A for solving problem 3) of applying to space X algorithms for classifying auxiliary indices $\tilde{X}^{(l \cdot q)}$ that use the metric $\rho_{\tilde{X}}^{(W)}$ given by (38). We give below (see section 3 of chapter 2 [not included here — Ed.])

an account of what are, from our point of view, the most convenient classificatory algorithms of this type.

Optimization problem (39) and the associated procedure for find-
ing an extremum of function $d\,(W) = d\,(S_Y, S_{\widetilde{X}}\,(\bar{W}))$ in the p' variables $w^{(1)}$, $w^{(2)}$, . . . , $w^{(p')}$ is difficult enough. In this particular
case, however, we can use approaches that simplify this procedure
substantially and at the same time reduce the computer time needed
to acceptable limits. We describe one of these approaches here.

We consider the vectors of indices found to carry most information; these vectors increase in size from 1 to p' and are
found by solving problem 5, i.e.,

$$\widetilde{X}\,(1) = (\tilde{x}^{(1)}\,(1)), \quad \widetilde{X}\,(2) = (\tilde{x}^{(1)}\,(2),\ \tilde{x}^{(2)}\,(2))',$$
$$\ldots, \widetilde{X}\,(p') = (\tilde{x}^{(1)}\,(p'),\ \tilde{x}^{(2)}\,(p'),\ \ldots,\ \tilde{x}^{(p')}\,(p'))'. \tag{40}$$

We choose components $\tilde{x}^{(1)}\,(p')$, $\tilde{x}^{(2)}\,(p')$, . . . $\tilde{x}^{(p')}\,(p')$ from the
most informative p'-dimensional index $\widetilde{X}\,(p')$ (i.e., the vector
that is finally chosen) and see how often each of these components is encountered in the sequence of vectors (40). Let μ_l be
the overall number of "appearances" of index $\tilde{x}^{(l)}\,(p')$ in the
most informative sets $\widetilde{X}\,(1)$, $\widetilde{X}\,(2)$, . . ., $\widetilde{X}\,(p')$. Obviously, $1 \leqslant$
$\mu_l \leqslant p'$. Our original approximation $W_0 = (w_0^{(1)},\ w_0^{(2)},\ \ldots,\ w_0^{(p')})$
of the unknown extremal point $\bar{W}$ is

$$w_0^{(l)} = \frac{\mu_l}{\sum\limits_{l=1}^{p'} \mu_l}. \tag{41}$$

We choose a step size δ $(0.05 \leqslant \delta \leqslant 0.10)$ and in the sections
of the hyperplane $\Sigma w^{(l)} = 1$, where $w^{(l)} \geqslant 0\ (l = 1.2, \ldots,\ p')$,
we construct a lattice with nodes of the form

$$W\,(t_1, t_2, \ldots, t_{p'}) = (w_0^{(1)} + t_1\delta, w_0^{(2)} +$$
$$+ t_2\delta, \ldots, w_0^{(p')} + t_{p'}\delta), \tag{42}$$
$$\text{where} \quad \begin{cases} t_i = 0, \pm 1, \pm 2, \ldots, i = 1, 2, \ldots, p' \\ \sum\limits_{i=1}^{p'} t_i = 0. \end{cases}$$

We continue to search for the minimum point $\bar{W}$ of function $d(W)$ by a directed selection of the values of this function in the nodes of the lattice (42). The search finishes at the point where a movement from one lattice point to a "neighboring"[10] one fails to reduce the value of the function under investigation.

It is obvious from our method of solving the problem of finding the best metric of type (38) in space $\tilde{X}$ that we have also solved the problem of constructing the breakdown $S_{\tilde{X}}(\bar{W}) = \{S_{\tilde{X}}^{(1)}, S_{\tilde{X}}^{(2)}, \ldots, S_{\tilde{X}}^{(N)}\}$ that is closest, in the sense of (39), to S_Y, the breakdown into consumption types of the set of households O.

(c) The nature and purpose of problem 5 involve solution of the following major problem.

Problem 7. This involves determining the type of consumption behavior of a household on the basis of the value of its classifying index (or determining factor) $\tilde{X}$.

We start from the assumption that problems 1-6 are solved. We define a permutation

$$\Pi^* = \begin{pmatrix} 1 & 2 & \ldots & N \\ t_{(1)}^* & t_{(2)}^* & \ldots & t_{(N)}^* \end{pmatrix},$$

that shows the relationship between classes $S_Y^{(1)}, \ldots, S_Y^{(N)}$ in breakdown S_Y and classes $S_{\tilde{X}}^{(1)}, S_{\tilde{X}}^{(2)}, \ldots, S_{\tilde{X}}^{(N)}$ in breakdown $S_{\tilde{X}}(\bar{W})$ (see hypothesis (E) in section 1 of this chapter), in such a way that it satisfies the following requirement:

$$\min_{1 \leqslant k \leqslant N} \mathbf{P}\{Y \in S_Y^{(k)} \mid \tilde{X} \in S_{\tilde{X}}^{(t^*(k))}\} = \\ = \max_{\Pi} \min_{1 \leqslant k \leqslant N} \mathbf{P}\{Y \in S_Y^{(k)} \mid \tilde{X} \in S_{\tilde{X}}^{(t(k))}\}. \tag{43}$$

The experimental analogue or statistical estimate of the conditional probability $P\{Y \in S_Y^{(k)} / \tilde{X} \in S_{\tilde{X}}^{(t(k))}\}$ in this relationship will be the percentage of such households in all the households in class $S_{\tilde{X}}^{t(k)}$ that were allocated to the k-th type when households O were divided into classes in space Y, the maximum on the right-hand side being taken over all possible permutations Π.

Henceforth, for simplicity of exposition we shall renumber the classes in breakdown $S_{\widetilde{X}}(W)$ in such a way that $t^*(k) = k$. Knowing permutation Π^* which satisfies criterion (43), we automatically determine $1 - \beta$, the confidence level of classifying indices X (see assumption (E)); given the renumbering of classes, this can be expressed as

$$1 - \beta = \min_{1 \leqslant k \leqslant N} \mathbf{P}\{Y \in S_Y^{(k)} \,|\, X \in S_{\widetilde{X}}^{(k)}\}. \tag{44}$$

<u>Remark.</u> Classes $S_{\widetilde{X}}^{(1)}, S_{\widetilde{X}}^{(2)}, \ldots, S_{\widetilde{X}}^{(N)}$ could also be formed without searching for a metric $\rho_{\widetilde{X}}^{(W)}$ and a breakdown $S_{\widetilde{X}}(W)$ in space X, but by using the normal Bayesian approach. Indeed, the region of values of $S_{\widetilde{X}}^{(k_0)}$ which "signals" that a family should be allocated to consumption type $S_{\widetilde{X}}^{(k_0)}$ consists of those values of $\widetilde{X}$ for which

$$\mathbf{P}\{\widetilde{X} \,|\, S_Y^{(k_0)}\} = \max_{1 \leqslant k \leqslant N} \mathbf{P}\{\widetilde{X} \,|\, S_Y^{(k)}\}. \tag{45}$$

Our analysis shows, and available evidence from experimental calculations confirms, that in practice both methods yield identical results when households are classified by consumption type on the basis of the classifying indices $\widetilde{X}$. The latter approach, however (i.e., the approach relying on Bayesian criterion (45)), turns out to be less convenient in practice.

NOTES

1. Here and below, a prime and a superscript -1 mean, respectively, the operations of transposing and inverting a matrix; $|\Sigma|$ means the determinant of matrix Σ ; we shall use the symbols M, D and cov to denote, respectively, the mathematical expectation, the variance, and the covariance of the random variables that follow them.

2. If the quantities $y^{(1)}, y^{(2)}, \ldots, y^{(m)}$ of the goods consumed by the family are measured in monetary units, then obviously we must set $p^{(1)} = p^{(2)} = \ldots = p^{(m)} = 1$.

3. Here and below, we use symbols $P\{A\}$ and $P\{A \,|\, B\}$ to denote, respectively, the probability of random event A and the conditional probability of random event A given that event B occurs (has occurred). We note incidentally

that the value of β which appears in assumption (E) must obviously be positive and fairly small (in any case, no greater than 0.5).

4. Algorithms for computing I_m (Y) generally assume that we know the distribution of random variable Y; however, for most of the normal variants of I_m (Y) it turns out to be sufficient, when we compute the numerical value, for us to know the vector of average values of Y_0 and the covariance matrix Σ of the random variable Y under investigation.

5. ε_0 could be, for example, the maximum possible value of ε at which at least one value of θ (ε_0) can be found with a nonempty stability region.

6. In our experiments (see chapter 3 [not translated here — Ed.]), we used both Forel-type procedures and к-means procedures. For the case of realistic data arrays ($n \sim 10^3$, $m \sim 10^2$) rather than experimental ones, however, Forel-type algorithms require too much computer time; these algorithms have not proved themselves in practice, particularly with respect to criterion (17).

7. For moderate values of n (the sets to be classified), the outcome of using к-means type algorithms will depend also on the original choice of N_0 and the corresponding base points Y_{i_1}, Y_{i_2}, . . ., $Y_{i_{N_0}}$. This relationship practically disappears for large values of n, however (for the properties of the MacQueen algorithm, see [2, pp. 116-18]).

8. If the quantities $y^{(1)}$, $y^{(2)}$, . . ., $y^{(m)}$ of the goods consumed by the family are measured in monetary units, then obviously we must set $p^{(1)} = p^{(2)} = \ldots = p^{(m)} = 1$.

9. We note incidentally that, in the particular case of normal distributions (see the expression for density function f_k (Y) given by formulas (1)-(3)), the Kul'bak informational distance I (k_1, k_2) between classes numbered k_1 and k_2 can be put in the form

$$I(k_1, k_2) = \frac{1}{2} tr \{(\Sigma(k_1) - \Sigma(k_2))(\Sigma^{-1}(k_1) - \Sigma^{-1}(k_2))\} +$$
$$+ \frac{1}{2} (Y_0(k_1) - Y_0(k_2))' (\Sigma^{-1}(k_1) + \Sigma^{-1}(k_2)) (Y_0(k_1) - Y_0(k_2)),$$

with identical covariance matrices, this yields the Mahalanobis distance

$$I(k_1, k_2) = (Y_0(k_1) - Y_0(k_2))' \Sigma^{-1} (Y_0(k_1) - Y_0(k_2)).$$

10. Points $W(t_1', t_2', \ldots, t_{p'}')$ and $W(t_1'', t_2'', \ldots, t_{p'}'')$ are called neighboring if and only if $\max_{1 \leqslant i \leqslant p'} |t_i' - t_i''| = 1$.

REFERENCES

1. Aivazian, S. A. "O nekotorykh napravleniiakh primeneniia mnogomernogo statisticheskogo analiza v sotsial'no-ekonomicheskikh issledovaniakh." In Algoritmy mnogomernogo statisticheskogo analiza i ikh primeneniia. Moscow: Central Economic Mathematical Institute of the USSR Academy of Sciences, 1975.

2. Aivazian, S. A.; Bezhaeva, Z. I.; and Staroverov, O. V. Klassifikatsiia mnogomernykh nabliudenii. Moscow: "Statistika" Publishers, 1974.

3. Anderson, T. Introduction to Multivariate Analysis (Russian edition). Moscow: Fizmatgiz, 1963.

4. Apraushcheva, N. N. "Algoritm rasshchepleniia smesi normal'nykh klassov." In Programmy i algoritmy. Moscow: Central Economic Mathematical Institute of the USSR Academy of Sciences, 1976.

5. Vol'konskii, V. A. "Ekonomiko-matematicheskie modeli soglasovannogo planirovaniia platezhesposobnogo sprosa i roznichnykh tsen." Ekonomika i matematicheskie metody, 1973, vol. 9, no. 4.

6. Vol'konskii, V. A. "Ob ob'ektivnoi matematicheskoi kharakteristike narodnogo potrebleniia." In Narodnokhoziaistvennye modeli. Teoreticheskie voprosy potrebleniia. Moscow: USSR Academy of Sciences Press, 1963.

7. Kendall, M., and Stuart, A. Inference and Relationships (Russian edition). Moscow: "Nauka" Publishers, 1973.

8. Cramér, H. Mathematical Methods of Statistics (Russian edition). Moscow: "Mir" Publishers, 1975.

9. Kul'bak, S. Teoriia informatsii i statistika. Moscow: "Nauka" Publishers, 1967.

10. Kupershtok, V. L.; Mirkin, B. G.; and Trofimov, V. A. "Metody naimenshykh kvadratov v analize kachestvennykh priznakov." In Problemy analiza diskretnoi informatsii, part 2. Novosibirsk: "Nauka" Publishers, 1976.

11. Matiukha, I. Ia. Statistika biudzhetov naseleniia. Moscow: "Statistika" Publishers, 1967.

12. Mirkin, B. G. Analiz kachestvennykh priznakov. Moscow: "Statistika" Publishers, 1976.

13. Plotkin, A. A. "Ustoichivost' razbieniia kak kriterii optimal'nosti postroennoi klassifikatsii." In Statisticheskie metody analiza ekspertnykh otsenok. Uchenye zapiski po statistike, vol. 28. Moscow: "Nauka" Publishers, 1976.

14. Raitsin, V. Ia. Matematicheskie metody i modeli planirovaniia urovniia zhizni. Moscow: "Ekonomika" Publishers, 1970.

15. Rimashevskaia, N. M., and Rogova, O. L. "Modelirovanie struktury denezhnykh raskhodov naseleniia." Ekonomika i matematicheskie metody, 1972, vol. 8, no. 6.

16. Trofimov, V. A. "Modeli kachestvennogo faktornogo analiza matrits sviazi." In Problemy analiza diskretnoi informatsii, part II. Novosibirsk: "Nauka" Publishers, 1976.

17. Frisch, R. "A Complete Scheme for Computing All Direct and Cross Demand Elasticities in a Model with Many Sectors." Econometrica, 1959, vol. 27, no. 2.

18. Hartigan, J. A. Clustering Algorithms. London, 1975.

19. MacQueen, J. "Some Methods for Classification and Analysis for Multivariate Observations." In Proceedings of the Fifth Berkeley Symposium on Mathematical Statistics and Probability, vol. 1, 1967.

Part 4

Natural Resources Economics

INTRODUCTION

Judith Thornton

Soviet models of natural resource use have been developed to
meet specific needs of the planning system. The formal mathematical models are intended to serve as an institutional substitute for competitive product markets and capital markets to
generate information on the potential income streams from resources in their optimal uses and on the capitalized value of
such streams.

Since demands for resources are derived demands, resource
use cannot be modeled in isolation from the other variables of
the economic plan. So resource models usually figure as elements in large systems of integrated models in which the estimated results of one model become the assumed parameters
of the next model.

Although Soviet mathematical economists have kept abreast
of Western developments in economic dynamics in their literature in pure theory, few of the recent Western approaches have
found their way into the models for natural resources. The
typical Soviet resource planning model takes the form of a large
linear program or a set of fixed-coefficient optimizing models.
Dual to each of the primary optimizing problems is a valuation
problem whose solution yields the shadow prices of the constrained inputs — the marginal effect on the objective function
of relaxing a constraint by one unit. Sometimes the problem

is static, as in Gofman, Gusev, and Mudretsov [6], or in the selection by Antsyshkin and Polianskaia presented here. A common static formulation is the minimization of the cost of a vector of outputs subject to constraints on capacities capable of production at varying levels of constant cost. Sometimes the problem is dynamic, as in Sakhovaler and Eskin [17], or in the article by Golovin, Kitaigorodskii, and Fainshtein presented here. A typical dynamic model would posit the maximization of the present value of output or of rent over some plan period subject to constant costs and subject to constraints on available resource stocks, potential future resource stocks, and quantities of investment. Frequently, a system of models integrates a dynamic optimization problem with a set of local static optima, as in the selection by Maksimov presented here, or the dynamic optimization may be linked to national and regional balances, as in the application of the Raiatskas and Sutkaitis system presented here.

The recent evolution of Soviet resource models mirrors the development of all Soviet planning models. First, programming models involving the maximization of an objective function have gained in importance at the expense of stochastic models, such as estimates of production functions. Secondly, all types of models now treat maximization or optimization as the central economic problem. Even the input-output balances discussed here introduce a form of optimization in that individual elements of final demand are allowed to vary between minimum and maximum values to permit the maximization of the total value of final output.

The most important recent development has been the integration of individual models into large-scale systems of optimizing models for the whole economy. Indeed, virtually all economic modeling has been co-opted to the attempt to develop interrelated sets of mathematical models to solve the problems of planning and management of the socialist economy. The new approach aims to create a System for the Optimal Functioning of the Socialist Economy, or SOFE (sistema optimal'nogo funktsionirovaniia sotsialisticheskoi ekonomiki) that could form the

basis for a "scientifically substantiated" computer centralization of planned resource allocation. Many proponents of SOFE
expect their models to provide synthetic efficiency parameters
that can be used to generate proposed values for the decision
variables in the economic plan. Real economic units could then
be instructed to conform to planned targets, and the real economic system would replicate the hypothetical model.

The reader will sometimes wonder whether it is good fortune
or massage that guarantees the consistency of the results of
various subproblems. And, although he may find a Soviet author referring to the reconciliation of results, he rarely will
find a reference to problems of feasibility.

The authors of competing systems of models disagree as to
how the models should relate to the real world — on the extent
of divergence there should be between the information system
provided by the models and the incentive system of real costs
and payments. Early supporters of optimizing models like
Gofman seemed to hope that operational prices facing decision
makers would be adjusted toward the shadow values of the
models. Indeed, most of the models use actual cost-accounting
prices to value all of the unconstrained variables in their problems. However, it is now official practice that the shadow-
price valuations of the models will be used only in drawing up
perspective plans and in assigning the cadastral valuations of
resources in the State Register but not in actual transactions
between firms. In fact, some of the authors, such as Antsyshkin
and Polianskaia, provide models for estimating two separate
sets of prices.

The Antsyshkin and Polianskaia paper presents a static
branch optimizing model to determine the optimal structure of
production in an extractive industry, derive shadow prices for
fuels of varying quality, and impute rental incomes to the deposits from which the fuels are extracted. The objective function in the primary problem is the minimization of the total
costs of the extraction, concentration, transport, and use of
power station coal. The demand for coal by individual power
stations is given by the fuel and energy balance, which is

treated as a constraint. The technical productivity of deposits is modeled as a function of the size of stocks, extent of previous exploitation, engineering conditions, and time duration of mine construction. Extraction costs vary as a function of previous exploitation. There are constraints on the capacities of individual mines, which are differentiated by the qualities of their coal.

Solution of the dual yields vectors of the shadow prices of various types of raw and processed coal. Then, the difference between the marginal valuation of each type of coal and its local direct cost is estimated to provide measures of the annual unit rental earned by each site.

Overall, the marginal cost of coal in the model is only 10 to 15% higher than existing accounting costs of coal, but the regional structure of shadow prices differs markedly from the accounting structure. So the authors solve, next, for what might be called the optimal politically feasible set of prices. This new model minimizes the gross income received for coal deliveries in the whole country — minimizes the sum of wholesale price, transport cost, and use cost of the previously determined structure of coal deliveries. This is minimized subject to the constraints that no coal basin makes losses and all coal users are placed in a position of equal profitability from their use of coal. The set of optimal accounting prices derived in this model differs from region to region. Then an imputation of accounting rent is made by comparing the direct cost of each local mine with the cost of the marginal fuel in that region.

The authors recognize that price systems have incentive, as well as information, functions, for they argue that the rents earned by the mines should be divided among the producers, the state treasury, and the supply and procurement organizations responsible for the coal allocation plan. Otherwise, they argue, these organizations will have no incentives to draw up an efficient plan.

Most of the recent models for the natural resource industries pose dynamic or quasi-dynamic problems. Although they are set up as dynamic programming problems with a form much like Western resource models, the values of so many variables are specified at each point in time that the models seem deterministic by comparison with their Western counterparts. For example, a standard Western approach is found in Burt and Cummings [4] and Kuller and Cummings [8]. In "An Economic Model of Production and Investment for Petroleum Reservoirs," Kuller and Cummings maximize the discounted sum of net rents from a petroleum reservoir subject to an initial capital stock, gross capital investment, upper bounds on annual oil output, and a rate-dependent cost function. The maximization yields first-order conditions on four different margins. In each case, the present value of marginal net income is set equal to a marginal cost — a user cost of resource stock or future output, a boundary user cost, a user cost of capital consumption, and a production user cost measuring the effect of current production on future variable cost. This approach may be compared with Maksimov's multilevel model translated here.

The Maksimov selection describes the simplest version of his dynamic system — a two-level set of models for minimizing the costs of exploration, extraction, and transport of natural gas to consumption points. The upper-level problem takes the form of a network linking gas consumption points, specified by location and time, to actual and potential production points by means of actual and potential pipelines. The upper-level problem is solved for optimal levels of gas output plus accumulation of reserves, and it determines an optimal structure of gas deliveries through the pipeline system to specified consumption points.

The lower-level problem describes production decisions in individual regions or districts. Again, it is a cost-minimizing problem for supplying time-dated deliveries of natural gas. It yields estimates of the optimal timing and level of gas exploration, drilling of production wells, and construction of pipelines and facilities.

The Maksimov system is an example of the sort of modeling that is supposed to be performed for each branch of industry in the course of drawing up long-run plans. The structures of

some other approved branch systems are spelled out in the
Standard Methodology for Calculations to Optimize the Development and Location of Production in the Long Run [19], an official document worked out by a committee under the direction
of Aganbegian.

While the Maksimov system deals with a world of certainty,
the following article by Golovin, Kitaigorodskii, and Fainshtein
introduces uncertainty into determination of the long-run optimal plan of the natural gas industry. This latter system maximizes the difference between the marginal-cost value of oil
and gas discovered and the total cost of extracting that fuel
subject to constraints on levels of annual consumption. The
primary decision variables are rates of discovery and development of deposits. Optimal rates of consumption are also
estimated in the regional plan, and these rates are compared
with the given demands in a set of static fuel and energy
balances.

The discovery of fuel is described by a probabilistic model
that estimates the expected value of the summed growth of
stocks of fuel in a region as a function of capital investment
and prospecting effort. The probability of discovering new
stocks is a function of the ratio of deposits developed previously to a measure of potential deposits. Large deposits are
assumed to be discovered first, and the probability of discovering a particular deposit is assumed proportional to its size.
Costs of extraction depend on rates of production and on levels
of previous withdrawal.

The authors simulate the exploration process using data on
regional reserves, the time path of exploratory activity, inventories of discovered fields, investment in exploration, and average annual depth of wells. The outcome of the simulation is
a table showing the probability of securing an increase in reserves from a given level of exploratory investment applied
to an assumed level of total reserves.

The authors describe a set of computations made for the
Tiumen district that shows how desired rates of extracting and
proving new reserves depend on available investment and the

national marginal cost of fuel.

The Golovin et al. system embodies some of the features of a recent Western model by Arrow and Chang [1], in which discoveries occur stochastically in proportion to the level of exploratory activity, but the Golovin system does not treat exploration, itself, as a means of reducing uncertainty — a subject explored by Pindyck [12, 13], in the Western literature. Nor do the Soviet authors raise the question of how uncertainty about the size of stocks bears on the desired time path of resource use, the subject of recent work by Stiglitz and Dasgupta [18].

One of the most successful features of Soviet resource modeling has been the integration of environmental and traditional inputs into a single model. Publication of a paper by Leontief and Ford [10] in Ekonomika i matematicheskie metody in 1972 set a Soviet precedent for the inclusion of environmental variables in traditional input-output balances. Marginal approaches to identifying optimal levels of pollution and choosing optimal rates of use of environmental inputs were worked out in Gofman's laboratory at Central Economic-Mathematical Institute where much of the methodology in current use was elaborated by A. A. Gusev [7].

Rather than choosing between the approaches of constrained maximization and balancing, the resource economists built systems that incorporated both. Gusev estimates the optimal mix of pollution control investment by applying coefficients of damage per unit of effluent. He solves for the optimal location of production by minimizing the environmental damage from a given level of output. In a third case, he uses a 16-sector input-output matrix to maximize the value of final demand minus a measure of environmental damage. The input-output matrix specifies technological coefficients, including those for environmental damage as an input. Resource and labor constraints are given, as are maximum and minimum values of each item of final demand.

Ushakov [20] applies the Gusev procedure to estimate the optimal use of water in a river system. Decision variables in the problem are the location of production and water treatment facilities. The objective function minimizes the sum of production costs and economic damages of water pollution. There are constraints on labor and on total investment. Derived demands for inputs depend on choice of technology, with the final input set described by an input-output balance.

The largest and most complex system for modeling economic and environmental variables together is the set of regional models for Estonia developed by Raiatskas and Sutkaitis. The full system of static and dynamic models is described in a set of three papers, one of which is translated here [14, 15]. The Raiatskas and Sutkaitis system provides procedures for estimating input demands for resources, including environmental resources. Measures of social cost are broadly defined to include both direct and indirect environmental costs.

Environmental quality is treated as a form of capital. Reduction in the stock of environmental capital requires a substitution of other conventional inputs either to produce the same level of output directly or to replace environmental capital. Further, the marginal product of environmental inputs varies with the level of accumulated pollution, with the stock of pollution defined to be the sum of annual differences between pollution created and a vector of environmental absorptive capabilities.

Each set of choices as to the amount of pollution accumulated generates a different set of fixed-coefficient input demands. A more polluted state of the world uses less environmental capital and more conventional inputs and natural resources. So the technologies prevailing under different states of the world can be treated as alternatives in a linear program. In the linear programming model, the primal problem maximizes the output from a given stock of conventional inputs, natural resources, and levels of environmental capital. The dual minimizes the full resource cost of producing a given level of output. In this model, the marginal value of a less polluted state of the world is the marginal increment in output. The output vector consists of a vector of conventional products plus a vector of changes in environmental capital.

In addition, there is a conventional input-output balance corresponding to the solution of the maximization problem. The set of outputs in the maximization problem is treated as a vector of final demands in the input-output balance. Input coefficients are described by a matrix of per-unit demands for conventional and environmental resources. Raiatskas and Sutkaitis's 1978 article presents the optimization problem, and their 1979 article presents a dynamic input-output model designed to choose a path with an optimal level of pollution.

There is little room for innovation in the form of resource planning models, for basic procedures have been laid down in a series of official technical documents, called Standard Methodologies, each constructed by a committee of economists. The Standard Methodology for the Economic Valuation of Mineral Deposits [11] describes the set of models sanctioned for most resources. Approved are a maximization model to determine the marginal valuation of resource products, a set of deductions from cost to determine annual site rental, and a capitalization process for assigning capitalized values to resource deposits.

Since the state exercises the property rights in physical capital, resource allocation problems present the decision maker with all aspects of the principal-agent relationship, including information and incentive problems. So far, the modeling of incentives has not been integrated into general Soviet planning models. The Soviet literature offers nothing as interesting as the Western model by Bonin and Marcus [3], which, in effect, provides a two-part payment to a producer for the provision of correct information and subsequent output. Rather, the need for accurate primary information is handled by means of cadastral accounts for centralized monitoring of stock size and drawdown.

While monitoring is essential to the exercise of socialist property rights, it is equally important that administrators should see accurate information as being in their own interest. The Antsyshkin article presented here proposes that a portion

of resource rents should be assigned to the agencies of supply
and procurement. Gofman, on the other hand, favors estab-
lishment of regional resource-owning agencies to centralize
the collection of property rents and to pay for expansion of the
state's resource stocks. His proposal is translated below.

A survey of current Soviet resource models shows that they
share common features with Western forecasting and operations research models, but they have relatively little in common with current Western economics of natural resources.
The Soviet description of technical processes has little in common with the trans log demand functions of Berndt and Wood[2].
The dynamic planning models have more practical concerns
than the steady-state equilibria that have interested Western
economists (and Soviet mathematicians) from Hotelling to
Stiglitz. The discussion of rents and incentives gives only informal recognition to the principal-agent problems modeled
by Leland [9] and Ross [16]. On just one topic, valuation,
Gofman, Gusev, and their associates [21] address the subject
in a manner akin to the analysis of taxation by Dasgupta and
Heal [5].

The requirement that Soviet resource models should meet
specific planning needs has made the models standard and routine, although their operational role generates ingenuity in
treating large, complex problems. In sum, it seems to me
that Soviet resource economics has a place for the forecaster,
operations researcher, and pure mathematician. It remains
to be seen whether there is a place in Soviet science for the
economist who builds models in order to generate testable
hypotheses.

Judith Thornton

REFERENCES

1. Arrow, Kenneth, and Chang, Sheldon. "Optimal Pricing, Use, and Exploration of Uncertain Natural Resource Stocks." Department of Economics, Harvard
University, Report No. 31 (December 1978).

2. Berndt, Ernst, and Wood, David. "Technology, Prices, and the Derived

Demand for Energy." Review of Economics and Statistics, 1975, vol. 57, no. 3, pp. 259-267.

3. Bonin, John, and Marcus, Alan. "Information, Motivation, and Control in Decentralized Planning: The Case of Discretionary Managerial Behavior." Journal of Comparative Economics, 1979, vol. 3, no. 3, pp. 235-252.

4. Burt, O. R., and Cummings, R. G. "Production and Investment in Natural Resource Industries." American Economic Review, 1970, vol. 60, no. 4, pp. 576-590.

5. Dasgupta, Partha, and Heal, G. M. Economic Theory and Exhaustible Resources. Cambridge: Cambridge University Press, 1979.

6. Gofman, K. G.; Gusev, A. A.; Mudretsov, A. F. "Opredelenie zamykaiushchikh zatrat na produktsiiu prirodoekspluatiruiushchikh otraslei" (Determination of the marginal costs of natural resource products). Ekonomika i matematicheskie metody, 1975, vol. 11, no. 4, pp. 695-706. Translated in Matekon, 1976, vol. 12, no. 3, pp. 3-21.

7. Gusev, A. A. "Problemy sovmestnogo prognozirovaniia razvitiia ekonomiki i okhrany atmosfery" (Problems in the simultaneous forecasting of growth of the economy and reduction in air pollution). Ekonomika i matematicheskie metody, 1979, vol. 15, no. 1, pp. 31-44.

8. Kuller, Robert, and Cummings, Ronald. "An Economic Model of Production and Investment for Petroleum Reservoirs." American Economic Review, 1974, vol. 64, no. 1, pp. 66-79.

9. Leland, Hayne. "Optimal Risk Sharing and the Leasing of Natural Resources with Application to Oil and Gas Leasing on the OCS." Quarterly Journal of Economics, 1978, vol. 92, no. 3, pp. 413-437.

10. Leontief, W., and Ford, D. "Mezhotraslevoi analiz vozdeistviia struktury ekonomiki na okruzhaiushchuiu sredu" (Input-output analysis of the influence of the structure of the economy on the environment). Ekonomika i matematicheskie metody, 1972, vol. 8, no. 3.

11. "Metodicheskie osnovy ekonomicheskoi otsenki mestorozhdenii poleznykh iskopaemykh" (The methodological basis for valuations of mineral deposits). Ekonomika i matematicheskie metody, 1978, vol. 14, no. 3. Translated in Matekon, 1979, vol. 15, no. 4, pp. 3-27.

12. Pindyck, Robert. "The Optimal Production of an Exhaustible Resource when Price is Exogenous and Stochastic." Sloan School of Management, MIT Working Paper 1162-80 (November 1980).

13. Pindyck, Robert. "Uncertainty and Exhaustible Resource Markets." Journal of Political Economy, 1980, vol. 88, no. 6, pp. 1203-1226.

14. Raiatskas, R. L., and Sutkaitis, V. P. "K probleme modelirovaniia vzaimosviazei obshchestva i prirody" (On the problem of modeling the interaction of society and nature). Ekonomika i matematicheskie metody, 1978, vol. 14, no. 3. Translated in Matekon, 1979, vol. 15, no. 3, pp. 34-58.

15. Raiatskas, R. L., and Sutkaitis, V. P. "Modelirovanie ekonomicheskoi dinamiki s uchetom zagriazneniia okruzhaiushchei sredy" (A dynamic economic model incorporating environmental pollution). Ekonomika i matematicheskie

metody, 1979, vol. 15, no. 1, pp. 45-57. Translated in Matekon, 1979, vol. 16, no. 2, pp. 89-108.

16. Ross, Stephen. "The Economic Theory of Agency: The Principal's Problem." American Economic Review, 1973, vol. 63, no. 2, pp. 134-139.

17. Sakhovaler, T. A., and Eskin, V. I. "Optimizatsiia raspredeleniia zatrat mezhdu razvedkoi, dobychei i magistral'nym transportom nefti" (Optimizing the distribution of expenditure between exploration, extraction, and transport of oil). Ekonomika i matematicheskie metody, 1980, vol. 16, no. 6, pp. 1123-1130.

18. Stiglitz, Joseph, and Dasgupta, Partha. "Market Structure and Resource Extraction under Uncertainty." Econometric Research Program Research Memorandum No. 262 (March 1980).

19. "Tipovaia metodika raschetov po optimizatsii razvitiia i razmeshcheniia proizvodstva no perspektivu" (Standard methodology for calculations to optimize the development and location of production in the long run). Ekonomika i matematicheskie metody, 1977, vol. 13, no. 6. Translated in Matekon, 1978, vol. 15, no. 1, pp. 75-96.

20. Ushakov, E. I. "Optimizatsiia razvitiia i razmeshcheniia proizvodstva v regione s uchetom vosproizvodstva vodnykh resursov" (Optimization of the growth and distribution of production in a region taking the maintenance of water resources into account). Ekonomika i matematicheskie metody, 1978, vol. 14, no. 1, pp. 78-85.

21. Voronovitskii, M. M.; Gofman, K. G.; Gusev, A. A.; and Spivak, V. A. "Ekonomicheskie osnovy platy za zagriaznenie okruzhaiushchei sredy" (The economic basis for pollution payments). Ekonomika i matematicheskie metody, 1975, vol. 11, no. 3, pp. 483-490.

ON POSSIBLE WAYS OF USING
OPTIMAL BRANCH PLANS TO IMPROVE
THE PRICE SYSTEM—
THE CASE OF POWER STATION COALS

S. V. Antsyshkin and T. M. Polianskaia

Planned prices are an important tool for controlling the economy. Their role in ensuring organic consistency between
planning and financial accountability is enormous. Prices are
an important instrument for comparing costs and benefits.
They can only perform the latter function if they take account
of the two poles in the exchange process: they must reflect
the interests of the producer on the one hand and of the consumer on the other.

Prices as a category are an important means of implementing optimal plans. In the theory of optimal planning, prices
take the form of the partial derivative of the social welfare
function at the optimum with respect to the output of the corresponding commodity or input of the corresponding resource.
Hitherto it has proved impossible to implement these well-
known principles in practice, because of the considerable problem of modeling, procuring the necessary information, and
computation. One of these difficulties (and perhaps the most
important of them) is the lack of a formal analytical expres-

Russian text © 1978 by "Nauka" Publishers. "O vozmozhnykh napravleniiakh
sovershenstvovaniia sistemy tsen na osnove otraslevykh optimal'nykh planov (na
primere energeticheskikh uglei," Ekonomika i matematicheskie metody, 1978,
vol. 14, no. 3, pp. 518-530.
Presented as a discussion of the issue.

sion for the social welfare function. However, the fact that it is not possible at present to switch to optimal prices does not mean that we should not gradually bring existing prices into closer correspondence with them. The present article deals with possible ways of achieving this aim.

The economic literature frequently discusses the proposition that prices based on branch average costs should take account of such factors as the return derived by the customer, substitution possibilities, the relationship between supply and demand, and the need to provide adequate incentives for every enterprise working in normal conditions. In parametric terms these proposals can be expressed as:

$$c = F(z, \rho, v, \varepsilon, s) \tag{1}$$

where z is average branch cost; ρ is the normal rate of profit; v is a component which takes account of substitution possibilities between goods; ε is a term expressing the benefit yielded to the consumer by substitutes; and s is a term which incorporates in the price the relation between supply and demand.

Incorporating these factors in price formation need not mean that the general level of prices must go up. The point is that existing prices in many cases incorporate profits much larger than the level implied by $\rho \Phi$. This proposition is supported by the large size of the free remainder of profit paid into the state budget. The magnitude $F(s)$ is only positive for goods in short supply. In the cases of products which either are inferior substitutes or yield a low return, the values of $F(v)$ and $F(\varepsilon)$ will be zero. Prices based on the optimal national plan would incorporate all the components in equation (1).

In our view, the prices which are in actual use in a centrally planned and controlled economy should satisfy the following requirements: (1) they should be organically linked with the plan denominated in physical units and should act as an incentive for its fulfillment; (2) they should be an effective means of comparing costs and benefits; (3) they should act as a special kind of bridge between planning and the implementation of the plan, making these processes consistent with each other and with the global interests of the economy; (4) they should take account of all the factors included in equation (1).

In the present article we concentrate on research into the prospects for using the data and results of branch optimal plans to improve the price system. As an example we consider two possible ways of constructing a system of wholesale prices for power station coals.

The Optimal Branch Problem

The aim of an optimal plan for the development of the coal supply system is to choose levels for the production and processing of power station coals in each coal basin and coalfield and also to derive the optimal allocation of run-of-mine coals and by-products by user regions — i.e., to establish demand zones for coals from different basins and fields.

In formulating this problem in economic terms, we made the following assumptions: firstly, the optimization of development plans should take account of the special features of the coal industry as an extractive branch (these are exhibited in important differences between the costs or quality of coals in individual open-cast mines or pits, in the period required for construction and for achieving designed capacity, in changes in the level of current costs over the period of introduction and operation, and in the need for investment to maintain the level of output); secondly, the development of the coal supply system depends on the level of the economy's demand for power station coals and the technically feasible level of output.

To allow the problem to take account of the major differences in the cost and quality of coal, individual mining enterprises were taken as the basic unit. The length of the construction and start-up periods, the changes in current costs over the period of introduction and operation, and the need for investment to maintain output levels were taken into account in the definition of extraction costs. These were calculated as integrals (or as weighted annual averages in static problems) over the period for which the calculations were made; this period

covered construction of the mine and attainment of designed
capacity and part of the period of normal operation [1].

The coal industry is one of the branch subsystems in the fuel
and energy complex. Hence the level and structure of demand
for power station coal are determined in a way which takes account of the circumstances affecting optimal energy balance
for the country, particularly the level of demand for the more
efficient fuels — natural gas and fuel oil. The customers for
fuel in each region consisted of existing or new coal-dust-
burning installations (basically thermal power stations) and
also boiler and small-scale local installations for layer burning.

When account was taken of the requirements these groups of
customers impose with respect to fuel quality (particle-size
distribution), it turned out that the boiler installations for layer
burning could use only grades of coal with a large average size
and brickets (T^c) while dust-burning installations could use any
unsorted coals, siftings, industrial products, or slurry (T^n).

As far as the qualitative characteristics of coal were concerned, attention was paid to calorific equivalent and ash content, since these have the greatest impact on transportation and
combustion costs. From the users' standpoint these costs were
taken into account using coefficients of substitution between
energy sources; these take account of differences in the coefficients of effective use of coals of different quality.

Technically feasible output levels were established for each
enterprise on the basis of that enterprise's geological reserves, the extent to which these reserves were ready for use,
the engineering conditions in which the mine had to be constructed, the time taken to introduce designed capacity, and
the standard levels at which that capacity would be introduced.
There were additional sources of supply in the form of power
station coals produced in conjunction with coking coal, and by-
products from enriching the latter. The quantity of these was
determined in the course of solving the development and location problem for the output of coking coal.

The problem took account of the prospects for processing

all coals which are mechanically and thermally resistant. In the absence of differentiated data on how the costs of using fuel depend on its qualitative properties, the problem was limited to choosing the form of the processing and determining the optimal quantities of graded coal on the basis of given processing methods and given output coefficients for each method.

In order to get a compact description of mining conditions, we used a discrete representation of the cost function. For this purpose cumulative total costs and annual mining levels were found for qualitatively homogeneous groups of enterprises based on a ranking of their unit mining costs.

In the light of the margins of error tolerated in the original data, all coals were aggregated into qualitatively homogeneous groups, and delivery centers and consumption regions were identified.

The optimality criterion adopted for the development of the coal supply system was minimization of the total costs of mining, processing, delivery, and use of power station coal.

The mathematical model of the problem under consideration was constructed on the basis of a sequential representation of the processes of mining, processing, delivery, and use of power station coals.

The model is required to find variables $v_{i_l k}$, $x^T_{l f}$, $x^t_{i_l jr}$ which minimize total costs:

$$\Phi = \sum_{l=1}^{L} \sum_{i_l=1}^{I_l} \left[\sum_{k=1}^{K} v_{i_l k} z^T_{i_l k} + \sum_{f=1}^{F} c^T_{i_l f} x^T_{l f} + \sum_{t=1}^{T} \sum_{r=1}^{R} \sum_{j=1}^{J} (c^t_{i_l r} + c^t_{i_l jr}) x^t_{i_l jr} \right] \tag{2}$$

and satisfy the following conditions:

(a) a constraint on the quantity of run-of-mine coal produced at each enterprise (this depends on the enterprise's technical possibilities)

$$x_{i_l}^T = \sum_{k=1}^{K} v_{i_l} B_{i_l k}^T, \quad i_l = 1, \ldots, I_l, \quad l = 1, \ldots, L, \tag{3}$$

$$\sum_{k=1}^{K} v_{i_l k} = 1;$$

(b) an annual balance between the production of run-of-mine coal and its demand, either for processing or customers' direct demand

$$x_{i_l}^T - \sum_{f=1}^{F} x_{i_l f}^T - \sum_{r=1}^{R} \sum_{j=1}^{J} x_{i_l jr}^T = 0, \quad i_l = 1, \ldots, I_l, \quad l = 1, \ldots, L; \tag{4}$$

(c) a balance between processed output and its delivery to users

$$\sum_{f=1}^{F} \alpha_{i_l f}^t x_{i_l f}^T - \sum_{r=1}^{R} \sum_{j=1}^{J} x_{i_l jr}^t = 0, \quad t = 1, \ldots, T-1; \tag{5}$$

(d) a balance for the use of the various coals, taking account of their substitution possibilities

$$\sum_{l=1}^{L} \sum_{i_l=1}^{Il} \sum_{t=1}^{T} \gamma_{i_l jr}^t x_{i_l jr}^t = \Pi_{jr}, \quad r = 1, \ldots, R, \quad j = 1, \ldots, J; \tag{6}$$

(e) nonnegativity constraints on the variables

$$x_{i_l f}^T \geqslant 0; \quad x_{i_l jr}^t \geqslant 0; \quad v_{i_l k} \geqslant 0. \tag{7}$$

The following notation was adopted: i_l is the index of a qualitatively homogeneous group of coal mines attached to consignment point l, $i_l = 1, \ldots, I_l$; l is the index of a coal consignment point, $l = 1, \ldots, L$; t is an index of a grade of coal ($t = 1, \ldots, T-1$ for processed outputs, $t = T$ for run-of-mine coal); f is the index for a coal-processing technique, $f = 1, \ldots,$ F; j is the index for a group of coal users, $j = 1, \ldots, J$; r is the index for the region in which those consumers are located, $r = 1, \ldots, R$; $B_{i_l k}^T$ is the technically feasible production level for run-of-mine coal of a qualitatively homogeneous group of enterprises i_l, corresponding to point k of the discrete approximation of the cost curve; $\alpha_{i_l f}^t$ is the coefficient for the output of processed coal, which varies for each qualitatively homogeneous group of mines i_l and processing technique f; $\gamma_{i_l jr}^t$ are substitution coefficients for various types of coal for the various consumer groups j; Π_{jr} is demand for coal by customers j in region r; z_{ilk} is the total cost of producing run-of-mine coal at point k of the discrete approximation of the cost curve; $c_{i_l f}^T$ is the cost, including capital charge, averaged over the year, of processing run-of-mine coal, in rubles per ton of fuel equivalent — this depends on its quality (i_l) and the processing technique (f); $c_{i_l r}^t$ is the cost, including capital charge, of shipping coal, in rubles per ton of fuel equivalent, from consignment point l to the center of demand region r; $c_{i_l jr}^t$ is the cost, including capital charge but excluding energy costs, of using coal in the installations of the user groups j in rubles per ton of fuel equivalent; v_{ilk} is the level of use of run-of-mine coals of qualitatively homogeneous enterprises i_l, operating at point k in the discrete approximation of the cost curve; $x_{i_l f}^T$ is the quantity of run-of-mine coal going for processing; $x_{i_l jr}^t$ is the quantity of run-of-mine coal and processed coal, $t=1,\ldots,T$, going to customer j in region r.

The objective function (2) includes the costs of mining, processing, delivery, and use of the coal; these depend on its qualitative properties, the processing techniques used, and the firing conditions.

Dual Prices

On the basis of the above model, we consider a procedure for finding the system of shadow prices associated with the optimal plan. The vector of shadow prices is the optimal solution to a problem which is dual to the original problem. The dual to problem (2) to (7) has the following form.

Find the maximum of the linear function:

$$\Phi = \sum_{i_l=1}^{J_l} u_{i_l} + \sum_{r=1}^{R}\sum_{j=1}^{J} w_{jr}\Pi_{jr} \tag{8}$$

subject to

$$s_{i_l}^T B_{i_l k}^T + u_{i_l} \leq z_{i_l k}^T, \tag{9}$$

$$-s_{i_l}^T + \sum_{t=1}^{T-1} \alpha_{i_l f}^t s_{i_l}^t \leq c_{i_l f}^T, \tag{10}$$

$$\gamma_{i_l jr}^t w_{jr} - s_{i_l}^t \leq c_{i_l jr}^t \tag{11}$$

(It is assumed here that $c_{i_l jr}^t$ also includes costs $c_{i_l r}^t$).

The system of shadow prices includes: valuations of run-of-mine coal, $s_{i_l}^T$ and processed outputs $s_{i_l}^t$, in rubles per ton, corresponding to balance equations (4) and (5);[1] valuations u_{i_l}, in millions of rubles, associated with mining enterprises, and reflecting constraints (3), which keep coal production within technically feasible limits; and valuations associated with users w_{jr}, in rubles per ton, associated with balance equations (6). The relationships between the shadow prices at the optimal point are found using constraints (8) to (11).

The shadow prices of run-of-mine coals are given by

$$s_{i_l}^T = \frac{z_{i_l}^T - u_{i_l}}{B_{i_l}}, \quad i_l = 1, \ldots, I_l;\ l = 1, \ldots, L, \tag{12}$$

i.e., as the difference between the cost of mining coal and the rents of the mining enterprises.

Shadow prices for the output from processing run-of-mine coal,

$$s_{i_l}^q = \frac{s_{i_l}^T + c_{i_l f}^T - \sum_{t=1}^{T-1} \alpha_{i_l f}^t s_{i_l}^t}{\alpha_{i_l f}^q}, \quad t = 1, \ldots q, \ldots, T-1, t \neq q \tag{13}$$

are computed for each output on the basis of the shadow prices of processed run-of-mine coal, the prices of other outputs, and the processing cost; this expression incorporates output coefficients for all products.

Shadow prices $s_{i_l}^T$ and $s_{i_l}^t$ show how costs change if there is a unit change in demand for a particular type of coal. They define the marginal costs, including capital charge, of mining (or mining and processing) one ton of coal at enterprise i_l and have the same sign as the coefficients in the objective function.

The shadow prices u_{i_l} for each mining enterprise

$$u_{i_l} = z_{i_l}^T - s_{i_l}^T B_{i_l}^T, \qquad i_1 = 1, \ldots, I_l, \quad l = 1, \ldots, L, \qquad (14)$$

show the effect on the value of the functional of altering the technically feasible output level; these shadow prices reflect the differences between mines in their engineering condition, technical equipment, location, and so on — the factors which determine the comparative efficiency of the enterprise. Shadow prices u_{i_l} are in the nature of rents, and they depend on the productive capacity and quality of coal sold by the enterprise in question. For this reason they have to be expressed per ton of coal mined.

Shadow prices associated with the consumers are given by the equation

$$w_{jr} = \frac{c_{i_l jr}^t + s_{i_l}^t}{\gamma_{i_l jr}^t}, \quad j = 1, \ldots, J, r = 1, \ldots, R. \qquad (15)$$

They are the sum of the shadow prices of the coal and the cost the customer incurs in using that coal, and they take account of substitution coefficients; they express the change in the functional which would result from a unit change in the consumer's demand for coal.

The basis for these shadow prices is the valuations of the coals at the marginal mining enterprise and the marginal consumer's valuation of each qualitatively homogeneous group of coals. The marginal enterprise is the enterprise whose technical possibilities for coal production are not fully utilized in the optimal plan — i.e., the enterprise for which $v_{i_l} < 1$. The shadow price u_{i_l} for this enterprise is zero. In this case the shadow price $s_{i_l}{}^T$ of a ton of run-of-mine coal of a given quality type can be expressed, using (12), as

$$s_{i_l{}^3}^T = c_{i_l{}^3}^T = \frac{z_{i_l{}^3}^T}{B_{i_l{}^3}},\qquad (16)$$

i.e., it is equal to the unit cost, including capital charge, of producing coal at the marginal enterprise.

The marginal consumer of a qualitatively homogeneous group of coals is that enterprise which derives the smallest economic return from the use of the coal. The shadow price w_{j_3r} of the marginal consumer using coal from the marginal supplier i_{l3} is given by

$$w_{j_3r} = \frac{c_{i_{l3}j_3r}^T + c_{i_{l3}}^T}{\gamma_{i_{l3}j_3r}}.\qquad (17)$$

If the marginal consumer uses other coals as well as the marginal ones, this means that they must be as economical as the latter from the point of view of that consumer; i.e.

$$w_{j_3r} = \frac{c_{i_{l3}j_3r}^T + c_{i_{l3}}^T}{\gamma_{i_{l3}j_3r}^T} = \frac{s_{i_l}^t + c_{i_l j_3r}^t}{\gamma_{i_l j_3r}^t}.\qquad (18)$$

Hence the shadow price of these coals is determined via the shadow price of the marginal consumer:

$$s_{i_l}^t = w_{j_3r}\gamma_{i_l j_3r}^t - c_{i_l j_3r}^t,\qquad (19)$$

The shadow prices which the model yields for the coals determine the shadow prices of the marginal consumers, and so on. The chains of substitution possibilities thus formed allow us to determine the shadow prices of all coals. The overall shadow price of each type of coal is based on the cost, including capital charge, of producing the marginal run-of-mine coal. The correction for qualitative differences between the marginal grade of coal and any other grade is based on the delivered price at the marginal consumer of all possible substitutes.

From the expressions for the shadow prices, it is evident that they are both concrete and dynamic. The level of the shadow prices is determined by the formulation of the problem and all the initial data used, and that level changes if the data change. The extent of stability of the system of shadow prices depends directly on the stability in (12) to (15) of coefficient $B_{i_{l3}}$ — the technically feasible output levels of the marginal mines, and also on the stability of $c_{i_{l3}}$ — the production costs at the same mines. A change in the demand for fuel which is less than B_{i_l} does not change the identity of the marginal enterprise and consequently does not alter the production costs of the marginal fuel. The value of $c_{i_{l3}}$ basically determines how much the shadow prices change when demand for fuel changes and the identity of the marginal enterprise changes as well.

The effect which B_{i_l} and $c_{i\,_{l3}}$ have on the stability of the shadow prices depends principally on the extent to which the original data were aggregated in order to solve the problem. If the basic planning unit is a coal basin, a whole field, or a large development section of a field, each value of $c_{i_{l3}}$ will be associated with a large value of $B_{i_{l3}}$, which makes the system of shadow prices highly stable. But if individual mines are adopted as the basic units, then the degree of stability is sharply reduced.

The stability of the shadow prices also depends on the demand of the marginal customer. If a change in demand for or supply of fuel leaves the identity of the marginal consumer unchanged, the shadow prices are unaffected. If such a change occurs, however, then the ratio of the returns yielded by the different coals ($\gamma^t_{i_l j_3 r}/\gamma^t_{i_{l3} jr}$) changes, as do the total costs of delivery ($c^t_{i_{l3} j_3 r}$) and use ($c^t_{i_l j_3 r}$); this affects the shadow prices.

At present, increasing practical use is being made of shadow prices in the course of planning and design work. In particular, they are the basis for devising marginal costs for fuel, which show the actual costs the economy incurs if the demand for fuel changes in a particular region at a particular time. The concept of marginal costs is a development or revision of the cost of marginal fuel indices used previously for similar calculations, but the latter, as shown above, incorporate only part of the costs which are actually incurred if the demand for fuel changes.

Using the model we have described, the Central Mathematical Economics Institute (TsEMI) of the USSR Academy of Sciences, in conjunction with Central Research Institute for Economics and Scientific and Technological Information of the USSR Ministry of the Coal Industry, has calculated optimal development and location plans for the extraction and processing of power station coals of different qualities. The system of shadow prices which emerged exhibited the following features.

1. As well as covering the costs of mining, processing, and delivery of coals, the shadow prices also take account of the benefits the user receives from using coals of different qualities.

2. The shadow prices of coals at each mine depend on the quality of the coals produced there.

3. The relative levels of shadow prices in the various basins and fields reflect the presence in the optimal plan of several marginal basins and corresponding "marginal zones."

4. The resulting system of shadow prices depends heavily on the economy's demand for coal. If the latter changes by 5 to 10%, shadow prices increase by 20 to 40%, depending on the "marginal zone."

Methods of Price Formation

The properties of the shadow prices described above allow us to make some use of them to improve the system of wholesale prices for power station coals. This is the basis for the first of the approaches proposed here. Under this approach shadow prices $s_{i_l}^T$ and $s_{i_l}^t$ are used as a proposed price, bearing in mind that, when the appropriate bodies review the price, they take account of factors which are not incorporated in the model.

Specific shadow prices are found using a coefficient of calorific value for each grade of coal appearing in the corresponding official price list. An analysis of these indices reveals a number of interesting features which they embody; it also illustrates ways in which they might be used to improve existing prices.

The overall level of shadow prices for power station coals exceeds the existing price level slightly (by 10 to 15%) because of the high proportion of Kuznetsk and Donets coals. However, relative shadow prices for individual coals and grades of coal are significantly different from relative prices in the existing price list. For example, shadow prices are about 40% above current prices for a number of grades of Donets coals (PASH, ASH, ASHS, DMSSH, etc.) and 10 to 20% below current prices for certain grades. Shadow prices for Kuznetsk coals are about 10 to 15% above actual prices, while the shadow prices for Ekibastuz, Amur, Irkutsk, and Baikal coals are 25 to 30% higher. On the other hand shadow prices for all grades of coal from the Moscow region and the Pechora and Karaganda basins are 15 to 30% lower than their actual prices.

This is most important. Existing prices often fail to fulfill their necessary regulatory function not because the overall price level is wrong but because relative prices for different grades are incorrect. The shadow prices associated with an optimal development and location plan can be of great value in providing a basis for such relative prices. Moreover, prices based on shadow prices will provide an economic incentive for production units (open-cast mines, pits, trusts, or combines) to carry out the optimal plan.

The recent literature on price formation in the coal industry contains frequent discussions of the need for prices to take better account of the qualitative properties of power station coal (combustion temperature, ash content, moisture content, etc.) [2]. However the methods proposed for doing so normally have no connection with the techniques and information used for planning. Most of the authors of these proposals came out against using the shadow prices or marginal costs found in computing optimal branch plans. Their argument is based on the large differentiation of mining costs between individual open-cast mines and pits and also on the unrepresentative nature of enterprises with the worst indices. However these critics ignore the notion of marginal cost; moreover, it escapes their notice that an optimal planning problem can be solved in aggregate terms and that it yields shadow prices which are more stable, yet which take account in an objective way of the qualitative properties of the coal (provided that the planning model takes proper account of how producers' and customers' costs are affected by such quality differences).

Using shadow prices is a natural way of exploiting the information yielded by optimal branch plans to improve the price system. But it is not the only way. Since the optimization is at the local or branch level and since it relies in part on models and data which are imperfect, use can be made of other methods of putting forward price proposals based on the information in optimal branch plans. We consider one such experimental method below. We had the following major aims in devising it. We wanted: (i) to preserve in the price proposals the properties of the shadow prices associated with optimal branch plans — particularly their incorporation of substitution possibilities, the benefit derived by the customer, and the relationship between supply and demand (at the local, branch level); (ii) to generate an overall price level for power station coals lower than the shadow prices; (iii) to provide an incentive to fulfill the optimal branch development and location plan; and (iv) to take account of the special factors affecting the way in which the branch's output is used.

In devising the corresponding price model, we adopted the principle of ensuring equal profitability for all the enterprises in a region using the various qualities of power station coal. This is necessary because means of production are allocated through a centralized system. In these circumstances it is not up to the enterprise what type of coal it gets, while the costs of generating a unit of heat are different per equivalent ton of coal from the different fields.

A further important requirement on prices, which is incorporated in the model, is the need to ensure that no coal basin makes a loss. The existence of subsidized enterprises and associations is normally associated with a reduction in the prices paid to the extracting branches; this leads either to a lower overall price level or to unjustifiably high rates of profit in processing branches. This situation was very common prior to the 1967 price reform, but it has not been fully eliminated even after that date. A significant proportion of the surplus value created in the extractive branches is realized in the prices of the goods produced by the processing branches, and this applies primarily to the coal industry, which is the "price-leader" for fuels. Even if the prices ensure that no coal basin makes losses, this does not mean that there are no loss-making enterprises whose outputs are needed by the economy. To overcome this problem we would have to work out an appropriate system of prices within the basin. This problem is not considered in the present article.

The main requirement which our model of coal prices must satisfy is that they should be as low as possible while meeting the conditions set out above. Their level is calculated on the basis of the total coal produced and shipped, according to the optimal plan. This requirement arises from the fact that prices are being changed only locally, for the output of the branch in question; the stated condition must be fulfilled in order to prevent an increase in wholesale prices along the whole chain of production from natural resources to final output.

On the basis of the foregoing, our model for calculating wholesale prices for power station coal can be set out as follows. The constraints are:

(a) the need to ensure that it is equally advantageous in one region to use coal from any field:

$$x_{ij} + z_{ij} + u_i = y_j, \; i=1,...,m, \; j=1,...,n; \tag{20}$$

(b) the need to ensure that all coal-mining basins avoid losses:

$$x_{ij} \geqslant s_i \tag{21}$$

We are required to find values of x_{ij}, the price customers in region j pay for shipments of coal from basin i, which minimize the gross income received for all deliveries in the country as a whole (i.e., which minimize the price level); i.e.

$$\min F(x) = \sum_{i,j} v_{ij} x_{ij}, \tag{22}$$

Here x_{ij} is the wholesale price of an (equivalent) ton of coal, produced in basin i for shipment to region j; z_{ij} are transportation costs, including capital charge, of shipping one (equivalent) ton of coal from basin i to region j; u_i is the cost the customer incurs in using one (equivalent) ton of coal from basin i; y_j is a variable for region j, the meaning of which is discussed below; s_i is the cost, including capital charge, of mining an (equivalent) ton of coal in basin i; v_{ij} is the quantity of coal (in equivalent units) shipped from basin i to region j in the optimal branch plan.

In the model z_{ij}, u_i, s_i, and v_{ij} are given, being derived from the solution of the optimal planning problem for the development and location of the branch's enterprises. There is this difference, however: in the price model z_{ij}, u_i, and s_i are calculated by averaging the corresponding indices in the optimal plan. The x_{ij} and y_j are the unknowns, x_{ij} being the major unknown and y_j an auxiliary variable.

The model set out above for fixing the price of power station coal needs no special information apart from data used in the optimal branch planning model. This is one of its major advantages. Moreover, it makes effective use of information about the optimal structure of planned deliveries of coal throughout the country. Finally, since it minimizes the level of wholesale prices, the model does not conflict with the interests of other branches in the economy. It brings the wholesale prices generated by the model as close as possible to the average level of existing prices. Disaggregation to the level of products included in the approved price list is made on the basis of calorific value. Account can be taken of the qualitative properties of coals using the method adopted in setting those prices. The model also takes indirect account of coal quality by including as a component of total costs the costs incurred by the customer in using the coal.

The value of x_{ij} is an analog of the wholesale producer price; in addition users of power station coal pay supply and sales organizations for delivery. According to the model these prices should vary for different consumption regions. This is somewhat unusual in terms of current practice for fixing coal prices and is not acceptable to some economists. However, zonal pricing is not merely justified for all branches and particularly for extractive branches; it is also advantageous inasmuch as it takes account of regional and interregional aspects of planning and management [3, etc.]. We do not consider in the present article the problem of determining the prices at which accounts are settled with the supplier (the individual coal mine).

Let us consider in greater detail what the price x_{ij} generated by the model means in economic terms. When the problem has been solved, the auxiliary variable for each region can be interpreted at the overall marginal cost of mining, transportation, and use of the coal, as given by:

$$y_j = \max_{i_j \in I_j} (s_{i_j} + z_{i_j j} + u_{i_j}), \tag{23}$$

where I_j is the set of indices of the suppliers assigned by the optimal branch plan to consumption region j.

The price computed in the present model is based on marginal costs, and these differ from region to region (these are the costs of the marginal fuel); on the other hand prices computed from the shadow prices associated with the optimal branch plan are based on marginal costs for the country as a whole. The cost of the marginal fuel in each region is normally less than marginal costs for the country as a whole; only in rare cases is it the same. This creates an additional opportunity for the model to yield a lower price level than would be the case if prices were based on shadow prices. This is the basis of our view that, if we are using information from optimal branch plans to construct a price system, it is more correct to use the concept of the marginal fuel, rather than that of marginal costs.

Prices in the model are given by the formula:

$$x_{ij} = y_j - z_{ij} - u_i = \max (s_{i_j} + z_{i_j j} + u_{i_j}) - z_{ij} - u_i. \tag{24}$$

If we denote the magnitudes s_{ij}, z_{ij}, and u_{ij}, which maximize (24), by s^*, z^*, and u^*, it becomes clear that, as well as covering costs, prices x_{ij} contain components of profit (i) from mining operations (a rent from extraction):

$$r^g = s^* - s_i, \tag{25}$$

(ii) from transportation (a rent from transportation):

$$r^{\text{тр}} = z_j^* - z_{ij} \tag{26}$$

and (iii) from use of the coal (a rent from use):[2]

$$r^{\text{исп}} = u^* - u_i. \tag{27}$$

The coal basin with the largest total rent in a region is the most efficient basin within that region. The basin which incurs the marginal cost for mining, transportation, and use of coal earns zero rent. Shipments from that basin to a region with a large total rent are preferable from the standpoint of the economy. The sequence of calculations required to allocate the total rent is shown in the accompanying diagram.

We should examine the possibility of allocating some rent to the supply and sales organization which determines the coal allocation plan. The organization would then try to maximize the total rent and would have an economic interest in compiling and implementing an optimal distribution plan, i.e., in furthering the interests of the economy as a whole. The price system should also allocate some proportion of the rent to the supplier. Finally the largest share of the total rent component in the price of power station coal should go to central state funds — i.e., to the USSR state budget.

An analysis of the wholesale prices yielded by this model (which are based on the same original optimization problem as the shadow prices) revealed the following major features. The prices yielded by the model are higher than existing prices for most grades of Donets coal (by about 20 to 25%), and higher than existing prices for Moscow region and Kizel coals, for Kuznetsk coal (by 10 to 15%), and for Ekibastuz coal (by a factor of 2 to 2.5). At the same time prices calculated in this way

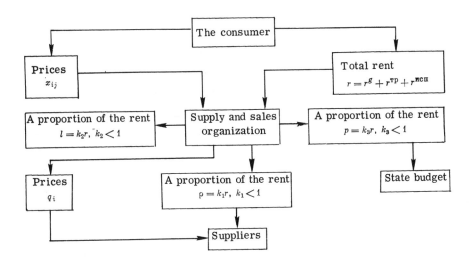

are significantly lower than shadow prices for Donets, Lvov-Volyn, and Pechora coals (by about 25 to 30%) and for Kuznetsk coal (by about 10%), but higher for coal from all the fields in the eastern part of the country. The prices calculated in this way would have the overall effect of slightly lowering the whole-sale prices of power station coal in the immediate future; this corresponds to an observed general tendency for mining costs to decline somewhat.

Donets coal shipped to the Western Ukraine and the Central Black Earth district yields the highest total rent. In these regions it competes very favorably with eastern coals, the mining of which is costly. Kuznetsk coal is the most efficient substitute for Kizel and Pechora coals in the Northern Urals, in the Komi ASSR, and in the Volga-Viatka district. It is not desirable on economic grounds (unless there is a general fuel shortage) to expand production of power station coals in Pechora, the Moscow region, Kizel, the Dnepr, and Karaganda, since the total rent in these basins is zero. In [4] we analyze in more detail the system of wholesale prices which we calculated using each of the methods set out above.

Whichever of the above two methods we use to compute wholesale prices for power station coal from the data in optimal branch plans, the resulting wholesale prices incorporate incentives for plan fulfillment in physical units.

If the first method, based on shadow prices, is more efficient in the context of a general revision of prices and the introduction of uniform coal prices for the whole country, then the second method is more suitable if prices are being recalculated at the local (branch) level and if a system of zonal prices at point of consignment is being introduced. In our view, both methods are capable of bringing the existing system of price formation genuinely closer to the optimal system.

NOTES

1. For brevity $s_{i_t}{}^T$ and $s_{i_t}{}^t$ are referred to below as the shadow prices of coal.
2. Rents are viewed here in the same sense as in a transportation problem in linear programming.

REFERENCES

1. Osnovnye polozheniia optimizatsii razvitiia i razmeshcheniia proizvodstva. Moscow/Novosibirsk: TsEMI AN SSSR; IEiOPP SO AN SSSR; SOPS pri Gosplane SSSR, 1969.
2. Tsenoobrazovanie i effektivnost' promyshlennogo proizvodstva. Materialy konferentsii. Leningrad: Leningradskii gornyi institut', 1972.
3. Granberg, A. G. Optimizatsiia territorial'nykh proportsii narodnogo khoziaistva. Moscow: "Ekonomika" Publishers, 1973.
4. Antsyshkin, S. V., and Polianskaia, T. M. Analiz vozmozhnostei ispol'zovaniia informatsii otraslevykh optimal'nykh planov dlia sovershenstvovaniia sistemy tsen (na primere energeticheskikh uglei). Moscow: TsEMI AN SSSR, 1976.

Received October 8, 1976

MODELING THE DEVELOPMENT OF
THE GAS INDUSTRY

Iu. I. Maksimov

We have to develop gas production in Siberia intensively because we need to solve the major problems of making up the
shortage of gas in the European part of the USSR and the Urals,
speeding up and intensifying the process of locating energy-
intensive industries in Siberia, switching the Siberian economy
to gas, and exporting natural gas.

For these reasons it is becoming increasingly urgent to improve the techniques and models used to plan the development
of this branch of the USSR's fuel and energy complex. One
major transition to be made is to switch from single-level
models to multilevel models, from a determinate approach to
a stochastic one, and from models for individual branches to
the modeling of multibranch systems, based on the principle
of planning and management by objectives. As noted in [1],
"under this system economic development is geared to the
achievement of final economic goals. The system for analyzing
and taking decisions is first established with this aim in view."

The present note discusses some results obtained at the Institute for the Economics and Organization of Industrial Pro-

Russian text © 1979 by "Nauka" Publishers. "Modelirovanie razvitiia gazovoi
promyshlennosti," Ekonomika i matematicheskie metody, 1979, vol. 15, no. 5,
pp. 978-982.

duction (IEiOPP) of the Siberian division of the USSR Academy of Sciences, using a model for the development of a branch system which includes the gas industry, geological exploration, and also construction of oil and gas facilities.

Natural gas is one of the most difficult raw materials to detect, and for this reason the costs of geological exploration are a significant component in the total cost of searching for, extracting, processing, and delivering natural gas. At present exploration costs are approximately equal to expenditure on installations in the same gas production region.

Geological exploration has been divided off as an independent branch within the economy; however, the return to this activity should be evaluated from the standpoint of its final economic results. By optimizing the fuel and energy complex we can evaluate the contribution that natural gas can rationally make to the country's fuel and energy balance. Analyzing the branch system allows us to optimize long-run plans for the development and location of facilities in the gas industry and, in particular, to find the regional breakdown of geological exploration for gas which is optimal from the standpoint of the economy's ultimate objectives.

We shall examine an upper-level network model for optimizing long-term plans for the development of the branch system defined above. This model can be used in either a two-level or a multilevel system. In the former case the lower-level units in the planning process are the districts where gas is extracted (this includes exploration), major gas pipeline systems, and construction enterprises, while the upper level consists of the branch system comprising the country's overall gas supply system, geological exploration, and oil and gas construction activity. A resource network diagram can be used as the upper-level model, the activities in the diagram being described in terms of four types of parameters: estimates of the time required to complete the activity, the resources required, the corresponding estimated costs, and finally the output level [1]. This choice of parameters has a number of advantages, chief of which are the following:

thanks to the special nature of network models, it allows the long-term plan for development of the gas industry to be optimized dynamically in a relatively simple way;

it establishes the necessary relationship over time between the stages involved in building or rebuilding a single unit (a major gas pipeline, facilities for working a field) and also between technologically related stages in the construction of several units;

it creates additional opportunities for taking account of links between the gas industry and neighboring branches (geological exploration, metallurgy, energy engineering, construction for the oil and gas industries, etc.);

in practice it imposes no strict requirements (such as linearity or concavity) on the nature of the relationships between the constraints considered and the objective function;

it makes it possible to use optimization algorithms which allow the size of the resource network diagram to be expanded at the cost of increasing the time taken for the calculations [2].

In what follows we shall discuss a directional graph Ω containing a set of arcs Ω_Q, without placing any special constraints on the structure of the latter. As noted above, activity $(\alpha, \beta) \in \Omega_Q$ is characterized by four parameters. For (α, β) they are specified by a matrix:

$$
M_{\alpha, \beta} = \begin{pmatrix} t_1^{(\alpha, \beta)} & \vec{r}_1^{(\alpha, \beta)} & S_1^{(\alpha, \beta)} & Q_1^{(\alpha, \beta)} \\ \cdot & \cdot & \cdot & \cdot \\ \cdot & \cdot & \cdot & \cdot \\ \cdot & \cdot & \cdot & \cdot \\ t_p^{(\alpha, \beta)} & \vec{r}_p^{(\alpha, \beta)} & S_p^{(\alpha, \beta)} & Q_p^{(\alpha, \beta)} \end{pmatrix}, \tag{1}
$$

which describes discrete cost relationships (including capital charges) and also the resources required to perform activity (α, β). Here $t_k^{(\alpha, \beta)}$ is the time required to carry out operation $(\alpha, \beta) \in \Omega_Q$, assuming that variant k is chosen for the development or reconstruction of the unified gas supply system, as derived from the optimizing model at the level below, where $1 \leq k \leq p$; $S_k^{(\alpha, \beta)}$ is the cost (including capital charge) of variant

k; $r_{l,k}^{(\alpha,\beta)}$ is the input of type l resources required to perform activity (α, β), assuming variant k is adopted for the development or reconstruction of the system, $l=1,\ldots, N$; $Q_k^{(\alpha,\beta)}$ is the productivity of a complete unit in the unified gas supply system corresponding to $t_k^{(\alpha,\beta)}$, $S_k^{(\alpha,\beta)}$, and $\vec{r}_k^{(\alpha,\beta)}$; p is the number of possible discrete values of the activity parameters in the network model; N is the number of resources for which constraints are incorporated.

Under the approach proposed, we make no special distinction between exploration districts, which can either be in current use or be districts where gas production is planned [2]. In order that each new gas-extracting district should begin to operate in the course of the period considered, the exploration strategy for that district should ensure that much of the investment is spent on increasing reserves in category C_1 (with the minimum possible share of increases in reserves in category B)[3]. If this is done, the return to increasing reserves in each district can be evaluated in terms of final output — i.e., from the standpoint of getting the maximum return at the national level from the use of natural gas.

Assume that there are n gas-producing districts, of which the first n_1 are in operation, $n_1 \leqslant n$. These are linked with gas consumption centers by an existing system of pipelines, specified by an aggregate connection matrix $A = \|a_{ij}\|$. Over the plan period the network of pipelines may be reconstructed, without changing matrix A [4].

If a resource network diagram is to be used as the upper-level optimizing model, an aggregate connection matrix $\bar{A} = \|\bar{a}_{ij}\|$ must also be specified, showing possible ways of developing the pipeline system. This network will allow the districts where gas production is planned to be linked with consumption centers. It will also create new routes for gas from districts already in operation.

In order to define the activities covered in the network diagram, we assume that the following relationships are known: the cost function for producing gas in existing or new districts; the relationship between surveying expenditure and increases in reserves; the relationship between operating costs and throughput for each major section of the pipeline system in operation; and the relationship between the cost, including capital charges, of constructing the major sections of the projected pipeline network and the flow of gas through those sections.

At the upper level of the network model the variables to be optimized are the production levels and changes in reserves of gas in the producing districts, and consignments of gas between districts through existing or projected sections of the pipeline network. If the solution does not provide for an increase in gas reserves in a producing district, this indicates (within the framework of the problem as formulated) that surveying in that district is not efficient (even local evaluations of the return to surveying may also turn out to be minimal).

Depending on which section of the unified gas supply system activity (α, β) belongs to, $Q_k^{(\alpha,\beta)}$ represents either the volume of gas produced in a production district or the throughput of a major section of pipeline, whether already in operation or projected, or the increase in the reserves of gas of a particular production district.

The annual volume of gas x_{it} produced in districts where extraction is taking place must satisfy a condition of the following form:

$$x_{it} \geqslant q_{it}^{\min} > 0, \quad i = 1, \ldots, n_1, \quad t = 1, \ldots, T, \qquad (2)$$

where T is the length of the plan period and $q_{it}^{\min}$ is the minimum feasible quantity of gas which can be produced in district i in year t. This figure is found on the basis of the capacity of existing wells in the operating fields of the district and the rate at which average pressure is declining. Thus $q_{it}^{\min}$ is the volume of gas in district i which can be extracted in any year of the period without additional capital investment.

We break Ω_Q down into nonoverlapping subsets: $\Omega_{\eta i}$ are activities associated with the operation of existing $(i=1, \ldots, n_1)$ or new $(i=n_1+1, \ldots, n)$ production districts; Ω_{mh} are activities associated with the operation of existing or projected pipeline systems; and Ω_{ri} are prospecting activities in production district i.

A constraint has to be placed on the total production of gas in existing and new districts:

$$\sum_{(\alpha, \beta) \in \Omega_{\pi}} Q_k^{(\alpha, \beta)} = F(t) \geqslant q_{\Sigma, t}, \quad 0 \leqslant t \leqslant T, \tag{3}$$

Here $q_{\Sigma, t}$ is the total planned volume of gas to be produced in year t over the whole country; $\Omega_{\pi} = \cup \Omega_{\pi i}, \quad i = 1, \ldots, n$.

We denote by Q_{i0} the reserves of gas in commercial categories available in district i at the start of the period, and by Q_{it} the reserves in the same district at the end of year t (the start of $t+1$). The Q_{it} must satisfy some recursive balance equations which link the optimal activity levels in subsets $\Omega_{\pi i}$ and Ω_{ri} :

$$Q_{it} = Q_{i\,t-1} - \sum_{(\alpha, \beta) \in \Omega_{\pi i}} Q_k^{(\alpha, \beta)} + \sum_{(\gamma, \xi) \in \Omega_{ri}} Q_k^{(\gamma, \xi)},$$

$$i = 1, \ldots, n, \quad t = 1, \ldots, T, \tag{4}$$

$$Q_{it} \geqslant 0, \quad i = 1, \ldots, n, \quad j = 1, \ldots, T. \tag{5}$$

Optimal values of the annual increase in gas reserves y_{it} are constrained from above:

$$y_{it} \leqslant M_i^{\max}, \quad i = 1, \ldots, n, \quad t = 1, \ldots, T, \tag{6}$$

where $M_i^{\max}$ is a magnitude determined by the long-run availability of geological deposits in production district i.

Thus the activities in the network model which belong to subset Ω_{ri} must satisfy:

$$\sum_{(\gamma, \xi) \in \Omega_{ri}} Q_k^{(\gamma, \xi)} \geqslant M_i^{\max}, \quad i = 1, \ldots, n. \tag{7}$$

No constraints are imposed on the throughput of major sections of the projected pipeline system, but the flow of gas through existing sections must satisfy:

$$\sum_{(\alpha,\,\beta)\in\Omega_{Tk}} Q_k^{(\alpha,\,\beta)} \leqslant G_k, \tag{8}$$

where G_k is the capacity of section k of the existing pipeline system.

In accordance with matrices A and $\bar{A}$, certain balance relationships have to be imposed on the variable $Q_k^{(\alpha,\beta)}$ to be optimized; there must be consistency between the flows of gas at each junction and at the termini of the existing or projected pipeline system [4].

There is a set of constraints covering resources (materials, labor) which have to be checked:

$$\sum_{(\alpha,\,\beta)\in\Omega} \vec{r}_{lk}^{(\alpha,\,\beta)} = \vec{D}_l(t) \leqslant \vec{R}_l(t), \quad 0 \leqslant t \leqslant T, \quad l = 1,\dots,N, \tag{9}$$

Here $\vec{D}_l(t)$ is a vector-diagram for the allocation of resource l, found by optimizing the upper-level model, and $\vec{R}_l(t)$ is a constraint on resource l, imposed by an adjoining branch. Constraints (9) can include limitations in the supply of pipes and pumping equipment and in the capacity of construction enterprises and of storage facilities for the oil and gas industries.

Finally, we note that it is necessary to take account of a constraint:

$$\frac{1}{q_{\Sigma,\,0}} \sum_{i=1}^{n} Q_{i,\,0} = \frac{\xi}{q_{\Sigma,\,T}} \sum_{i=1}^{n} Q_{i,\,T}. \tag{10}$$

The parameter ξ in (10) should be specified on the basis of calculations at the economy level. It follows from (10) that ξ controls the ratio between total exploration activity and gas production. If $\xi=1$, the multiplier for gas reserves is the same at the end of the period as it was at the start [5]. If $\xi<1$, then reserves grow more quickly than production; in the opposite case the multiplier is lower at the end of the period.

The objective function is minimization of the total costs (including capital charge) of constructing or rebuilding facilities in the unified gas supply system, of producing gas and shifting it in major pipelines, and of exploration.

We can ensure that the necessary connections are made between the various stages in the development and reorganization of the supply regions and of the associated pipeline system by introducing the appropriate relationships when the directional graph Ω is constructed.

Using the set of mathematical models we have developed, we calculated alternative projections of the development of the gas industry in Siberia over the period up to 1990.

One of the urgent problems in improving mathematical models for optimal long-term planning of the development of the gas industry is to incorporate various probabilistic factors affecting the branch's development. One approach to solving these problems within the framework of a deterministic mathematical model is to use the technique based on the adaptive properties of plans and to exploit certain properties of the network models [6, 7].

REFERENCES

1. Planirovanie otraslevykh sistem (Modeli i metody optimizatsii). Moscow: "Ekonomika" Publishers, 1974.

2. Maksimov, Iu. I. "Setevye modeli v perspektivnom planirovanii razvitiia gazovoi promyshlennosti." Ekonomika gazovoi promyshlennosti, 1975, no. 11.

3. Instruktsiia po primeneniiu klassifikatsii zapasov k mestorozhdeniiam nefti i goriuchikh gasov: Moscow. "Nedra" Publishers, 1971.

4. Maksimov, Iu. I. "Setevye modeli v perspektivnom planirovanii otraslevykh sistem." In Modelirovanie proizvodstvennykh protsessov. Novosibirsk: IEiOPP SO AN SSSR, 1977.

5. Maksimova, I. F. "Stokhasticheskoe modelirovanie sroka funktsionirovaniia gazodobyvaiushchego predpriiatiia." In [4].

6. Smirnov, V. A.; Maksimov, Iu. I.; Konstantinov, V. I.; and Maksimova, I. F. "Spetsializirovannye modeli perspektivnogo planirovaniia gazovoi promyshlennosti." In Optimizatsiia razvitiia i razmeshcheniia neftegazovoi promyshlennosti. Novosibirsk: "Nauka" Publishers, 1977.

7. Maksimov, Iu. I. "Ispol'zovanie setevykh modelei dlia analiza potentsial'noi adaptivnosti perspektivnykh planov razvitiia gazovoi promyshlennosti." In Optimizatsiia planov razvitiia i razmeshcheniia syr'evykh otraslei promyshlennosti. Novosibirsk: IEiOPP SO AN SSSR, 1976.

Received December 4, 1978

FORECASTING GAS RESERVES AND
OPTIMIZING REGIONAL PRODUCTION LEVELS
WITHIN THE FUEL AND ENERGY COMPLEX

A. P. Golovin, V. I. Kitaigorodskii,
and I. Ia. Fainshtein

The oil and gas industry is one of the most important branches
in the country's fuel and energy complex. The quantity of oil
and gas produced has a major impact on the structure of the
optimal long-run balance of the fuel and energy complex. Reference [1] discusses various aspects of the problems encountered in investigating this relationship.

In the method for optimizing the development of the fuel and
energy balance set out in [2], it is assumed that the possibilities
for producing oil and gas in major regions (such as Tiumen
province, Central Asia, etc.) can be represented by highly aggregated piecewise-linear functions relating unit costs to the
increase in production levels. However, this formulation, combined with a quasi-dynamic model of the development of the fuel
and energy complex (consisting of a series of static models),
misrepresents the true costs of developing an oil- and gas-
bearing region, and this can lead to a situation in which the
wrong production levels are chosen. There are methods of determining field development costs which yield correct cost indices and which enable us to choose the optimal strategy for

---

Russian text © 1979 by "Nauka" Publishers. "Prognozirovanie zapasov i optimizatsiia regional'nykh urovnei dobychi gaza i ramkakh toplivno-energetiche-
skogo kompleksa," Ekonomika i matematichesie metody, 1979, vol. 15, no. 5,
pp. 940-950.

developing the oil and gas resources in a region, but these only apply for a given sequence of production levels [3]. Hence a method is needed which takes sufficient account of both the time and the cost aspects of developing a field, which expresses production possibilities as a function of reserves in the region, and which also allows us to choose the time path of output in that region which is optimal for the economy.

A Formulation of the Problem of Optimizing Long-Run Gas Production Levels in an Oil- and Gas-Bearing Region[1]

Finding the optimal production levels for any resource presupposes some knowledge of the circumstances in which it is produced — in particular the level of commercial reserves in the region, possible methods for developing fields and their associated costs, and also the costs of discovering and surveying reserves and preparing them for commercial exploitation. Moreover, since the return to using the resource depends on its quantity, we require information on this relationship. The problem of finding optimal extraction levels over time can then be solved with the help of a model — we shall call it a regional development model — which can be formulated as a linear programming problem. The major constraints in the model cover the conditions in which the reserves have to be proved and developed, and the objective function to be maximized is the difference between the benefit yielded by the resource and the total cost of recovering it. The variables in the model are the rates over time at which fields are worked, reserves proved, and the resource used. By the returns to using the resource we mean its marginal cost in the particular region. Thus the model's objective function is based on the economic valuation of the resource [4].

A dynamic function expressing the return to the economy from using the resource can, in principle, be found by solving a static model of the fuel and energy complex in variant form for each five-year plan in the period for which calculations are made. However, the optimal production levels generated by the model for developing the fuel and energy complex may not correspond with the levels yielded by the regional model. Hence we must ensure that the models interact in such a way that the costs of increasing extraction levels over a five-year period are found by solving the regional development problem, while a new dynamic benefit function is constructed which takes account of cost changes.

One of the major problems in optimizing the production of hydrocarbon fuels in an oil- and gas-bearing district is identifying the prospects for recovering the raw material. The most reliable resource basis for oil and gas production is recoverable reserves which have been surveyed and assigned to commercial categories ($A+B+C_1$). However, demand for oil and gas has grown so fast over recent years and the return to exploration has declined so quickly with the growing complexity of geographical and geological conditions that in many regions estimates of recoverable commercial reserves in fields which have been explored have turned out to be quite inadequate for long-term planning and forecasting in the oil and gas industry. For this reason, qualitative estimates of the oil and gas potential of deposits in different regions have become important as a basis for scientific forecasting of oil and gas production.

As is well known (see [5]), the overall oil and gas potential of a field (i.e., the maximum oil and gas content of the deposits in the ground) is determined on the basis of accepted geological criteria for estimating the long-term potential of individual regions in the country; the estimate is made by crystallizing all the geological information available at the time. Hence quantitative estimates of the oil- and gas-bearing potential are dynamic and change over time. At the same time potential resources (including the quantity already recovered at the time the evaluation is made) incorporate both surveyed reserves and fields in operation (categories $A+B+C_1+C_2$) and also unsurveyed (or predicted) reserves (categories $C_2+Д_1+Д_2$). The importance of the latter in providing a basis for oil and gas production increases as the planning horizon is extended and the role of commercially explored reserves declines. This explains why it is of national importance to have a correct and reliable estimate of the prospects for switching predicted reserves of oil and gas to commercial reserves in each period in the long run. This depends on how much is spent on geological exploration.

After solving the regional development problem, we can not only calculate optimal regional production levels but also devise strategies for developing fields and preparing (or exploring) reserves. In planning practice, estimates of the output of crude oil and gas are normally made on the basis of the average increases in reserves which would be achieved by discovering fields of average size on the assumption of average levels of prospecting and exploration activity. This yields a deterministic forecast but does not take account of the stochastic nature of reserve increases in the long term and of their distribution about the mean. Essentially such forecasts only entitle us to expect that the planned level will be achieved "on average," and this often leads to large errors. Such forecasts are substantially less reliable than the other types of information used to predict the level of oil and gas production. We have therefore made an attempt to establish the link between additional investment in exploration and the increased certainty of attaining given rates of growth of output.

We thus face the problem of defining a conditional function for how the probability distribution of the total increase in oil and gas reserves in a region depends on investment on geological exploration. The problem is solved by simulating the process of exploration on a computer using Monte-Carlo methods. In developing the simulation model we make the following major assumptions.

1. We assume that in the long run the prospects for discovering fields in various possible areas are independent of their location within the region. We note that the plausibility of this assumption depends heavily on the geological homogeneity of the region. If we are forecasting increases in oil and gas reserves in a large region which is not geologically homogeneous, we should break the region up into homogeneous subregions.

Otherwise there will be a downward bias in the estimates which the model yields of future increases in reserves in the region as a whole.

2. The range of exploration activities involved in investigating a particular potential area (hereafter referred to as testing a possible area) is treated as a single activity. At the same time the costs of exploring the area are not assumed to be constant. For example, we take account of the relationship between the number of test wells and the success rate in drilling, of how the average depth of test wells increases as the region is more fully explored, and so on.

3. The tests in a single potential area can discover a maximum of one field.

4. The probability distribution of the level of reserves in a field is log-normal, with the following density function:

$$\varphi(z) = \frac{1}{\sigma\sqrt{2\pi}} \frac{1}{z} \exp\left\{-\frac{1}{2\sigma^2}(\ln z - \mu)^2\right\},$$

where μ and σ are respectively the expected value and the standard deviation of the logarithm of the reserves in a field.[2]

Many authors have asserted that the distribution of reserves in oil and gas fields is adequately described by the log-normal distribution (for a detailed bibliography, see [6]). Moreover, the function's success in describing the actual distribution of reserves is borne out by statistics for the overwhelming majority of oil- and gas-bearing regions in the USSR with a fairly large number of fields already in operation.

We adopted the following major assumptions concerning the sequence of major stages in the exploration process.

1°. The probability of discovering a field does not remain constant as a potential area is tested, but declines as the resources of the region come on stream. We express the rate of utilization by $\rho = Q/R$ where Q is the level of total proved reserves at any time (reserves of fields in operation, including total quantities lifted) and R is an estimate of the oil- and gas-bearing potential of the region. Thus the probability q of discovering a field — which we subsequently call the success rate — is a declining function of ρ, where $\lim_{\rho \to 1} q[\rho] = 0$. It is easy to see that the simple relationship we have adopted — $q = q_0(1-\rho)$, where q_0 is a constant estimated by least squares — satisfies all these requirements; moreover, it closely matches available empirical data.

2°. The expected quantity of reserves in a new field also changes as the exploration process continues. In most geologically homogeneous regions there is a general tendency for the major fields to be discovered in the earlier phase of exploration.

Some possible ways of confirming this proposition empirically are described in [6], which also puts forward the stronger hypothesis that the probability of discovering a field is directly proportionate to the reserves it contains.

In the present article we assume that average reserves in the $(n+1)$-th field (since exploration of the region began) are proportional to the average reserves in the n fields already discovered and to the level of predicted reserves. In other words, we assume the following relationship:

$$z_{n+1} = k \frac{Q_n}{n} \frac{R - Q_n}{R},$$

where z_{n+1} is the expected value of the reserves in the $(n+1)$-th field; Q_n is the level of total reserves in the n fields already discovered; $(R-Q_n)$ are predicted reserves in the region, the difference between R, the estimate of potential oil and gas reserves in the region, and Q_n, the reserves already discovered; k is a positive constant, estimated by least squares.

This equation not only matches existing empirical data; it also closely matches (for $0 < k \leqslant 1$) the pattern of average reserve levels implied by the assumption made in [6].

As well as the above, we make some additional assumptions about the costs of the exploration process, particularly the change of the average depth of exploratory wells.

3°. Exploration takes place from the top down; i.e., the average depth of exploratory wells increases as a region is explored more fully.

$4°$. The extent of exploration at various depths is proportional to the potential reserves estimated to lie at those depths.

In order to check these assumptions, generate the basic relationships, and estimate the model's parameters, we used the following types of information: (1) the level of potential reserves in each region and their distribution at various levels; (2) the program for exploring potential areas over time, broken down by year; (3) the rate of change and distribution of the mean number of wells needed to test a single potential area: this depends on the test results; (4) a list of fields discovered in each region, with their reserves, depths, and date of discovery; (5) the time path of exploration activity and the change in the average depth of test wells in the various years; (6) the time path of investment in exploration, broken down by year and type of work.

A Brief Account of the Algorithm for Modeling the Exploration Process

We consider briefly a simulation of the exploration process based on our assumptions. (See the diagram.)

Block 1 simulates the testing of one potential area; i.e., it models a uniformly distributed pseudorandom variable $\eta \in (0, 1)$ and compares it with the current value of the success coefficient q. If the area turns out not to be productive $(\eta > q)$, then we proceed to block 4, which computes the economic consequences of abandoning exploration of that area without success. This takes account of ρ, the extent to which the region's resources are currently being utilized. If however a field is discovered in the course of exploring the potential area in block 1 $(\eta \leqslant q)$, we proceed to block 2.

When a field has been discovered, block 2 models its reserves as a log-normally distributed pseudorandom variable ξ with parameters corresponding to ρ, the current rate of utilization of the region's resources. Reserves in the "discovery" are added to the total reserves in the region. However a ceiling operates if the total computed in this way exceeds the level of

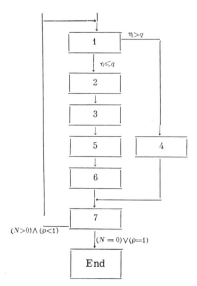

A diagram of the major stages in the algorithm for modeling the exploration process.

total reserves set a priori.

Block 3 determines the range of depths to which the discovery belongs, on the basis of assumptions $3°$ and $4°$. Block 5 computes the costs of surveying and exploring the field, while block 6 computes a new value for the level of exploitation of the region which takes account of the reserves in the field "discovered" in blocks 1 and 2.

The success coefficient is then recalculated in accordance with the new value of ρ, together with the parameters of the distribution of reserves and a number of other cost indices.

Block 7 examines the remaining potential areas. Unless they are exhausted ($N = 0$) or unless all possible reserves are being utilized ($\rho = 1$), we go back to block 1 and continue the simulation on the basis of the new information. If the number of potential exploration areas is exhausted (or if $\rho=1$), the simulation is concluded.

We ensured that our calculations were accurate by running the simulation many times over ($L=1000$). However $L=1000$

was excessive. For example, reducing L from 1000 to 500 gives results which differ from the previous ones only by tenths of one percent.

The output of the simulation is a table. In the table $\tilde{z}_j$, $j=1,\ldots,l$ are given levels of overall increases in reserves in the region; $\tilde{W}_i$, $i=1,\ldots,m$ are given levels of investment on exploration; f_{ij} is the probability of securing an increase in reserves of $z\geq\tilde{z}_j$ with investment equal to $\tilde{W}_i$ (the f_{ij} are estimated on the basis of the frequency with which the given increase in reserves was exceeded, as calculated in block 2); $E_i(z)$ and $\sigma_i^2(z)$ are respectively the mathematical expectation and variance of total reserves discovered for a level of investment of $\tilde{W}_i$; $E_j(\bar{W})$ and $\sigma_j^2(W)$ are the mathematical expectation and the variance of the level of investment which yields an increase in total reserves of $\tilde{z}_j$.

Thus the rows in the table give the probability distribution of reserve increases for a given value of investment on exploration, while the columns are probabilities of getting a given

How the Probability of Increasing Reserves Depends on the Levels
of Reserves and Investment

Investment on exploration	Increases in reserves				Mathematical expectation of total reserves	Standard deviation of total reserves
	$\tilde{z}_1$	$\tilde{z}_2$	...	$\tilde{z}_l$	$E_W(z)$	$\sigma_W(z)$
$\tilde{W}_1$	f_{11}	f_{12}	...	f_{1l}	$E_1(z)$	$\sigma_1(z)$
$\tilde{W}_2$	f_{21}	f_{22}	...	f_{2l}	$E_2(z)$	$\sigma_2(z)$
...	...	...	...	...	...	...
$\tilde{W}_m$	f_{m1}	f_{m2}	...	f_{ml}	$E_m(z)$	$\sigma_m(z)$
Mathematical expectation of investment $E_z(W)$	$E_1(W)$	$E_2(W)$	...	$E_l(W)$		
Standard deviation of investment $\sigma_z(W)$	$\sigma_1(W)$	$\sigma_2(W)$	...	$\sigma_l(W)$		

increase in reserves for alternative levels of investment. The
simulation model also yields information about the expected
distribution of future increases in reserves broken down by
fields in various sizes, types, and depths.

The Data and Algorithms Used in
the Regional Development Model

Each technique for recovering the resources in a field is associated with a time path of output, capital investment, and current costs. However, investment inputs and current costs are
related to the quantity produced in a nonlinear way. In order
to eliminate, or at least to reduce, the error introduced by
representing a nonlinear relationship by a linear one, we propose that the following procedure is adopted for preparing the
initial data on production methods for the regional development
model.

All reserves in a given region are grouped by type of field;
fields can be classified according to a number of criteria, such
as the reserves per field, the depth of the deposit, the well
yield, the type of field (gas only, oil only, oil and gas, gas condensate, etc.), the presence of by-products (sulphur, helium,
condensate, etc.), location, and so on. These properties are
largely responsible for the nonlinearity of the relationship between costs and the quantity produced in each field.

Data concerning possible projects (or technological sequences)
for developing the fields in a particular region are expressed in
the form:

$$(g_k^1, \ldots, g_k^{T_k}), \ (h_k^1, \ldots, h_k^{T_k}), \ (s_k^1, \ldots, s_k^{T_k}). \tag{1}$$

Here $k \in K$, where $K = \cup K_i$, and K_i is the set of possible projects for developing a field of type i, $i = 1, \ldots, I$; g_k^t is a coefficient expressing what proportion of the field's maximum capacity will have been recovered under project k in the final
year of the t-th five-year period after development has started;
h_k^t is the level of investment per unit of capacity output required to equip the field by the t-th five-year period on the

basis of project k; $s_k{}^t$ is the current cost of production (averaged over the t-th five-year period); T_k is the period of utilization of the field as given in the project. By maximum capacity
here we mean the level of output which can be maintained
permanently.

On the basis of this information, we can use a statistical approximation (the method of least squares, for example) to formulate the set J_i of possible ways of working fields of type i:

$$\left.\begin{array}{c}(a_j{}^1, \ldots, a_j^{T_j}) \\ (f_j{}^1, \ldots, f_j^{T_j}) \\ c_j\end{array}\right\} \quad j \in J_i, \quad i = 1, \ldots, I, \qquad (2)$$

Here $a_j{}^t$ and $f_j{}^t$ have an interpretation similar to $g_k{}^t$ and $h_k{}^t$,
and c_j is the unit cost including capital charge (in the final
year of the first five-year period) of equipping the field only.

In the case of fields already in operation at the start of the
period under consideration (we call this group K^0), we use (1)
to establish c_k, the unit cost including capital charge (in the
final year of the first five-year plan of the period under consideration) of continuing to operate the field.

The function expressing the benefit derived from the resource
is given in piecewise-linear form by variables $r_l{}^t$ and $d_l{}^t$,
$t=1,\ldots,T$, $l=1,\ldots,L$, where $r_l{}^t$ is the benefit from using a unit
of the resource in the final year of the t-th five-year plan, when
the output level lies in the interval

$$\left[\sum_{\tau=0}^{l-1} d_\tau{}^t, \ \sum_{\tau=0}^{l} d_\tau{}^t\right] \quad \text{where} \quad d_0{}^t = 0.$$

(Here l is the number of the interval in the piecewise-linear
function.)

The functions for switching predicted reserves to commercial reserves and for classifying such reserves by type are
found by simulating the exploration of the region. In order to
specify the transfer function we fix the total amount of investment on exploration, the total level of reserves to be switched,
and the probability of the transfer.

Using these parameters and the results given in the table we compute p_m and d_m $(m=1,\ldots,M)$; p_m is the investment cost of switching a unit of predicted reserves to commercial reserves when the reserves available for transfer lie in the interval

$$\left[\sum_{\tau=0}^{m-1} d_\tau, \sum_{\tau=0}^{m} d_\tau\right] \text{ where } d_0 = 0.$$

(Here m is the number of the interval in the piecewise-linear function for exploration costs.)

The reserves switched to the commercial category are broken down by type using coefficients $(\beta_{m1},\ldots,\beta_{mI})$, where the β_{mi} satisfy $\beta_{mi}\geq 0$ and $\sum_{i=1}^{I}\beta_{mi} = 1$, $m = 1,\ldots,M$. For a given sequence of investment resources allocated to development (R_1^t), and to exploration (R_2^t), we can formulate a mathematical model of the region's development.

A Mathematical Formulation of the Model

The (nonnegative) variables in the model are as follows: x_k is the permanent level of production in a field k which is already in operation; x_{kj}^t is the permanent level of output for a field k $(k \in K^1)$ which is discovered but not yet in operation, on the assumption that method j of working the field is used, starting in the t-th five-year period; x_{ij}^t is the permanent production level of a field of type i, which will be discovered and explored in the course of the period under consideration and will come into operation in the t-th five-year period using method j; z_m^t are the reserves switched to the commercial category in the t-th five-year period at interval m of the piecewise-linear function, $m=1,\ldots,M$; y_l^t is demand for the region's output in the final year of the t-th five-year period at interval l of the benefit function.

The objective function to be minimized is the difference between the costs of exploration and recovery and the benefit yielded by the resource, summed over the period T. This can be written as:

$$\sum_{k \in K^0} c_k x_k + \sum_{\substack{t=1 \\ k \in K^1, \, j \in J_i}}^{T} c_j(t) x_{kj}^t + \sum_{\substack{t=1, \, i=1 \\ j \in J_i}}^{T, \, I} c_j(t) x_{ij}^t +$$

$$\sum_{\substack{t=1, \, m=1}}^{T, \, M} p_m(t-1) z_m^t - \sum_{t=1, \, l=1}^{T, \, L} r_l^t(t) y_l^t. \tag{3}$$

A symbol of type $c(t)$ in this context means that the variable c has been discounted from the final year of the t-th five-year plan to the final year of the first five-year plan in relevant period $[1, T]$.

Balances for the production of and demand for output take the form:

$$\sum_{k \in K^0} g_k^{t+t_k^0} x_k + \sum_{\substack{\tau=1 \\ k \in K^1, \, j \in J_i}}^{t_0} a_j^\tau x_{kj}^{t-\tau+1} + \sum_{\substack{i=1, \, \tau=1 \\ j \in J_i}}^{i, \, t_0} a_j^\tau x_{ij}^{t-\tau+1} -$$

$$\tag{4}$$

$$\sum_{l=1}^{L} y_l^t \geqslant 0, \quad t = 1, \ldots, T,$$

where t_k^0 is the number of five-year periods for which existing fields have been worked prior to the start of the period under consideration; $t_0 = \min\{T_j, \, t\}$. In order to describe the constraints on the permanent output level of each field, we introduce the magnitudes α_k and α_j, which equal the period a field can be worked if it operates continuously at maximum capacity. Let B_k be the reserves in field k. Then constraints for existing fields, known fields, and fields which are yet to be discovered can be written:

$$\alpha_k x_k \leqslant B_k, \quad k \in K^0, \tag{5}$$

$$\sum_{t=1, \, j \in J_i}^{T} \alpha_j x_{kj}^t \leqslant B_k, \quad k \in K^1, \tag{6}$$

$$\sum_{j \in J_i} \alpha_j x_{ij}^t - \sum_{m=1}^{M} \beta_{mi} z_m^t = 0, \quad i = 1, \ldots, I, \ t = 2, \ldots, T. \tag{7}$$

Constraints on the investment required for production and the exploration of reserves are as follows:

$$\sum_{k \in K} h^{t+t_k^a} x_k + \sum_{\tau=1}^{t_0} f_j^{\tau} x_{kj}^{t-\tau+1} +$$

(8)

$$\sum_{\substack{i=1, \tau=1 \\ j \in J_i}}^{I, t_0} f_j^{\tau} x_{ij}^{t-\tau+1} \leqslant R_1^t, \quad t = 1, \ldots, T,$$

$$\sum_{m=1}^{M} p_m z_m^{t+1} \leqslant R_2^t, \quad t = 1, \ldots, T-1. \tag{9}$$

The final constraints in the regional development model are conditions defining the "steps" of the piecewise-linear cost functions for switching predicted reserves to commercial reserves and fixing the time path of the benefit from using the resources recovered in a particular region:

$$\sum_{t=2}^{T} z_m^t \leqslant d_m, \quad m = 1, \ldots, M, \tag{10}$$

$$y_l^t \leqslant d_l^t, \quad l=1, \ldots, L, \quad t=1, \ldots, T. \tag{11}$$

In order to organize the supply of data, to formulate and solve model (3) to (11), and to analyze the results, the Siberian Energy Institute of the Siberian Division of the USSR Academy of Sciences has prepared a set of programs which allows the researcher to carry out the stages listed above in what is almost an interactive regime; this substantially simplifies the experimental calculations.

In order to verify the feasibility of our method for optimizing the regional output plan and also to provide data for a model of the development of the fuel and energy complex [1], we have done some computations of the long-term level of gas production in the northern districts of Tiumen province. By using the model for simulating exploration, we were able to establish the relationship between unit exploration costs and predicted reserves. Using the criteria of the size, depth, and location of reserves, we distinguished five types of fields, and a breakdown of predicted reserves was found on the basis of a simulation of exploration activity. We estimated marginal cost functions for gas in the northern districts of Tiumen province by computing various solutions of a model for optimizing the development of the fuel and energy complex in the final year of each five-year plan.

We devised techniques for working all types of field, expressed in form (2), using existing projects and technological programs. The cost (including capital charge) per unit of output at maximum capacity depended on the type of field and the period over which each technique was operated. In each case model (3) to (11) included 271 equations and 1,238 variables. The calculations were done on the basis of a fairly highly probability (0.9) of switching predicted reserves into commercial categories.

The first matter to be investigated was the prospect for producing gas in the absence of any constraint on investment in extraction and exploration, and with no limit on the demand for gas from the northern districts of Tiumen province. The outcome of the calculations was trajectories of the optimal output of gas in the regions under consideration and the economically justified marginal costs. The marginal costs grew over time as a result of depletion of reserves and the utilization of inferior fields.

Our analysis showed how the time path of gas output and the strategies for working reserves and for exploration were affected by such factors as the probability of transferring predicted reserves into the commercial category, the overall level of marginal costs for gas, and the level of the investment constraint. We reached the following conclusions.

1. The most effective constraints are those on investment on extracting the resource. Tightening these constraints not only changes the strategy for bringing known fields into operation and the pattern of output over time; it also increases the

overall level of economically justified marginal costs, as well as altering their time path.

2. The effect of raising the overall level of marginal costs for gas in the northern districts of Tiumen province is to raise the level at which the gas is extracted (a switch to more expensive but quicker methods) and to increase the rates at which predicted reserves are transferred to the commercial category.

3. Adopting a lower (or higher) probability of transferring reserves to the commercial category has no impact on the time path of the indices for gas production in the first five-year plans of the period under consideration.

Our joint examination of models for optimizing the fuel and energy complex and of regional optimization models has shown that the latter are viable in principle; it has also allowed us to identify some weaknesses in the assumptions. In particular, as noted above, when we calculated the costs of working fields, we took only equipment costs in account. This had the effect of ensuring that intensive use was made of fields which had fairly low equipment costs but which could operate only if the appropriate infrastructure was created. This has clearly raised production levels. The model is at present being redesigned to incorporate new variables covering infrastructural investments in a region.

NOTES

1. This formulation can also be applied to oil resources.

2. Mathematical expectation $E(z)$ and dispersion $D(z)$ of reserves of a single deposit in this case are expressed by μ and σ^2

$$E(z) = \exp\ (\mu + \sigma^2/2), \qquad D(z) = \exp\ (2\mu + \sigma^2)\ (\exp(\sigma^2) - 1).$$

REFERENCES

1. Makarov, A. A. "Rol' Sibiri v toplivno-energeticheskom komplekse strany. Metody i nekotorye rezul'taty issledovaniia." Ekonomika i matematicheskie metody, 1979, vol. 15, no. 5.

2. Metodicheskie polozheniia po optimizatsii razvitiia toplivno-energetiche-skogo kompleksa. Moscow: "Nauka" Publishers, 1975.

3. Garliauskas, A. I., and Feigen, V. I. Dinamicheskie ekonomiko-matemati-

cheskie modeli optimizatsii edinoi gasosnabzhaiushchei sistemy. Moscow: Ministry of the gas industry, VNIIEGAZPROM, 1975.

4. "Metodicheskie osnovy ekonomicheskoi otsenki mestorozhdenii poleznykh iskopaemykh." Ekonomika i matematicheskie metody, 1978, vol. 14, no. 3. Translated in Matekon, 1979, vol. 15, no. 4, pp. 3-27.

5. Metodicheskoe rukovodstvo po kolichestvennoi otsenke perspektiv neftegazonosnosti. Moscow: Vsesoiuznoi nauchno-issledovatel'skii geologoraz-ved. institut; Vsesoiuznoi nauchno-issledovatel'skii geologicheskii neftianoi institut; Institut geologii i razrabotki goriuchikh iskopaemykh; Vsesoiuznoi nauchno-issledovatel'skii institut prirodnogo gaza, 1973.

6. Kaufman, G.; Balcer, J.; and Kruyt, D. "A Probabilistic Model of Oil and Gas Discovery," Studies in Geology, 1975, vol. 1.

Received December 4, 1978

A SYSTEM OF ECOLOGICAL AND ECONOMIC MODELS FOR ENVIRONMENTAL PLANNING AND CONTROL

R. L. Raiatskas and V. P. Sutkaitis

According to contemporary genetics the state of the biosphere depends to a significant extent on the genetic information which organisms inherit from previous generations. It has also been established that many environmental pollutants are capable of generating mutations (or changes in genetic information) which can lead to undesirable consequences. In particular, by eliminating some of the planet's genetic stock today, we may be deprived of the opportunity in the future of managing the biosphere in a way which will enhance its stability and productivity, and this in its turn will have a negative effect on food supplies.

The scale of this genetic effect depends not only on the absolute level of pollution but also on the period over which moderate or even very slight concentrations of harmful substances take effect. The methods which health experts and toxicologists currently adopt are geared chiefly to establishing the absolute impact of pollution on living organisms. Correspondingly, current practice in planning environmental protection is based in the branches and is limited to supervision of the major forms of pollution. Indices of environmental quality are merely cal-

Russian text © 1980 by "Nauka" Publishers. "Sistema ekologo- ekonomicheskikh modelei dlia planirovaniia i upravleniia sostoianiem okruzhaiushchei sredy," Ekonomika i matematicheskie metody, 1980, vol. 16, no. 6, pp. 1081-1093.

culated rather than imposed as plan targets. This is clearly
unsatisfactory for a number of reasons. Firstly, from the
standpoint of the global approach we need forecasts of how the
environment will change in the long run, under the impact of
technogenic emissions. This is clearly necessary if we are
going to forecast the consequences of pollution in a way which
takes account of society's social, economic, and ecological development goals. Secondly, we need a system of valuations
and indices which allows us to evaluate and compare social,
economic, and ecological aspects of the state of the environment and to identify ways of controlling it which best meet
those global goals. Thirdly, it is vitally necessary to find ways
of consciously controlling the factors which affect pollution, so
that we can keep the environment in the state we desire. In
other words there is a need for a system for ecological and
economic planning and control which will allow us to take coordinated decisions which satisfy at least two criteria, one
concerned with the quality of the environment and the other
with the quantity of natural or man-made goods, whenever the
use or manufacture of the latter to satisfy society's socioeconomic needs currently depends on an imperfect technology
with many by-products.

In the present article we focus on the principles underlying
the construction of a system of ecological and economic models,
an outline of which is set out in [1, 2]. We shall formulate a
set of requirements on a system of ecological and economic
models. In our opinion these requirements ensure that the
model can be used to plan and control the environment in a
way which is satisfactory, in the sense that it embodies a general approach to solving the problem of pollution. The first of
these requirements is that the models must incorporate all the
causal relationships in the ecological economic system. Secondly, the system of models must incorporate the closed loops
caused by direct effects and feedbacks between the various
components of the ecological and economic system. Thirdly,
there is a need for a combination of formal and informal criteria which will enable decisions to be taken which are consis-

tent with the targets for environmental quality over the plan period and which are balanced in socioeconomic and ecological terms. Fourthly, the system must contain both formal and substantive models for evaluating and selecting ways of keeping the environment in the desired state. Fifthly, all the ecological and economic models which make up the system must be dynamic.

In addition, the models in the system should be coordinated in terms of their inputs and outputs with the models in an integrated system for planning and forecasting [3] and also with certain other special models which we discuss below. This approach enables us to introduce major simplifications into the structure of the system of ecological and economic models and to clarify the relationships to be modeled; it also relieves us of the need to introduce here the separate models (or groups of models) which are studied by other branches of science and are discussed in the specialist literature.

In order to formulate the general conception underlying the construction of the system of models, we examine the causal relationships in the ecological and economic system. The major ones are presented in the accompanying diagram.

The basic principle of the diagram is a division of society's needs into two major groups: socioeconomic needs and ecological needs. These groups differ in the way in which the goods which satisfy those needs are derived. The first group is satisfied by goods, whether natural or man-made, and society organizes the use or manufacture of such goods using scarce natural resources and labor. The second group of needs is satisfied by goods which are derived wholly from nature and are obtained by direct interaction between man and the natural environment (sunlight, clean air, etc.). These ecological needs impose certain requirements on the quality of the natural environment. The extent to which both groups of needs are satisfied determines the supply and quality of the labor which is available at any time for use in production.[1]

The state of the environment depends on the level of technogenic emissions — pollutants which are not eliminated and any additional pollutants emitted in the course of utilizing

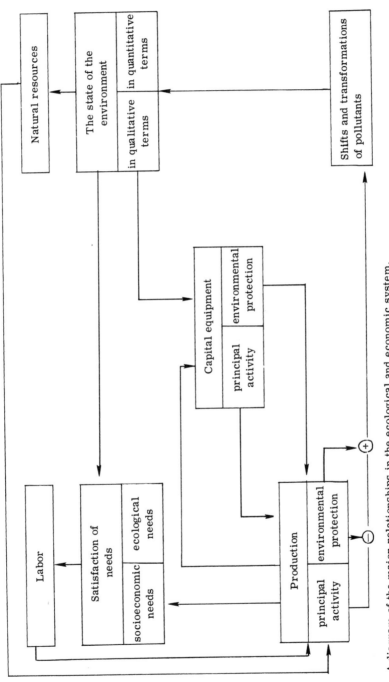

A diagram of the major relationships in the ecological and economic system.

waste products. However, the final concentrations of pollution depend on shifts and transformations of pollutants in the geo-biophysical sphere.

The impact of production on the environment generates a number of responses in the latter, the nature and mode of oper-ation of which are obvious. These are the direct and feedback effects in the ecological and economic system, and together they form a closed loop which has to be taken into account in environmental control. This proposition enables us to identify the following major groups of models in the system:

models of social production;

models of the impact of technology on the environment (the direct relationship);

models of changes in the factors of production brought about as a direct and indirect result of environmental pollution (the feedback);

consultative models.

We consider each of these groups separately, beginning with the second. This approach will allow us to identify the param-eters through which the environment regulates production and to devise ways of taking these factors into account in models of production.

Models of the impact of technology on the environment can be divided into two types: models of the time path of techno-genic emissions and models of the shifts of pollutants. The first are intended to relate technogenic emissions to the pro-duction process and to environmental protection measures; the second link technogenic emissions with processes in nature. Together these models should allow us at each moment of time to compute the level of pollution, as measured by the concen-tration of pollutants in different parts of the environment.

If we assume that the output of by-products is proportional to gross output of useful commodities or to the quantity of pol-lution eliminated, we can represent the time path of technogenic emissions of different types of pollutants by a set of differen-tial equations:

$$\frac{dz_q}{dt} = \sum_{j=i}^{n} b_{qj}x_j + \sum_{g=i}^{m} b_{qg}y_g - y_q - \hat{y}_q, \qquad q=1,\ldots,m, \qquad (1)$$

where x_j is gross output of useful commodity j; y_g is the quantity of pollutant g eliminated; y_q is the quantity of pollutant q eliminated; $\hat{y}_q$ is the quantity of pollutant q absorbed (detoxified) by the environment; b_{qj} and b_{qg} are coefficients expressing the output of pollutant q per unit of output of useful commodity j or per unit of pollutant g eliminated. The derivative on the left-hand side of (1) shows the rate of change of the emission of pollutant q over time.

Equations (1) are essentially expressions for the output of by-products of the economic system, and they allow us to determine at each time t the levels of pollutants which can be modified and transformed in the environment. Assuming as a first approximation that the coefficients b_{qj} and b_{qg} are constant,[2] the level of pollution can be expressed as a function of three variables, of which the first two (x_j, y_q) are based on human activity (social production), while the third $(\hat{y}_q)$ is a property of the environment and, we can assume, depends upon the state of the environment.

By shifts of pollutants we mean the process by which they are displaced or filtered from one part of the environment to another in a way which is specific to each kind of pollutant. As this shift takes place under the impact of various environmental factors, the pollutants are also transformed; as a result changes may occur in their composition which worsen the harm done by the original emission. If there are no external sources of pollution, then in the course of time a dynamic equilibrium is reached in which the "receipts" and "expenditure" of pollutants in each part of the environment cancel each other out. The structure attained then establishes where pollutants are concentrated, and this determines the state of the environment.

Reference [2] describes some principles for modeling shifts and transformations of pollutants, based on the use of Monte-Carlo methods to construct a random homogeneous Markov chain. The model proposed incorporates many assumptions

which have not yet been formalized and needs to be supplemented and extended in the appropriate ways. This should not
be done at the cost of complicating the random process on
which it is based, but should be done by supplementing the description of the geophysical, geochemical, hydrometeorological,
and other processes occurring in the environment. In other
words, the original model should be integrated with a number
of specific models of natural processes associated with the
movement of pollutants, where those processes have an effect
on the overall level and structure of environmental pollution.
Since it is not part of our aim to give a detailed account of
models of this type, we note only that, according to [2], the outcome of the group of models for shifts in and transformations
of pollutants will be defined by a vector with $m \times n$ components

$$\hat{Z}_k = (\hat{z}_{1k}, \ldots, \hat{z}_{qk}, \ldots, \hat{z}_{mk}), \quad k = 1, \ldots, \bar{n}, \qquad (2)$$

where $\hat{z}_{qk}$ gives the concentration of pollutant q in part k of the
environment.

If we know vector $\hat{Z}_k$, we can proceed to the next or third
group of models in the system under consideration. Vector $\hat{Z}_k$
is the outcome of the group of models covering the impact of
the technology on the environment and provides the information needed to model the changes in the components of the ecological and economic system which occur under the direct or
indirect impact of changed external conditions. Since the elements in the ecological and economic system are extremely
varied in composition and content we cannot set out a unified
theory here; still less can we propose concrete models of how
those elements change under the impact of environmental pollution. The exposition below should rather be viewed as setting
out basic principles or as an illustration of ways of modeling
these changes within the context of our overall conception of how
to construct a system of ecological and economic models. Developing such models is a difficult and lengthy process, requiring the participation of specialists from different branches
of science; the task must be organized independently and must
have its own special methodology, information, and technology.

When we model the changes in the factors of production taking place under the direct or indirect impact of environmental pollution, we distinguish three subgroups: capital, natural resources, and labor.

For obvious reasons it is natural to assume that the simplest task in conception (if not in scale) is analyzing the impact of environmental pollution on capital. We shall examine ways of solving this problem by taking one model of the development of fixed capital as an example. We denote the fixed capital of type i coming into operation by Φ_i' and we denote by Φ_i'' the quantity of capital going out of service over the same period. The increase in fixed capital at time t is thus:

$$\Phi_i(t) = \Phi_i' - \Phi_i'', \quad i = 1, \ldots, n. \tag{3}$$

We also use a system of differential equations to show the rate at which fixed capital comes into operation and goes out of service:

$$\frac{d\Phi_i'}{dt} = f_i'(\Phi_i', \Phi_i'', \hat{Z}_k),$$

$$\frac{d\Phi_i''}{dt} = f_i''(\Phi_i', \Phi_i'', \hat{Z}_k), \quad i = 1, \ldots, n, \tag{4}$$

Here $\hat{Z}_k$ is a vector expressing the level of environmental pollution. Then:

$$\frac{d\Phi_i}{dt} = f_i'(\Phi_i', \Phi_i'', \hat{Z}_k) - f_i''(\Phi_i', \Phi_i'', \hat{Z}_k). \tag{5}$$

If we know the values of Φ_i' and Φ_i'' at any time t, together with the value of each component of vector $\hat{Z}_k$, and if we also know the form of functions f_i', f_i'', and $\Phi_i(t_0)$, then we can establish the principle determining the rate of change of fixed capital $\Phi_i(t)$. Let us assume that the form of functions f_i', f_i'' is known; then system (4) formally allows us to derive solutions which express Φ_i' and Φ_i'' as functions of $\hat{Z}_k$; i.e.

$$\Phi_i' = g_i'(\Phi_i', \Phi_i'', \hat{Z}_k),$$

$$\Phi_i'' = g_i''(\Phi_i', \Phi_i'', \hat{Z}_k), \quad i = 1, \ldots, n. \tag{6}$$

By substituting these solutions into (5) and making simple transformations for $\Phi_i(t)$, we derive

$$\Phi_i(t) = \Phi_i(t_0) + \int_{t_0}^{t} G_i(\Phi_i'(t_0), \Phi_i''(t_0), \hat{Z}_k)\, dt. \qquad (7)$$

Clearly the left-hand side of (7) is a function of $\hat{Z}_k$; consequently (7) allows us to study the behavior of $\Phi_i(t)$ for alternative forecast values of $\hat{Z}_k$. As we know how environmental pollution affects fixed capital, we should regard an increase in the absolute values of components of $\hat{Z}_k$ or in the duration of a constant level of pollution as doing extra damage — i.e., as speeding up the rate at which fixed capital goes out of service. This treatment of the damage done by environmental pollution may create the impression that in order to study the time path of fixed capital we need only to know the time path of the function for $\Phi_i''(t)$. This would be correct if the ecological and economic system under investigation contained no measures for environmental protection; but the speed at which the latter take effect clearly depends on the level of pollution. Thus the model under consideration is of more general character.

In the absence of counteracting measures, the impact which environmental pollution has on capital lowers output and consequently lowers the level of technogenic emissions into the environment. The environment thus has a regulatory impact on production. The instrument here is the damage done to the economy — the capital lost through accelerated write-offs brought about by accelerated obsolescence, corrosion, amortization, loss of quality, and other consequences of the impact of harmful substances in the environment. References [1, 4] discuss various methods of incorporating this kind of regulation in models of economic activity, and these methods will be examined below.

More complex problems arise when we try to model the development of natural resources. As noted above, the availability and state of natural resources depend on the state of the environment; i.e., an analysis of the development of natural resources presupposes a preparatory study of the changes

which occur in the environment as by-products are emitted into
it. It is worth mentioning that vector $\hat{Z}_k$ is quite acceptable as
an index of the quality of the inorganic natural environment.
This allows us to study the development of a number of inorganic natural resources (or processes) using various modifications of models similar to (3) to (7) in [5]. The remaining (or
organic) natural resources require a different and special approach, which is set out below, though not in comprehensive
form.

We shall describe a simplified model of a natural ecosystem
which consists of a total of four elements (see [6]): (I) auto-
trophic plants; (II) herbivorous animals; (III) predators; and
(IV) parasites, which consume the biomass of the first three
groups of organisms. The balance equations for living organic
matter in this ecosystem are:

$$\frac{dB_I}{dt} = P_I - \gamma_{II} B_{II} - D_I, \tag{8}$$

$$\frac{dB_{II}}{dt} = P_{II} - \gamma_{III} B_{III} - D_{II}, \tag{9}$$

$$\frac{dB_{III}}{dt} = P_{III} - D_{III}, \tag{10}$$

where B_I, B_{II}, or B_{III} is the biomass of the corresponding group
of organisms per unit of the area they occupy; P_I, P_{II}, or P_{III}
is the productiveness of or addition to the biomass per unit of
time, from which the amount spent on maintaining the organism
is subtracted; D_I, D_{II}, and D_{III} is the biomass required by
parasites; γ_{II} and γ_{III} are coefficients expressing the consumption of biomass by groups II and III, per unit of their biomass.

If we assume that coefficients γ_{II} and γ_{III} are constants,
equations (8) to (10) contain nine unknowns. Consequently, in
order to solve them we must use empirical data to establish
six additional relationships. If we introduce the level of environmental pollution, these can be written as:

$$P_I = P_I(B_I, B_{II}, \hat{Z}_k), \tag{11}$$

$$P_{II} = P_{II}(B_{II}, B_I, B_{III}, \hat{Z}_k), \tag{12}$$

$$P_{\text{III}} = P_{\text{III}}(B_{\text{III}}, B_{\text{II}}, \hat{Z}_k), \tag{13}$$

$$D_{\text{I}} = D_{\text{I}}(B_{\text{I}}), \tag{14}$$

$$D_{\text{II}} = D_{\text{II}}(B_{\text{II}}), \tag{15}$$

$$D_{\text{III}} = D_{\text{III}}(B_{\text{III}}). \tag{16}$$

Relationships of the type $P_{\text{I}}(B_{\text{I}}, B_{\text{II}})$, $P_{\text{II}}(B_{\text{II}}, B_{\text{I}}, B_{\text{III}})$, and $P_{\text{III}}(B_{\text{III}}, B_{\text{II}})$ have been widely studied in ecology and have a well-defined interpretation. In order to define the nature of relationships $P_{\text{I}}(\hat{Z}_k)$, $\dot{P}_{\text{II}}(\hat{Z}_k)$, and $P_{\text{III}}(\hat{Z}_k)$, in contrast, we need to do further empirical research on various ecosystems. This is essential if we are to study the development of the biomass of the system's components in a way which takes account of the factors affecting that biomass. In fact, if we solve system (8) to (10) in conjunction with additional equations (11) to (16), at each moment of time t we can determine the biomass of each group of organisms in a way which takes account of the structure of the nutritional interrelationships between them and impact on them of environmental pollution. It is reasonable to assume that if there is a change in the value of the components of $\hat{Z}_k$ or in the duration of a constant level of environmental pollution, there will be changes in the biomass of the components of the ecosystem. Let us consider the consequences of these changes on production.

We assume that the ecosystem is of industrial use: i.e., its biomass or the biomasses of its separate components are an input used in the production of material goods and are also used to eliminate harmful by-products. Then if we incorporate the negative effect of environmental pollution on the productivity of the separate components of the ecosystem, the change in the biomass which is used for production purposes can be expressed in a balance equation:

$$B(t) = \sum_{i=1}^{n} r_i x_i + \sum_{g=1}^{m} r_g y_g + \sum_{q=1}^{m} r_q \hat{z}_q, \tag{17}$$

where r_i and r_g are inputs of biomass into the respective activities; r_q is a coefficient for the loss (or shortfall) of biomass resulting from environmental pollution; $B(t)$ is one of the components of the general solution to the system of differential equations (8) to (10).

Thus the final summation in (17) takes account of the damage to nature caused by environmental pollution and makes a correction for this in the balance for the use of the particular natural resource in production. Coefficient r_q can be determined on the basis of equations (11) to (13), which are estimated using the empirical data for two dates t' and t'', which are characterized by different pollution levels or a different period of operation of the same level of harmful pollutants.

As can readily be seen, in formal terms equations (8) to (17) make up a closed loop in an ecological and economic system consisting of the direct impact of the flow of technogenic emissions and the feedback onto production caused by the impact of pollution on resources. Using this description of the system we can identify the damage to nature resulting from environmental pollution and incorporate it in the balances of the resources used in production. Thus resource losses are a second parameter through which the environment regulates the very productive system which pollutes it with numerous waste products.

We now consider changes in the biomass of the components of the ecosystem from the standpoint of environmental quality — understood not only in terms of the purity of the inorganic components but also in terms of the makeup of the natural ecosystems which comprise the environment. Any ecosystem or any system in nature reacts to external stimuli in its own way, so that our remarks below should again be understood as a set of basic principles rather than a list of detailed proposals for one of the most important and complex subsystems in the overall system of ecological and economic models for planning and control of the environment.

According to the theory of ecosystem stability, any change in the biomass of an individual component which exceeds the level acceptable for a stationary state will lead to the elimination of those components. In fact this means the destruction of the ecosystem. However the system's overall reaction to environmental pollution does not end there: components which are eliminated are replaced by others which are more adapted to the new and changed circumstances. The process of so-called exogenous succession begins, as a result of which an ecosystem is formed with a new qualitative composition which is normally inferior to its predecessor [7, 8].

All processes and phenomena in nature are related by various biogeochemical cycles; they do not exist in isolation. Consequently, qualitative changes in the ecosystem or in its separate components may become the cause (or the start) of more fundamental ecological transformations which may have a detrimental impact on environmental quality. In order to study the dynamics of global cycles of this kind (water, carbon dioxide, oxygen, etc.) under the impact of environmental pollution, we can use systems of type (3) to (7), modified in various ways, and taken in overall conjunction with relationships of the type (8) to (16) and models of ecological succession. Obviously it is also appropriate to incorporate informational models of natural systems, since there is a view that an exhaustive account of how the biosphere changes under the impact of technogenic emissions must be based on models which reflect the transformation in nature of information as well as of matter and energy [9]. Naturally a final list of the groups of models describing qualitative changes in man's natural environment can only be established in the course of detailed studies which take account of the whole range of natural processes and phenomena. Such an interdisciplinary problem cannot be solved at once or by specialists in any single discipline; it requires a special program of work by specialists of various types and holding various qualifications [10].

Let us assume that a set of such models is available and that we can forecast the state which the natural environment will be in as a result of the vector $\hat{Z}_k$ of concentration of pollutants. We address ourselves to the principles for incorporating and evaluating the impact of the qualitatively new state of the environment on the ecological needs of the population and on the supply and composition of labor. We introduce a new vector

$$E=(e_1, \ldots, e_M; \hat{Z}_k), \tag{18}$$

each component e_l, $(l=1, \ldots, M)$ of which is a particular ecological parameter showing the state of the living part of the environment with respect to "free" good l, provided to mankind by the environment;[3] $\hat{Z}_k$ is a known vector showing the state of the inorganic components of the environment in the same respect.

We assume further that the supply and composition of labor depends on the level of the population and on its state of health. In view of the aims of the present study, and also because the connections and interrelations between mankind and the environment are continuous and always have an impact on human health [11], we only take account of the effects of purely ecological factors on health; i.e.:

$$L(t)=L(N, E), \tag{19}$$

where $L(t)$ is labor supply at time t; N is the population level; and E is a vector determined by equation (18).

Population $N(t)$ is treated as an exogenous variable, the value of which is given by the forecasting block in the integrated system of models for planning and forecasting the economy [3]. Forecasts of labor supply are provided in the same way. The task of the system of ecological and economic models is to specify the relationship $L(E)$, the nature of which can only be established by investigating man's biological reaction to ecological factors and by analyzing the mechanisms underlying these reactions [12]. The result of this process should be the identification of optimal values for the parameters of vector E; this corresponds to our conception of the standard of health.

In what follows we shall view any departure from $E_{опт}$ as resulting in a loss of labor input caused by temporary inability to work through sickness or reductions in labor productivity, by premature deaths, and by other consequences of environmental pollution. These losses should also take account of the impact of a polluted environment on the health of that part of the population which is not working at that particular time. This is quite appropriate, since the effect of the environment on this part of the population is linked with general consumption levels via increased demand for health services. An increase in the overall level of consumption creates an extra "shortage" of labor.

We denote the labor input lost through environmental pollution by $\Delta L(t)$. In view of the above it can be represented by the obvious relationship:

$$\Delta L(t) = L(N, E_{\text{опт}}) - L(N, E). \tag{20}$$

In principle, (20) enables us to determine coefficients l_q showing the amount of labor lost per unit of a pollutant of a particular type in the environment. This in its turn allows us to represent the change from the forecast level of labor utilization (ignoring environmental pollution) in terms of a balance equation:

$$L(t) = \sum_{i=1}^{n} l_i x_i + \sum_{g=1}^{m} l_g y_g + \sum_{q=1}^{m} l_q \hat{z}_q, \tag{21}$$

Here l_i and l_g are labor input coefficients for production and environmental protection respectively. Equation (21) clearly shows the labor input lost through the deterioration in public health; this is a third channel through which environmental pollution regulates production. This impact (or feedback) is a major and highly complex relationship in the ecological and economic system. It has been little investigated in practice since it is hard to formalize, but some studies show that this problem can be successfully solved within certain limits (see, for example, [13, 14]).

We now proceed to consider the first group of models, describing the process of social production. All the necessary preconditions for this are satisfied, since the basis of the direct relationship is the model (1) of the time path of technogenic emissions into the environment, while the two feedback relationships investigated subsequently are closed by the loss of (or damage to) natural resources or labor incorporated in balance equations (17) and (21) respectively. Essentially this means that we have identified and found the environmental link between the by-products of and two inputs into the productive subsystem, which is regarded as a "black box." In order to close the loop we have to set down the basic nature of the trans-formations of inputs and outputs which take place within the black box. We can assume that this can be done in various ways. However, the need to take account of environmental pol-lution limits the scope for making direct use of existing models in mathematical economics without modifying them first. As we desire to demonstrate both operations simultaneously, we use a dynamic input-output equation:

$$x_i - \sum_{j=1}^{n} a_{ij}x_j - \sum_{g=1}^{m} a_{ig}y_g - \sum_{q=1}^{m} a_{iq}\hat{z}_q - \sum_{j=1}^{n} k_{ij}\frac{dx_j}{dt} - \qquad (22)$$

$$\sum_{g=1}^{m} k_{ig}\frac{dy_g}{dt} - \sum_{q=1}^{m} k_{iq}\frac{d\hat{z}_q}{dt} = c_i, \quad i=1,\dots,n,$$

Here x_i is gross output of good i; y_g is the quantity of pollutant g eliminated; $\hat{z}_q$ is the level of pollutant q emitted into the en-vironment; a_{ij} and a_{ig} are material input coefficients; a_{iq} is a coefficient showing the loss of product i per unit of pollutant q in the environment; k_{ij} and k_{ig} are respectively incremental capital-output ratios in production and in the elimination of pollutants; k_{iq} is a coefficient measuring the loss of capital resulting from the increase in the level (or concentration) of pollutant q over period t; c_i is net final output of good i.

Equation (22) illustrates the dynamics of expanded reproduc-tion in a way which incorporates the resources required to eliminate harmful by-products and compensates for losses re-sulting from the impact of environmental pollution on the capi-tal stock. It is linked with (1) through the first two variables, and through these variables it incorporates the constraints in equations (17) and (21). Consequently, (22) meets the require-ments formulated above and can adequately represent the mod-els in the first group.

In order to give a general account of the consultative models, we have to consider how the system of ecological and economic models may be used to plan and control the environment.

There is no doubt that preliminary calculations of the state of the ecology and the economy should begin with a forecast of exogenous variables: the size of the population, the availability and breakdown of labor and natural resources inputs, and the autonomous function for net final output $c_i(t)$, which in dynamic model (22) reflects the aims of economic growth. From the ecological standpoint, models (22) and (1) translate these objectives into a vector of technogenic emissions z_q which in turn is converted via a set of models for shifts and transformations of pollutants into a vector $\hat{Z}_q$ of pollution levels. This provides the information required for forecasting the time path of the state of the biosphere in qualitative and quantitative terms and for forecasting changes in the quantity of capital and of inorganic natural resources, in health levels, and in the time path of labor supply under the impact of environmental pollution. Representative models of this kind were discussed above.

By modeling the time path of the components in the ecological and economic system we determine a vector of losses of materials of various kinds and of the damage done by harmful technogenic emissions. In order to reduce these various magnitudes to a common denominator, we need valuations of the labor and natural resources which are in some way affected by a polluted environment. The need for such valuations was explained in mathematical terms in [4], where the problem of ecological and economic equilibrium is formulated in terms of primal and dual linear programming problems for a given system of social preferences expressed in terms of aggregate demand functions for output and for the elimination of pollution, and supply functions for primary resources. Substantive aspects of these valuations are considered in theoretical work on the problem of optimal functioning of the economy. From the standpoint of ecological and economic planning and management, such valuations would allow us to derive a single indicator of the losses from environmental pollution — the hidden social costs of production.

The authors of the present article have developed a dynamic optimality criterion for environmental protection measures, which makes it possible to estimate the hidden costs of production in a way which is economically correct [1]. The essence of this method is a comparison of the costs and benefits of eliminating pollution. In formal terms the optimality criterion can be expressed as a nonhomogeneous system of linear differential equations:

$$\frac{dy_q}{dt} + \alpha_{qg} y_g = \beta_q (\hat{z}_q' - \hat{z}_q''), \quad q, g = 1, \ldots, m, \tag{23}$$

where α_{qg} and β_q are nonnegative coefficients; $\hat{z}_q'$ and $\hat{z}_q''$ are two different concentrations of pollutants of type q.

Model (23) is essentially a consultative model, with which one can determine the economically justified level for eliminating pollutants or the hidden costs of production. Whether society is willing to incur such costs or not is a question which requires special consideration. It is significant that (23) allows us to take a decision from among the alternatives available which in the final analysis serves as a "point of departure" for taking other decisions. Moreover (23), in conjunction with (1) and (22), is an integrated model which allows us to find balanced values of the variables included, given the structure of final demand, the level of environmental pollution, and constraints on labor and natural resources. These show the relationships between flows of goods, pollution, and the capital investment, especially in production, needed to ensure the production of net final output and to maintain the environment in the desired state. Consequently they can be used as control figures to compile long-term plans for economic development which take account of worsening ecological problems. The figures can finally be revised to take account of new information concerning the state of the ecological and economic system at any time t. These changes should be reflected in disaggregated form in long-run and short-run plans; in this way the principle of closed-loop control, which lies at the basis of our system of ecological and economic models, will be implemented.

The fact that the system of ecological and economic models is not fully developed prevents us at present from giving a full list of indices for environmental planning and control. However the major groups of indices of this kind can be specified even on the basis of the outline of such a system which we have presented. They comprise: indices covering the major resources used for environmental protection; indices of technology's impact on the environment; indices of the state of the environment; indices of the hidden social costs of production; and indices of the return to improving the environment (expressed in both physical and monetary units).

The first three groups are related in some way with indices currently used in environmental planning. In our view the last two categories should ensure that environmental protection measures are integrated with the targets of other sections of plans for economic development. For example, if the hidden social costs of production were included in enterprise production costs in a way which depends on that enterprise's "contribution" to environmental pollution, and if profit and profitability were planned to take account of return in terms of environmental improvement, this would positively encourage the implementation of planned measures to protect nature.

The present article does not give an exhaustive account of all the problems of devising and implementing a system of ecological and economic models for environmental planning and control. We have only considered the outline of such a system, and the separate parts of this system differ in the extent to which they have been developed either scientifically or technically. Some of the methodological assumptions which underlie our analysis and interpretation both of economic and of purely ecological processes and phenomena may turn out to be open to question.

NOTES

1. Obviously environmental pollution also has a direct impact on labor supply. Other factors which lie outside the system under consideration are not considered here.

2. This assumption is equivalent to excluding the impact which scientific and technical progress may have on the time path of technogenic emissions.

3. As noted above, these benefits could be clear air, fresh water, the aesthetic value of the countryside, the contribution made by the landscape to health and recreation, and other phenomena associated with man's ecological needs.

REFERENCES

1. Raiatskas, R. L., and Sutkaitis, V. P. "Modelirovanie ekonomicheskoi dinamiki s uchetom zagriazneniia okruzhaiushchei sredy." Ekonomika i matematicheskie metody, 1979, vol. 15, no. 1. Translated in Matekon, 1979-80, vol. 16, no. 2.

2. Raiatskas, R. L., and Sutkaitis, V. P. "K probleme planirovaniia i prognozirovaniia sostoianiia okruzhaiushchei sredy." Izvestiia AN SSSR, Seriia Ekonomicheskaia, 1979, no. 3.

3. Raiatskas, R. L. Sistema modelei planirovaniia i prognozirovaniia. Moscow: "Ekonomika" Publishers, 1976.

4. Raiatskas, R. L., and Sutkaitis, V. P. "K probleme modelirovaniia vzaimosviazei obshchestva i prirody." Ekonomika i matematicheskie metody, 1978, vol. 14, no. 3. Translated in Matekon, 1979, vol. 15, no. 3.

5. Gorstko, A. B., and Surkov, F. A. Matematika i problemy sokhraneniia prirody. Moscow: "Znanie" Publishers, 1975.

6. Bubiko, M. I. Global'naia ekologiia. Moscow: "Mysl'" Publishers, 1977.

7. Commoner, B. The Closing Circle (Russian edition). Leningrad: Gidrometeoizdat, 1974.

8. Antonovskii, M. Ia., and Semenov, S. M. Matematicheskie metody ekologicheskogo prognozirovaniia. Moscow: "Znanie" Publishers, 1978.

9. Armand, A. D. Informatsionnye modeli prirodnykh kompleksov. Moscow: "Nauka" Publishers, 1975.

10. Moiseev, N. N., and Svirezhev, Iu. M. "Metody sistemnogo analiza v probleme 'chelovek-biosfera.'" In Imitatsionnoe modelirovanie i ekologiia. Moscow: "Nauka" Publishers, 1975.

11. Raikh, E. L. "Geograficheskie aspekty optimizatsii sistemy 'chelovek-prirodnaia sreda' (Antropoekologicheskii podkhod)." In Problemy optimizatsii i ekologii. Moscow: "Nauka" Publishers, 1978.

12. Koval'skii, V. V. Geokhimicheskaia ekologiia. Moscow: "Nauka" Publishers, 1974.

13. Lave, L. B., and Seskin, E. P. Air Pollution and Human Health. Economics of the Environment. New York: Johns Hopkins, 1972.

14. Barkalov, N., and Tatevosov, R. "O vzaimosviaziakh okruzhaiushchei sredy i narodonaseleniia v modeliakh rosta." In Naselenie i okruzhaiushchaia sreda. Moscow: "Statistika" Publishers, 1975.

Received April 20, 1979

FINANCIAL ACCOUNTABILITY AND
THE RIGHT TO USE RESOURCES

K. G. Gofman

Differential valuations of natural assets can be used for accounting and analytical purposes and also in planning and design
work. They can be used for such purposes as compiling State
Registers of natural resources, placing a money value on the
natural resource component of the national wealth, finding the
economic return to the activity of branches, enterprises, and
organizations concerned with the use, conservation, or development of natural resources, and finding appropriate standards
for the recovery of minerals when they are mined and processed or norms for using forest and water resources, or they
can be used in the allocation of agricultural land and woodland
for building purposes.

In addition, economic valuations of natural resources can be
used to devise incentive systems which will encourage enterprises and organizations to improve the use they make of natural resources and to amend the penalties imposed for breaching plan targets or standards for rational environmental use.

The procedures for using such monetary valuations of natural resources in the economic field should be fully consistent

Russian text © 1977 by "Nauka" Publishers. This selection is excerpted from
Chapter 1 of Gofman's book Ekonomicheskaia otsenka prirodnykh resursov v
usloviiakh sotsialisticheskoi ekonomiki (The economic valuation of natural resources in the socialist economy). Moscow: "Nauka" Publishers, 1977, pp. 61-67.

with existing environmental protection legislation. Differential valuations of natural resources are based on a special system of cadastral prices (or marginal costs) for the output of branches using natural resources; this is quite distinct from the existing system of wholesale prices for those goods. Cadastral prices differ from wholesale prices not only in respect of the methodology by which they are computed (cadastral prices are based on marginal costs, while current wholesale prices are based on branch average costs) but also in the length of the planning horizon. The system of cadastral prices should normally take account of long-term circumstances affecting the production of and demand for output, "cleansed" of short-term effects operating in the immediate plan period.

In present conditions, marginal costs and the economic valuations of natural resources which correspond to them should, in our view, be a special subset of the monetary valuations used in the economy. This subset should not be used to organize actual trade between enterprises (i.e., it should not be used as a price system); it should rather be used to create an informational basis for the appraisal of planning and project decisions which involve the use of natural resources. In other words, natural resource valuations should be fully taken into account only at the planning and design stage; this does not require any change in the existing level of wholesale and retail prices, nor in financial relationships within the economy. Standard estimates in money terms of the differential valuation of natural resources should be used in State Registers of the nation's assets and also in the balance sheets of the fixed capital of enterprises and organizations which use natural resources; but they should not be taken into account in fixing the price level or estimating production costs.

Of course, such a procedure for using monetary valuations of natural resources makes it more complicated to control their use. Planning and design decisions based on the full economic value of natural resources may turn out to be financially disadvantageous to the enterprise working the resource, since its output will be sold at existing prices and not at marginal

costs. To avoid this contradiction a procedure should be
adopted under which any departures from established standards
for using a natural resource (either savings or overexpenditure)
would be charged at the full cadastral valuation of the resource
irrespective of the monetary valuation adopted when planned
costs were computed.

Thus, irrespective of existing scales of charges for water,
minerals, standing timber, and so on, any overexpenditure (or
saving) of the corresponding resources should be charged at
their cadastral valuation. If this is done it will be financially
advantageous to enterprises that use natural resources to adhere to rational levels of utilization, even if we maintain the
existing level of prices for the output of branches using natural
resources and the corresponding charges for use of those
resources.[1]

Over the long term, as the appropriate financial resources
are created in the economy, it will become possible to bring
the charges for using natural resources more closely into line
with their differential valuations without significantly increasing the price level of branches with natural resource inputs.
At the same time there will be greater opportunities for introducing more effective forms of financial accountability in relations between enterprises and organizations which use natural resources. In our view, one possible way of organizing
the use of natural resources on the basis of complete financial
accountability is as follows.

A network of financially accountable regional organizations
would be established whose function would be to establish well-
defined quantitative and qualitative parameters for all the natural resources in a particular region. The income of the regional organization would be derived from two sources:
(i) rental payments from enterprises exploiting the natural resources of that region — i.e., charges for the right to deplete
those resources; (ii) payments for maintaining specified parameters in the natural resources — i.e., payments for conserving
natural assets. If we ignore the income received for the use
of natural resources in production, the regional organization

would, as it were, dedicate these resources to the (present or future) needs of society as a whole, thereby carrying out an operation similar to the storage of assets in a bank.

Thus it is desirable that a special bank should be created which would finance and allocate credit for the opening up of natural resources and take measures to economize on their use; in what follows, we provisionally christen this organization the bank of the biosphere. One of its functions would be to pay the regional organizations for natural assets which they conserve (or deposit in the bank, as it were). The proposed dual source of income for the regional organizations makes it economically advantageous for them both to exploit and to conserve the resources in the biosphere. By changing the ratio of the payment for using resources to the payment for conserving them (these scales should be fixed centrally), the socialist state would have an economic means of controlling the process by which resources are reproduced and of achieving the position which is optimal from the standpoint of society's long-term objectives. Since the income of the regional organizations would depend on the composition of the natural resources entrusted to them, those organizations would have an economic interest in devising conservation programs and in developing and using all kinds of natural assets in an integrated way. Being financially accountable, the regional organizations would have to finance their expenditure from their own resources and might also use credits which the bank of the biosphere would make available to them to carry out programs to conserve and develop their natural resources.

Making payments for the conservation of resources would be a passive operation on the part of the bank of the biosphere. Its active operations would consist in offering credits for (in some cases financing) measures to develop and conserve natural resources whether taken by a regional organization or directly by the enterprise exploiting a resource. The assets of the bank of the biosphere could be derived from special payments made by enterprises into a Fund for the Development of the Environment (FDE) and also through the repayment

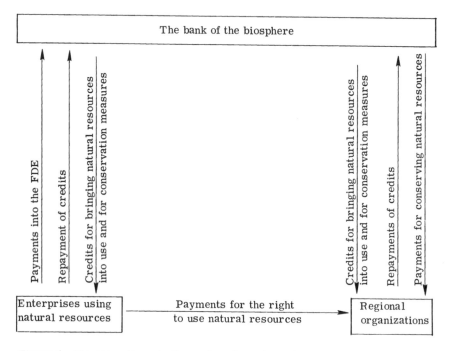

Figure 1. Monetary flows in the system for using natural resources.

of loans by the regional organizations and by enterprises using natural resources. Another possible source of funds for the bank of the biosphere is for it to issue special environmental protection bonds to the public (on a strictly voluntary basis, of course).

The accompanying diagram (Figure 1) shows the monetary flows implied if the system for resource use which we are proposing came into operation.

As is clear from the diagram, an enterprise which exploits a natural resource must pay two kinds of charges: a charge for the right to use the natural resource and a payment into the FDE.

The desirability of charging for the right to use a natural resource arises in the final analysis because using the natural resources in a particular district for one purpose makes it either difficult or impossible to use them for another: the land

occupied by a factory cannot be used for agriculture; forests
in water-preservation zones cannot be used (or can only spar-
ingly be used) for lumber, and so on. Hence an enterprise
which occupies a certain piece of land must earn some standard
rate of return on that resource, to justify the land's being used
by that enterprise, rather than in another way. The size of the
return is determined by the opportunity cost of using the land
for other purposes (for example, the possible return which land
in industrial use would yield if it were devoted to agriculture).
In economic terms the standard embodied in the charge for the
use of natural resources is nothing other than differential land
rent mentioned above.

If we are to ensure that the resources of a region are optimally allocated among different uses, it is very important that
the charge for the right to use a natural resource is not based
on the actual return it yields to a particular enterprise: enterprises pay for the right to use water from a supply irrespective
of the actual intake; the right to cut timber in a particular area
is independent of the actual amount cut, and so on. Thus charges
for "the right to use" a natural resource should provide an incentive for a rational allocation of land among possible uses.

As for ensuring the most effective regime for the exploitation of natural resources, incentives for this should be provided
by the scales of payments into the FDE, which are set up per
unit of natural resource used (a charge for the minerals extracted in mining industries, a felling charge in the lumber industry, and so on).

The function of payments into the FDE is a dual one; on the
one hand they should ensure that financial resources are accumulated to maintain the process of reproduction in the field
of natural resource use; on the other hand they should provide
an incentive to optimize the scale of an activity which uses natural resources. Thus by varying the charge for depleting mineral deposits, we can influence the quantity of ore wasted in the
extraction process; by varying the level of charges for water
collection we can control the quantity of water wasted in irrigation schemes, and so on.

Charges for the right to use natural resources and payments into the FDE together make up a system of pricing for the use of resources which is based on a double tariff; in our view this is the most rational system for charging for the use of most types of resources.

NOTE

1. At present there is a system of charges (or compensation payments) for forestry, mineral deposits in solid form, and land taken away from agriculture for building purposes (compensation payments go into a fund for reclaiming new land in place of the old). However existing payments for the use of resources only cover (and usually only partially cover) the development costs for the corresponding natural resources and hence do not reflect their differential values.

About the Editors

Martin Cave is Lecturer in Economics at Brunel University. He is the author of Computers and Economic Planning (1980); co-author of Alternative Approaches to Economic Planning (1979); and since 1979 editor of Matekon.

Alastair McAuley is Senior Lecturer in Economics at the University of Essex. Besides many articles in journals, he is author of Women's Work and Wages in the Soviet Union (1981) and Economic Welfare in the Soviet Union (1979).

Judith Thornton is Professor of Economics at the University of Washington. She edited Economic Analysis of the Soviet-type System (1976) and Matekon (1978), and she is the author of numerous scholarly articles.

303007725R